3 and 5 door models, in V8 petrol or turbodiesel, with a choice of manual or automatic transmission.

And although Discovery is as reliable as night following day, you're secure in the knowledge that Land Rover's Customer Care Assist plan provides 24-hour emergency roadside assistance anywhere in Australia.

When you consider style, value and performance, Discovery offers more than any other 4WD on the market. The best way to

shops.

discover it for yourself is to visit your Land Rover dealer for a test drive.

It's just the thing for nicking down to the shops. Wherever they are.

If you'd like to know more about the Discovery post this coupon to Reply Paid AP32, Rover Australia, PO Box 3846, Parramatta, NSW 2124.

Name

Address

Postcode

Phone (Home)

Phone (Business)

DISCOVERY
"4WD OF THE YEAR." AGAIN.

GENERAL STORE

manual, $47,275. These prices exclude statutory, dealer and on-road charges. Land Rover has a network of 85 Sales/Service outlets nationwide. (02) 687 2266. Land Rover is distributed by Rover Australia, a subsidiary of the Rover Group Ltd.

Palm Valley

Desert Oak

Kakadu – flood plain in the 'Wet'

OUTBACK AUSTRALIA

AT COST

A TRAVELLER'S GUIDE TO THE NORTHERN TERRITORY AND KIMBERLEY

Malcolm Gordon

©*Malcolm Gordon, 1989, Revised edition 1991,*
Revised edition, 1994.

Maps and Illustrations

©Little Hills Press,pp 15, 33, 43, 74, 114, 217, 227, 229, 243, 311, 315, 493, 531 ©Conservation Commission of the Northern Territory, pp175, 193, 326, 437, 483, 485. © Alice Springs Regional Tourist Association Inc, p88 © Northern Territory Tourist Commission, pp293, 306, 389, 425, 457 © Australian National Parks & Wildlife Service, pp342, 349, 351, 353 © Palmerston Town Council, p467 © Broome Tourist Bureau Inc, pp497, 500-1, 508 © Darwin Region Tourism Assoc. pp392-3 © Dept. of Conservation and Land Management (CALM), p511 © Derby Tourist Bureau, Inc, p515 © Kununurra Visitors' Centre, pp554-5 © Wyndham Tourist Information Centre, p571

Diagrams © Hospital Benefits Association Ltd. pp59-60 © Ian Morris, Aboriginal Season Calendar, p312 © Department of Mines, p519

Photographs © Northern Territory Tourist Commission, © Peter Ackland, ©Malcolm Gordon, © Arnold Dix © Uluru Experience.

Little Hills Press Pty Ltd
Regent House, 37-43 Alexander Street,
Crows Nest, NSW, 2065, Australia.
ISBN 1 86315 046 3

Published in the United Kingdom by
Moorland Publishing Company
Moor Farm Road,
Airfield Estate,
Ashbourne, Derbyshire DE6 1HD, England,
086190 335 8
Printed in Singapore

All rights reserved. No part of this publication may be reproduced, stored in a retrieval system, or transmitted in any form or by any means, electronic, mechanical, photocopying, recording or otherwise, without the prior permission in writing of the publishers.

DISCLAIMER

Whilst all care has been taken by the publisher and author to ensure that the information is accurate and up to date, the publisher does not take responsibility for the information published herein. The recommendations are those of the author, and as things get better or worse, places close and others open, some elements in the book may be inaccurate when you get there. Please write and tell us about it so we can update in subsequent editions.

Cover Photograph: The Lion's Camel Cup Race held every May, Alice Springs.
Back Cover Photograph: A perspective of Ayers Rock.

ACKNOWLEDGEMENTS

Without the generous help and encouragement of many organisations and individuals, this book would not have been possible, and I sincerely thank the following for their contribution, and for the kind use of material: The Australian Tourist Commission; Northern Territory Tourist Commission; West Australian Tourist Commission; local Tourist or Visitor Information Centres in Alice Springs, Tennant Creek, Katherine, Pine Creek, Darwin, Kununurra, Derby and Broome; The Northern Territory Conservation Offices at Katherine, Alice Springs and Darwin; Conservation and Land Management (Kimberley); The Central Land Council, Alice Springs; Tiwi Land Council; The Australian National Parks and Wildlife Service; The National Trust; The Bureaux of Meteorology, Northern Territory and Western Australia for the use of their data; Fire Authorities, Northern Territory and Western Australia; The NT Department of Mines and Energy for use of their excellent detailed geological material on the National Parks; The NT Government Information Centre for the use of the NT Profile material; The Department of Transport and Works Roads Division, Alice Springs; Royal Automobile Associations of Victoria and South Australia; The Royal Flying Doctor Service in Alice Springs; The WA and NT Police Departments; Mornington Disposals for camping advice and the camping checklist; Glen McCullough Photography, Mornington, for photographic advice; **Ian** and **Sue Sinnamon**, Home Valley Station, and **Margaret Salerno**, El Questro Station, both Gibb River Road, Kimberley; Hospital Benefits Association, Victoria, for permission to use their first aid material and diagrams, **Mark Butler** and the team from **Uluru Experience** for Ayers Rock Resort details and photographs.

To individuals: **Leigh Goldsmith**, Alice Springs; **Noel Fullerton**, Outback Camel Safari, for camel details; **Roger Vale**, Alice Springs, for Ghan Preservation Society details; **Jan Heaslip**, Bond Springs

Station; **Rod Steinert**, Alice Springs; **George Kemble**, Kununurra; **Nelly Dykstra** and **Stefan Hampel**, Hobart; **Peter** and **Sue Ackland** and **Karl Leskovec**, of Mornington, all of whom helped plug some of the gaps; for initial advice, **Roy Farrell**, Mornington; for help with the first aid section and fluid intake information, **Dr David Price**, Mornington; **Charles Burfitt** and **Fay Smith**, Sydney, for encouragement and putting me and things in order; **Elspeth Noxon** for art advice; **Neil Taylor**, Mornington. And to the station and roadhouse owners, the tour operators and the many others in the tourist industry with whom I met, or had long telephone conversations.

A special thanks to **Douglas** and **Joyce Stephen** for all their help, and above all, to my **Family**, without whose support the project would have been impossible, in particular to my wife **Gill** for her valuable advice on the manuscript, and for her much needed support when the task at times seemed overwhelming; to **Hannah** for reading parts of the script; and to **Simon** who waited so patiently for that game of golf with his Dad.

Along the Gibb River and Kalumburu Road section is taken from WATC booklet 'Kimberley Region', with permission.

Maps
For their kind permission to publish maps:
NT Conservation Commission - Maps of the NT Parks and Reserves. Australian National Parks and Wildlife Service - Kakadu and Uluru. Alice Springs Regional Tourist Association - Alice Springs maps. NT Department of Transport and Works Roads Division - Road Classification and Surface Types Road map. Tennant Creek, Katherine, Darwin - NTTC and regional associations.

Kununurra, Wyndham, Halls Creek Fitzroy Crossing, Derby, Broome - WA Tourist Commission and regional/local associations.

Department of Conservation and Land Management - Geike Gorge Geological Map.

ABOUT THE AUTHOR

Malcolm Gordon was born in New Zealand where he attended
Victoria University, Wellington, and graduated with a Bachelor of
Arts degree in geography. He then taught at secondary schools in
New Zealand before moving to London for a four year teaching and
travelling stint. Like many antipodeans, he found it difficult to settle
down after his return to New Zealand and moved to Melbourne with
his family in 1976. A trip around Australia with his wife Gill,
daughter Hannah and son Simon began a fascination with the outback
which prompted further research visits, the culmination of which is
this book which has now gone to a third edition. Now an Australian
citizen, Malcolm teaches at Camberwell Boys' Grammar School
(Melbourne), where he is Head of Geography, and lives with his
family at Mount Martha on the Mornington Peninsula.

LIST OF MAPS

CONTENTS

****

PREFACE

A six month camping trek around Australia was originally intended as a research trip for a geography text book - somewhere along the way it became a Travel Guide instead. While it contains a fair amount of geographical content, I have seen my role largely as an assembler of a massive amount of information, packaged in a readily accessible format to suit all types of visitors.

Regional boundaries at times are arbitrary and I hope that no offence is taken by those who consider they are more Red Centre or Top End, rather than the transitional zone dwellers in the region where they are included called The Barkly. I have also tried to redress an imbalance noted in much written material on the Northern Territory; namely the scant attention given to the smaller, out of the way places. Highlighting these as well as the main tourist centres and attractions, is a way of acknowledging a much wider and colourful outback.

The book makes no claim to being a complete guide (is there such a thing?), and although I have listed most places of interest, other excellent material produced by State and Local Tourist Centres, Conservation and Motoring Organisations, and The National Trusts, to name some, should be consulted, too.

The outback is a beautiful mosaic of colour, mood, space, freedom, frontier, dreamtime and characters that along the way, and at the end, form amazing, often indescribable patterns that evoke deeper awareness.

This is The Outback, take time to enjoy it.

Malcolm Gordon

HOW TO USE THIS GUIDE

Planning

Read through *Introducing the Outback* and regional introductions for a general picture of the Northern Territory and Kimberley. Refer to *Practical Information* and *Advice* sections, both before and during your visit. Plan your itinerary with the help of maps and touring suggestions. Select places to stay from maps, detailed *Places and Attractions* listings. The inclusion of costs assists with budgeting. An *Index* lists all towns, parks and other places included in the guide.

Visiting Places

Read through the *Places and Attractions* listings, alphabetically presented within the regions, to help choose worthwhile spots to visit, and appreciate their often fascinating pasts.

Exploring Areas

Where an outstanding range of features give a particular identity to an area, the special attractions are grouped and arranged in order of appearance.

INTRODUCING THE OUTBACK

At its simplest, 'outback' is an Australian word that describes the remote, sparsely populated back country. But it is much more than that. While all mainland states have their outback, nowhere is it more closely associated than with the Northern Territory, and the Kimberley region of Western Australia. Even vehicle number plates in the Territory boldly proclaim "NT Outback Australia".

The varied, perhaps even comfortable, conceptions of where and what the Outback is, are likely to be shattered when confronted with the real thing. While it is difficult to define and map, road travellers in particular will definitely known when they have arrived there. A few random pictures and incidences suggest something of its unique character and colourful lifestyle.

It begins when fences and farmhouses slip off the landscape. A sand-blasted road sign points along a red track to a homestead, 100km (62 miles) into the lonely horizon. On the highway, on-coming drivers who are strangers, wave, reassured by fleeting communication. On a dirt road, a 50m-long road train bellows and bursts through a huge ball of red dust. At Timber Creek, two policemen patrol their beat - an area nearly the size of Tasmania. A character called 'Scrubber' shaves by a rain-barrel in the main street of a small, dusty cattletown. A millionaire businessman from New York is captivated by a 40,000-year-old Aboriginal culture in Arnhem Land, and finds revelation in their art and continuing way of life. A tourist becomes lost near Kata Tjuta (Olgas), and in four hours dies alone from dehydration, while 35km (22 miles) away, hundreds relax in the bars and pools of the air-conditioned Ayers Rock desert resort. On the McArthur River at Borroloola, children are prevented from getting to school because the boat which carried them across the river is threatened by huge crocodiles. An Aborigine saunters from the side of the Great Northern Highway in the vast wastes of the Great Sandy Desert and politely asks for the time. In the Kimberley at a remote homestead on the Gibb River Road, a pastoralist and his family dine formally in the high-ceilinged, corrugated iron, partially open-walled dining room with a party of overseas tourists, while at one of the property's outstations, stockmen cook over a fire and prepare for another night under the wide, starry skies. At Katherine, a teacher begins a lesson in the world's biggest 'classroom' - the School of the Air where children on the far-flung station homesteads receive their schooling by radio. The Outback is where the mailman and the doctor do their rounds by air. The milk arrives in Darwin on the world's longest milkrun - by roadtrain from the Atherton Tablelands near Cairns, just under 1000km (1860 miles) away. A Kimberley bushfire burns for five months, razes 4 million hectares (9,880,000 acres) - an area one-third the size of Tasmania - and is finally extinguished with the onset of The Wet. In Alice Springs, an upside-down boat regatta is held - the river flows underneath its sandy bed and the boats have no bottoms. The images roll on...

The Outback too, is space, freedom and wilderness: a landscape of colours, botanical oddities, stunning wildlife, electrifying landforms, an ancient, mystical culture and deep blue, piercing blue skies. Symbol of it all is the sometimes benign, sometimes brooding rich-red monolith, Uluru (Ayers Rock), which guards the ochre-dusted desert and anchors to its heart the soul of a continuing Aboriginal culture. After a visit to Australia, Mark Twain's general comments perhaps best sum up too, the Outback of today "... it is full of surprises, and adventures and incongruities, and contradictions, and incredibilities, and they are all true".

OUTBACK PEOPLE

The first Outback people, the Aborigines, form a significant group, and attitudes towards them since the time of the first white explorers and settlers have been ambivalent to say the least. Underlying racial tensions exist in places, as Aborigines get new found independence through the return of their traditional land via Aboriginal Land Rights. Whatever the views and feelings engendered by this, the reality is that Aborigines now own in contemporary law, a significant proportion of land in the Territory today. Since land rights implementation, options to live traditionally, semi-traditionally, operate economic enterprises, administer with white organisations some national parks and to continue a significant role in the tourist industry through their art and heritage, have been exercised. In contrast, the town fringe-dwellers form a small but highly noticeable minority.

Aboriginal people have occupied these lands for at least 30,000 years, some suggest even 60,000 years, and most retain the long-established ancestral bonds with their traditional areas, even although modification to their lifestyle through which contact has occurred. The essence of Aboriginal outlook is best outlined in the Australian National Parks and Wildlife publication *Kakadu National Park, Plan of Management 1986*, from which the following description is taken.

"According to Aboriginal tradition, the relationship to the land is an amalgam of spiritual, economic and physical bonds. These bonds are inextricably interwoven, and are set into a time frame which is sometimes referred to as 'dreaming' or 'dreamtime'. These expressions are inadequate attempts in the English language to explain a system of belief which perceives the past, present and future as interacting with each other in an eternally dynamic relationship affecting the affairs of men and women in their everyday lives. A major aspect of the past which affects the present and future, is the creative behaviour of beings, said to have moulded the landscape into its present forms and to have set in place people's languages and social organisations and values."

Some landscape features are the temporary or permanent residences of these beings, and so are regarded as significant by Aborigines and continue to reinforce their ancient system of belief today, through membership of a clan or local descent group, the major common element of which is language. A few sites are seen as sacred and these are off-limits to visitors. While highly debatable, a curious parallel may be seen between the Aboriginal view of creation and the Christian one.

There are plenty of opportunities to meet Aborigines, either through organised tours or at places like Uluru. In more remote areas, as elsewhere, accord them the respect you would expect given to yourself and don't photograph them unless you have permission. Cross-cultural experiences can be enlightening provided you are open, have time and patience, and are prepared to accept differences. Jeff Carter has an interesting chapter on this in his book *The Australian Explorers' Handbook*.

One of the delights of the Outback is meeting the roadhouse owners, stockmen, pastoralists (men and women) or tour operators, and some are real characters. Often unsung, these people are among the prized assets which give the Outback some of its unique flavour.

The 'tyranny of distance' which fostered a particular outlook on life in earlier times is often reflected in these men and women today, despite the advent of modern communications. While much Australian history focuses on the eastern and southern States, it is clear that those much revered character traits of Australians regarded as typically 'Aussie' today, stem largely from Outback roots.

Friendliness, a dry sense of humour and plenty of good stories, best experienced in the quaint, often ramshackle bush pubs, characterise

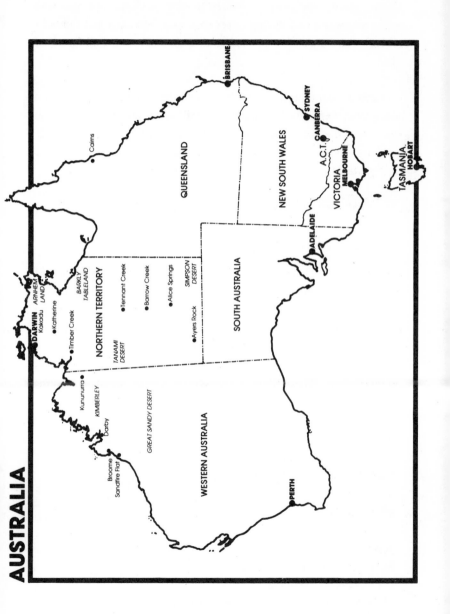

AUSTRALIA

many of the outback people. When the 10-year drought broke in the Centre, there's the story of Ashley Severin at Curtin Springs, who was a youngster and having never seen rain, panicked and fainted - revival was quick after his father threw a bucket of bulldust over him!

Outback people have strong links with the past and you can learn much from them; in some places they will tell of fascinating things to see, where the best fishing is, and some good yarns. It's worthwhile catching some of the races, rodeos and campdrafts for some unforgettable Outback entertainment and people, too.

INFORMATION SOURCES

Outside Australia

The Australian Tourist Commission (ATC) is the first point of contact for intending visitors from overseas. It is a government body that functions externally in a promotional capacity, so get the materials they offer before you leave. Frequently their offices are conveniently shared with the Northern Territory and Western Australian Tourist Commissions, which also have overseas representation. These three organisations are information centres only.

Singapore
Suite 2602, 17th Floor
United Square, 101 Thomson Road
Singapore 1130
ph 253 6811.

Japan
8th Floor, Sankaido Building
9-13, Akasaka 1-chome
Minato-ku, Tokyo 107, Japan. ph (3) 3582 2191.

(Opposite)
A view of Ayers Rock

Road Train

Ormiston Pound

Hong Kong
Suite 6, 10th Floor
Central Plaza
18 Harbour Road
Wanchai, Hong Kong
ph (2) 802 7700.

New Zealand
Level 13
44-48 Emily Place
Auckland 1, NZ
ph (9) 379 9594.

USA
Suite 1200
2121 Avenue of the Stars
Los Angeles, CA 90067, USA
ph (310) 552 1988.
31st Floor, 489 Fifth Avenue
New York, NY 10017, USA
ph (212) 687 6300.

UK
Gemini House
10-18 Putney Hill
Putney, London, SW15
ph (81) 780 2227.

Australia
Sydney (Head Office)
Level 3, 80 William Street
Wooloomooloo NSW 2011
ph (02) 360 1111.

Within Australia

Northern Territory Travel Stations are located at accredited travel agents throughout the country, and can provide information and booking services.

Travel Stations in the capital cities are:
Sydney
Fantastic Aussie Tours
Shop 3, 323 Castlereagh Street,
ph (02) 281 7100.

Thomas Cook Travel
175 Pitt Street,
ph (02) 229 6611.

Canberra
Westpac Travel
cnr Mort & Alinga Streets,
ph (06) 275 5388.

Perth
Thomas Cook Travel
760 Hay Street,
ph (09) 321 2896.

Adelaide
Australian National Travel Centre
132-136 North Terrace,
ph (08) 231 4366.

Brisbane
Travelworld
71 Grey Street
South Brisbane 4101
ph (07) 846 5566.

Melbourne
V-Line Travel,
589 Collins,
ph (03) 619 1549.

The Western Australian Tourist Commission (WATC) no longer has offices in the other states. It's only office is at Forest Place, cnr Wellington Street, Perth, ph (09) 483 1111.
Whilst touring, visits to local information centres are good value for finer detail and maps. You can discover places of interest by talking to locals, particularly in the smaller centres.

National Park Organisations

Northern Territory parks are administered by the Conservation Commission, the exceptions being Uluru (Ayers Rock and Olgas) and Kakadu, which are run by the Federal Organisation, The Australian National Parks and Wildlife Service (ANPWS). The West Australian Conservation and Land Management Department (CALM) controls Kimberley Parks. These organisations provide a great service up front, where at the actual parks information literature, displays, advice and provision of amenities are some of the things offered. Wildlife and Plant Identikit booklets are produced by the NT Conservation Commission, and are highly recommended. Address and telephone numbers are listed in the appropriate sections.

National Trust

The Trust, with its affiliated state organisations, is a voluntary body that aims to preserve and maintain for future generations, Australia's heritage of buildings, landscapes and sites. It owns a number of properties which are open to the public while others privately owned are classified to ensure their preservation. Offices in Darwin and Alice Springs have excellent material, particularly historic walk guides.

Membership is worth considering as it entitles free entry to all Trust properties in Australia and the UK.

Direct enquiries to your state office, or write to: National Trust of Australia (NT), GPO Box 3520, Darwin NT 0800, ph (089) 812 848. For Western Australia: The Old Observatory, 4 Havelock Street, West Perth 6005, ph (09) 321 6088.

Automobile Associations

Reciprocal arrangements operate between the state associations in Australia and their equivalents overseas. Up-to-date print-outs of road information, route maps, accommodation/camping guides and books are some examples of what is available. Membership has advantages of discounted prices and access to material, apart from the road services offered and their technical advisory section. Contact your respective state association office. NTAA is at 81 Smith Street, Darwin, ph (089) 813 837.

Maps

Map producers do their best, but some things on the ground change quickly making accurate depictions very difficult. A useful map is the

NT Touring Map. Strip maps and road maps of the Northern Territory, Northwest and Kimberley are available from Automobile Associations. 4WD enthusiasts will welcome RAC maps of the Canning Stock Route and Gunbarrel Highway, also available from Automobile Associations. Pastoral maps of the Northern Territory and Kimberley detail station properties and land uses - enquire at local tourist offices or respective State Department of Lands.

For those going off the beaten track or bushwalking, Topographic 1:250,000 and 1:100,000 may be purchased from Surveying and Land Information Group, PO Box 2, Belconnen ACT 2616, ph (06) 252 7099. (Send for a series grid map first so you can select required maps.) Local tourist offices have specialised local interest maps.

HOW TO GET THERE

By Road

Coach

Pioneer Express, Bus Australia and Greyhound coaches run regular
services to the Northern Territory and Kimberley, entering via the
Stuart Highway from Adelaide, the Barkly Highway from Townsville
(Queensland) to where it connects with the Stuart, or go around the
Western Australian coast from Perth via the Great Northern Highway
to Broome.

The Great Northern Highway crosses the Kimberley and joins the
Duncan Highway near Kununurra which leads to the western entry to
the Northern Territory.

Sample generalised costs are shown for adult one way fares, but there
are discounts for pensioners and children, and various passes for up
to 60 days are offered.

From Perth to Darwin via the West Coast costs around $325. From
Sydney to Alice Springs $234.
From Melbourne to Alice Springs $192.
Brisbane to Darwin $245.
Darwin to Kununurra $87, and from Katherine to Kununurra $43.
Pioneer Aussiepass offers 21 days $840, 30 days $1020, 60 days
$1520.

It's worthwhile checking out Aussie Explorer Passes if you are
going to stick to a set route, as they offer even greater savings.

Motoring

For motorists, all main entry roads referred to under *Coach* are sealed and present no problem. The Tanami Track and Gunbarrel Highway from the West, and the Plenty Highway and Burketown Road from Queensland are rugged four-wheel-drive entry points. Hired campervans are an interesting alternative to taking your own - check costs with Budget or the other major rental companies.

By Rail

The famous *Ghan* runs between Adelaide and Alice Springs (1559km - 965 miles) and links the Outback town by rail to the rest of Australia. It takes 21 hours (sleepers 1st class around $435, economy $229, seat $139 one way), and has a motor rail service too, for vehicles. Connections are available with transcontinental trains from Sydney and Perth.

Australian Railways have an Austrail Pass and a Flexible Pass for overseas visitors obtainable in Australia on presentation of passport at capital city booking offices, or overseas from travel agents (Thomas Cook and Co in UK).

Current prices are:

Austrail Pass -

	1st Class	Economy
14 days	$690	$415
21	850	535
30	1050	650
60	1460	930
90	1680	1070

Flexible Pass - **8 day travel within 60 days** - $530 1st Class - $320 Economy (not accepted on the Indian Pacific or the Ghan)
15 days travel within 90 days - $750 1st Class. $475 Economy.

By Air

Ansett Australia and Qantas Airlines are the two major carriers.

> Ansett Australia is the only carrier in The Kimberley, and has an extensive network of services to and within The Territory.

Ansett associate airlines, EastWest and Ansett Express, also operate services in the NT. Both major carriers offer a range of packages (conditions apply), child/student concessions, and airpasses. For details of discounted fares ph Ansett 13 13 44 (national) and Qantas Airlines ph 13 14 15 (national).

> Ansett Australia's and Qantas have discounted adult fares for economy class starting at about $488 from Sydney to Alice Springs, and to Darwin around $600.

Combinations

Combinations of transport modes can have cost and time advantages, as well as providing greater opportunities for seeing and experiencing the landscape. Air/coach or fly/drive combinations are worth considering. Apart from the 'Big Three' coach companies, there are many coach operators who run a variety of tours to the Territory and Kimberley from capital cities.

PRACTICAL INFORMATION

Best Time to Visit

The accepted tourist season is between April and October, when desert and tropical weather conditions are more tolerable. **June and July are ideal months,** as temperatures and humidity are lower (refer to outlines of climate for each of the regions). Generally, at these times places are more accessible, and conditions for outdoor sightseeing are best. However, popular tourist spots do get crowded so it is advisable to book early.

Out of season visits are worth considering. Some advantages are often reduced rates, fewer tourists, the lush green of Top End tropical vegetation, and the spectacular water expanses and falls of the Wet or Green Season. Despite the Wet Season, Darwin has high sunshine hours (check tables), and air-conditioning and many all-weather roads reduce the impact of climate conditions. Off season in the Red Centre is hot, but visits are possible.

Older visitors and young children may well find heat discomfort levels of the Outback in summer too stressful, and are best advised to plan their visits in the 'cooler' periods.

What to Wear

Light casual clothing, worn year-round, is a part of the Outback lifestyle. Cottons or similar are best as high synthetic content clothing can cause 'prickly heat' in the humid tropics. Drip dry, non-iron are most convenient.

Reasonable dress standards are maintained in restaurants and hotels in the larger centres, where in the evening for men, open-necked shirts, trousers and shoes are acceptable. Casino standards are stricter in the evening - no denim or corduroy trousers, shirts with collar and dress shows.

The 'Darwin Rig' is common for men: shorts (or long trousers), long socks, shoes and open-necked shirt with collar. So take a pair of dress trousers. For women, light dresses, tops and skirts, tops and shorts are worn, and a dress to suit the occasion in the evening.

In The Centre, nights are cold to freezing in winter, so take warm clothing. For the bush, light trousers (jeans or similar), strong comfortable rubber-soled footwear and wide brimmed hats are advised for protection. Jeans are not advised for camel or horse riding - track suit trousers are better as they don't chafe.

What to Take

Health insurance documents are easily forgotten, as are vehicle insurance policy and spectacles prescription (in case of lost or broken glasses).

Protect Yourself

Sun strength and light intensity, particularly in The Centre, are much warmer and stronger than people from other climates expect. Hats, sunglasses (for the children, too), sun lotions and block out creams are essential for comfort and skin protection. Bushflies and mosquitoes are plentiful in places, so take supplies of reliable repellents. Face nets are an effective bush fly deterrent. Take supplies of any medication you may require. Attune yourself as much as possible to the climate conditions - in and out of air-conditioned environments can increase discomfort levels.

Disabled Persons

Visitors confined to wheelchairs will welcome the attention given to their needs in recent years. Most new accommodation places have facilities, as do the major national parks. Many local Tourist Information Centres have listings of facilities.

Pets

Domestic cats are prohibited from all Northern Territory Conservation Commission parks and reserves. Dogs are not permitted in most (see also under National Parks, page 44).

The ANPWS have banned all pets from Kakadu National Park. In the Kimberley, no pets are allowed in national parks. Many caravan parks don't allow pets, and there's a shortage of kennels in many places. Given the restrictions, and climatic conditions (even crocodiles take a fancy to dogs), it's not much of a holiday for them! Dog owners are advised to have the animal checked for heartworm - the mosquito carriers are rife in the tropics. Those taking dogs should seek preventative advice regarding heartworm (tablets can be administered). Cattle tick is another problem for pets in the tropics. Kennels are few and far between, and most will not accept animals that have not been recent inoculated, i.e. within 3 weeks. Kennel arrangements must be made several months in advance.

Accommodation

A wide variety is available from luxury hotels to youth hostels, and well-appointed caravan parks to basic camping grounds. Many hotels, resorts and motels offer family group concessions, and have lower rates during the summer off-season period.

Hotels

Premier class are found in Darwin, Alice Springs, Ayers Rock, Jabiru and Broome. Old established and less expensive hotels are available for the budget-minded. The requirement of public bar among its facilities distinguishes a hotel from a motel.

Motels

They are well represented in cities, towns, resorts, and along the major highways. Developed to meet the needs of the travelling motorist, the motel industry now offers plenty of choice and fine facilities, particularly in Darwin, Alice Springs, Katherine, Tennant Creek, Broome and Kununurra. Like hotels, many have restaurants and swimming pools. In the Kimberley, many private hotels have standards similar to medium priced motels.

Roadhouses

On the highways, and in the rural areas of the Outback, roadhouses offer comfortable overnight accommodation, including motel-style rooms, or cabins called dongas, or demountables and camping. They are relatively cheap, particularly camping.

Cattle Stations

Some enterprising station owners offer ranch style (bunkhouse) accommodation at their homesteads as an adjunct to normal station operation.

Hostels

Youth hostels offer an inexpensive alternative, but membership, irrespective of age, is needed. YHA Hostels handbook outlines membership conditions, lists locations, and is obtainable from National Head Office at 10 Mallet Street, Camperdown, NSW, 2050, ph (02) 565 1699.

State office addresses applicable to this guide are 65 Francis Street, Northbridge, WA, 6003, ph (09) 227 5122, and Darwin Hostel Complex, Beaton Road, Berrimah, (PO Box 39900 Winnellie) NT, 0821, ph (089) 84 3902.

Hostels are located at Darwin, Border Store (Kakadu), Pine Creek, Katherine, Mataranka Homestead, Tennant Creek and Timber Creek, Alice Springs. In the Kimberley, there is one at Kununurra. YWCA has hostels in Darwin and Alice Springs.

Camp-o-tels

A new concept in budget accommodation is a cross between a motel and tent. The capsules consist of a raised A-frame structure, moulded fibreglass floor and fittings, and strong fabric for the walls. It has beds. Lake Bennett was one of the first resorts to introduce these new designs.

Caravan Parks and Camping Grounds.

Sometimes called tourist or holiday parks in the major centres, and despite frequent omissions from tourist literature, many do have areas set aside for tents.

Cabins and on-site vans are available for renting at some.

Powered sites are common in virtually all; shady grassed areas are not so common in arid areas. Facilities include at least toilets and showers, and larger parks in towns and cities offer a range of recreation facilities and services.

> It is still the cheapest type of accommod -ation, but fees vary, as do the quality of facilities.

Extras in the Top End and Kimberley are air-conditioning and power. Most roadhouses offer campsites - some free.

Many national parks permit camping (fees now apply in all), with facilities varying from pit toilets only, to modern amenities. Alternatively, you can camp 'bush' - this is definitely the cheapest, provided you are geared for it. (See also practical advice section on Camping).

Tourism Marketing Duty (bed tax)
A duty of 5% of basic accommodation is placed on hotel and motel charges by the NT Government. Caravan Parks are exempt.

Bookings and Guides.
Advance bookings are advised for places of your choice at popular spots, particularly during peak season months. Availability, types and costs are included for all places in regional sections.

Local Visitor Centres are helpful. The Automobile Associations also handle bookings, and the RACV annually publishes *Australian National Tourguide*, which is its recommended list of all types of accommodation - available from all AA offices.

For Overseas Visitors

Electricity
Power in Australia is 240 volts AC. Some of the large hotels provide a variety of power outlets at 240, 220 and 110 volts AC. However, it is advisable to include a small 110 volt transformer and plug conversion kit for the Territory.

Tipping
This is not obligatory in Australia, but visitors are quite at liberty to leave a tip if they so desire.

Currency
Australian currency is dollars and cents. Notes come in denominations of $100, $50, $20, $10 and $5, and coins in $2, $1, 50c, 20c, 10, and 5c. Overseas currency and travellers cheques may be exchanged at any bank and some larger hotels.

Driving

Vehicles in Australia are right hand drive, and travel on the left hand side of the road. A valid overseas driver's licence allows visitors to legally drive on Australian roads. Refer also to Traffic Regulations and Road Surface Types (pages 32-38) in the Practical Information Section.

Shops, Services, Costs

Larger centres offer a wide range of goods and services, and have excellent modern shopping facilities. Trading hours are generally between 9am and 5.30pm (in the Kimberley shops are open 8am to 5pm) during weekdays. Weekend trading is widespread, particularly in Alice Springs and other prime tourist centres.

> **Great distances mean higher costs for a range of goods, particularly in the outlying areas.**

Some foodstuffs, such as fresh vegetables, are expensive, but it's not all bad news - a random survey showed some items only a few cents dearer in comparison with a Mornington Peninsula supermarket (near Melbourne), a few items were cheaper, most about 10% to 20% dearer, others up to 30% more. Fuel costs are higher. For the budget-minded, it is possible to save on some durable food, photographic and vehicle items by purchasing in the supermarkets of Darwin or Alice Springs. Cold drinks can be a budget-biter for families, and takeaway beer can be expensive in some remote places.

Shopping

If you are looking for something different and indigenous, you will not be disappointed. Fly home with a special container of fresh barramundi or buffalo steak (cheaper direct from NT Exports than

from Darwin Airport), and for wine buffs, a Chateau Hornsby red from the desert winery near Alice Springs. If beer is preferred, then try the world's largest bottle - the Darwin Stubby. Buffalo horns, replicas of outback road signs and crocodile warning signs, locally crafted leather, gemstones, and other items from natural sources, make interesting reminders. Genuine Aboriginal artifacts can be purchased throughout the Territory. Some fine bookshops in Alice Springs and Darwin have a fascinating range of Outback titles. Broome offers pearls and related items, while Kununurra has diamonds from the 'local' Argyle mine, and 'zebra rock'. Otherwise, for those gifts to take home there is the usual, often terrible, cheaper range of souvenirs.

Medical Services

Most visitors will never be too far away from medical help. Many small settlements have nursing clinics, providing initial care with a visiting doctor service on some days. The Flying Doctor Services are for everyone, including tourists, and are only a phone or radio call away for advice or action. They are called The Royal Flying Doctor Service in the Centre, Aerial Medical Service in the Top End, and Royal Flying Doctor Service in the Kimberley. A full range of services are available in the larger centres, and in emergencies, medical services in the Aboriginal communities can be used. Full facility hospitals are in Darwin and Alice Springs; smaller regional or district hospitals at Tennant Creek, Katherine, Gove, Broome, Kununurra and Derby, Fitzroy Crossing, Halls Creek and Wyndham.

Banks and Credit Cards

Banks, while well represented at branch level in the major centres, may have an agency only in smaller centres.

Banking hours are Monday to Thursday 9.30am to 4pm, Friday 9.30am to 5pm.

Locations of auto-tellers are listed in facilities for each settlement. Major national and international credit cards are widely accepted. It is advisable to carry sufficient cash for those long stretches between towns, as some roadhouses do not accept credit cards for fuel or other services. Electronic Funds Transfer/Point of Sale (EFT/POS) facilities are becoming more widespread.

Fuel and Vehicle Services

Petrol (super, ULP) and diesel are available on all major routes, and on some remote tracks. LPG for vehicles is now more widespread in its availability. Unless you go off the beaten track, there are few places where distances between services exceed 200km (124 miles). 24-hour fuel is available, and some places have varied opening hours (usually ranging between 6am and 11pm). Always check availability of fuel if travelling at night, as opening fees may be charged for after hours service. Supplies at some more remote places are unreliable, so check beforehand. The Automobile Associations provide detailed fuel availability print-outs. Bottled gas is widely available. Aviation fuel is limited to a few locations. It is best to get spares and have your vehicle serviced in larger centres, as smaller places are not geared for this - some will undertake emergency repair work, but you may have to wait for parts.

Roads

First-time motorists may well be surprised by the extent and quality of bitumen, all weather-roads. In fact, most drivers see what they want to without leaving the bitumen. Road names can be misleading: don't always associate highways with sealed roads - the Gunbarrel Highway is a track; the Sandover Highway is a formed road; and part of the Buchanan Highway is a gravel road. Road surface types fall into three categories.

(Opposite)
Mt. Connor

(above) Kings Canyon
(left) Aboriginal Art (Kakadu)

Hotel, Kakadu

ROAD SURFACE CROSS SECTIONS

Sealed, bitumen or blacktop:

Fig 1. Two Lane all weather highway (eg. Stuart Hwy)

Fig 2. One Lane sealed highway. Note frayed edges. (eg Victoria Hwy)

Unsealed

Fig 3. Unformed, flat bladed. Become more channel – like in sand country. Pot holes, bulldust and corrugations common.

Fig 4. Unformed rarely graded track. Deep wheel ruts and centre hump.

Fig 5. Formed earth or gravel road

Sealed

Sometimes called bitumen or blacktop (Figs 1 and 2), these are mainly two-lane all weather highways, e.g. The Arnhem. Most sections of the Stuart and many sections of The Great Northern Highway are to this standard. But, some may reduce to a width barely sufficient for two vehicles to pass. Other highways may have just one lane of sealed surface. Upgrading is a continuing process, and sealed roads generally present no problem for drivers.

Unsealed

Unsealed or gravel, dirt or sand surfaces may be formed, i.e. engineered, to shed water quickly (Fig 5), while unformed are cut into the surface by a grader blade (Figs 3 and 4). The latter, in particular, can deteriorate rapidly after rains causing dangerous surfaces. After grading (usually once or twice a year after the rainy season), they can be good, passable even for some conventional vehicles. Many unsealed roads were built as 'beef highways', replacing the old stock-routes for the motorised roadtrain haulage of cattle.

Tracks

Generally have little traffic, and many are more akin to pathways worn by vehicles. Sometimes, sections of tracks are barely distinguishable from the surrounding terrain, while others are similar to unformed roads. Tracks are best suited to 4WD vehicles only.

Users of all unsealed roads should always seek local, tourist authority, AA or police advice. Police stations have road condition postings, and regularly patrol major Outback highways in the Territory and Kimberley. Road conditions can alter rapidly, and many unsealed roads have 4WD only recommendations.

Up-to-date road reports for the Territory can be obtained by telephoning (089) 843 585; for the Kimberley ph (091) 911 133, after hours 911 389.

Computer print-outs of road conditions are available from AAs and Tourist Offices.

Driving Hazards

Driving can be safe if the driver is aware of potential hazards, extends courtesy to others, and above all, adjusts speed to suit road conditions.

The main hazards are:

Tiredness

Distances and long straight stretches can have a mesmerising effect. Break your trip into realistic proportions, stop frequently, and change drivers to prevent 'dropping off'. Don't drink alcohol and drive.

Wandering Stock

Most station properties are unfenced, and dead, desiccated animals along the roadside are a grim reminder of stock and wildlife hazards. Camels, donkeys, horses, cattle, kangaroos and emus are very unpredictable in their movements, particularly at night. They sometimes seek the warmth of the bitumen to sleep on also. Best advice is to avoid night driving if you can.

Single-lane Bridges

There are a number of these on the Great Northern Highway between Derby and Wyndham. Others may be encountered too, on some unsealed roads. Slow down and be prepared to give way.

Cattle Grids

On some roads, cattle grids occur at intervals, and may be set above road surface levels. Iron-grid joins in the middle can be out of line, with one edge protruding. Slow down to prevent damage.

Road Surfaces and Edges

If you are unfamiliar with driving on dirt roads, reduce speed until you get used to travelling on such roads. Speed generally on dirt roads should be about half that you would normally travel. Dust from passing or on-coming vehicles on unsealed surfaces obscures vision, so slow down or stop and close your windows. Pot holes, sand, corrugations, ruts left by heavy vehicles, jump-ups, rough creek crossings, flash flooding and 'bulldust' (fine deposits of soil and dust of varying depth) are all possible hazards on unsealed roads. Edges can become soft and cause bogging after rains. One-lane sealed road edges may drop sharply to the natural surface (see Fig 2).

Single Tracks

Many roads have been constructed for one vehicle at a time. On unsealed roads, shoulders are sloped more to effect run-off after rains, so slow down to have complete control when you are passing vehicles approaching from the opposite direction. Loose gravel from road verges may be flung at your windscreen when passing on narrow, sealed roads - again slow down to reduce the danger.

Road Trains

These mammoth haulers of freight are often 50m long, and consist of a prime mover towing up to three trailer sections. Be careful when passing or overtaking, especially on sections of the Stuart, Barkly and Victoria Highways where the seal width is only 4m, and the road trains need 2.5m of that! There's not going to be much room for you - slow down and pull over. This action will also reduce the chances of stone damage to your vehicle. If following one, be patient - they take a long time to overtake, and at least a clear kilometre ahead is needed before doing so. Often drivers will assist by signalling when the way is clear. And don't expect road trains to move over for you - they are more difficult to control if driving on two surfaces at once.

Traffic Regulations

They are much the same in the Kimberley and Northern Territory as in other parts of Australia. The main differences are:

Northern Territory

Speed limits of 60km/h in built-up areas unless stated otherwise, with open limits on some roads. 'P' plate licence holders must have 0% blood alcohol level, and not exceed 80km/h. Blood alcohol limit is .08%, and random breath tests are conducted. Seat belts are compulsory. Interstate vehicles that stay for more than three months require NT registration. All accidents must be reported within 24 hours to police. Motorists turning right must give way to all vehicles from opposite direction, including those turning left.

Kimberley

Speed limit has a 110km/h maximum. 'P' plate holders must not exceed 80km/h and .02% blood alcohol levels - others .08% blood alcohol level. Accidents involving injury or damage over $300 in value must be reported to police as soon as possible. The wearing of seat belts is compulsory, and the NT turning right rule applies.

Crossing State Borders

Two things happen here - you need to adjust your watches as Eastern and Western Territory Borders are also Time Zone boundaries, and certain fruit and plant quarantine regulations apply.

Time Differences

Australia is divided into three time zones. Central Zone (South Australia, Northern Territory) is half an hour behind Eastern Time Zone (Queensland, NSW, Victoria, Tasmania) and 1.5 hours ahead of Western Time (WA). This means when travelling east across the

WA/NT Border, advance watches by 1.5 hours; going the other way, turn back by 1.5 hours. Across Eastern and Central Time Zones, advance by half an hour if travelling East, turn back half an hour if going West. Make further allowances when Eastern States adopt Daylight Saving during summer.

Fruit and Plant Quarantine

Manned stations on some state borders and other points of entry may be annoying, but necessary, to prevent pests and diseases from entering these parts of Australia, and to stop the spread to 'clean areas' of those already there. Multi-million dollar agricultural enterprises could be jeopardised by travellers unwittingly bringing infected plants or fruits. The WA Agricultural Department is strict at their WA/NT border station, about 40km (25 miles) east of Kununurra. Vegetables, fruits, seeds, soil, plants and honey are some of the prohibited items, so don't stock up with fresh foods at Katherine if you are heading to the Kimberley. Acquaint yourself with the regulations by reading *Travellers' Guide to Plant Quarantine*, available from Agricultural Department Offices throughout Australia.

Aboriginal Land

Land previously designated "Aboriginal Reserve" became Aboriginal Land with the declaration of Aboriginal Land Rights (NT) Act in 1976. Aborigines now have freehold title, accepted in traditional and contemporary Australian law. In short, it is now privately owned land, the title of which is no different in law to that of suburban blocks in the cities, and subject to the same laws of trespass. The fact that it is not fenced, as with cattle stations, does not alter its status. Visitors must obtain a permit and have it in their possession, whilst on Aboriginal land.

Permits

When making application for entry to any Aboriginal Land, applicants must state the reason for entry, dates and duration of intended stay, names of persons travelling, and itinerary and routes to be used while on these lands. Permits can only be issued after consultation and approval of the relevant Aboriginal communities. Processing permit applications can take 4-6 weeks.

It should be noted that, as a general rule, Land Councils have been asked by Traditional Owners not to issue entry permits for unaccompanied tourist travel. This does not affect visitors travelling on one of the organised tours onto Aboriginal Land, where tour bookings include the necessary permit.

It is the right of Traditional Owners of Aboriginal Land to refuse entry permits. Applications and any enquiries must be directed in writing to the relevant Land Council listed below.

Public roads that cross Aboriginal Land are exempt from the permit provisions. However, the exemption covers the immediate road corridor only, and if there is a likelihood of a need for fuel stops, travellers should seek transit permits from the relevant Land Councils. Many roads across or on Aboriginal Lands are not designated as public roads, so please seek advice from the Land Councils before travelling.

Permits are NOT required on the following roads in The Central Lands Council Region:

1 Tanami Road (Alice Springs to Western Australian border)
2 Stuart Highway
3 Tanami to Lajamanu Road
4 Barkly Highway
5 Alice Springs to Haasts Bluff Road (natural feature not community)
6 Sandover Highway (through Utopia Land Trust)
7 Larapinta Drive (Alice Springs to Hermannsburg)
8 Namatjira Drive (Larapinta Drive to Glen Helen)
9 Finke River (Hermannsburg to Palm Valley)
10 Hermannsburg to Areyonga Road
11 Simpsons Gap National Park access road
12 Standley Chasm access road
13 Lassetter Highway (Erldunda to Ayers Rock)
14 Ayers Rock to Olgas Road
15 Allambi Road (Alice Springs to Allambi Station)

Access on the above roads 1-15 provide access 50m either side of the centre line of the road specified. You may camp on the side of these roads, or at roadside stops or parking bays.

Direct enquiries to the appropriate Councils at the following addresses.

Red Centre & Tanami (Alice Springs and Tennant Creek regions)
Permit Officer
Central Land Council
PO Box 3321
Alice Springs NT 0871
Ph (089) 516 320

Top End and Tablelands (Darwin, Nhulunbuy or Katherine regions)
Permit Officer, Northern Land Council, PO Box 42941, Casuarina,
NT 0811, Ph (089) 205 172.

Melville or Bathurst Islands
Tiwi Land Council
Nguiu, Bathurst Island
via Darwin NT 0822
Ph (089) 783 957 or
Darwin Office (089) 410 224

South Australia
Pitjantjatjara Council
3 Wilkinson Street
PO Box 2584
Alice Springs NT 0871
Ph (089) 505 411

The Kimberley, Western Australia
Aboriginal Affairs
Planning Authority
35 Havelock Street
West Perth WA 6005
Ph (09) 483 1222

Sacred Sites

A large number of places and features have special, often spiritual significance to Aborigines. These sacred sites are protected, and visitors should be aware that penalties exist for entering or interfering with them. Some areas that have historic significance to Aborigines are open to the public, and while visitors are welcome to visit such sites, respect should be shown for them.

Photography

Commercial photography is not allowed in Aboriginal Lands, unless prior permission has been granted by CLC. Photographs for personal collections are okay. If these photographs involve the people who live in the areas, please observe the normal courtesy you would expect for yourself. In fact, because this has not always happened, some areas do not allow photography or videos.

Alcohol
Most Aboriginal Lands prohibit the importation and/or consumption of alcohol. If travelling to, or through, these Lands, check with the NT Liquor Commission.

Information
Come Share Our Culture is a NTTC Guide to Aboriginal Tours, Arts and Crafts.

Cattle Stations and Homesteads

Cattle stations are business enterprises that are not geared to meeting requests for supplies from tourists. However, owners are reasonable and willing to help in cases of genuine trouble, but expect a cool reception if, through poor planning, you have run out of fuel. Station property is private land, and while it may be unfenced and wilderness-like, accord it the respect you would to your own. Some owners have closed access to attractions because of wilful damage to fences and bores, and there is some measure of exasperation behind the blunt "No Shooting, Camping or Trespassing" notices erected on some properties.

If you wish to use station land, always, if possible, seek permission. Very few stations permit shooting, and permission is definitely required.

(In the Kimberley, no shooting is permitted.) Cattle, sheep, donkeys, buffalo, horses and goats are usually the property of the land owner, and must not be shot. A few stations in remote areas offer mainly basic services to tourists.

Water and Fluid Intake

In remote arid regions, water is a scarce commodity. Always carry adequate supplies of drinking water, and motorists, don't forget to allow for the car too. In The Centre, campers should allow at least 4 litres (one gallon) per person per day. The amount you carry in the vehicle will depend on how far off the beaten track you go, the degree of physical activity, time of the year, and the number of people.

Take water on walks, no matter how long. You'll be surprised how thirsty you get, and how much moisture the body loses. Alcohol (beer, etc) is not recommended as a thirst quencher on walks - in fact it hastens dehydration, as most will know!

Facts clearly indicate the need to replace moisture lost mainly through the skin pores (moisture is also lost through the lungs by expelled air). The normal fluid requirement is around 4 litres per day in temperate climates (less for children, but remember their regulatory system is more sensitive than adults' and so need frequent smaller intakes). Under normal temperate climate conditions, e.g. Melbourne, about 1.5 litres is lost per day. In the arid and Top End regions, higher temperatures and the nature of activities are going to increase the loss at a faster rate, e.g. in the Top End at least twice the normal intake is needed, and up to 3 times more with strenuous exercise. On longer treks and under hot conditions, walkers are advised to drink 1 litre every 3 hours (a rough guide). Also, they need to counter salt and sugar loss - use salt tablets and barley sugar (or similar), as well as some solid food such as raisins or nuts (muesli bars are ideal).

Always boil water from natural pools and billabongs before drinking, after all you don't know who, or what, has had their feet in the trough! Water purifying tablets are a practical way to ensure adequate drinking water for bush campers.

National Parks

They aim to preserve and protect the natural environment, including features of scenic, historical, archaeological, geological and other scientific interest, in a system of parks and reserves open for public enjoyment, education and inspiration. Parks exist for heritage preservation and rangers work hard to keep them in pristine condition - help them by following park rules. Larger parks have well appointed visitor centres and ranger stations; others have visiting rangers.

Fees

All Northern Territory Commission Parks and Reserves charge camping fees (between $1 and $4 pp night, or $3-10 per family). The ANPWS has entry and camping fees for Kakadu. Camping fees are also charged for some Kimberley National Parks.

Camping

While some parks are day use only, many permit camping.

Pets

Pets are prohibited from all Kimberley National Parks. Northern Territory Parks do not permit cats, but some allow animals by permit only, and subject to designated areas. Pets are not permitted at Kakadu. It is advisable to check with the NT Conservation Commission regarding pets, as new regulations are in force.

Facilities

Many have well appointed facilities; others, in keeping with the nature and usage of the park, are limited.

There are no bookings taken, and camping areas can get crowded. Always check water supplies. Restrictions on night use of generators apply in some. Wood for campfires is scarce in arid areas, and dead litter, if used, destroys a micro-habitat for many small creatures - gas for cooking is preferred. Refer to regional sections for detailed outlines on Parks.

Wildlife and Environmental Respect

All native animals (kangaroos, euros, wallabies and other marsupials, etc), reptiles (lizards, fresh water and saltwater crocodiles and snakes, etc) and birds (all parrots, cockatoos, finches, eagles, emus, bustards, etc) are fully protected in both the Northern Territory and Kimberley. Most trees, shrubs and wildflowers are similarly protected (refrain from picking wildflowers, photograph them instead).

The environment is a fragile resource, and while crocodiles, snakes and the like, may give you the 'horrors', each has a vital role in the ecological balance of things. The landscape beauty is often marred by unsightly litter cast off along the highways, in rest areas, and along bush walking trails, by thoughtless people. The ancient Kimberley boabs and rocky outcrops on the way west, have not escaped crude desecration either by 20th Century vandals. The only things you should take are photographs, while footprints should be the only traces of your visit.

At all natural waterways, falls, holes and dams, do not pollute these wildlife and cattle drinking spots by using soap and detergents when camping. This causes fouling, kills unseen aquatic life, and has a negative ripple effect on the food chain and ecosystem.

Wildlife and Marine Dangers

With good sense and a preventative approach, such dangers need not mar your visit. Potentially dangerous snakes are around (as they are in all Australian states) but will rarely attack unless provoked. Wear appropriate protective clothing in the bush. Snakes capable of killing humans include taipan, king brown or mulga, western brown, eastern or common brown, Ingram's brown snake, speckled brown or Down's tiger snake, desert whip snake, yellow-faced whip snake, curl snake, desert death adder and common death adder. Despite the lengthy list, most are rarely seen. Crocodiles, both freshwater and saltwater, inhabit coastal and inland waters of the Top End and Kimberley regions, and the latter type is lethal (refer to Top End Region introduction for crocodile outlines). Feral buffalo and boar (wild pig) inhabit large areas of the Top End, and can be dangerous. Bull camels can be temperamental, too. Get your close-ups with a telephoto or zoom lens to avoid trouble. Dingoes and goannas can be unpredictable.

Tropical coastal waters harbour an array of nasty species. Between October and May, box jellyfish (sea wasp) invade the coasts, and stings from their tentacles can be traumatic and lethal. The simple precaution is don't swim or paddle in the sea during these times. Darwin beaches have warning signs posted. Other marine nasties are sharks, sea snakes, blue-ringed octopus, cone shell and stone fish. On the brighter side, some areas are relatively free of these, but always seek local advice.

Other things to avoid are scorpions, an ugly-looking larger insect that gives a nasty sting, and is found in the arid regions. Leeches, on the other hand, are not so easy to avoid in the tropical, damp rainforests. They latch onto lower leg areas in particular, and if these flat slug-like things attach themselves, scrape them off, or discourage them with a bit of vinegar.

By far the greatest natural danger to tourists in the Outback is Ayers Rock. In 1987, over 15 people died within a 6-hour period of climbing the rock - a most physically demanding walk for the not-so-fit. Heart attacks were the main cause of death, as they continue to be (those with a heart condition, high blood pressure, or who are asthmatic, should not climb). In the same period, 2 people were killed by crocodiles! Perhaps these statistics place wildlife and marine dangers in proper perspective.

Safe Swimming

Despite the marine and crocodile dangers, it is not all bad news for swimmers. A range of safe swimming can be found: Cable Beach

(Broome), Berry and Howard Springs (outside Darwin), some natural rock holes in the gaps and gorges of the Centre and Kimberley, Mary Ann Dam (Tennant Creek), Low Level Park (Katherine), Mataranka Thermal Pool, and Lake Jabiru (Kakadu), to name some. Many hotels, motels and caravan parks have pools for guests, and larger towns have superb public swimming pools. If in any doubt about places to swim, seek local advice. And, if you feel uncomfortable about a place, be guided by your instinct - don't swim.

Fire Danger Period

Northern Territory

A sign near Kulgera, near the South Australian/Northern Territory border, reads... "We like our lizards frilled not grilled", and warns of the bush fire dangers, even in the arid zone. Bushfires in Australia are usually associated more with the southern states. It may be of surprise to many visitors to learn the extent of this hazard in the northern regions during the Dry season, when large areas can be ravaged. Between July and December, a fire danger period is declared north of the 21st parallel (about 350km [27 miles] north of Alice Springs) at which times there are restrictions on fires in the open - camp fires can only be lit in constructed fireplaces, or on properly cleared areas (at least 4m distant from flammable matter), and must be extinguished after use. In extreme fire danger periods, a total fire ban may be declared, when no fires in the open may be lit. Fire danger months in the Centre occur between October and March. Please note the "Fire Danger" index signs, and act accordingly.

Controlled burning in the north takes place in late April/early May to reduce rank grass and encourage regrowth.

Kimberley

Here they say "Beef runs on grass", so help the great Kimberley pastoral industry to prevent bushfires by strictly observing the following regulations. Camping and cooking fires must not be lit within 3m of a stump or log, and a 3m radius from the fire must be clear of all inflammable material. Someone must always be in attendance, and the fire must be properly extinguished before leaving. Total prohibition for all fires in the open operates in all shires of the Kimberley during the Dry Season. Check with local authorities for the exact dates, as they differ from shire to shire.

Fossicking

Fossicking in the Kimberley is allowed on Crown land, and a Miner's Right is required ($20 for life). For details, write to The Department of Minerals and Energy, Mineral House, 100 Plain Street, Perth, WA, 6000, ph (09) 222 3333.

In the Northern Territory, there is plenty of scope for rock hounds, too, and a Miner's Right costs $20 for life. Check grids for locations. The Department of Mines and Energy has an excellent book available, *A Guide to Fossicking in the Northern Territory*. At $10, it is great value. For details write to their head office at Centrepoint Building, Smith Street Mall, Darwin, NT, 0800, ph (089) 895 511.

Hunting and Shooting

There's a misconception in many quarters that shooting is 'open go' in the Outback - this is simply not so! While the Top End is one of the few wilderness hunting areas in the world, stringent regulations apply. Strict rules on firearms also apply, and on the way they are carried and used. Every shooter must have a licence, and every firearm registered. Check with the Northern Territory Police. No

Ayers Rock

Road to the Olgas

Jim Jim Falls

hunting or shooting is permitted in the Kimberley, and all firearms carried in WA must be registered with the Police.

Hunting Areas

Hunting is permitted on some areas of vacant Crown land in the NT. Contact The Surveyor General, Department of Lands, Housing & Local Government, Nicholls Place, Cavenagh Street, (PO Box 1680) Darwin, NT, 0800, ph (089) 895 511.

On private property, including Aboriginal Land, permission of the owner or lessee must be obtained prior to entry. As buffalo, cattle, sheep, goats, donkey and horses are usually the property of land owners, they cannot be shot. Buffalo are classed as stock, and any unauthorised shooting of them, as with cattle, incurs heavy fines, or even confiscation of vehicles and rifles. No hunting or shooting is permitted on land managed by the Conservation Commission (i.e. parks, reserves, sanctuaries) with the exception of designated hunting reserves, and where licensed safari operators have special hunting concessions. Two safari companies have concessions to shoot limited numbers of banteng cattle, sambar deer, buffalo and pigs in Gurig National Park, Cobourg Peninsula. A duck and magpie goose hunting season is declared annually by the Minister for Conservation. The Conservation Commission manages a duck and goose hunting reserve at Howard Springs in the Top End (refer to that listing for details).

Before You Shoot is a NT Government publication that should be read. The Conservation Commission has detailed information on hunting, as do the Police.

Firearms

There is an impression, too, in some quarters that the Territory and Kimberley are wild places, and some first-time campers think it is necessary to carry a rifle for protection. This misleading notion and practice is definitely not encouraged - statistics show you are more liable to be attacked in Melbourne or Sydney than in the Outback.

Fishing

Northern Territory waters, in particular, offer some of the best year round fishing in Australia. Fishing with hand lines or rods is generally permitted in rivers and billabongs throughout the year, without a licence. Amateur fisherman are not permitted to sell their catch. The prized fish is the barramundi, currently under a stringent management programme. Bag limits for barramundi are: 5 fish per person per day. Special limits for barramundi apply to the Mary River System, including Shady Camp and Corroboree Creek - 2 fish per person per day, 4 fish for any trip of more than one day, and a minimum size of 50cm (20 inches). The Mary River System is closed to fishing between October 1 and January 31 of the following year. It is probable the 2 fish bag limit will apply to all waters in the near future. Refer to Top End regional introduction for further details.

The Northern Territory Fisheries Department has a detailed guide booklet to recreation fishing, and they will answer any angling questions. It pays to check too, for any changes in licence policy. Write to Fisheries Division, Department of Primary Industry and Fisheries, GPO Box 990, Darwin, NT, 0801, ph (089) 894 517.

Fishing is good in the Kimberley, too. A recreational fishing licence is required, and the Fisheries Department produces an excellent booklet detailing types of fish and regulations. Write to Fisheries Department, 108 Adelaide Terrace, East Perth, WA, 6004, ph (09) 220 5333.

Geology

Those with an interest in natural history may find the Geological Time Scale useful when visiting ancient geological landforms.

GEOLOGICAL TIME SCALE

Years Ago	Epoch	Period	Era
10 000	Recent	Quaternary	
1 000 000	Pleistocene		
12 000 000	Pliocene		
25 000 000	Miocene		
35 000 000	Oligocene	Tertiary	Cenozoic
	Eocene		
60 000 000			
70 000 000	Paleocene		
		Cretaceous	
130 000 000			
		Jurassic	Mesozoic
165 000 000			
		Triassic	
200 000 000			
		Permian	
235 000 000			
		Carboniferous	
285 000 000			
		Devonian	Palaeozoic
325 000 000			
		Silurian	
350 000 000			
		Ordovician	
410 000 000			
		Cambrian	
500 000 000			
3 000 000 000			Pre-Cambrian

Emergency and Road Information Telephone Numbers

For medical, fire, police and ambulance, dial 000 in all of the Kimberley Region and the Northern Territory.

For Marine Stinger Emergencies, ph 008 079 909 (free call).

For advance Road Information, ph (089) 843 585, for Northern Territory recorded message. For Kimberley, ph (091) 911 133, after hours 911 389 (Main Roads Department). Alternatively, contact the nearest police station in the proposed area of travel.

For vehicle breakdown, contact the nearest service - these are listed in the Regional Sections under places.

PRACTICAL ADVICE

Motoring

A reliable vehicle is essential for safe and enjoyable motoring in the Outback states. Conventional 2 wheel drive vehicles are quite suitable, and research shows that most 2WD travellers see what they want to by rarely leaving the bitumen. While a 4WD vehicle and Outback touring are often strongly associated, it is not necessary to outlay such an expense - for the few tracks and dirt roads you may want to venture on, it would be more economical to hire a 4WD.

We camped our way around Australia for nearly six months covering 27,000km (16,740 miles) in a 1977 Station Wagon (no trailer) that carried all our gear, including a camping fridge. Helper springs were the only modification to the vehicle. Perhaps we were fortunate in encountering relatively few mechanical problems and unbelievably, no punctures (I had steel belted radials and, on advice, bumped pressures up to 40lb per square inch).

However, the 4WD used on our most recent trip to the Territory had these advantages: comfort and security, flexibility to explore unexpected places along the way, ample power with a high performance capability in the rough, and, as my wife commented - very easy to drive and plenty of space for the kids.

Preparation

Have your vehicle systems thoroughly checked. For older vehicles, replace all hoses, fan belts, filters, plastic sections of fuel lines; check electrical system - coil, condenser, plugs, points, and replace if required; check and repack wheel bearings with grease; check brakes; and undertake a systematic check for loose wiring and nuts. After travelling on corrugated roads in the Outback you will be surprised how the jarring loosens things. Give attention to the cooling system, and flush out. Trailers and caravans should be checked thoroughly, too - often light, city trailers require strengthening before being suitable for outback conditions.

It is a good idea to acquire some mechanical skills, too. Local TAFE Colleges generally offer excellent courses for beginners that give confidence, and allow identification of many potential and real mechanical problems. In fact, with these skills you may be able to rectify simple problems without the expense of getting outside help, and to do your own basic servicing. I enrolled in such a course and, under guidance, did most of the car preparation work during these classes.

By all means listen to the loads of advice you are likely to receive. Cross-check with mechanics, Automobile Associations, etc, and a sensible, practical list of spares and tools to take will emerge. Otherwise, you will end up towing a complete repair workshop!

Spares

For most travellers, tyre and spare tubes, tyre repair kit, coil, condenser, distributor points, fuses, fan belt and radiator hoses would be adequate. If you travel off the main roads, an extra tyre and tube is advised. Obviously, the extent of spares will depend on how long, and where you plan to go. Roof-racks should be of a heavy-duty type to withstand vibrations on corrugated dirt roads.

Tools

A good set of tools is strongly advised. Socket set, open-end and ring spanners, shifting spanner, screwdrivers, pliers, insulation tape, hammer, jumper leads, jack with wide base plate for sand surfaces, wheel spanner, pump, fire extinguisher, tow rope, axe, shovel, tarpaulin (for shade) and a good torch, are suggested.

Fuel, water, lubricants

Much depends on where, and for how long, you are going. Extra oil, fuel, water (out bush allow 4 litres [1 gallon] per person per day) and brake fluid are advised.

Maps and Manuals

Always carry an up-to-date set of maps (see Information section on maps). Carry vehicle insurance documents. A car manual is useful, as are several specialist books on the market about Outback motoring, including how to solve vehicle problems and survival skills. Jack Absalom's *Safe Outback Travel* is good value.

General Advice

In the arid areas in particular, never leave children or pets in a parked car, and always leave the windows down a bit if parked in the sun, to avoid windscreens being blown out by expanding air. A patent sun shade for windows (or towels and the like) keeps the car cooler when parked. (When travelling, sun blinds or similar make life more comfortable in the back seat, and prevent sunburn too.)

Be aware of driving hazards. In remote areas, check the fuel availability beforehand. Keep a weather eye out and, if off the main roads, check road conditions prior to leaving. Summer in the arid zones and in some Top End and Kimberley places, is not the time to travel off the bitumen. Keep your load to a minimum, as excessive loads are a frequent cause of breakdowns. Carry plenty of food and water in case of breakdown.

> If planning to drive across remote country, let reliable people know your plans and estimated arrival time, and don't forget to report in (searches are costly and endanger other lives too).

On long driving stretches, it is a good idea to change drivers if possible every hour or 100km, to avoid tiredness, particularly in warm conditions and with no air-conditioning. Also 'water' the children every hour or so.

Outback motoring is not as hazardous as made out to be, provided you plan well. Automobile Associations are extremely helpful, and should be consulted. Check that your membership is current!

Breakdown

No matter when you break down, always stay with your vehicle. Erect some shade, conserve energy, and wait until you are able to attract attention. If you have good supplies of food and water as suggested, there will be little danger.

Four Wheel Drive (4WD)

There are many publications, including magazines, which give a good guide to this specialist form of motoring. Well off the beaten track stuff requires thorough preparation and good equipment, including RFDS radio transceivers. At least two vehicles should make up treks along remote tracks such as Gunbarrel Highway, Tanami Track and Canning Stock Route. Escorted 4WD treks are an alternative for treks in the remote areas. 4WD Clubs are a good source of information, and way to acquire skills, so contact those in your local area.

Extended Touring with Children

Education

Many Australian families camp their way fully or partially around Australia for periods of 3 months or more. Get school work guidance from teachers. The trip will be ideal for much project work, and there is plenty of scope for parents being teachers - costs of things, distances, map reading, etc, can be a practical form of maths and geography. Keeping a diary helps with English. It is not necessary to enrol at correspondence school, and your local school will provide worksheets for subjects. It is surprising how enthusiastic children do get when travelling.

Travelling

On the long journeys, have frequent breaks to allow children to run off a bit of energy. Avoid too many sweets as too much sugar can cause hyperactivity - better to chew on some dried meat strips (Jerky) or dried fruit and nuts. To counter the heat, have water in the car. A water filled contained with a spray nozzle is a good way to keep refreshed. If you carry ice in a fridge or esky, cubes are good to have in a small cooler in the car for the children to suck. Rotate the children to reduce boredom - let them have turns sitting up front with one adult in the back. Above all, have plenty of games, tapes (Walkman ideal), etc, to keep them occupied, including 'school work'. Children's books (adults too) can be easily and cheaply purchased at book exchanges along the way, and many children (depending on age) enjoy making things from a kit containing glue, sticky tape, scissors, paper, cardboard and coloured pencils.

For toilet stops in the bush along the roads, a whistle is a good idea if people have to walk a fair distance away for privacy (both on the walker and in the vehicle so they can call each other) - it is easy to get lost and lose a sense of direction in flat scrublands. A trowel rather than a shovel, is better for children for bush toilet stops.

First Aid

A first aid kit is essential for motorists and campers, and a reputable first aid book is strongly suggested too, and don't forget health insurance. The St John Ambulance and Red Cross produce good first aid books. A first aid kit should include a broad crepe bandage, an antiseptic, vinegar or other acetic acid (apple cider vinegar is good for minor insect bites and stings, and urine is a good vinegar substitute for bull ant bites too), band-aids, scissors. Ideally, all general problems such as burns, cuts, gashes, blisters, sunburn and minor injuries, should be provided for.

First aid treatment for less common injuries from potentially lethal venomous creatures and dehydration are given below. In all cases, seek medical attention urgently.

Snake Bite

While a few hundred get bitten each year in Australia, fatalities are few and there are antivenoms available.

Steps taken should be:

*Lay the victim flat and immediately apply a broad pressure bandage over the bitten area. As much of the limb should be bound up as possible. Crepe bandages are ideal, but strips of clothing will do (see diagram). Tourniquets are no longer used.

*DO NOT wash, cut or suck the wound. Washing may delay venom identification and the administering of antivenom. Completely immobilise the limb by binding some type of splint to it - any rigid object will do. Leave bandages and splint intact until medical care is reached.

*Reassure and calm the victim and arrange transport as quickly as possible to the nearest hospital or medical centre.

If the victim suffers from asthma, any allergy, or has received antivenom before, inform the doctor or hospital. (Doctors can monitor the victim closely for serum reaction.)

If breathing fails, apply mouth-to-mouth resuscitation.

As doctors can determine the type of snake from the venom by use of identification kits, there is no need to kill the snake and take it to the hospital (it can be helpful to identify and/or describe the snake).

Stone Fish

Occurs in shallow pools at low tide and, as the name suggests, it is very well camouflaged. A human hand or foot placed firmly on its back is likely to be pierced by one or more of the fish's 13 dorsal spines, and injected with deadly venom. Prevention is to wear strong shoes when exploring reefs and shores of known stone fish areas. A victim feels unbearable pain, and may collapse. Apply hot towels to the punctured area, or immerse in hot water to relieve the pain. Antivenom is available and medical help must be urgently sought.

Box Jellyfish or Sea Wasp

They inhabit northern coastal waters during the summer months from October to May, and they are deadly. Their venom has been known to kill within a few minutes. It is a jelly-like creature, box-shaped, and trails venomous tentacles several metres long. They

Techniques that save lives

There are two basic life saving techniques that may be used in the case of a venomous bite.

However, if they are applied incorrectly, they can be dangerous.

Any person who is out and about regularly should get a more thorough knowledge, perhaps making use of the many excellent first aid courses available.

Pressure Bandage and Limb Immobilisation.

1. Immediately apply a broad firm bandage around the limb to cover the bitten area as tightly as one would bind a sprained ankle. As much of the limb should be bound up as possible. Crepe bandages or any flexible material can be used.

2. Keeping the limb as still as possible, bind some type of splint to it – any rigid object will do.

3. Leave bandages and splint intact until medical care is reached.

1. Apply a broad pressure bandage over the bite site as soon as possible. Keep the bitten area still.

2. The bandage should be as tight as you would apply to a sprained ankle.

3. Extend the bandages as high as possible.

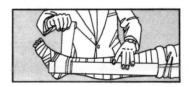

4. Apply a splint to the leg.

5. Bind it firmly to as much of the leg as possible.

Bites on hand or forearm. 1. Bind to elbow with bandages. 2. Use splint to elbow. 3. Use sling.

Mouth to Mouth Resuscitation

To be commenced immediately in all cases where breathing has stopped.

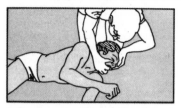

1. Lay the patient on one side. tilt head backwards and while supporting the jaw, use fingers to clear mouth of all foreign matter.

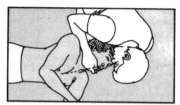

2. Look for breathing movements. Listen and feel for patient's breaths. If breathing leave on side.

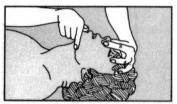

3. If breathing stopped turn patient on back, tilt head backwards and, while supporting the jaw, seal nose with fingers.

4. Place your widely open mouth over patient's slightly open mouth and blow until the chest rises.

5. Watch the chest fall and listen for air escaping from the mouth. Then repeat steps 4 and 5 at a rate of 15 times a minute.

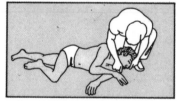

6. When breathing begins, turn the patient on to one side with head back, the jaw supported and the face pointing slightly towards the ground.

Continue resuscitation until the patient recovers and keep under observation until medical assistance arrives. For infants, cover the mouth and nose with your mouth and blow at the rate of 20 times a minute until the Chest rises.

are difficult to see. If stung, apply liberal doses of vinegar to the affected area (this action renders the tentacles harmless). Do not rub, as this triggers off more venom capsules. Do not suck the wound. Get the victim to medical help quickly. Apply mouth-to-mouth resuscitation if the victim collapses. Antivenoms are available. Marine Stinger Emergencies, Northern Territory, ph 008 079 909 (free call).

Dehydration
Lack of fluid intake has caused many deaths in the Outback. In serious cases, administer water or some other liquid (non-alcoholic) in very small sips. Add some salt and sugar to the liquid, too. Make sure the patient drinks slowly by only pouring small quantities into a utensil. Sponge the person down to lower body temperature. Medical attention depends on the recovery rate.

Camping

Commercial caravan parks
It is advisable to book ahead, during peak season periods, for sites at popular tourist spots such as Alice Springs, Mataranka, Katherine, Darwin, Kununurra and Broome. Better parks in Darwin tend to be further out of the city - in and around the Howard Springs area (inner parks tend to have a number of 'permanents'). Tent sites are usually available at caravan parks.

National Parks
There are no bookings for sites, and many do get crowded. Check regional listings for those where camping is permitted.

Bush Camping
In the Territory and Kimberley, camping in the bush, alongside roads and in rest areas, is allowed. But camping is not allowed in the latter two areas if they are within a 16km (10 miles) radius of an established caravan park. Camping in rest areas and along main roads

is not advised. Apart from traffic noise and feelings of insecurity, many are not attractive places (some resemble rubbish tips!).

> **Choose a spot well off the main road - along dry creek beds is ideal, but keep in mind the following:**

* do not camp in dry creek beds (flash flooding from storms miles away is a real danger);

* don't pitch your tent directly under a tree (falling limbs, insect dwellers and moisture drip can pose problems),

* keep sites well away from waterholes and bores (drinking habits of wildlife and cattle may be disturbed, and you may be in the midst of a cattle stampede if they are frightened);

* be prepared for mosquitoes in many sites near water in the Top End (mosquito nets are advised);

* seek permission where practicable of station owners to camp (it is private land);

* do not pollute waterholes or dams by using soaps, etc; be careful with fire, and do not cut down any vegetation for wood (all regions are fire prone and strict regulations on fires in the open apply - see Information section);

* store food away at night (dingoes and others enjoy a free meal!); deeply bury toilet waste (dingoes easily scrape out shallow or covered sites);

* do not bury rubbish (take it out with you); and remember that shooting is prohibited unless you have permission (all shooting in the Kimberley is illegal).

Camping under the stars in the bush is one of the delights of the Outback, and provided bush campers do the right thing, this freedom to camp out will continue. When you leave the site, there should be no evidence of your stay.

Camping Equipment

The checklist included provides a starting point. Talk with your local camping dealer, most of whom offer better advice than the larger supermarket retailers, and have had experience in the bush. Tents should be dried before packing up - wet canvas will produce mildew and damage if not dried within a few hours. In the Centre, hard, sometimes stony ground can puncture the inner floor of tents - use a tarpaulin for underneath, but don't have it extending beyond the tent boundaries otherwise if it rains water will collect underneath! In hard ground, steel pegs are needed - use a mallet for driving them. Sand pegs are useful in sandy terrain. Blowing up airbeds each night can be a chore - alternatives are thick foam rubber rolls or self-inflating mattresses (the latter are ideal and less bulky).

Camping gas bottles are date stamped. Check that yours is valid, otherwise service stations will refuse to fill them. Older ones may need replacement fittings, and leaking gas is not desirable.

A camping fridge is highly convenient, but not absolutely essential; a 3 way type (gas, electricity, car battery) is ideal, and it can be run off a lead from the cigarette lighter fitting when travelling, then converted to gas or electricity at the campsite. If you do run it off the car battery, don't forget to turn it off when you stop the vehicle.

An extension lead is useful for caravan parks where many charge $1 per night for such power needs. It is not advisable to run it on gas while travelling - in fact, it is dangerous. If you do, it must be turned off at service stations. Also, gas should be kept out of inner tents where not only is there the risk of fire, but more significantly potentially lethal leaking gas. You should be thoroughly familiar with all gas accessories, and for first-time campers, a trial run is a good idea. A cooler or esky packed with ice is an alternative to a fridge for storing perishable foods.

Hire camping equipment is available from Darwin for visitors wishing to camp out, and many tours include bush camping in their itinerary. Hire campervans are another alternative.

Campers, in particular school groups, must observe rigid hygiene with respect to cleaning utensils after a meal. Bacteria love hastily-washed plates in the tropics, and sometimes outbreaks of stomach trouble can be traced to this source, or inadequate cold storage of perishable goods.

Camping Checklist

Tents
  Family Tents
  Hike Tents
  Pegs
Sleeping
  Sleeping Bags
  Air Beds
  Camp Stretchers
  Space Blankets
Cooking
  Stove
  Barbecue
  Gas Bottle
Lighting
  Gas Lights (and spare mantles)
  Pressure Lantern
  Kero Lantern
  Gas Lantern
  Torch
Cooking Utensils
  Camp Oven
  Frypan
  Jaffle Iron
  BBQ Hot Plate
  Kettle
  Billy
  Toasting Fork
  Sausage Grill
  Eating Utensils

NOTES

Trouble Shooters
Wax Stick (for tent seams)
Spare Tent Pegs
Air Bed Patch and Plug
Puritabs
First Aid Kit
Insect Repellent
Waterproof Tape
Waterproof Matches

Other Equipment
Fridge or Cooler
Folding Table
Camp Chairs
Water Container
Bush Shower
Extension Pole for gas light
Stove Stand
Bucket
Porta Potti
Folding Toilet
Folding Spade
Air Bed Pump
Pocket Knife
Ground Sheet
Coil Rope
Fire Extinguisher

Clothing
Hat and Fly Veil
Poncho
Sturdy Clothing and Boots

NOTES

Photography and Films

In the Outback, particularly the Centre, light intensities are much greater. Even with automatic exposure, it will in most cases be necessary to 'stop down' one or a half-stop to compensate for brilliance, unless you use a lens hood.

For those with a new camera, get familiar with it before leaving; shoot some film and check results. Discuss and seek advice from your local camera dealer, who will advise on film types, speeds and accessories you should take. Stock up with sufficient film as costs can be higher there. The major centres in the Territory have fast print-processing services.

Camera Care

Avoid leaving cameras for lengthy periods in hot sunshine or in a confined space where it can get hot, as a car glove box. A good inexpensive way to store camera and films is in a 6-pack polystyrene beer cooler! Protect your equipment from dust and sand by using lens covers, and use a sealed camera bag or similar for out and about. Use a blow brush, not a tissue, for cleaning lens. Do not break seals on films until ready to use. Get your films processed as soon as possible - if this is not practicable, then store exposed film in a cool spot, even in a refrigerator (camping fridge), provided the film is in a sealed container. Where camera and film have been in an air-conditioned (films in a fridge) environment for some time, avoid problems of moisture condensation by allowing them to 'warm up' at least one hour before use.

Processing

There are differences in fast print-processing machine settings between northern and southern states. If you have your prints processed away from the Territory, ask for a test print run to make sure the colours are right. Record roll numbers and shots taken to make for easier identification when you get home. For those taking slides, check that the brand of film used numbers the mounts in the processing - it makes for efficient cataloguing later. Ask the processor to number film bags so that these match your roll numbers.

For photography in Aboriginal Lands and of Aborigines, see Information section.

THE NORTHERN TERRITORY

A SUMMARY

Size

The Territory covers 1,346,200 sq km (519,633 sq miles), which represents about a sixth of the Australian continental land mass. It extends 1610km (1000 miles) from north to south, and 934km (580 miles) from east to west. Eighty percent of its area lies within the tropical zone, north of the Tropic of Capricorn.

Population

It has just under 1% of Australia's population with around 175,900 people, 104,000 of whom live in the two major centres, Darwin (78,000) and Alice Springs (26,000). The remaining population is spread thinly, mainly in the smaller towns, tiny wayside settlements, station homesteads, and mining areas.

About one quarter of the population is Aboriginal; living mainly in communities in the remote areas. The main self-contained settlements are: Galiwinku (Elcho Island, 1076); Wadeye (Port Keats, 1232); Nguiu (Bathurst Island, 957); Yirrkala (410); Milingimbi (699); and Angurugu (584).

The curious blend of British, European, Asian and Aboriginal cultures and lifestyles gives the region a distinctive flavour and character, with Darwin being the most cosmopolitan. Another distinctive population characteristic is that it is weighted towards the young - 80% are below 40 years, and 50% below 25 years.

Political Status

The Commonwealth of Australia is a federation of six States (New South Wales, Victoria, Tasmania, Queensland, South Australia, Western Australia) and two territories. The Northern Territory, while established as a self-governing territory in 1978 with most Commonwealth powers transferred to it, has yet to reach full statehood. It has some differences in titles: instead of a Governor and Premier, there is an Administrator and Chief Minister respectively, and the 25 member Parliament sits at Darwin. Two major problems have yet to be resolved before statehood is declared.

One is the emergence of a cultural dualism in the Territory as a result of self-determination restored to Aborigines, and how to bridge cultural gaps for the social unity and cohesiveness that statehood demands. Another is financial. The small population is seen as being insufficient to generate the finance needed for statehood status.

Flags

The Territory flag incorporates 3 colours - black, white and red ochre. The five stars on the black panel represent the Southern Cross constellation, while the 7 petals of the Territory's floral emblem, Sturt's Desert Rose, are etched on the ochre. The 7 petals represent the 6 Australian States and Northern Territory.

The bird depicted on The Tourist Centre logo is the delightful brolga (Grus rubicunda). In the Dreamtime, according to Aboriginal legend, there lived a beautiful girl named Bralgah, who loved to dance. She would dance all day long, whirling around with her arms outstretched as she fluttered about. Bralgah rejected the advances of one of the clan and was banished in the form of a whirly-wind. She returned as the dancing Brolga. Also known as the Native Companion, Brolga is one of the few Aboriginal names retained after European settlement.

Economy

The Territory's vibrant economy is reflected in above the national growth rate figures in many sectors. Plentiful reserves of natural resources provide a strong base for the mining, pastoral, agricultural, fishing and tourist industries - the most rapidly growing being the tourist. Defence establishments are another important activity.

The Arts

The variety and quality of the Arts in the Territory come as a surprise to most visitors. The region is rich in multi-cultural experiences, and various Arts organisations are active in Alice Springs and Darwin, where they have fine facilities. Festivals add further colour, museums at Alice Springs and Darwin provide further cultural interest.

Sport and Recreation

The Territory climate and outdoor lifestyle are conducive to sport. Along with the younger age characteristics, there's a high degree of participation in organised sports, and as a consequence there are magnificent facilities. Visitors can share these, too.

Top End activities include fishing, canoeing, hunting, swimming, water-skiing, sailing, skin diving or pleasure cruising. Darwinites involve themselves in sporting activities from indoor bowling to football, athletics to cricket. Racquet sports and golf are popular, too. Alice Springs has over 40 sporting clubs, and even tiny Outback settlements might have a golf course - a 1-hole desert course! Horse racing, rodeos and campdrafts are popular and important social events in the Outback.

TERRITORY HISTORY

The First Australians

Aborigines have occupied these lands for at least 30,000 years, possibly 60,000. Where they came from is not known, and various theories of migration waves from Asia have been suggested.

Europeans

The Dutch ship *Arnhem* is the first authenticated European contact, made in 1623. Long before the Dutch, however, Macassan fishermen were known regular visitors. Abel Tasman, another Dutch navigator, explored the northern coast in 1644, naming a number of features including Groote Eylandt. It's thought the Portuguese may have circumnavigated Australia in the early 1500s. While the Dutch showed spasmodic interest to the mid 1700s, they made no attempts at colonisation. Matthew Flinders charted sections of the coast in 1803, and navigator Phillip King did a more elaborate survey in 1817.

British Settlement

The British began the colonial garrison era when in the name of King George IV, Captain Gordon Bremer claimed the land as part of New South Wales on September 20, 1824, at Port Essington. Three days later, he moved his party of 57 soldiers and 44 convicts to a new site at Fort Dundas (Melville Island). Neither this, nor a settlement established at Raffles Bay (Fort Wellington) in 1827, were successful. While fear of French settlement and the spread of Dutch Trade prompted this British action, the harsh climate, isolation and miserable conditions caused the abandonment of both settlements in 1829. The trade that these settlements were supposed to encourage did not happen either.

All the old arguments for settlement were revived when Bremer again was ordered to establish a settlement in 1838. Port Essington was chosen and Victoria settlement eventually, like its predecessors, was abandoned in 1849. The northern coast was neglected until the landward approaches of the 1860s.

Overland Exploration

Leichhardt was the first of the overland explorers to cross any part of the Territory after a 5000km (3100 miles) journey, which took nearly 14.5 months from the east to Port Essington, in 1845. Explorer John McDouall Stuart's epic south-north crossing of the continent effort, in 1862, paved the way for development.

Development

In 1863, control of the Northern Territory was vested in the Colony of South Australia, and known as Northern Territory of South Australia. Escape Cliffs, near the Adelaide River mouth, was the site of the colony's first attempt at settlement. Established by the Territory's first Government Resident, Colonel Boyle Finniss, it was a dismal failure and was abandoned in 1866. Surveyor-General George Goyder finally established the first permanent settlement on the north coast at Palmerston (Darwin) in 1869. Gold discoveries at Pine Creek, the Overland Telegraph Line in the 1870s, and the railway later to Pine Creek, assured Darwin's permanence. The importation of Chinese labour at this time marked the beginnings of the Territory's cosmopolitan population.

Along the Overland Telegraph Line came the pastoralists, overlanders and drovers with their mobs filling up the vast, rich pastoral lands of the Barkly Tablelands, Victoria and Roper River regions, thus laying the foundation for the cattle industry. In 1877, the first mission at Hermannsburg was established, and in 1888, the Northern Territory became a separate electorate. Mineral finds widened the developing Northern Territory economic base.

In 1911, The Northern Territory formally passed to the control of the Commonwealth Government. 1912 brought the appointment of Dr J.A. Gilruth as the Territory's first Administrator, whose leadership saw industrial and social unrest emerge, culminating in the Darwin Rebellion of 1918-19. Between 1926 and 1931, the Territory was divided into two administrative regions; Northern Australia and Central Australia. The war years saw military rule in the north, and after the bombing of Darwin in 1942, it was the first area to experience war on the mainland. Aborigines became eligible to vote in Federal and Territory elections in 1962, and the historic Aboriginal Land Rights Legislation was passed in 1976. The devastation of Darwin by Cyclone Tracy on Christmas Day in 1974, saw a new city emerge from the rubble soon after, and the first big step towards statehood was in 1978, when self-government was proclaimed.

Two books well worth reading for their historical insights and Outback character are: *Far Country - A Short History of the Northern Territory* by Alan Powell, and *Outback* by T. Keneally.

"The Track"

National Route 87 (Stuart Highway) is Australia's 3188km (1977 mile) transcontinental highway that runs from Adelaide to Darwin, and basically follows the original trail of explorer Stuart in 1860, and the subsequent Overland Telegraph Line laid in 1872. Although it's now sealed from Adelaide to Darwin, many Territorians still call it 'The Track', while some 'truckies' used to endearingly refer to it as 'Bitch-o-mine'.

David D. Smith was the engineer responsible for the highway's construction between Alice Springs and Darwin in the early 1930s. With little more than shovels, picks, crowbars and a 'motley crew', construction began. Road plant was non-existent, and camels were used for transport. Anticipating war, Smith exceeded his budget by over $130,000 when he straightened and widened sections of the track, and his only comment when reprimanded was "Too bloody bad!". Smith was in charge of the upgrading and sealing of the road during the war (1943); a task undertaken by Australians, not the United States as widely believed. It must have been a good road, too. Taylor and Rendle drove an XK120 Jaguar from Darwin to Alice Springs in 10 hours in 1951, averaging 155km/h (96mph).

Upgrading in recent years has resulted in what is virtually a two-lane, all-weather highway, along which the various isolated settlements are like chapters in a book that unfold a fascinating history, captured best of all by Douglas Lockwood in his book *Up The Track*.

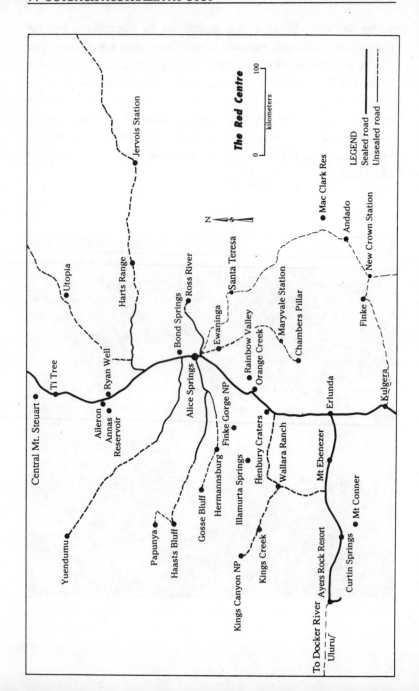

The Red Centre

LEGEND
Sealed road
Unsealed road

0 ———— 100 kilometers

THE RED CENTRE

Characteristics

The Red Centre is most associated with the mighty monolith, Uluru (Ayers Rock), red sand-soils, and the best-known Outback town in Australia, Alice Springs. It is a vast sun-drenched desert region. The features of the landscape evoke a powerful sense of pre-history, and leave lasting impressions for their vibrant colours; reds and golds at sunrise and sunset, blues and purples during the day.

About a quarter of the population are Aborigines. Thriving threads of their ancient culture continue, mainly in the outstations or small communities in the arid interior, and some are also involved with cattle stations, arts and crafts industries and tourist ventures.

The heart of this uncompromising and sparsely populated region is Alice Springs. Today, it's a modern, small city that clings to legacies of its legendary pioneering days, despite rapid growth and sprawl brought about by the tourist boom. From its strategic, scenic setting, it has a thriving economy based on regional administration, pastoral, oil and gas, and tourist activities. Apart from Yulara, other settlements are small and relatively few in number.

While Uluru is the best known and most popular scenic attraction, there are many other outstanding natural features: Kata Tjuta (the Olgas); Kings Canyon; gaps and gorges of the MacDonnell Ranges; Mt Sonder; Palm Valley; Chambers Pillar; and Rainbow Valley.

The mysteries surrounding pre-historic Aboriginal rock engravings and Lasseter's lost gold reef, old mining settlements, Outback pubs, cattle stations, prolific flora and fauna, an almost overwhelming sense of space and friendly locals, are other facets of this great arid region.

There are unlimited activities for visitors, from camel trekking to living traditionally with Outback people, and if you wish to just relax, some ideal places are Alice Springs, Yulara, Ross River and Glen Helen.

Climate

Using Alice Springs as a guide, summers have long hot days, of which over 80 are above 35C (95F) and around 13 are over 40C (104F). Nights are mild to warm and humidity is low. Ground temperatures during the hottest parts of the day are higher in many places due to heat radiation from surface sand and rocks (temperatures can reach 50C [136F] at the Olgas), and strenuous activities are not advised during these times. Winter months have mild to warm days around the low 20C (54F), but a few can be cold at around 10C (27F). Skies are clear and there's plenty of sunshine. Nights and early mornings are cold, often freezing, particularly during June, July and August.

Rainfall is very erratic. The 285mm (around 11 ins) average, while tending to fall mainly in summer, can come at any time; occasionally it is in cloud bursts which cause dry creeks to rapidly become raging torrents.

The climate table for Alice Springs, on page 101, details patterns.

Landscape

Sand dunes, salt lakes, clay pans, rocky outcrops, small plateaux, low mountain ranges, and dry sandy creek beds provide relief, colour and fascination to a landscape dominated by relentless red sand and gibber (stony) plains.

The distinctive reddish-brown colour results from rainwater mixing with iron-oxides contained in the rocks to form a common rust. Along with the weathering of rock over millions of years, the huge amounts produced have effectively stained most surface soil, sand and rock in rich ochre tones. Walkers and campers will soon find that clothing is quickly pigmented, and bare limbs rapidly acquire a golden tan!

Unlike most desert regions in the world, the Centre is clothed with a moderate but nevertheless distinctive cover of vegetation. In fact, after major rains, the 'Green Centre' is a more suitable description.

In one respect, the early explorers were right about the great inland sea - they were just a few million years too late! Immense geological forces associated with various orogenies (major mountain building periods between 350 and 450 million years ago) distorted the ancient sea bed, wrenched and uplifted, inclined and split great sandstone slabs, while buckling the more flexible bands of limestone and siltstone. Molten rock (magma) welled to the surface, fused and changed rock compositions creating complex structures for geologists to ponder over, and a wealth of minerals to tantalise prospectors.

Millions of years of heat, wind and water have worn down, sculptured or exposed rock into some of Australia's best known landmarks - Ayers Rock, The Olgas, The MacDonnell Ranges, Kings Canyon and Chambers Pillar. Sand resulting from the breakdown of rock provided substance for the great deserts. If you wonder how those infrequently flowing creeks carved great gaps through the MacDonnell Ranges, much of the wearing away and grinding down action occurred during times when the climate here was sub-tropical, and rainfall was much higher.

It is a land of infinite mood, enormous in scope and scale, yet also sharp and fine in detail and best understood by Aborigines, whose spiritual attachment to it through their Dreaming adds another dimension to its character.

Flora

The Red Centre is a botanical wonderland, not only for its variety of vegetation, but also in the adaptation of plants to withstand the arid conditions and drought cycles. Against a background of dominant red soil, the variety, shape and form of tree, shrub and ground plant soften and enhance the aesthetic quality of the desert landscape. More than 1000 species have been recorded, and the ability of the plants to avoid, counter and endure droughts is quite remarkable.

Tough, leathery and wax-coated; thick, fleshy and succulent; needles, spikes and thorns and fine hair-covered, are some of the leaf forms designed to counter and endure dry periods by reducing moisture loss or conserving water. Root systems of ghost gum and cyprus pine probe deeply into the most unlikely precipitous rock faces to tap moisture sources from seepage, or condensation from and air and soil trapped in the crevices. Shaded valleys and water in the MacDonnell Ranges allow the continued survival of relic cycad and cabbage palm. Large river red gums and coolabah, amongst others, line the sandy creek beds, indicating moisture presence deep below.

Masses of daisies, pea flowers, pussy tails, parakeelya are some annual and ephemeral wildflowers and grasses that grow rapidly after rains, and climax in a sweep of colour. They avoid the droughts; their seeds germinate only when adequate moisture is available, and can change the red desert to green in a matter of days. Whilst plants in the Centre can flower at any time, noticeable peaks coincide fortunately with the popular tourist months of April and September. Depending on winter rains, wildflowers are at their best around August and September.

Drought, rain and fire are the major elements that regulate vegetation cover. In fact, Aborigines developed a system of patch burning to promote new growth to attract animals and so ensure an adequate food supply - a practice which the Wildlife Service is now using for conservation purposes. Grasses, roots, seeds, berries and fruits are a rich food and medicine source, and Aborigines have exploited this vast natural 'supermarket' for thousands of years. However, unless you have a good knowledge of edible 'bush tucker', it's best not to experiment as some plants are poisonous.

Some distinctive trees on the sand plains are: *desert oak* (Casuarina decaisneana) a 'droopy' willow-like tree that grows particularly in the Ayers Rock, Kings Canyon area; *corkwood* (Hakea suberea), noted for its cork-like bark and delicate yellow flowers; *desert poplar* (Codonocarpus continifolius), a tall thin tree similar in shape to the English variety; *ironwood* (Acacia estrophiolata) with tough wood and drooping foliage; and *beefwood* (Grevillea striata). On both plains and rocky slopes are: *bloodwood* (Eucalyptus terminalis), noted for its red sap; *mulga* (Acacia aneura) matures from shrub to tree and has yellow flowers; and *white-wood* (Atalaya hemiglanca) characterised by small white cup-shaped flowers and waxy leaves.

Some common shrubs on the plains are: *colony wattle* (Acacia murrayana) with small, fluffy, yellow ball-like flowers; *desert grevillea* (Grevillea juncifolia) distinctive for its long yellow flowers loaded with nectar and a source of honey for Aborigines and honey-eating birds; and *saltbush* (Atriplex nummularia). Common to plains and rocky slopes are: *witchetty bush* (Acacia kempeana) and several species of *cassia* with their 5-petalled yellow flowers. *Native fig* (Ficus platypoda) thrives on the rocky slopes; *tea-tree* (Melaleucas) are associated with watercourses and soaks, and *spinifex* is widespread on plain, rocky slope and sand dune. Refer also to flora cross-section under MacDonnell Ranges Region for further plant characteristics.

A visit to the Olive Pink Flora Reserve in Alice Springs is a worthwhile introduction to plants of the Centre. Buy the *Plant Identikit* booklet (Conservation Commission) - good value at $3.00.

Fauna

Wildlife is prolific, and like the vegetation, has adapted ingeniously to cope with the cycles of heat, drought and rain.

Larger animals include those of the kangaroo family which are marsupials (young raised in a body pouch): *red kangaroo* (Macropus rufus), the world's largest marsupial, two metres in height, very mobile and ranges the grassy shrub plains; *euro* or *wallaroo* (Macropus robustus), smaller, adapted to rocky outcrops and less mobile than the red kangaroo, survives for lengthy periods without water, and, like all kangaroos, the female raises three different aged young ('joeys') at a time - at about 6-months-old, the joey leaves its mother's pouch and is replaced within a month by a newborn, hairless one about 2-3cm in length, whereupon the female gets pregnant again (joey number one suckles for another three months from outside the pouch which is occupied by joey number two). This 'production line' can be slowed down during drought periods. The black flanked *rock-wallabies* (Petrogale lateralis) are highly agile in their rocky habitats, and best seen at Simpsons Gap.

Other larger animals are: *dingo* (Canis familiaris dingo), a dog thought to have been brought to Australia by Aborigines, howls rather than barks, hunts mainly smaller animals, usually belongs in packs although mainly seen alone, coloured sandy-yellow with an occasional black and tan, and extremely cunning; *feral cats* (Felis catus) are larger than domestic varieties and have adapted well to arid conditions; *fox* (Vulpes vulpes) is an introduced species as are the more observable *donkey* (Equus asinus), *horse* (Equus caballus), *camel* (Camelus dromedarius) and *rabbit* (Oryctolgus cuniculus).

There are many smaller animals which avoid heat stress by sheltering in burrows and the like during the day, and so are rarely seen. Some of these ***nocturnal species*** are: *brushtail possum*

Darwin

Mataranka Thermal Pool

Dragon

(Trichosurus vulpecula) a tree living marsupial; *bandicoot* (Macrotis lagotis), bilby or rabbit-eared are the only species now left; *marsupial mole* (Notoryctes typhlops), sandy-coloured, lives in desert sands; *spiny anteater* or *echidna* (Tachyglossus aculeatus), a porcupine-like, spine-covered creature; and several special of *bats* that live in caves, crevices and in tree trunks. Once rid of prejudices, native rats and mice are attractive little animals, and unlike their distant city relatives are disease and dirt free. The *spinifex hopping mouse* (Notomys alexis), among others, is fun to watch at night when spotted by torchlight. Small carnivorous mouse-like marsupials include the *stripe-faced dunnart* (Sminthopsis macroura), like many species can go into a type of suspended animation when food is scarce; fat-tailed *marsupial mouse* and hairy-footed *pouched mouse*.

Reptiles are plentiful and the spinifex habitats support the world's greatest variety of lizards, which include *goannas*, *skinks*, *geckoes* and *dragons*. Being cold-blooded, they rely on heat absorption to regular their body temperature and seek shelter when it's really hot or cold. *Perentie* (Varanus giganteus) grows to 2.5m and is the world's largest lizard - they are harmless, but like all reptiles, give them space!; *Goulds goanna* (Varanus gouldii), grows to 1.3m and is the most common variety in the arid region. *Skinks* are a varied group, and best known as they are common throughout Australia. They generally have smooth skins and large headscales - the Central Australian *blue-tongued lizard* (Tiliqua multifasciata) with its striking blue tongue, is one example. *Geckoes* are small velvet-skinned nocturnal lizards with large eyes and the ability to detach their tails as a protective mechanism. *Dragons* are distinguished from skinks and geckoes by their dull, thick, rough scales, spiny projections and lidded eyes. Some species include: *central bearded dragon* (Pogona vitticeps); *long-nosed dragon* (Lophognathus longirostris), long bodied and a fast mover when disturbed; *central netted dragon* (Ctenophorus nuchalis) has distinctive mesh patterning; the *thorny devil* (Moloch horridus), the most fearsome in appearance with its yellow-brown colouring and projecting spines, while the *frilled-neck dragon* (Chlamydosaurus kingii) has a folded frill that can be raised into a wide collar around its neck as a protective device designed to scare.

While rarely seen, be mindful that **snakes** do exist and you are best advised to give them a wide berth. Main snakes are: *king brown* or *mulga snake* (Pseudechis australis) which is widespread, grows up to 2.5m and is the largest and most dangerous; the *western brown* (Pseudonaja nuchalis) is about 1m, timid, moves quickly, and is dangerous if provoked; the *children's python* (Liasis childreni) and *carpet python* (Morelia bredii) grow to 0.75 and 2m respectively, are night hunters, timid and non-venomous. Reptiles of the Centre are well represented in Graeme Gow's Reptile World in Alice Springs, and this reptile house is a useful way to get an introduction to the range of species.

Bird life is plentiful with over 200 types being recorded. *Ground birds* include: Australian bustard (Ardeotis australis); emu (Dromaius novaehollandiae); crested pigeon (Ocyphaps lophotes); spinifex pigeon (Petrophassa plumifera); brolga (Grus rubicundus); willie wagtail (Rhipidura leucophrys); zebra finch (Poephila guttata); and painted firetail (Emblema picta). Some *shrub and tree dwellers* are: black-faced cuckoo-shrike (Coracina novaehollandiae); grey shrike-thrush (Colluricincla harmonica); red-backed and sacred kingfisher (Halcyon pyrrhopygia and sancta); spiny-cheeked honeyeater, yellow-throated miner, white-plumed honeyeater and mistletoe bird (Dicaeum hirundinaceum). *Aerial birds* include: rainbow bee-eater (Merops ornatus); varieties of woodswallows and martins.

The most colourful are the *parrots*: red-tailed black-cockatoo, little corella, pink cockatoo, galah, cockatiel, Port Lincoln ringneck, mulga parrot and budgerigar. Raven, crow, magpie, magpie-lark and butcherbirds are distinctive black and white birds.

Main *waterbirds* are: pelican, cormorant, duck, egret, heron, plover and grebe. Barn owl and southern boobook are *night birds*. *Birds of prey* include: wedge-tailed eagle, brown falcon, black and whistling kite, black-shouldered and letter-winged kite and Australian kestrel.

Aquatic life includes fish, frog and crustacea, which generally bury themselves and suspend body functions when the waterholes dry up. Desert squalls called 'willy-willies' have been known to suck fish, tadpoles, frogs, shrimps and crabs into the air where they eventually fall some distance away as 'fish rain'.

> Best times to see wildlife are early morning, evening, or just after storms, when animals are more active, and waterhole localities are ideal spots.

Take your time on walks; frequent stops and patience may well be rewarded by wildlife activity happening around you, and there's much truth in the saying, "happiness isn't found at the end of the track, but along the way".

The Conservation Commission also has an excellent *Wildlife Identikit* booklet available (costs $3) that covers birds, reptiles, mammals, aquatic life, spiders and insects. A detailed bird checklist brochure for Central Australia is useful, too. *The Living Centre of Australia* by Alec Blombery is an illustrated field guide to the region and recommended for those seeking greater detail on landscape, flora and fauna.

Attractions and Conservation

Most of the scenic attractions of the Centre are protected by Conservation Commission Park or Reserve status. The accessibility and popularity of many parks, particularly those in the MacDonnell Ranges, places pressure on facilities and the environment. These can be minimised if visitors are mindful of regulations with respect to litter, fire, firewood, flora and fauna, and use of vehicles.

The Conservation Commission provides a wide range of interpretive displays, information boards, literature and facilities at the parks, and fees are levied. The Department of Mines and Energy has excellent coloured brochures covering the geology and landforms of some of the parks.

Driving

Always check the condition of unsealed roads. 'Off the beaten track' travellers are advised to check fuel availability, road conditions and Aboriginal land permit requirements prior to leaving. The granting of land rights to Aborigines means that they now legally own large areas of land, so make sure you don't trespass. Keep to designated tracks, and users of all roads should be alert to livestock and roadtrains. Refer to Information and Advice Section for detailed Outback travel comments.

Touring Suggestions

Most of the Centre's attractions are natural features and, although widely separated (Ayers Rock is 450km [279 miles] from Alice Springs!), are located in distinct areas that with careful route planning can be seen without too much back-tracking.

Day and extended tours of the MacDonnells can be undertaken, but it's best to have at least one overnight stay both east and west. Ormiston Gorge and Glen Helen Lodge in the Western MacDonnells, and Ross River Homestead in the Eastern, are suggested bases for exploration. Further west from Glen Helen, a round trip including Red Bank Gorge, Gosse Bluff, Hermannsburg, Finke Gorge National Park (Palm Valley), back to Namatjira Drive, allows you to see a range of Centralian scenery, but you will need a 4WD in places.

There is much to see and do in Alice Springs, and a good starting point is the Spencer and Gillen Museum where fascinating displays provide good background information before visiting places.

Another good round trip is the Lasseter Highway to Ayers Rock, then back to Angus Downs Road to old Wallara Ranch and Kings Canyon, returning to the Stuart Highway via Henbury Meteorite Craters. Try the revitalised Old Ghan Train for a trip to Ewaninga Siding, or visit Rainbow Valley by camel-back; a couple of novel ways to see landscape features.

There's plenty of 'off the beaten track stuff' for 'explorers' - Old Andado Station in the Simpson Desert (Simpson Desert Loop Track) and Chambers Pillar. Roads deep into western deserts are definitely for the well-equipped 4WD traveller only.

Many tours are available, including escorted 4WD and safari type. Vehicle rentals are worthwhile considering if you wish to be independent - major and local firms offer a good range in Alice Springs. Hire bicycles is an idyllic way to tour around the MacDonnells. Balloon, helicopter and light aircraft flights are interesting alternative ways to see things.

Specialist interest tours worth considering are: Discovery Ecotours' natural history treks, and Rod Steinert's Dreamtime Tour (Aboriginal Culture tour). Cattle station tours and stays are further touring options. Check with a Northern Territory Travel Station for details.

PLACES AND ATTRACTIONS

AILERON

Population 8

Location

Half a kilometre off the Stuart Highway, 133km (82 miles) north of Alice Springs.

Characteristics

Ian McCormack runs this modern roadhouse that offers a well-stocked general store, licensed restaurant (main course $7-13), accommodation, and a couple of entertaining kangaroos. There used to be a hotel here, but that was burnt down in 1980, and the homestead of the 4,000 sq km (1520 sq miles), Aileron Station, is next door. Of interest in the area are Ryans Well and Annas Reservoir (see separate listings) and Native Gap, 20km (12 miles) south.

Accommodation

Motel style - single $45, double $55.
Camping/Caravans - powered sites $12 per power point, unpowered $5 per van. Sites grassed and shaded; pets allowed, dogs must be leashed.

ALICE SPRINGS

Population 24,000

Location

In the heart of the MacDonnell Ranges, 1482km (918 miles) south of Darwin and 1543km (958 miles) north of Adelaide, on the Stuart Highway. It also lies 25km (15 miles) south of the Tropic of Capricorn.

Characteristics

It is Australia's premier Outback town destination, but don't expect to find hitching rails, 'ringers', or ramshackle pubs. Alice Springs, *The Alice* or simply *Alice*, has long since shed her frontier appearance, and with her sparkling shopping plazas, pedestrian mall, palm-fringed resorts and suburban sprawl, has become quite a modern, sophisticated Miss.

Dramatic growth brought about by the tourist boom has led to the destruction of all but a few remnants of the Old Alice; with the 1988 brutal removal of Marron's Newsagency (the first glass fronted shop in *Alice*, and over 50 years old), the only Outback reminders in the main street are the Inland Mission (Adelaide House) and the waft of leather from the saddlery.

In itself, the town is not Outback any more, and the place projected in Neville Shute's novel *A Town Like Alice* no longer exists - in fact, some long-time residents suggest that it was far from being the bonza (good) town which Joe Harman reminisced about. But the real Outback is not too far away, and this stark discovery fosters an acute awareness of the past, as well as lessening any conflicts between town image and city reality. Despite the outward changes in character, the continuation of The Flying Doctor Service, the intriguing legends of a thriving Aboriginal culture, and a host of new explorers and pioneers, such as the tour operators, still lend an air of excitement to Alice Springs.

Qualities too, such as the lurking Outback reality, an upside-down river where the water flows mainly underneath its sandy bed, surrounds of ancient ranges and red desert, isolation highlighted by over 1100km (682 miles) road distance from a comparably sized settlement, and always sunshine, piercing blue skies and star-filled nights, make *The Alice* a mecca for tourists.

City Centre

It's attractive, treed and compact, with modern shopping plazas, art galleries, museums, information centres, restaurants, essential services and historic buildings all within easy walking distance. Focal point is the Todd Mall with Yulara type 'sails' as its centrepiece. Some hotels and motels fringe the centre, while most other accommodation places, Casino and Cultural Centre are within 3km (2 miles). Apart from tourism, the commercial centre serves a thriving cattle and mining industry, as well as personnel from the highly secretive US communications establishment at Pine Gap. Government administration and railhead are other functions.

History

The area in and around Alice Springs is the traditional homeland of the Aranda people whose ancestors have lived her for thousands of years, and whose total culture is enigmatic to non-Aborigines.

The original Alice Springs was founded in 1871 as a Telegraph Station, situated alongside a Todd River waterhole thought to have been discovered by surveyor W.W. Mills. He named it after the wife of the Superintendent of Telegraphs, Charles Todd. To the Aranda, the waterhole is known as Tjanerilji. The completion of the Adelaide to Darwin Telegraph Line established a well defined and watered route through the Centre. Along its umbilical-like line came explorers, prospectors and pastoralists, and the beginnings of 'The Track'.

The tiny settlement was not designed to cater for outsiders (it received once yearly supplies by Afghan camel strings) and the influx associated with mineral discoveries in the Eastern MacDonnell Ranges, among other factors, led to the establishment of Stuart Town. It was sited midway between the station and Heavitree Gap in 1888. Despite the promise of a railway, the first 96 blocks of land offered for sale saw only five buyers. William Benstead had confidence though, and built Central Australia's first pub, The Stuart Arms, which remains in name only today.

Francis Gillen described *The Alice* of 1901 as having nine buildings; three breweries, a pub, three stores and two houses. The breweries were closed, not through lack of demand for beer, but because the brewers drank the amber liquid before it had time to cool - or so it was claimed!

The railway came in 1929. Population rose from 40 Europeans in 1926 to 250 by 1932. Consolidation of the cattle and mining activities gave it a sound economic base. But it was also a tough, frontier cattle-town with a dusty street and the rowdy weather-board Stuart Arms Pub, which offered the only accommodation in town, including beds on the veranda for latecomers!

Between 1926 and 1931, Stuart Town was a seat of government for the separate Territory of Central Australia, and the name was changed officially to Alice Springs in 1933. The population at this time was only 467.

During World War II, Alice Springs was a major military base and, with the bombing of Darwin in 1942, became the administrative headquarters for the Northern Territory. Supreme Allied Commander, South West Pacific Area, US General Douglas MacArthur spent some time here. Australia, north of Alice Springs, was under military control and many civilians were moved out of the town. In 1943, the Stuart Highway was sealed between Alice Springs and Darwin to facilitate rapid troop movements. On the lighter side, one Brigadier claimed that liquor constituted one-third of civilian supplies coming up from Adelaide - the Tennant Creek pub was selling beer at $28 a case, and the lessee at Dunmarra was buying grog in 30 to 50 case lots. In the interests of efficiency, the Brigadier restricted soldiers' drinking in Alice Springs hotels to just one hour a day, and placed a ban on all licensed places along the Stuart Highway. It's doubtful, though, if this order affected the rate of beer consumption by Aussie troops!

Partly due to glowing reports by ex-servicemen, the tourist industry started to develop after the war. There were tough times between 1957 and 1962, when virtually no rain fell and cattle numbers dropped dramatically from over 350,000 to below 175,000. Population in 1961 was 4648, rising to over 18,000 twenty years later.

If you find the name Blatherskite Park intriguing, it was once a stockmen's meeting place or camp, where they used to yarn or blather. In other words, a spot where they talked a 'load of bull'.

Alice Springs

Water and Floods

Aquifers (layers of rock which hold water) surround Alice Springs and supply the city's needs. Most water is drawn from the Mereenie Sandstone formation where bores at Roe Creek satisfy daily demands of around 50 million litres (2500 litres per person, making consumption rates at Alice Springs amongst the highest in Australia). Future water will be piped from greater distances to prevent depletion, maintain quality, and allow natural recharge of aquifers.

Todd River flooding, while infrequent, was awesome on the three occasions it happened in the 1980s. Alice Springs gets most of its rainfall in summer (so it's unlikely that floods will occur during peak tourist periods), generally as a result of tropical monsoonal depressions moving inland across Central Australia. Heavy rainfall, rocky terrain and steep slopes combine to produce rapid run-off and flash flooding - a good reason not to camp in any creek beds. The flood height peaked at 1.73m (5.5 ft) at Wills Terrace in 1983, while in 1988 it was 1.80m (6 ft) at the same location. But rest assured, Alice Springs is well geared to meet any flood emergency.

Tourist Information

The Telephone Area Code is 089.

Central Australian Tourism Industry Association - detailed local information. Excellent monthly information booklet *This Month In Alice*, and separate map of the city and Red Centre. They are very much up front at their airport booth, which is open 7 days a week, and at the railway station booth, which is open when The Ghan rolls in. Main office is open daily 9am-5pm, cnr Hartley Street & Gregory Terrace, ph 525 199.

Automobile Association (NT), 58 Sargent Street, ph 521 087, and Shop 4, 105 Gregory Terrace, ph 531 322.

National Trust - heritage information and books. Open Mon-Fri 10.30am-1pm. Old Hartley Street School, Hartley Street, ph 524 516.

Northern Territory Conservation Commission - national parks information and brochures. Stuart Highway, 7km south of town, ph 518 211, open Mon-Fri 8am-4.20pm. They also have a desk in the Tourist Association office.

Attractions

Around Town

Anzac Hill. Either walk up via the 'Lions' walk (starts opposite Catholic Church), or drive up for the best viewing and orientation point. Located just north of the city centre.

Spencer and Gillen Museum. After Anzac Hill, this is a starting point to learn something of the natural history, pioneering days and Aboriginal culture of Central Australia. First Floor, Ford Plaza, Todd Mall. Open 9am-5pm 7 days, $2 admission. Children free.

Adelaide House. Built as the first Alice Springs Hospital by the Australian Inland Mission between 1920 and 1926, under the direction of the late Reverend John Flynn. It incorporates an ingenious cooling system. With the establishment of a government hospital in 1939, it became a convalescent home for Outback women and children, and was declared a museum in 1980. The stone radio hut behind the building was where Traeger and Flynn conducted their first radio transmission in 1926. Traeger invented the first pedal radio transmitter used by Flynn for his Flying Doctor Service in 1929. This development gave the Outback stations a 'mantle of safety' for the first time. Todd Mall, open 10am-4pm weekdays, 10am-noon Sat. Adults $2, children $1, family $5.50.

Flynn Memorial Church. Built in memory of the Reverend John Flynn. Todd Mall.

Old Court House. Was originally built as the Administrator's Council Rooms when Central Australia had its own government, between 1926 and 1931. Viewing from Parsons Street only.

The Residency. Built in 1926 for John Cawood, the first Government Resident of Central Australia. It now functions as a museum of Northern Territory history. Parsons Street.

Stuart Town Gaol. Completed in 1908, it's the oldest building in Alice. The gaol's first white prisoners were put away for such offences as horse stealing, and the last two for riding on the Ghan without tickets! The gaol closed in 1938, and it is now a National Trust property. Parsons Street, open Sat 9am-11.30am, Tues and Thurs 10.30am-12.30pm (Mar-Nov), $2.

Hartley Street School. This first government school opened in 1929 with Miss Pearl Burton as teacher. The building reflects contrasting styles of architecture, with the addition of the octagonal room in 1946. It now houses the National Trust.

Panorama "Guth". Dutch artist Henry Guth started an art studio here, and conceived and executed an impressive 360 degree landscape painting of the Centre. You view it from a central elevated observation point. Also, there's an art gallery featuring many of the Hermannsburg School of water colourists. Open 9am-5pm Mon-Sat, 2pm-5pm Sun. Hartley Street. Adults $2.50, children $1. Closed Sun (December-February).

Tunk's Store. A good example of an old-type store built in 1940 and run by Ralph Tunks until 1979. Corner Hartley Street and Stott Terrace, and now the town office of Hertz NT.

The Old Government Homes. Built for government officers in the early 1930s, they give an idea of period styles. Hartley Street.

Royal Flying Doctor Base. Offers a window on Outback isolation and a visit is worthwhile. Open 9am-4pm Mon-Sat, 1-4pm Sun. Tours half-hourly. Adults $2, children 50c. Stuart Terrace, ph 521 129.

Olive Pink Flora Reserve. A unique assemblage of Central Australian native plants in a reserve south-east across the river from the town centre. It was established by a rather remarkable woman, Olive Pink, who lived with the Aranda and Walpiri people in the Tanami, worked hard for their advancement, and was a great stirrer of Government Departments. There are fine displays at the visitor centre. Open 7 days 10am-4pm. Access via Tuncks Road.

Aboriginal Art. Aboriginal paintings and artifacts by artists from the desert regions have captured the interest of art galleries from London to New York. This recent fascination with its subject matter and style has spawned a large number of galleries in Alice Springs. See also page 107.

Technology, Transport & Communications, including Aviation Museum and Kookaburra Memorial. Houses reminders of the early days of aviation in the Red Centre in the former Connellan Hangar. It's the site of Alice Springs' first airport. Recent extensions to the Hangar provide a home for the original AEC roadtrain, built in the UK as part of a joint military/civil engineering project. It was found rusting away along with three 'dogs' (trailers) in Darwin and has been restored. Open 10am-4pm, 7 days. Memorial Drive.

Memorial Cemetery. Contains the graves of Lasseter (of Lasseter's lost gold reef fame, see Docker River listing), Albert Namatjira, a famous Aboriginal artist, and E.J. Connellan, founder of Connellan Airways, the Territory's first. Memorial Avenue, just beyond the Aviation Museum.

(Opposite)
The Olgas

A jetty in Broome

Bungle Bungle

Stuart Memorial Cemetery. A small area of pioneer graves. The headstones of some have disappeared in this original Stuart Town Cemetery. George Crescent, off Larapinta Drive.

Diarama Village. Outlines myths and legends of Aborigines and has artifacts and local crafts. Open 7 days, 10am-5pm. Adults $2, children $1. Larapinta Drive.

Araluen Arts Centre. Centre for visual and performing arts. Art and exhibition galleries open 9am-5pm weekdays, 10am-4pm weekends. See also under Nightlife listing. Larapinta Drive, ph 525 022.

Around North Alice

RSL Club War Museum. An interesting collection of war memorabilia is located at Schwartz Crescent. Open 10am to late, Sun from 11am.

School of The Air. This is where teachers communicate with pupils who live on the remote Outback stations. It's a fascinating place that first started radio education in 1951. Open 8.00-noon weekdays during term time, costs $1. Head Street, ph 522 122.

The Old Telegraph Station Historical Reserve. Covers 570ha (1407 acres) and is administered by the Conservation Commission. It's the original settlement site, and there are ideal places for picnic lunches along the banks of the Todd River. It features the waterhole from which Alice Springs takes its name, a visitors centre, and many restored buildings that comprised the original Telegraph Station Settlement. There's an interesting walk to Trig Hill Lookout, which is a good spot for photographs and views. The Larapinta long distance Trail Walk links to Simpsons Gap National Park. Facilities include shaded grassy picnic areas with tables, barbecues, toilets, including disabled, and water. A wildlife enclosure adds interest, and rangers are most helpful. There's plenty of literature about the reserve available, too, and the area gives an insight into the pioneering lifestyle of a century ago.

It functioned as the main station of a telegraph line laid across 3000km (1860 miles) of rugged, inhospitable and unknown desert terrain between Adelaide and Darwin. It was erected in 2 years, used 30,000 telegraph poles, involved hundreds of construction men, and was masterminded by Charles Todd. Opened in 1872, the line connected Australia to the rest of the world, which suddenly reduced the isolation of the country. Messages which took weeks could now be relayed in hours, and legendary cattleman, Sir Sidney Kidman, used it effectively for relaying instructions to his drovers moving herds down the stock routes (see Bond Springs listing for Kidman story). Stations were needed at intervals to boost the flagging signals, and as you travel up 'The Track', you'll see a few more smaller ones.

Guided tours are available, and it's located 3km (1miles) north of town. Open October-April, 8am-9pm, May-September 8am-7pm. Entry is adults $2.50, children $1.

Around South Alice

Pitchi Richi Sanctuary. Features an extraordinary collection of relic machinery, station implements, and artifacts of a bygone era, in an outdoor bush setting. There are also sculptures by William Ricketts. The original owner, C.H. Chapman, made a fortune from gold in the Tanami, and built the strange cement house which he called 'Pearly Gates'. Leo Corbett took over in 1955, and established a sanctuary and developed the outdoor museum. Corbett was a rather remarkable man. His prompt action prevented Heavitree Gap from being quarried, scarred and widened by government contractors in the 1960s - he took out a miner's right, pegged the area as a gold-mining lease, and called on Police Inspector Bill McKinnon to "eject all those people who are interfering with my mining lease". There was quite a fuss, but there has been no quarrying since. For many years afterward, Leo still held the mining right and 'worked' his claim the statutory one day a year. He was also called the 'modern Saint

Francis of Assisi' for saving thousands of parrots and finches which descended on his dam during the terrible drought of the early 1960s. He had plenty of water, but no food, so he appealed to four Southern newspapers for bird seed. A few days later, an airline van arrived with a tonne of seed with another 2.5 tonnes on its way! Birdseed arrived by mail too, and with many broken packages it caused a mice plague in the Post Office. Leo solved that problem by shovelling a mixture of birdseed and mice into his truck! There are still plenty of birds which add further interest to the museum.

It's located across the Southern Todd River Causeway along Palm Circuit, and is worth a visit. It has a kiosk and sells souvenirs. Admission - adults $3, children $1. Open 7 days, 9am-6pm, ph 521 931.

Stuart Auto Museum. Houses a number of restored vintage cars, motor bikes, as well as old telephones, phonographs, etc. It also has a restaurant and caters for light meals. Located at Palm Circuit, open 7 days during season, 9am-4pm. Admission - adults $2, children free.

Mecca Date Gardens. Date palms, the oldest known cultivated tree crop, established as early as 3000BC, were introduced to Central Australia by Afghan camel drivers. This 2ha (5 acre) date plantation is the only one of its kind in Australia. There's no entry fee. You can purchase dates and enjoy afternoon tea under the palms. Palm Circuit. Open Mon-Sat 9am-5pm, Sun 10am-4pm, ph 522 425.

Frontier Camel Farm and Reptiles of Arid Australia. Two enterprises on the one site offer a camel museum, camels and camel rides and tours, while Reptile World houses a fascinating collection of desert snakes, goannas and lizards, all of which can be viewed closely (and safely). There's an informative talk by staff. The entry fee (adult $7, children $3.50) includes a short camel ride, reptile house and museum. Camel tours cost $22 per hour for adults, $15 for children (6-12 years). Take a Camel out to Dinner incorporates a one-hour camel trek down the Todd River to Chateau Hornsby

Winery, where you indulge in wine tasting before a meal. Costs $60 per person. Ross River Highway, open 7 days, 9am-5pm, ph 530 444.

Wallaby Rock. At Heavitree Gap Motel you can watch these delightful creatures in the wild when they make their evening descent from the rocky slopes for feeding.

Old Timers' Museum. A museum with exhibits of the pioneering days. South Stuart Highway, open 7 days during season, 2-4pm. Admission $1, groups by appointment, ph 522 844.

Ghan Preservation Society. The society has not only built a station to the original design specifications, but has also restored 26km (16 miles) of the Old Ghan train track, and a 'W' Class and 'C17' Class Steam and Diesel locomotives. The MacDonnell Siding location features a Station which has tea rooms, souvenir shop, museum, and toilets, including for the disabled; a bbq picnic area with tables, and of course, train and tracks. Train trips to Ewaninga Siding (26km-16 miles) operate. Locomotives used are mainly diesel; steam is used 2-3 times per month for special events. Trips can be undertaken either from MacDonnell or Ewaninga Siding. Future plans include a dining car and period dress. At Ewaninga, there's a restored fettler's cottage (railway worker's house) which has a kiosk and toilet. Future plans will possibly incorporate visits to Ewaninga Rock Engravings.

The Old Ghan Railway and the Overland Telegraph Line once formed the Territory's two life lines, and the name Ghan honours the Afghan Camelmen who plugged the gap between Oodnadatta railhead and Alice Springs. A statue in the city railway station foyer bears the inscription: "In 1878 work started on the planned 1800 mile railway. It got to Oodnadatta where it stopped for nearly 40 years during which time camel trains run by hardy Afghans worked the country to Alice Springs ferrying passengers and freight up from Oodnadatta. The railway reached Alice Springs in 1929 and the train was affectionately known as the Ghan. It was variously known as

Afghan Express, Afghan Special, The Royal Ghan, The Flash Ghan". For more on Afghans and camels, see Orange Creek listing.

This attraction offers a unique and nostalgic desert journey that is a must for visitors. Phone the Society (555 047) for times and costs. South Stuart Highway, open 7 days, 9am-5pm, admission adult $3, children and pensioners $1.50. Dogs are not allowed.

Chateau Hornsby Winery. The only winery in the Territory has five grape varieties: Shiraz, Cabernet Sauvignon, Riesling, Semillon and Chardonnay. It's open from 9am to 4pm for lunches and wine tastings, and there's some lively evening entertainment with Dave Berman and Ted Egan (see also Nightlife listing). There is a restaurant, too. Located in Petrick Road, off South Stuart Highway, ph 555 133.

Flower Farm. "Wintercarn" is a commercial flower farm located next to the Winery. Open weekdays 7am-3pm for flower sales. Tours 2.30pm. Admission $1.

Fossicking. There is an amethyst field along Ilparpa Road (turn off from South Stuart Highway almost opposite the Old Timers' Home). The area is 4.6km (3 miles) from the turn-off. The Gem Cave, Todd Mall, will identify rocks and provide information, as will the Mines and Energy Department, Minerals House, 58 Hartley Street. Refer also to Information and Advice Section on Fossicking.

Alice Springs	J	F	M	A	M	J	J	A	S	O	N	D	Ann. av.
Temperature: C°													
Av. monthly max.	36	35	32	28	23	20	19	22	26	31	33	35	28
Av. monthly min.	21	21	17	13	8	5	4	6	10	15	18	20	13
Rainfall:													
Av. monthly mm.	38	45	34	14	17	15	17	12	10	22	25	36	285

The MacDonnell Ranges. See MacDonnell Ranges Region following Alice Springs listing.

Organised Tours

There is a great variety of tours of varying duration that cover scenic attractions, geography, historic places, Aboriginal Culture, cattle stations, and special interests, many of which are 'off the beaten track' stuff. Alice Springs is the main departure point and base for Red Centre exploration, and large tour operators such as AAT Kings and Australian Pacific, are complemented by a host of smaller local companies, each with their own specialist niche and mode of transport. You can see and experience things by bus or coach, 4WD safari, camel, horse, chauffeured limousine, aircraft, helicopter and balloon. There are even operators who tailor tours to meet your specific needs. Most day and extended tours include a meal in the cost. Some tours offer last minute stand-by rates, and 'off season' touring can be a bit cheaper.

Staff at the Alice Springs Regional Tourist Association office will point you in the right direction.

A sample of the types of tours, times, costs and operators, is as follows. Bookings - Tourist Association, or direct using telephone numbers listed.

Coach Tours

AAT Kings, ph 525 266: 3 hour town tour, around $36 adult; 3 day Ayers Rock and Kings Canyon, around $475 adult (includes motel/lodge accommodation, meals, entry fees); Palm Valley day tour, around $79 adult.

Centre Highlights, ph 531 733: half-day Standley Chasm/Simpsons Gap, around $30 adult; 1 day Western MacDonnells, around $59 adult; Kings Canyon 1 day Safari from $100 adult; 2 day Ayers Rock/Olgas, around $150 adult.

Camp Oven Kitchen, ph 531 411: 4 hour Evening Bush Dinner Tour, around $45 per person.

Trek-About, ph 530 714: 5 day camping tour, fully inclusive (just bring yourself and sleeping bag), around $439 per person.

Smaller Operators and Four Wheel Drive (4WD)

Many visit similar places to coach tours, but they have advantages of smaller groups and are more flexible in Outback terrain.

Rod Steinert Tours, ph 555 000: Aboriginal Dreamtime Bushtucker Tour, 4 hours, 7 days 8am-noon, self drive, $42 adult, coach $62 adult. It's highly recommended.

Bond Springs Homestead: Cattle station tour - see under alphabetical listing of places for detail.

Outback Experience, ph 532 666; Day Trip Chambers Pillar, Rainbow Valley, Simpson Desert, $95 adult; 2.5 day Simpson Desert tour to Old Andado Station, from $275 adult.

Sandrifter Safaris, ph 532 126, is a 4WD private charter that offers groups of like interest a range of specialist tours (artists, geologists, photographers, field naturalists, etc) - prices negotiable.

Air Tours

Skyport, ph 526 666: offers the Outback Mailrun, which drops the post to the remote cattle stations, costs $205 per person; all day air safari covers Uluru, Kings Canyon, Palm Valley, Lake Amadeus, costs $270. Short flights are negotiable.

Outback Ballooning, ph 528 723: champagne breakfast with sunrise trips. Costs - half-hour adults $110, one hour adults $170, children half price.

Special Interest Tours

Discovery Ecotours, are specialists in science adventure and cultural tourism, and you don't have to be an expert to join one of their natural history or Aboriginal Cultural Odysseys into the desert. This is a welcome, new approach to tourism in Australia, and each tour is led by an expert.

Tours are exceptional because participants mix with Wildlife Scientists who are studying unique wildlife, giving people a special opportunity to see, touch and photograph wildlife in the wild. Traditional Aboriginal culture is a feature of many of these tours. Aboriginal people guide tours through their country, culture and art, providing rewarding encounters and first-hand understanding of Aboriginal people and culture in many parts of Australia. It is necessary to book ahead for all of the Discovery Ecotours, and for more information, ph 528 308, fax 531 308. **Some examples:** Kakadu, Arnhem Land & Cobourg Peninsula, 7 days, $1955 adult; Simpson Desert, Coongie Lakes & Flinders Ranges, 14 days, $2699 adult; Sail Arnhem Land to Nhulunbuy, 9 days, $2437.

Events

The Lions Camel Cup: Australia's premier camel races. Second weekend in **May.**

Bangtail Muster: A lively parade of floats. First Monday in **May.**

Shell Oils Finke Desert Race - Alice-Finke-Alice: 240km race over unmade fast roads, through sandhills and over rocky outcrops. Queen's Birthday weekend in **June.**

The Great Train Race: Man v Machine. The Old Ghan Train takes on runners along a 6-10km (6 miles) stretch of the track. Followed by open day fete.

In **July/August** at the Ghan Preservation Society, MacDonnell Siding.

Alice Springs Rodeo: **August/September,** at Blatherskite Park.

Henley-On-Todd: A boat regatta with a difference - no water and bottomless boats! In the Todd River next to Anzac Oval in **September/October.**

Corkwood Festival: features Central Australian arts, crafts, music and entertainment. Anzac Oval in **November.**

How To Get There

Refer also to Northern Territory *How To Get There* section.
By Air
Ansett Australia and Qantas operate daily services from all states.
By Coach
Pioneer Express, Greyhound and Bus Australia run regular services.
By Rail
The Ghan, between Adelaide and Alice Springs, takes around 21 hours, and offers a motor-rail service.
By Road
While it's a long way from anywhere, major roads from other States are bitumen.

Local Transport

Taxis and a bus service are the only forms of public transport. Many hotels offer courtesy coach transfer to and from the city centre.
Taxis
Alice Springs Taxis, ph 521 877.
Alice Radio Cars, ph 523 700. Both companies offer tours.

Airport Shuttle Service

Bus transfers from the airport to your accommodation destination cost $7. You must book for pick-up service to airport, ph 531 011.

Vehicle Rentals

Renting can be an economical way to see attractions, especially for groups. Rates are competitive, and there are variable concessions. Mokes or similar are popular, but some have distance restrictions - costs from $18 per day.

Budget, 64 Hartley Street, ph 524 133.

Hertz, Gap Road, ph 522 644.

Avis, 78 Todd Street, ph 524 366.

Territory Rent-A-Car, Hartley Street, ph 529 999.

Thrifty, 64 Hartley Street, ph 526 555.

Brits, Stuart Transit Plaza, Stuart Highway, ph 528 814.

Mopeds and Bicycles

There are a number of bicycle tracks, and many attractions are within easy cycling range. Bicycles cost from about $10 per day ($20 deposit), while mopeds (motor scooters) are around $18 per day, $11 half-day, and generally require $50 deposit.

Some places: Shell Todd Service Station, Todd Street, ph 522 279 - mopeds, $12 for 3 hours; Melanka Lodge, 94 Todd Street, ph 522 233 - bicycles.

Shopping

There are many outlets for traditional and contemporary Aboriginal artifacts, weapons and paintings, produced by Central Australian craftsmen. Prices are reasonably uniform, but while you can expect to pay more than at the smaller settlements along 'The Track' and Outback places, there's a greater range. It pays to shop around, and genuine items should have the artist's name, place of origin, and descriptive notes, as a measure of authenticity. Some prices: boomerangs from $25; didgeridoos from $60; bark paintings from $50; sand paintings from $25; and Namatjira prints from $15.

Todd River

Opals, gemstone, jewellery, crafts from local natural materials, pottery, fine arts, books on Central Australia, and Outback clothing, are further options.

Accommodation

With the recent flurry of buildings in Alice Springs, accommodation supply has now caught up with demand, but it is still advisable to book ahead for the place of your choice during the busy months. All categories of places to stay are well represented.

Most places have swimming pools, and newer ones have facilities for the disabled. Here are some options.

Sheraton, from $175, Barrett Drive, ph 528 000;

Vista Alice Springs, from $110, Stephens Road, ph 526 100;

Diplomat, from $89, cnr Gregory Terrace & Hartley St, ph 528 977;

Heavitree Gap Motel, from $70, Palm Circuit, ph 524 866;

Midland Motel, from $55, Traeger Avenue, ph 521 588;

Elkira Motel, from $63 (disabled, pool), 65 Bath Street, ph 521 222;

Red Centre Resort, motel from $116, bunkhouse accommodation available, North Stuart Highway, ph 528 955;

Melanka Lodge, from $35, 94 Todd Street, ph 522 233.

Stuart Lodge YWCA, single $27, Stuart Terrace, ph 521 894;

Pioneer Youth Hostel, from $12, cnr Parsons Street & Leichhardt Terrace, ph 528 855; *Youth Hostel,* $9 per person, cnr Todd Street & Stott Terrace, ph 525 016.

Camping/Caravans

MacDonnell Range Tourist Park - on-site vans from $40, caravan sites $16 for 2 persons, tents $13 for 2. Pets not allowed. Sites are grassed, swimming pool, fuel, shop. Palm Place, ph 526 111.

Heavitree Gap Park - on-site vans from $30, powered sites $15 for 2 persons, unpowered tent-site $6 per person. Grassed sites, no pets, swimming pool, shop, camping gas. Palm Circuit, ph 522 370.

Stuart Caravan Park - caravan sites $14.50 for 2 persons, un-powered tent sites $12 for 2, cabins and on-site vans from $32, pool, shop, camping gas, no dogs. Larapinta Drive, ph 522 547.

Wintersun Gardens Caravan Park - caravan sites $14.50 for 2 persons, tent sites $10 for 2. No pets. North Stuart Highway, ph 524 080.

Carmichael Tourist Park - cabins from $35, caravan sites from $13 for 2 persons, tent sites from $5 per person. Shade, pool, shop, camping gas, dogs allowed (leashed). Tmara Mara Street (off Larapinta Drive), ph 521 200.

Other caravan parks are G'Day Mate Tourist Park, Palm Circuit, ph 529 589; and Greenleaves Caravan Park, Burke Street, ph 528 645. The latter allow pets (leashed). Check well in advance.

Pets

Most accommodation establishments do not allow pets. The only cat and dog boarding kennels are at Triple Star Ranch, ph 521 587, but you must contact them well in advance, and their hours are strictly between 11am and 2pm Monday to Saturday. Refer also to Information and Advice section on Pets.

Eating Out

In and around Todd Mall there are plenty of take-aways and coffee bars, and **Kentucky Fried Chicken** is not too far away. At Eastside Shopping Centre, across the river in Lindsay Avenue, there is an excellent Fish and Chips shop, while next door is **Le Coq En Pate,** a delightful French Delicatessen that specialises in Brittany style food. It's run by Jacques and Francois Cocheu, who also offer a superb take-away evening menu - open Tuesday to Thursday until 7pm, Friday to Sunday until 8.30pm, ph 529 759.

Joannes Cafe is highly regarded by locals for lunches, Reg Harris Lane.

For counter-style pub meals, **The Stuart Arms Bistro** (steaks and the like around $10) in Todd Mall, and **The Old Alice Inn,** located at the top of Todd Mall, are good value.

The Hindquarter Steakhouse, Melanka Lodge, 94 Todd Street, ph 522 233, has relatively inexpensive meals. An interesting alternative is offered by **The Red Centre Resort** - they supply a bbq meat package, and you cook it on their pool-side bbq. I saw a few backpackers enjoy a swim while their $11.50 worth of meat was sizzling away! It's an ideal family spot too, and you don't have to be a guest to enjoy it. North Stuart Highway, ph 528 955.

You'll be hard pushed to find a better restaurant, for intimate atmosphere and fine food, than **Midlands**. The walls are lined with life-sized photographs and sculptures of Central Australia's Outback characters, while its range of meats (kangaroo, emu, camel, buffalo, lamb and fish) are an imaginative delight. Main course between $11-$15. Located at 4 Traeger Avenue, ph 521 588.

Some other medium priced restaurants that reflect the range of food styles are: **Lilli's** - specialises in Australiana (buffalo with witchetty grub sauce) and has a family emphasis, main course around $12; **Heavitree Gap Motel,** ph 524 260; Stuart Auto Museum, **Capone's,** where you can dine a la carte with a vintage wine and car, Ross River Highway, ph 524 844; **Golden Inn Chinese Restaurant,** a variety of Asian food, Undoolya Road, ph 526 910; **Overlanders Steakhouse** - plenty of Territorian flavour here with camel, kangaroo, buffalo steaks and bush music, good value from $12, 72 Hartley Street, ph 522 159; **Bojangles Bar and Grill** - excellent steaks and salad bar from $12, Todd Street, ph 522 873; and **La Casalinga,** Italian, 105 Gregory Terrace, ph 524 508.

Most resorts and motels also have restaurants, while The Bradshaw Room at the Sheraton, and The Retreat at The Territory Motor Inn, are more elegant establishments.

For unusual eating out, the **Bushman's Night** features a few bush tucker surprises and plenty of fun, orchestrated by the inimitable Rod Steinert. It's highly recommended, ph 555 000.

A bush setting and sunset campfire, four course dinner, an informal chat about the Centralian landscape, and star identification, is offered by the **Camp Oven Kitchen.** Naomi and Chris have resurrected some of the old bush cooking skills and implements, as well as fostering a good Aussie yarn around the campfire. Costs from $40, ph 531 411.

Night Life

Lasseters Casino: poker machines and Keno from 1pm to close, gaming tables from 7pm to close. They are strict on dress - neat clean trousers (no denims or cords), shirt and dress shoes for men, and no denims or cords for women, either. (Refer also to Dress standards in the Information section.) Barrett Drive, ph 525 066.

Trumps Nitespot: features disco and latest releases on a huge screen. Open Friday and Saturday nights to 6am. Located at the Casino.

Simpsons Gap Bar: live entertainment from 8.30pm, Mon-Sat. Sheraton Hotel, Barrett Drive, ph 528 000.

The Old Alice Inn: live entertainment Wed to Sunday in the Piano Bar, 8pm-1am. Disco, Thursday and Saturday, 8pm-4am. Muzo's Jam Session, Mondays 9pm-4am. Folk Club Concert, Sundays 8-11pm.

The Other Pace: live entertainment, Tuesdays until 11pm. Corner Todd Street & Wills Terrace, ph 521 255.

Chateau Hornsby Winery: 'Bard of the Outback' Ted Egan performs here in the cellar every Tuesday, Thursday, Saturday and Sunday nights during the tourist season. Also on Saturday nights there is a Bush Night with poet Dave Berman and a local band, Bloodwood. Bookings essential for a unique entertainment experience in the cellar. It costs $15 for the show, $35 for a meal and show, ph 555 133.

Aboriginal Corroboree: every Friday between June and November at The Red Centre Resort, North Stuart Highway, ph 555 000. Costs include bbq, adults $48, child $32.

Araluen Centre for Arts and Entertainment: this cultural centre has live theatre, films, and on the first Saturday of every month presents a cabaret in the Bistro. Larapinta Drive, ph 525 022.

Alice Springs Cinemas: in Todd Mall.

Services and Facilities

There's a full range of shopping services including big supermarkets (Coles New World, K Mart, Woolworths). Most open every day of the week and credit cards are widely accepted.

Banks

ANZ (corner Todd & Parsons Street); State (Ford Plaza), auto teller; Commonwealth (Parsons Street), auto teller 7am-11pm; National (51 Todd Street), flexi teller 6am-midnight; Westpac (Todd Mall) auto teller.

Vehicle needs

24-hour fuel at Shell Truckstop (North Stuart Highway), Shell Todd (Todd Street) 24-hour fuel Fridays only; LPG for vehicles at Mobil Palms Service Station (Wills Terrace), open 6.30am-8pm (closes Sunday at 7pm), Ampol Roadhouse (North Stuart Highway) and BP Red Centre (North Stuart Highway). There are plenty of places for specialist vehicle services.

Radio Stations and Frequencies

8AL 783 (ABC); 8HA 900; 8CCC FM 102.0.

Churches

Anglican, Baptist, Catholic, Church of Christ, Jehovah Witness, Uniting, Lutheran, Salvation Army, Seventh Day Adventist, Latter Day Saints and Pentecostal.

Emergency Services

Dial 000 (for police, fire or ambulance) or: **Police:** Parsons Street, ph 518 888; Fire, ph 521 000; Ambulance, ph 522 200.

Hospital, ph 502 211 (also poisons).

Doctors: Bath Street, ph 522 000 (all hours); 76 Todd Street, ph 521 088 (all hours).

Dentists: Department of Health Dental Clinic, ph 524 766; Reg Harris Lane, Todd Street, ph 526 055.

Chemists: Alice Springs Pharmacy, Hartley Street, ph 521 554 (AH 523 369); Plaza Amcal Chemist, Fort Plaza, ph 530 089.

Chiropractor: 6 Winnecke Avenue, ph 523 333 (AH 523 826).

Veterinary Surgeon: Bath Street, ph 529 899; 52 Grevillea Street, ph 526 966.

Vehicle breakdown: AANT 24 hours service, 58 Sargent Street, ph 521 087.

Recreational Facilities and Activities

Racing: every Saturday, Turf Club Racecourse, South Stuart Hwy.

Bowls: Gap Road, visitors welcome, ph 522 875.

Tennis: public courts for hire, Traeger Park, Traeger Avenue.

Golf: visitors are welcome at the Golf Club, Cromwell Drive.

Gliding: Bond Springs Airstrip, 25km (15 miles) North Stuart Highway, ph 526 384. Weekends only.

Swimming: Swimming Centre, Speed Street (October to April).

Bowling: 10-pin bowling at The Dustbowl, Gap Road, weekdays 9am-11pm.

Squash: courts in Gap Road, ph 521 179.

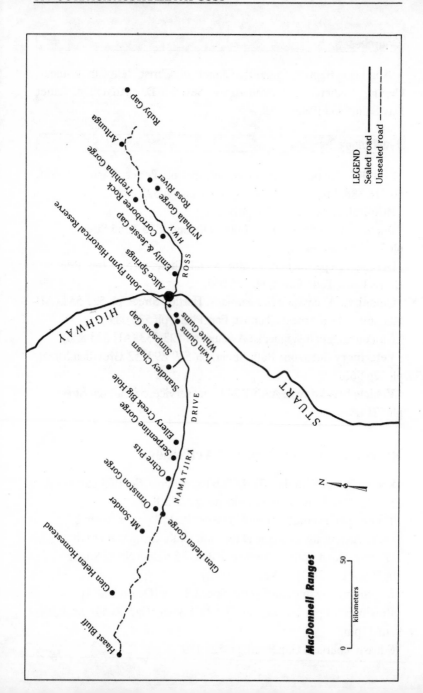

MacDonnell Ranges

LEGEND
Sealed road ———
Unsealed road - - - - -

THE MACDONNELL RANGES

Characteristics

The MacDonnells, which extend east and west of Alice Springs, have some of the best known and most accessible ranges in the Centre. They consist of a number of rises that reach for about 400km (248 miles) between their eastern and western margins, with a maximum north-south width of 160km (100 miles). There are two main parallel groups which, like all the ranges in the MacDonnells, have a distinct east-west trend or axis. They are formed from mainly quartzite (sandstone) with some limestone layers that, along Namatjira Drive, are exposed as serrated ridges. This contrasts with the more rounded profiles that the sandstones and siltstones tend to produce.

The Northern MacDonnells are dominated by the Chewing, Heavitree and Waterhouse Ranges to the west of Alice Springs, and contain many of the main scenic spots. To the east, they include Harts Range. Within this northern group are the highest points in the Centre, all to the west: Mt Leibig, 1527m (5010 ft) is the second highest, with Mt Zeil the highest at 1531m (5023 ft). Mt Sonder, the most picturesque peak in the MacDonnells, is 1380m (4526 ft).

The Southern MacDonnell group includes the James and Krichauff Ranges (near Finke Gorge National Park) and further south-west, the George Gill Range (Kings Canyon country).

Today the ranges are the titled, contorted stumps of mountains that once towered over 3000m (10,000 ft) above sea level. The average height now is less than 500m (1500 ft) above the surrounding land level, which is itself about 600m (1968 ft) above sea level. Erosion since their formation by the Alice Springs Orogeny in Devonian

Times (350-450 million years ago), has left long parallel belts of steep-sided ridges and deep valleys that from the air resemble the crests and troughs of waves.

The evolution of the MacDonnell Ranges is well explained by a Conservation Commission interpretative display at Simpsons Gap.

Altjira, the eternal land, is the name given to the MacDonnell Ranges by the Aranda Aborigines. John McDouall Stuart was the first non-Aboriginal here when he explored the region in April, 1860, and named it after Sir Richard MacDonnell, the Governor of South Australia. Stuart missed Heavitree Gap, the largest break in the centre of the ranges, that is now the southern entrance to Alice Springs, as well as the route for the Todd River, Stuart Highway and the railway. Stuart, in fact, followed the Hugh River to break through the Chewings Range just east of Standley Chasm at what is now called Stuart Pass. The number of features having Teutonic place names in the MacDonnells is attributed to explorer Ernest Giles on the instruction of his 1872 expedition patron, Baron Von Mueller, a botanist from Melbourne.

Because the ranges are lightly vegetated, the delineations and varied colours of the rocks dominate and, along with gaps, gorges and chasms, make the MacDonnell Ranges a place of unlimited, often startling, scenic beauty.

Attractions

Attractions listed for the Western and Eastern MacDonnell Ranges are arranged in order of occurrence from Alice Springs.

Pets

Most parks do not allow pets. Check with the Conservation Commission, ph (089) 508 211.

Fees

All parks are now subject to camping fees. For current fees phone the Conservation Commission (089) 508 211.

Flora and Fauna

Plants and wildlife of the Centre are generally well represented in the MacDonnell Ranges, and reference to them is made under the Attractions listings. The most common types of plants and their respective locations are shown on the cross-sectional diagram. A wildlife feature is the small colony of black-flanked rock-wallabies at Simpsons Gap. The best times to see wildlife are early mornings and late afternoons, and crowded tourist spots are not the ideal locations for observation as most animals are shy. Don't forget to take your Conservation Commission Identikit booklets for plant and wildlife.

WESTERN MACDONNELL RANGES

JOHN FLYNN HISTORICAL RESERVE

0.5ha (1.2 acres)

Location

On Larapinta Drive, 7km (4 miles) west of Alice Springs.

Characteristics

The ashes of Reverend John Flynn, who founded the Australian Inland Mission, The Royal Flying Doctor Service, the first inland medical centre, and an outback padre patrol system, are encased here in a stone cairn. A large boulder from the Devil's Marbles crowns the cairn, and Mt Gillen stands sentinel-like in the background.

The memorial plaque inscription sums up the achievements of this Outback humanitarian: "The Very Reverend John Flynn, OBE, DD, of the Presbyterian Church of Australia 1880-1951. His vision encompassed the continent. He established the Australian Inland Mission and founded the Flying Doctor Service. He brought to lonely places a spiritual ministry and spread a mantle of safety over them by medicine and radio".

****

SIMPSONS GAP NATIONAL PARK

30,950ha (76,447 acres)

Location

On Larapinta Drive, 18km (11 miles) west of Alice Springs.

Characteristics

The park protects and includes a sample of typical MacDonnell Ranges environments, and its closeness to Alice Springs is convenient for those on a strict time budget and who wish to see some gaps and gorges. Centrally located Simpsons Gap is the main feature of the Park, described by OTL surveyor Gilbert McMinn in 1871 as "one of the finest pieces of scenery I have met for a long time". Wide white sands, majestic river red gums and pale ghost gums lead to a quiet pool sheltering beneath some mighty cliffs. The remnants of huge quartzite slabs, sheared from the walls, lie jumbled at the entrance base, and provide a precipitous playground for a colony of black-flanked rock-wallabies. Picnicking here in the late afternoon is a delight when the mellow sun enhances the contrast between big and bold, soft and gentle.

Interesting wildlife around the spinifex, mulga and witchetty bush plains include dingoes, euros, long-nosed dragons and the harmless little children's python, while for keen bird watchers there are eagles, kites and Port Lincoln ringneck parrots, among many others. Bond, Wallaby, Spring and Rocky Gaps, while lesser known, offer further variety and provide access to northern wilderness areas.

History

To the local Aranda people, the Gap is Runutitjirba, the Dreamtime home of the Giant Goanna Ancestors or Big Lizard People. The ridge through which the gorge is cut retains this Aboriginal name today.

The main road and Finke River have something in common; the name Larapinta, a mythological white snake. Who the gap is named after is a mystery. There is no connection between the naming of the Simpson Desert and the Gap.

Before the park was established in 1970, it was part of a large cattle station. Years of overgrazing severely damaged the landscape, and Alice Springs took the brunt of dust storms that originated from here when tonnes of top soil was blasted away by the westerly winds. Careful land management practices and removal of cattle by the Conservation Commission have largely restored the delicate natural balance between soil, plant and wildlife.

Geology

Here the quartzite (metamorphosed beach sand) of the Heavitree Range is down-faulted into 2000 million-year-old rocks of the Arunta block below. Massive earth movements during a major mountain building period about 350 million years ago resulted in faults or fracture lines running north-south at various intervals through the east-west trending quartzite ranges. Simpsons Gap is thought to be the last of an extensive continuous arched sheet of quartzite that unified the Heavitree Range before major faulting and erosion occurred. The gap was cut along a fault-line by the erosive power of Roe Creek, which maintained its relative level as the surrounding land was lowered by erosion.

Even although Roe Creek flows intermittently, this fact accounts for the gorge and the often deep scour pools that characterise this and other gorges of the MacDonnells. Sometimes, a series of gentle creek flows will cause the pool to silt up until it's scoured out again by the next raging flood.

Conservation

While you are encouraged to walk anywhere in the park, please leave your pets at home, drive only on designated roads (as in all parks) and be mindful that it is a rather fragile environment.

Early mornings and late afternoons are best times to see the rock-wallabies, and please observe the "Do Not Feed" signs. Fires are not permitted, and swimming in Simpsons Gap is now allowed.

Walking Tracks

Tracks start from the Visitors Centre, and include a 20-minute marked trail in the vicinity of the Centre; a 19.5km (12 miles) unmarked nature walk west takes you to Eagle Hill, Rocky Gap, Bond Gap and Spring Gap, where you can climb the 1068m (3492 ft) Mt Lloyd; a round walk of approximately 18km (11 miles) east, leads to Wallaby Gap, Fairy Spring, Scorpion Pool and Euro Hill; Cassia Hill Walk is 500m where the summit gives fine views of Larapinta Valley, and starts from the road just over half-way between the Visitors Centre and Gap. For longer walks, the Alice Springs 1:100,000 topographic map should be taken. Also refer to the Information and Advice Sections. See the Ranger for finer details and maps before leaving.

How To Get There

A 6km (4 miles) sealed road leads to the Gap.

Services and Facilities

The Park is open for day use only between 8am and 8pm. One kilometre from the turn-off is the Visitors Centre which has a Ranger's office, excellent interpretive display, and park literature. Well appointed picnic facilities include gas barbecues, tables, water and toilets, including for the disabled. Animals by permit only. Ranger Guided Tours, ph (089) 550 310. Wheelchair access.

****

WHITE GUMS PARK

Location

At Honeymoon Gap, approximately 2km (1 mile) south of Larapinta Drive from the Bullen Road turn-off, just past the Simpsons Gap turn-off.

Characteristics

Scott and Margaret McDonald own this 9 sq km (3 sq miles) park, situated between outlying ridges of the MacDonnell Ranges, that provides an attractive setting for tea rooms and licensed restaurant. The park features some glorious ghost gums, walks where birdlife is abundant, lookouts, and a walk through a 6ha (15 acres) wildlife enclosure that has kangaroos, dingoes and emus.

A continuation along Bullen Road takes you past Temple Bar, along Ilparpa Road at the foot of the Blatherskite Range and back to Alice Springs via Heavitree Gap. There's a designated area along Ilparpa Road for amethyst gem fossicking (4.6km [3 miles] west of Stuart Highway) and the diggings and scrapings on the lower slopes can be seen from the road.

It is a scenic drive and the road is suitable for all vehicles.

Services and Facilities

Picnic, bbq, toilets, tea rooms and caravan/camping ground are the facilities available. There is a fee for entry to the wildlife enclosure, and families are most welcome to picnic on the lawns. The tea rooms/restaurant provide a lunchtime main course for around $15 (entrees $6-$8.).

Open 7 days from 9am-5pm, ph (089) 550 366.

****

TWIN GHOST GUMS

Location

Approximately 18km (11 miles) west of Alice Springs, just past the Simpsons Gap turn-off.

Characteristics

Here stand two majestic ghost gums (Eucalyptus papuana), highlighted by the changing colours of Burt Bluff in the background, and captured best of all on canvas by Aboriginal artist, Albert Namatjira.

Twin Gums is a popular subject for painters and photographers. There are no facilities.

****

STANDLEY CHASM

Location

In the Chewings Range, 50km (31 miles) west of Alice Springs.

Characteristics

Standley Chasm is a five to nine metre wide rock cleft which features sheer rust-stained walls of quartzite that blaze vivid red when fired by the sun's 10-minute mid-day passage. It's a dramatic climax to a comfortable 1500m walk along the creek bed where you can see some magnificent cycad plants. The Chasm's a popular spot around mid-day, but despite the crowds, the 'magic moment' is well worth seeing and photographing.

Geology

Nearly 900 million years ago, enormous pressures within the earth squeezed magma (molten rock) into vertical fractures that extended north-south in much of the rock of the MacDonnells. The intruding magma forced the fractures apart, and when it cooked, a dark green rock called dolerite was formed between the quartzite. Such intrusions are called dykes, and as dolerite is much less resistant to weathering and erosion than quartzite, it was eroded away completely by a south-flowing creek, leaving the near vertical 80m high walls you can see today.

History

The Chasm was named after Alice Spring's first school teacher, Ida Standley, who moved to Jay Creek in 1925 to teach Aboriginal children, and became the first white women to walk through the spectacular gap. Originally, it was known as Gall Springs, after Charles Gall, manager of one of the earliest pastoral leases taken up in the Centre, the 3625 sq km (1377 sq miles) Owen Springs Cattle Station. The creek and waterhole still bear his name.

Today, the Chasm is on land owned by the Iwupataka Aboriginal Community, and while no permit is required, an entry fee is charged.

How To Get There

The 10km (6 miles) road into the Chewings Range from Larapinta Drive is sealed all the way. 6km west from the turn-off is the Namatjira Drive junction; south-west on Larapinta Drive leads to Hermannsburg, while Namatjira Drive takes you to Glen Helen. It's possible to do a round trip (see Touring Suggestions).

Service and Facilities

It has a kiosk where you can buy refreshments, light meals, souvenirs, and local crafts and artifacts; toilet and shaded picnic area with water and bbq facilities; wheelchair access. Opening hours are between 8.30am and 4.30pm.

****

ELLERY CREEK BIG HOLE NATURE PARK

1766HA (4362 ACRES)

Location

93km (58 miles) west of Alice Springs on Namatjira Drive.

Characteristics

Another spectacular gorge characterised by high, red rock faces, a large deep waterhole, and a sandy creek fringed by red river gums. Explorer Ernest Giles came this way in 1872 and named it after Government Astronomer and Director of the Melbourne Observatory, R.L.J. Ellery. To distinguish the rock pool from others along the creek, locals added Big Hole to the name, while to the Aborigines, it's Udepata.

It's an appealing spot that's popular with picnickers and campers alike, and if you are energetically inclined, a climb to the top of the flanking ridges is well rewarded with magnificent views. The shapes and colours of the steep and narrow gorge walls are reflected in the still waters, creating fine subject matter for artists and photographers.

Geology

The gorge was formed by the south-flowing Ellery Creek, which cut across rock strata and carved a gap through a Heavitree Range quartzite ridge. Faulting has offset the alignment of the ridge across the waterhole, breaking the rock formation and causing a line of weakness which has been exploited by the creek. A few fine examples of folded rock strata here can be seen, giving some idea of the enormous energy associated with its formation. At the main road, directly across from Ellery Creek turn-off, an interesting lizard-like formation called 'Julie' highlights the ridge. This feature consists of a single two metre wide band of limestone in siltstone, and since the latter is more easily erodible, the limestone has been left projecting like a wall. Weathering of the limestone wall has produced the lizard-like silhouette.

Services and Facilities

Wood barbecues, toilet and picnic facilities are provided. While it may be very hot here, the water can be ice-cold for swimmers and an air mattress is advised for support, should cramp occur. Camping is allowed, and access is suitable for conventional vehicles. No animals are allowed. There is wheelchair access.

****

SERPENTINE GORGE NATURE PARK

518ha (1277 acres)

Location

On Namatjira Drive, 104km (65 miles) west of Alice Springs.

Characteristics

The park features two winding gorges where a south-flowing creek has cut through two quartzite ridges that have a fold between them. At the upstream site, the very narrow gap suggests that the creek has eroded along a nearly straight vertical joint, or fracture.

The gorge has an impressive, wide entrance, 60m high walls, and a deep permanent waterhole at the far end. At the entrance, another waterhole can prevent access after rains, but in summer, it dries up quickly. Many cycads (Macrozamia macdonnellii) make low green fountains of palm-like growth at the base of the cliffs.

Services and Facilities

Picnic, wood barbecues, and toilet facilities are provided, and camping is allowed. An air mattress or similar support is advised if you wish to swim here, as the water is extremely cold and deep, even in summer. Access is okay for conventional vehicles, but care is needed. No animals allowed.

****

OCHRE PITS

Location

11km (7 miles) on the right past Serpentine Gorge, on Namatjira Drive.

Characteristics

A very rough track leads down to the exposed cliff face consisting of various earthy coloured clays, used by Aborigines as colour pigments for a range of decorative purposes such as rock painting and body decorations. The colours were derived from the changes to the folded siltstones and shales by weathering, which caused iron oxides (common rust), aided by water, to be moved. The various colours from yellow to deep ochre, emerged when different iron oxides mixed with water and stained the mineral particles in the soft rock.

There are no facilities, and you need to measure the distance carefully from Serpentine Gorge as the road sign often disappears. The half a kilometre track is narrow and rocky. Care is needed with conventional vehicles. Caravans and trailers are not advised. The pits are a short walk to the right and are worth seeing, but please don't remove the coloured clays.

****

ORMISTON GORGE AND POUND NATIONAL PARK

4655ha (11,498 acres)

Location

132km (82 miles) west of Alice Springs.

Characteristics

Ormiston Gorge and Pound National Park is the largest in the Western MacDonnell Ranges, and its awesome 2km long red wall, permanent pool, and Pound wilderness, make it one of the most memorable parks in the Centre, and deserving of 'Jewel of the Centre' description. The dominant feature is the gorge, a deep cut carved through a quartzite range by floodwaters of Ormiston Creek, leaving sheer 250m high walls towering above the boulder-strewn creek. High above, ghost gums and cypress pine cling tenaciously, while the rock face gives a remarkable parade of colour when struck by the sun.

The Pound is a rugged natural enclosure that measures about 10km across, and is almost completely surrounded by high ridges. The 3 to 4 hour, 7km (4 miles) walk through this area unfolds a stark beauty that can touch the spirit. It must be one of the most inspiring wilderness walks in Australia. Dominating the eastern end of the Pound is the hump-shaped 1283m (4207 ft) Mt Giles.

Ormiston Creek is the most northerly catchment which, together with the Davenport River, form the Finke River a few kilometres north of Glen Helen. Ormiston Creek is thought to have been named by R.E. Warburton, son of explorer Colonel P.E. Warburton.

Geology

The area is a geologist's delight. Needless to say, it's very complex with much folding and bending back or overthrusting of rock strata. There's an anticline outlined by the Heavitree quartzite immediately past the park entrance gates, while at the main waterhole, this quartzite in the base of the cliff has been overlaid by more of the Heavitree quartzite which was pushed southwards from a few kilometres away. The change of slope, about half-way up the main rockface, indicates the thrust surface on which this movement occurred. The quartzite or sandstone is the main rock type in the gorge area, while outcrops of schist, gneiss and igneous can be seen in the Pound. The Pound rocks are over 1700 million-years-old and belong to the Arunta Complex - one of the Territory's oldest grouping of rocks.

Flora and Fauna

Many types of acacias can be identified around the public facilities area; red river gums line the creekbeds; bean trees and bloodwoods give scant shade in the Pound; and spinifex is widespread. In the spring and after rains, wildflowers add a delicate touch to the ground cover, particularly Sturt's desert rose.

The wildlife is varied. Rarely will you see dingoes, but you may hear them at night. Euros, rock-wallabies and smaller marsupials are shy. Reptiles include skinks, geckoes and the occasional perentie. In the pools, heron, grebe, teal, darter and cormorants may be seen. Plumed pigeon, spotted bower bird, mistletoe bird, Port Lincoln parrot and honeyeaters are other birds seen in the park. When the creek dries up, the spangled perch, one of the Centre's 30 species of fish, bury themselves deep in the mud where they survive until the rains come.

How To Get There

An 8km (5 miles) gravel-surfaced road, suitable for all vehicles, trailers and caravans, leads to the park. But, sudden flooding can temporarily close it.

Services and Facilities

Superb facilities are provided here. There's a ranger station and information centre, well appointed camping ground (fireplaces, showers, toilets including for the disabled), picnic and wood and gas barbecues. Rangers have made noteworthy efforts to tune visitors to the bush by providing a sensory trail and a litter awareness track (try them out!). You don't have to be an experienced bush walker to use the two main walks: Ghost Gum (2.5km-1.5 miles) and the Pound Walk (7km-4 miles). Both are well worthwhile and, for the longer one in particular, take plenty of water and don't forget your Plant Identikit booklet. You can also climb Mt Giles, but check with the ranger first. The permanent rock-pool is ideal for swimming. Supplies can be obtained from Glen Helen Lodge, from where scenic helicopter flights of the park may be undertaken. Animals allowed by permit only. Camping fees apply.

Western MacDonnell Ranges

GLEN HELEN GORGE NATURE PARK
386ha (953 acres)

Location

133km (83 miles) west of Alice Springs.

Characteristics

Erosion by the Finke River, thought to be the world's oldest having flowed along the same course for 350 million years, has produced the park's major feature; an impressive gorge and large, 30m deep waterhole. A short distance through the gorge you can see two interesting rock formations: 'window in the rock' on the eastern side, and the 'organ pipes' on the western. The latter are the result of weathering along the bedding planes of vertical sandstone strata. A climb over the range, or a swim through the icy waters, allows access for views of these two features. It was here that Ernest Giles found his way north blocked by the waterhole in 1872, and attempts to build a causeway on the western side for a shortcut for vehicles to Hermannsburg, have met with failure. After the floods of 1975, the waterhole silted up and for a while it was possible to walk through on dry sand.

To the Aranda people it was known as Yapalpe, the home of the Giant Watersnake, and according to Aboriginal mythology, it's from these icy depths that the first shapeless Dreamtime beings emerged.

Geology

The sedimentary rock beds cut by the Finke were more resistant, thus causing a deeply scoured pool that's kept full by water permeating through the sand in the bed of the river. The rock faces reveal Pacoota sandstone or quartzite that is distinctive by its coarser grain, and formed during major earth movements about 350 million years ago, when white sandstone was broken and mixed with brown sand and rock fragments. It's also called breccia, and the weathering process, with the help of water, has caused the rocks to be coloured by the iron oxides.

Facilities

There's a park and walking track with an information sign. From the car park, it's a pleasant walk alongside the ancient riverbed, and the date palms along the base of the red cliffs should not be mistaken for cycad or red cabbage palms found in the Finke Gorge National Park. Services and facilities are available at Glen Helen Lodge next door to the park. No animals are allowed in the Park. Wheelchair access is available.

****

GLEN HELEN HOMESTEAD LODGE
Population 10

Location

On Namatjira Drive, 133km (82 miles) west of Alice Springs.

Characteristics

The long, low, white-washed lodge nestles comfortably by the Finke River on what must be one of the most envied locations going. Massive, red quartzite cliffs provide a startling backdrop, while to the north-west, a softer landscape spread directs the eye to the beautiful Mt Sonder. The homestead has been restored and rebuilt with a 1930s atmosphere inside, and offers travellers a good base from which to explore the western part of the MacDonnells.

History

It is possible that the station was named after Helen Bakewell, a relation of Grant, one of the partners who established the property in the late 1870s. The original homestead was built alongside Ormiston Creek and was called Munga Munga. It now lies in ruins. Cattleman Fred Raggart built the first homestead on the Lodge site in the early 1930s, and a later owner of the property, Bryan Bowman, recalls the days of sheep, cattle and thoroughbred horses in his fascinating book, *The Glen Helen Story*. The 2165 sq km (823 sq miles) Glen Helen Station surrounds the lodge, and the homestead is 55km (34 miles) to the north-west. You may wonder about those donkeys on the road; no-one left the gate open, they are feral.

Attractions

National parks and features in the vicinity. The Glen Helen amethyst fossicking locality is near Redbank Gorge Nature Park. Scenic helicopter flights over Ormiston Gorge and environs are offered, $40 for 15 minutes. Cloudy's Restaurant was voted Australia's top restaurant in 1989.

How To Get There

Namatjira Drive is good bitumen surface to the Homestead.

Accommodation

Motel: double $72. Bunkhouse: $10 per bed ($8 YHA members).
   Camping/caravans: powered sites from $10; unpowered from $3. Sites have natural bush settings; pets allowed, dogs must be leashed.

Services and Facilities

It has a licensed restaurant (around $30 for 3 courses), bbq lunches, bar, bistro, outdoor patio overlooking Finke, sometimes country and western style live music, take-away food, ice, souvenirs and sells some basic foods. Super, diesel, ULP and oil are the only vehicle services. Opening hours 7am-11pm, credit cards accepted (Mastercard, Bankcard, Visa), ph (089) 567 489.

****

REDBANK GORGE NATURE PARK

1295ha (3199 acres)

Location

30km (19 miles) west of Glen Helen.

Characteristics

The park features a delightful gorge that is permanently blocked by several very deep and cold pools along is 800m length. It's a most attractive park in an area of superb scenery that includes Mt Sonder.

The sheer walls of the gorge rise to 40m, and its 5m maximum width narrows at one point to just one metre. From the car park, it's a 30 minute walk, and if you intend exploring the chasm be warned; the water is ice-cold, there are few natural footholds underwater, and the walls are slippery. Unless you are a very strong swimmer, cold-blooded or both, an inflatable mattress to provide support in case of chill-induced cramp, is strongly advised.

How To Get There

From Glen Helen, it's a formed road surface for 20km (12.4 miles) to the Redbank Gorge turn-off, then its 4km (2.5 miles) of flat bladed road to the car park. 4WD is recommended, but with care others can get through. Further west, the road continues to Haast Bluff (see Haast Bluff listing), while the southern branch leads 10km (6 miles) to the Gosse Bluff turn-off at Tyler Trig Point. The flat bladed road continues 53km (33 miles) to Hermannsburg. No permits are required for this route, but you are not welcome at Areyonga Aboriginal Settlement.

Services and Facilities

Picnic and wood barbecues only in this quite, remote location. Camping is allowed. No animals are allowed.

Redbank Gorge

MT SONDER

Location

15km (9 miles) north-west of Glen Helen.

Characteristics

Mt Sonder rises majestically and dominates the skyline north-west of Glen Helen. While it's not the highest peak at 1380m (4525 ft), it's certainly the most picturesque, and landscape painters and photographers will be hard-pressed to find a more aesthetically pleasing subject. Mt Sonder's steep faced peaks provide a challenge to the few who climb it, but they are rewarded with an astounding view of the ancient Finke and its tributaries, as well as the serene sweep of Centralian landscape. Redbank Nature Park, with its fine camping spots along the sandy, gum-shaded creek bed, is an ideal base for the climb.

Ernest Giles named the mountain after Dr William Sonder of Adelaide, and the local Aborigines call it Rutjipma. It's also known as 'sleeping women mountain' - from certain angles it resembles a woman lying on her back. The geology of Mt Sonder is very complex with much folding and bending back of rock strata, particularly where Heavitree quartzite is overthrust onto itself.

****

HAAST BLUFF

Location

Approximately 221km (137 miles) west of Alice Springs.

Characteristics

A prominent craggy peak with sheer faces that was a favourite landscape subject of Albert Namatjira and other Aranda watercolour artists who lived in Hermannsburg. It was discovered by Ernest Giles, and named by him after Julius van Haast, German geologist and explorer.

The surrounding land was once part of a huge pastoral lease. As Aborigines here had had minimal contact with Europeans, Lutheran Missionaries lobbied the Government not to allow any more pastoral developments on Tribal Lands. Missionaries feared it would lead to the demise of Aborigines. The Government responded by proclaiming the area, including the pastoral lease, an Aboriginal Reserve in 1937. Haast Bluff settlement was established soon after.

Access to the feature does not require a permit, but tourists are not welcome at the settlement. From Redbank Gorge, it is a flat bladed road that has a 4WD recommendation.

****

EASTERN MACDONNELL RANGES

EMILY AND JESSIE GAP NATURE PARK

695ha (1717 acres)

Location

On the Ross Highway, 10km (6 miles) and 17km (10.5 miles) respectively, east of Heavitree Gap.

Characteristics

Two gaps in the Heavitree quartzite, sand-fringed waterholes and river red gums are the main attractions here. The area is of significance to local Aborigines, and some well preserved rock paintings can be seen on Emily Gap's eastern wall - to get there you may have to swim. Camel teams hauled rock from here to help build the Telegraph station north of Alice Springs. Both gaps are popular picnic and swimming spots. You may also climb and walk along the top of the range between the gaps for some great views and wildlife encounters.

Services and Facilities

Wood barbecues and picnic facilities are provided. Access is okay for all vehicles. Dogs allowed in designated areas only.

****

CORROBOREE ROCK CONSERVATION RESERVE

7ha (17 acres)

Location

On the Ross Highway, 46km (29 miles) east of Alice Springs.

Characteristics

This prominent outcrop of vertical dolomite strata (a pillar of limestone), which has been more resistant to the ravages of erosion than the surrounding shale, was a place of Aboriginal manhood rituals. It was also where sacred stones, used by the Aranda Elders to teach their children the Dreamtime stories, were once stored. The Aranda people call the rock Antanangantana, and Corroboree is the name given to an Aboriginal meeting of festive, sacred or warlike character.

Services and Facilities

A sign and short walking track help appreciation of the area, and wood barbecues, picnic and toilet facilities are provided. Camping is allowed. Animals are not allowed.

****

TREPHINA GORGE NATURE PARK

1770ha (4372 acres)

Location

80km (50 miles) north-west of Alice Springs, via the Ross Highway.

Vegetation - Macdonnell Ranges

Characteristics

If you are looking for some wilderness, solitude and attractive scenery, this park will not disappoint. It features two quite different gorges. Trephina Gorge is more open and less awesome than the gaps of the Western MacDonnells, but its wall of upstanding quartzite formation is visually impressive, particularly when brushed pink by the low evening rays. A wide sandy creek bed, towering river gums and tranquil pool make it a delightful spot for campers.

By contract, John Hayes Rock Hole is protected by low cliffs, and its shaded seclusion provides an ideal refuge from the 44C temperatures summer can bring. Nearby, in the area below Mt Hayes, wedge-tailed eagles were so common that it was called the Valley of the Eagles.

History

Trephina Gorge was named after the wife of former prospector and cattleman, William Benstead, who also built Alice Spring's first pub. In 1907, the Hayes family established Undoolya Station that still surrounds the park, and the rock pool was named after their son. The park was once part of the Undoolya lease, and any encounters you may have with a few wild horses, donkeys and cattle, are legacies of those earlier station days.

Flora and Fauna

Flora around the gorges and valleys includes river red gums, ghost gums, whitewoods and ironwoods, while precariously clinging to the cliff tops and faces are white cyprus pine, ghost gums and native fig. Spinifex is widespread, and delicate rock ferns thrive around John Hayes Rock Pool, home to tadpoles and other small aquatic creatures.

Common larger animals are dingoes (you will hear their nightly howls), euros on the spinifex slopes, and the large reptilian perentie.

Smaller species include lizards and some bat colonies in the deep rock recesses (one roost entrance can be seen half-way up the left hand wall as you walk into the John Hayes Rock Hole).

Birdlife is rich and varied. In the bush are Port Lincoln parrots, mistletoe birds, western thrush, pied butcher birds and grass wrens, to name a few, while dainty fairy martins build mud nests in the rock crevices. Birds of prey include little falcons, goshawks, kestrels and wedge-tailed eagles, while white-faced herons frequent the pools. You don't have to walk great distances to see the wildlife. Find a shady spot away from other people, sit quietly, and let the wildlife resume normal activities. This approach is quite rewarding.

How To Get There

It's a sealed road to the turn-off, and 4km into the gorge. The remaining 4km is a formed gravel road suitable for all vehicles. Access to John Hayes Rock Hole requires a high clearance vehicle.

Services and Facilities

There are three picnic areas. John Hayes Rock Hole, and the two in the vicinity of Trephina Gorge, have wood and gas barbecues, tables, toilets and water. Superb campsites, climbs and bushwalking (no marked tracks) are features of the park. Animals allowed by permit.

****

ROSS RIVER HOMESTEAD

Population 20

Location

85km (53 miles) east of Alice Springs, via the Ross Highway.

Characteristics

The white-washed old homestead has a backdrop of time-worn hills from its creek side site where giant river red gums provide welcome shade. Formerly the headquarters of Loves Creek Station established in 1898, the homestead now offers visitors an economical base from which to explore the ancient Eastern MacDonnell's landscape. Although slightly altered to meet tourist needs, its bar and dining room still have plenty of rustic charm, while the self-contained red gum cabins are an imaginative compromise between old and new. Managers, Geoff and Marg Adler, are affable hosts who aim to ensure the character of the homestead is in keeping with the region's pioneering past.

History

The river and homestead were named after explorer, surveyor and pastoralist, John Ross, a six foot, black-bearded Highlander who along with Harvey, Alfred Giles, Hearn and Tom Crisp, in 1871, were the first men to follow John McDouall Stuart's trail-blazing route. Their brief was to survey a route for the Overland Telegraph Line, and some time was spent in the MacDonnell Ranges surveying.

Ross traced a northern trail from Adelaide for over 1500km (930 miles) using a prismatic compass, a tracing of Stuart's map, a lead pencil, and a two-foot ruler. Food consisted of flour, tea and 400 pounds of jerked meat ('boot-lace' or dried strips), and the medical supplies were Holloway's pills ('cure-all' patent tablets), boracic based eye lotion and castor oil. Water was collected and stored in canvas bags which were soon torn by scrub riding, so they shot wallabies, ate the meat, and used the ill-cured skins for water carriers.

At Chambers Pillar, a phallic symbol in Aboriginal mythology, they carved their names in the soft sandstone base before spending some time in the Eastern MacDonnells. Another survey party found Heavitree Gap and the Alice Springs. Further north, Ross unearthed

Stuart's papers at Central Mt Stuart, and to Harvey, this was the appropriate time and place to open a bottle of rum that he had carried from Adelaide. They drank here in silent memory of a fellow Scot. They completed their survey work, and met up with engineers who were already pushing the line of telegraph poles south from Darwin. Plans for the route, and stations across the Centre, were based on Ross' survey work. The Highway, River and Homestead named after him, are fitting tributes to this hardy explorer.

The Ross River Homestead was built in 1898 by Wallis, who named his station Loves Creek after a pastoralist of the same name who grazed his weaners (yearling cattle) around the waterholes here. Wallis also bred horses called Walers (a cross between Clydesdale and thoroughbred), a practice continued by the new owner Louis Bloomfield when he took over in 1908. These horses were bred as remounts for the British Army in India, and very few of this unusual breed now remain.

The homestead, bounded by Loves Creek Station (nearly 4000 sq km - 1520 sq miles) and The Garden Station (2064 sq km - 784 sq miles), is on a small lease originally developed by brothers Gil and Doug Green as a tourist resort in 1959.

Attractions

Visits to gorges and Arltunga can be undertaken individually or with guided tours from the Homestead, and there's plenty of landscape interest around here for artists, geologists, naturalists and photographers. A wildlife enclosure has some euros and a red kangaroo. Billy tea, damper and boomerang throwing; horse riding, wagon rides, and camel riding, are some activities. There are overnight camel or horse trail-rides, and evening talks on the area's history, Aboriginal culture, geology and station life. Sometimes rodeos are held.

How To Get There

By vehicle it is via 78km (48 miles) of sealed road and approximately 7km (4 miles) of good formed surface to the Homestead.
Conventional vehicles are okay.

An airstrip has been upgraded for light plane travellers (check the Homestead for details).

There are plenty of tours from Alice Springs - check with the Government Tourist Bureau.

Accommodation

Red gum cabins - single $90, double $100, family $125.
  Bunk house - $12 per person.
  Camping/caravans - powered sites $15 x 2.
                      unpowered, $4 per person.
  Disabled - 2 fully equipped cabins are available.
  Pets allowed, but dogs must be leashed.

Services and Facilities

The Homestead caters for casual and overnight visitors. Facilities

include a bar and restaurant (3 course meal around $30, menu includes kangaroo and beef steaks and specials), casual meals ('roo burgers), bbq lunches. Fuel - super, ULP, diesel and oil. Barbecue fireplaces are provided, and there's a swimming pool for guests and patrons.

Open all year, hours as required. Credit cards accepted (Bankcard, Mastercard, Visa), ph (089) 569 711.

N'DHALA GORGE NATURE PARK

501ha (1237 acres)

Location

92km (57 miles) east of Alice Springs, via the Ross River Highway.

Characteristics

A Ross River tributary has sliced a passage through the quartzite, and while the gap has a rugged beauty, it is the prehistoric rock carvings, sheltered by the gorge walls, that are the main interest of the park. Several thousand engravings, conservatively thought to be around 35,000-years-old, have been noted throughout the gorge, and local Aborigines today have no knowledge of the artists or the meaning of the designs. The carvings have been affected by weathering, and the best time to see and photograph them is early morning or late afternoon, when the low angle sun highlights the shallow engravings.

The local geology is complex and has been described as an open book on earth's history. The curious rock formations and ancient rock carvings combine to give an awesome sense of prehistory to the Ross River region.

How To Get There

4WD is necessary from Ross River Homestead. The Homestead offers various tours to the park, including horseback. Check with the Homestead or Tourist Centre for details.

Services and Facilities

There's a short walk to the rock carvings and an information sign. Wood barbecues, picnic and toilet facilities are provided. Camping is allowed. You need to take in your own water. No animals allowed.

ARLTUNGA HISTORICAL RESERVE
5506ha (13,600 acres)

Location

120km (75 miles) north-east of Alice Springs, via the Ross Highway.

Characteristics

This reserve protects the scattered and rather eerie remains of an old gold-mining town that was one of Australia's most isolated and desolate. Within the reserve, the old Government Stamp Battery and Cyanide Works, mine offices, police station and gaol, assayer's residence, and other historic buildings, are being restored. Many other ruins of houses exist at the old camp and mine sites throughout the reserve, and its two cemeteries and isolated graves are grim reminders of the hardships at the diggings.

History

In April 1887, Joseph Hele and Isaac Smith found alluvial gold in a dry watercourse downstream from the region's best natural waterhole, Paddys Rockhole, called Arltunga by the local Aborigines. But the 'ruby rush' at the nearby Hale River (Ruby Gap Nature Park area) was at its peak, and news of gold at Arltunga did not attract any immediate rush there.

Not surprising really when the red stones were bringing $2.50 a carat (5 carats=1 gram) on the London market, until chemical tests on the 'rubies' proved them to be near worthless garnets. The ruby rush collapsed. A few miners tried their luck at Arltunga, but hardships brought about by unreliable water supplies and periods of fierce droughts, deterred all but the hardiest and most desperate.

Although the field was not a particularly rich one, its spasmodic development, sometimes fired by the floating of short-lived mining companies, sustained a population of between 50-80 people for about 20 years. According to H. Brown, a South Australian Government geologist who visited the diggings in 1890, there were 12 men including a shopkeeper and a butcher, in residence at the shanty town beside the rockhole, and 15 diggers working only 5 of the 16 registered claims on the alluvial fields. Even though reef gold had been discovered at Mt Chapman, he found an equally bleak picture in these fields, too. After noting inadequate crushing and treatment equipment, and the band of dispirited diggers battling heat and flies for pitiful returns, Brown concluded that unless water supplies and equipment were improved, the field was doomed despite the good potential of the reefs. Consequently a 10 stamp battery and cyanidation plant for treating tailings was hauled 600km (372 miles) from Oodnadatta railhead and was in operation by 1898. It encouraged an influx of diggers at about the same time that Henry Luce discovered reef gold in the nearby White Range.

Between 1898 and 1916, the battery crushed 11,672 tons of ore-bearing rock, which produced 14,912 ounces of gold valued at $111,444. Luce's mine was the richest in realising 2,556 ounces.

Conservation

A few years ago, many of the remaining buildings were still intact, but with the deliberate removal of door and window frames for firewood, and the rumour of gold in the stone walls, most of the structures are now heaps of rubble. Visitors are asked to help preservation by not pushing or climbing on stone walls, and by leaving historical artifacts where they lie.

Care needs to be taken when wandering through the reserve as there are many old mine shafts and wells. Young children should be well supervised.

Fossicking

Fossicking, metal detectors, or mining of any description is not permitted in the reserve. A Mines and Energy Department gold fossicking locality is set aside in the bed of Paddy's Creek to the south of the access road, between the camping ground and Arltunga Bore. Small gold nuggets have been found there.

How To Get There

Via the Ross Highway, the Arltunga turn-off near Trephina Gorge is a formed gravel road suitable for most vehicles. East from the Stuart Highway, and 49km (30 miles) north of Alice Springs is an alternative route via The Garden and Ambalindum Cattle Stations. It is a flat bladed track often rough and impassable after heavy rains. 4WD only.

Services and Facilities

Within the reserve, wood barbecues (please bring your own firewood), picnic, toilet and water facilities are available (it's wise to bring additional supplies of water). Walking tracks and information sign-posts have also been provided. Information Centre and Museum are open daily, slide shows at 1pm. Animals by permit only. Wheelchair access.

Just outside the park entrance is the Arltunga Tourist Park, which includes what has been described as the 'loneliest pub in the scrub'. It's a corrugated iron and stone structure, and the owners also sell basic supplies, and run a small camping ground.

RUBY GAP NATURE PARK

9257ha (22,865 acres)

Location

140km (87 miles) east of Alice Springs, via the Ross Highway and Atnarpa Road.

Characteristics

A timeless, rugged beauty surrounds a system of gorges and startling geological formations along the winding course of the Hale River. Ruby Gap is at the south-western entrance to the park, but the main Gorge, Glen Annie, is located about 6km (4 miles) further upstream. It's well off the beaten track, a quiet spot that requires 4WD vehicles to get there.

History

It was here that explorer David Lindsay found some bright red gemstones in 1885. He named Glen Annie for his wife, rode off to break the news of his find, and started the 'ruby rush'. They came by camels, horses, or simply pushing hand-carts, and the area saw hundreds of diggers sifting through the river sands for rubies. Twenty-three companies were floated and the first gems to arrive in London were greeted with enthusiasm. However, when they arrived in increasing quantities, jewellers got jittery, and more detailed analysis revealed they were garnets. But some made money out of them and it certainly put Alice Springs on the map. Little remains at this desolate site today except for a long grave, and garnets can still be found in the river sands north of the gap.

Geology

Of particular interest is the geological structure at Ruby Gap. During a major mountain building period some 350 million years ago, a huge slab of Heavitree quartzite was forced southwards, sheared and rose over existing layers of quartzite. A second slab or slice was then thrust over the first and these piggyback structures are called nappes. Each quartzite slice was topped with thin tan-brown layers of limestone and siltstone, and being relatively flexible under pressure compared to other rocks, they have been contorted into many tight folds. Erosion has now cut through the nappes which can be seen as cliffs to the west and south of Hale River.

Many interesting folded rock strata can be seen between Ruby Gap and Glen Annie Gorge. North of Glen Annie, the river bed widens and here many fascinating river-worn stones can be found.

How To Get There

Rugged, 4WD access only from Arltunga.

Services and Facilities

There are fine camp-sites along the river, but there are no facilities or water. Please remember to take your litter with you when you leave, and bury toilet waste. No animals are allowed.

ANNAS RESERVOIR CONSERVATION RESERVE

85ha (210 acres)

Location

About 150km (93 miles) north-west of Alice Springs, 30km (19 miles) west of the Stuart Highway from the turn-off near Aileron.

Characteristics

It features a natural rockhole, 10m wide and 2m deep, surrounded on three sides by rocky walls, reserved for its aesthetic and historic interest.

History

It was discovered in 1960 by explorer Stuart, who named it after the youngest daughter of his patron, James Chambers. On his return from his final and successful expedition to the northern coast in 1862, Stuart rested here, seeking relief from the agony of scurvy. Alfred Giles saw the reservoir as an ideal watering place for sheep on their way to Springvale Homestead near Katherine. He even estimated that it contained enough water for two drinks each for 12,000 sheep. Giles achieved the remarkable feat of droving 12,000 sheep, broken into several mobs, across a 174km (108 miles) dry stretch between Alice Springs and here in 1878. It took 2 days to water the thirst-crazed creatures, and only 150 sheep were lost either by drowning in the reservoir or wandering off into the mulga scrub.

The waterhole also supplied construction gangs working on the Overland Telegraph Line, while in 1884 it was a homestead site for A.M. Woolridge's property. However, the rockhole was of importance to the Anmatjera people, and one night in 1886 they attacked the homestead with fire and sticks. The two occupants escaped, and Woolridge consequently moved his homestead to Barrow Creek. Today, little remains of the homestead except for the rock ruins of one building and walls of another.

The reserve is fenced, but damage by cattle has made it less than the idyllic spot that Stuart found, and the Conservation Commission is working on its restoration. There are no facilities, and visitors are asked to take out their litter. Camping is allowed. Animals are not allowed.

How To Get There

Getting there is complicated and requires a good mud-map. It's on private property; you can easily get confused by the number of station tracks, and the last 200m (218 yds) is by walking. For advice, check with the Conservation Commission.

BOND SPRINGS HOMESTEAD

Population 20

Location

Approximately 25km (15 miles) north of Alice Springs.

Characteristics

This privately-owned homestead is headquarters of the 1515 sq km (576 sq miles) Bond Springs Cattle Station, which features the original settlement buildings and a working station atmosphere in an undulating, sometimes rocky, arid landscape. Grant and Jan Heaslip own the station, and the tourist side of things is very much Jan's 'baby' - Grant's too busy getting the bovine beasts into shape for the bbq! Visits are on an appointment only basis, and groups are offered two to four hour tour options which may include breakfast, bbq lunch, dinner, historic station tour, swimming and tennis. Conveniently located close to Alice Springs, it not only provides accessible station experience, but also gives you a 'break' from gaps, gorges and chasms.

History

The station was established in 1872 by Mr Bond, who, with his family, had a pretty torrid 12 month bullock cart trek from Adelaide. Their mulga slab house with wattle-and-daub is basically as it was when first built and is a rare example of an authentic settler's dwelling. Straight sticks cut from mulga, ironwood or witchetty bush were used for the walls and called 'wattles' - in fact, Australia's wattles got their name when these early settlers built wattle-and-daub huts using acacia saplings woven or 'wattled' together and daubed with wet clay.

Other historic buildings include a saddlery and leather room, a 1930s two-roomed galvanised iron homestead and original school room and meat house. The present rambling homestead was built in 1940 by the Chisholm family from whom the Heaslips acquired the property in 1964. For a time, in the 1920s, Bond Springs was part of the Kidman Cattle Empire.

The Cattle King

The late Sir Sidney Kidman was a pioneer and visionary cattleman who, during the early 1900s, acquired a vast network of sheep and cattle stations spanning Outback New South Wales, Queensland, South Australia, Northern Territory and Kimberley. He eventually controlled, or had interests in, more than 100 stations covering well over 161,000 sq km (100,000 sq miles) - an area larger than the UK. He made the Birdsville Track famous, and the sheer scope of his organisation earned him the title, 'The Cattle King'. Ion Idriess write a vivid, although romantic account of Kidman's life in his book of the same title. Kidman's entrepreneurial approach to cattle raising was matched only by James ('Hungry') Tyson, who preceded him, and his methods were a forerunner to such big meat company operations as Vesteys from the 1920s. At 13, Kidman ran away from home in Adelaide with only a tiny swag (bundle of belongings), a one-eyed horse called Cyclops, and 50c in his pocket. He headed north. This was during the 1870s; the last phase of exploration and when settlement began to push towards the vast unoccupied tracts of the Centre, Top End and Kimberley. Through all manner of Outback jobs and experiences, he became an expert bushman and a fine judge of horses and livestock. With his acute memory he retained the most intimate mental maps of the interior, and his later fortune was based upon this vast store of knowledge and astute droving.

It was his bold plan to get cattle in prime condition to the coastal

New South Wales, Victorian and South Australian markets, and to the scattered mining settlements, that makes this man an extraordinary cattleman. His plan was remarkably simple: develop a system of stations through the Centre that would enable the owner to buy stock cheaply from anywhere in the north, bring them down through the 'chain' (strategically located and owned stations) where they could rest, feed and water until they reached the railhead from where they were taken to Adelaide. In this way, droughts could be beaten, the stock would be in prime condition and premium prices obtained at market. 'Chains' were eventually established down along the three great rivers of Western Queensland, the Georgina, Diamantina and Cooper; across the north-west to the Kimberley; and down through the Centre, of which Bond Springs was a later link in the 1920s.

There were inevitable disasters, but Kidman's conception of the Outback as being divided into a number of 'paddocks' in which livestock were moved from one to another, was innovative and successful. R.M. Williams, who founded the well-known empire based on boots and bush clothing, said of Kidman "... you have to remember he created his world, his empire in the horse and buggy days when there were no aeroplanes and no motor cars or trucks. He must have either ridden a horse or driven a buggy throughout the whole of Outback Australia". Kidman, along with Thomas Elder and others, also helped initiate the commercial use of camels, and his contribution to the pastoral development of Outback Australia is legendary.

Apart from the settlement aspects, there's some interesting natural history there, too. It was under the flight path of a meteorite shower some thousands of years ago, and attained astro-geological prominence when a six gram stone meteorite was found. The source of the Todd river that finally empties the water it infrequently carries into the Simpson Desert, is located on the station property.

How To Get There

By arrangement only. For transport, tour type and time, phone the station (089) 529 888, or NT Holiday Reservations Centre, ph 008 808 244.

Tours

Station tour plus morning or afternoon 'smoko' with fresh scones straight from the oven - $45; Station tour plus a bushman's lunch of either home-grown steaks or rare roast beef washed down with complimentary wine, beer or orange juice - $60. These prices include transfer by coach from Alice Springs, with a minimum of six persons per tour. Silver service dinners are available by prior arrangement.

Accommodation

You can also take a private station tour and then relax for the night in Corkwood Cottage, a beautifully appointed private cottage full of early Australiana furniture. Included are pre-dinner drinks, dinner with a complimentary bottle of wine, and breakfast. Price is $150 per person per night, with a maximum of four persons. Return transfers from the airport ($100) or from Alice Springs ($50) can be arranged. There are also a swimming pool and a tennis court. Bond Springs Station, PO Box 4, Alice Springs, NT, 0871.

CENTRAL MT STUART HISTORICAL RESERVE

0.3ha (0.74 acres)

Location

On the Stuart Highway, 216km (134 miles) north of Alice Springs.

Characteristics

Explorer John McDouall Stuart, along with companions William Kekwick and Benjamin Head, discovered the feature that lies closest to the continent's geographical centre on April 22, 1860. His dairy entry states: "I find from my observations of the sun that I am now camped in the centre of Australia. I have marked a tree and planted the British flag. There is a high hill about two and a half miles to the north-west. I wish it had been in the centre, but on it tomorrow I shall raise a cone of stones and plant the flag, naming it Mount Sturt". Captain Charles Sturt was his old leader, explorer and friend. Stuart also buried some papers in a bottle, no more than names and dates, under the stones.

Subsequently an 'a' was added to the name, probably due to cartographic error, a fitting tribute anyway to the man whose expeditions established a route from south to north across the continent. The reserve and stone cairn alongside the highway commemorates their discovery, and the actual 'mountain' is about 12km (7 miles) to the north-west from here.

Explorer Stuart

John McDouall Stuart, who was born in Scotland in 1815, was a member of Charles Sturt's expedition of 1844 which attempted to find the continent's heart, and had led minor expeditions west of Lake Eyre in search of grazing lands in 1858 and 1859. Surveyor and explorer, Stuart was fascinated by the mysterious interior, and it took three determined efforts to finally reach the Gulf. Turned back by hostile Aborigines and sickness at Attack Creek in 1860, and by harsh terrain and low supplies at Newcastle Waters the following year, Stuart's resolve to reach the north was successful in his final expedition, when the party struck the coast at Mary River mouth on July 24, 1862. But it was not without great personal cost. The epic pioneering success almost killed him; his eyesight impaired from taking solar observations rendered him blind in one eye, and such was his scurvy affliction and exhaustion, he had to be carried for much of the return journey. He never fully recovered, and died in London in 1866.

Following his 1858 expedition, the Royal Geographical Society had recognised this achievement by the presentation of a gold watch. For his subsequent efforts, the Society awarded him the Patrons' Medal, and only African explorer, Dr Livingstone before him had been twice honoured by this august body. Stuart had ridden over 16,000km (9,920 miles) in his relentless search for an overland route, and the 3025km (1875 miles) Stuart Transcontinental Highway between Adelaide and Darwin is a fine memorial to his indomitable spirit.

The Real Centre of Australia

Australia's precise mathematical centre of gravity has been calculated, and the point is on a virtually inaccessible tract on Lilla Creek Cattle Station, 335km (208 miles) east of Ayers Rock, and 300km (186 miles) south of Central Mt Stuart. The nearest settlement in its Simpson Desert location is Finke. The spot, located at a latitude 25 deg 36 min 36.4 sec south; longitude 134 deg 21 min 17.3 sec east, was determined by a team of three computer programmers, two Government surveyors and personnel from Queensland University

Geographical Studies Department in 1988. They used the South Pole as a reference point, and marked off more than 22,000 points around the continent and criss-crossed the country with lines, taking into account such variables as the rugged coastline. The Queensland Royal Geographical Society wanted something of value for its contribution to the Bicentennial. The place has been called the Lambert Centre, after Mr Bruce Lambert a noted surveyor and the first chairman of the National Mapping Council, and it's the precise point at which Australia can be divided into quarters.

CHAMBERS PILLAR HISTORICAL RESERVE

340ha (840 acres)

Location

165km (102 miles) south of Alice Springs, via the Old South Road.

Characteristics

This reserve features a prominent column of red and yellow sandstone, which, including its 25m (82 ft) high pedestal, towers 58m (190 ft) above the surrounding plain. An eerie quality pervades, and the names carved into the pillar's soft sandstone base by the explorers and early settlers, are a record of hardship and tenacity that gives it a genuine sense of history. The pillar was formed from sandstone sediments laid down under a shallow sea about 400 million years ago. Since then, wind, heat and rain have eroded away the weaker material, leaving this solitary column of pebbly sandstone.

Stuart discovered it in April, 1860, and simply described this giant pillar rising majestically from the scorched desert sands as a 'remarkable hill'. He named it after James Chambers, one of the expedition's sponsors. Stuart used the Pillar as a landmark on subsequent journeys, as did others such as Ernest Giles and John Ross, and it retained this function until the coming of the railway in the 1920s.

To the Aborigines, it has long featured in their Dreamtime as Itirkawara, the Gecko ancestor whose modern day descendants are the commonly seen knob-tailed geckoes. Mythology has it that Itirkawara left the Finke River, journeyed north, and grew into a man of huge stature, strength and extreme violence. On his return home he killed other ancestors, then disregarded strict marriage codes and took a wife from the wrong kin group, which incurred the wrath of relatives who banished him and the girl. They slunk off into the desert, Itirkawara in fury while the girl shrank from him in deep shame. Eventually they were turned into prominent rocky formations; Itirkawara into the pillar, and the girl into the low outcrop 500m to the north-east, called Castle Rock.

The colour is a pale cream-yellow except for the tip where oxidation of iron in the sandstone column has stained it a deep-red. Early mornings and late afternoons are best times for photography, when the pillar glows like a burning ember. It's a magic geological and historical place, and the only sad note is that a few visitors have added their names or graffiti to the sandstone. This action is not only illegal, it also lessens the historical significance of the reserve. Prosecutions have resulted in fines of over $5000!

How To Get There

It takes about 4 hours on a flat bladed surface that is not recommended for trailers or caravans, even when towed by 4WD vehicles. It's 4WD from Maryvale Station. A number of tourists are causing inconvenience and annoyance to pastoralists on Maryvale, Idracowra and Horseshoe Bend Stations by using private roads to cut across to the Stuart Highway, rather than using the authorised access road through the station. Understandably, prosecutions may result if travellers ignore advice and show disrespect when crossing private property.

The road to Maryvale Station is reasonable with sandy patches and plenty of dust. From the station, the first 12km (7 miles) is very dusty with bulldust patches; the next 23km (14 miles) slightly better, but care is needed at the washouts. At the 12km (7 miles) post, the road turns sharp left near a boundary fence and becomes rocky as it climbs to the top of a rise. Here the road divides - the right hand track is not recommended, so follow the other along the top of the rise (this section is very rough and requires extreme care during descent). The final 10km (6 miles) to the Pillar is over red sandhill terrain. If this is off-putting, there are plenty of tours to the Pillar from Alice Springs. For Stuart Highway entry see page 175 (Maryvale Station).

Services and Facilities

Barbecue fireplaces, tables and toilets are provided. Travellers are asked to bring their own firewood, as it is scarce here. As well, any locally collected material destroys habitats in this extremely fragile ecology and best advice is to use gas for cooking. Camping is allowed, but there is little shade and no water. The area has high temperatures, particularly in summer, so ample supplies of water are needed. There is a visitor information shelter.

Chambers Pillar

CURTIN SPRINGS

Population 12

Location

On the Lasseter Highway, 80km (50 miles) east of Ayers Rock Resort.

Characteristics

There's plenty of character and hospitality at this working cattle property and roadside inn that offers travellers refuge from heat and highway in a comfortable station setting. A pleasant brush-shaded area between the roadhouse and homestead has an interesting aviary, and even lush green grass; quite a contrast to the surrounding red sandhill, spinifex and desert oak country.

Peter and Ashley Severin not only opened the roadhouse in the late 1950s, but also the station homestead, where you can breakfast, lunch or dine with them. Ashley tells me they began tourist services here to help them through the drought years and only had six customers in their first year! Included within the boundaries of this 4162 sq km (1582 sq miles) station, is the Mt Conner monolith, as well as around 5000 Aberdeen Angus and shorthorn cattle. Apart from sharing their table, you can also join tours of the station and Mt Conner (see also separate listing). After the hype of 'The Rock', this establishment offers a more down to earth Outback experience that's a lot cheaper!

History

Curtin Springs was founded in 1943 by Mr Andrews, when the vacant Mt Conner Crown lease (abandoned by Paddy De Connlley, whose homestead ruins can be seen near Mt Conner), was incorporated into the new title. The station takes its name from the nearby brackish springs and the Prime Minister of the day, the late The Right Honourable John Curtin.

The Severins took over in 1956, managed to survive the drought years, built up the herds, and today run their own abattoir on the property.

Attractions

Tours that include Mt Conner and Curtin Springs, with dinner and champagne at the homestead are operated daily by Uluru Experience, ph 008 803 174.

Accommodation

Deluxe from $64.55; Budget from $32.15; Camping/Caravans - $10 per powered site, $2 for unpowered sites. Sites ungrassed. Pets allowed, dogs leashed.

Services and Facilities

The roadside inn has a bar, general store, meals in the homestead (breakfast $7, lunch $8, dinner $10), swimming pool (guests only), 1.2km airstrip, and showers for travellers ($1). Take-away food, ice, artifacts and souvenirs are available. Fuel includes super, ULP, diesel, camping gas and oil. Basic spares, mechanical and tyre repairs, tyres and tubes, and towing services are offered.

Credit cards accepted (American Express, Bankcard, Mastercard, Visa), opening hours 6am-10pm, 7 days all year, ph (089) 562 906, fax (089) 562 934.

DOCKER RIVER

Location

In the Petermann Ranges, 215km (170 miles) west of Ayers Rock on the Northern Territory/Western Australian border.

Characteristics

An Aboriginal settlement that has transit fuel services (super, ULP, diesel) and basic store available 9am-noon and 2-5pm weekdays, 9am-noon Saturdays. It's cash only and there's a $10 after-hours opening fee. A permit is required for the road and fuel. (See Information section.) The road through Pitjantjatjara lands leads to an abandoned section of the Gunbarrel Highway and the Warburton turn-off, about 80km (50 miles) west of the border at Giles. (An excellent map of the Gunbarrel Highway, produced by the RAC, is available from Automobile Associations throughout Australia.) Travellers crossing the border into Western Australia must have necessary permits.

History

Of interest, 41km (25 miles) east of Docker River is Lasseter's Cave and memorial plaque. Lewis Hubert Lasseter, better known as Harold Bell Lasseter was the central figure in one of the Territory's most intriguing mysteries - **the legend of Lasseter's lost gold reef.** His claim to have found a rich gold-bearing reef in central Australia was so convincing that the Central Australian Gold Exploration Company (CAGE) was formed in 1930 to find it. The expedition headed westwards from Alice Springs in July, 1930, and Lasseter was included in the party led by Fred Blakeley. Distrust of Lasseter's story by Blakeley, confusion and arguments over locations (Lasseter claimed their position in the Ehrenberg Range, about 150km [93 miles] due west of Haasts Bluff was nearly 200km [124 miles] too far north), and aerial reconnaissance halted by a plane crash, was enough for CAGE to order their return to Alice Springs. The fortuitous arrival of Paul Johns, a dingo trapper with a camel team, prompted Lasseter to engage him and together they struck out for the Petermann Range. But luck ran out soon after for Lasseter. Johns left him after a fight, his camels bolted away, and his supplies were almost depleted. Despite some help from Aborigines, he eventually made his way to Winters Glen where, in an emaciated and pitiful state, he lived for some weeks before his lonely death. His body was later found by Bob Buck who buried him at nearby Irving Creek. In 1957, the grave was reopened and the remains taken to Alice Springs and buried at the cemetery.

In his last letter found in his diary, Lasseter claimed to his wife that he had found the reef again. Since his death, many have tried in vain to find it, and the legend is either supported or refuted in some books that make interesting reading: *Hell's Airport* by Cootes, *Lasseter's Last Ride* by Idriess, and more recently, Stapleton's *Lasseter Did Not Lie*. In 1981, The Melbourne Sun (February 11, 1981) reported that two men had sighted a lengthy metre-high gold quartz blowout reef to the north of the Petermann Range. Yet another expedition in July, 1988, reported finding 'oceans' of quartz and four buried items specifically referred to in Lasseter's diaries. Over 30 people have died in previous expeditions, something that Lasseter's fabled reef refuses to do!

How To Get There

It's a flat bladed road, with care, suitable for conventional vehicles. Check road conditions before leaving. The road by-passes Docker River. Take the turn-off to the settlement for fuel. A permit to travel through this Aboriginal Land is required.

Lasseter's cave and plaque are near the settlement. Permission to visit is advised.

ERLDUNDA DESERT OAKS RESORT

Population 30

Location

On the corner of the Stuart and Lasseter Highways, 198km (123 miles) south of Alice Springs.

Characteristics

Erldunda means lime or salty water, and the resort established here in 1980 is a combination of motel, hotel, roadhouse, tavern and caravan park. Its strategic location 95km (59 miles) from the South Australian border, and 258km (160 miles) from Ayers Rock Resort, makes it a convenient rest, refuelling or stop-over point. Surrounding the resort is the large 6705 sq km (2548 sq miles) Erldunda Cattle Station covering vast expanses of red sand and desert oak country. For those travelling to Ayers Rock on the Lasseter Highway, a rest area 0.5km from the junction has an information bay that is worthwhile checking.

Accommodation

Motel - $61 single, $72 double, $82 triple per night.
 Budget - $26 single, $36 double, $47 triple.
 Camping/Caravans - powered sites $16 x 2, unpowered $12 x 2. Sites grassed and shaded.
Pets allowed, dogs leashed.

Services and Facilities

The resort has tavern/bistro bar, dining room (fully licensed a la carte menu approximately $16 for 3 course meal, bistro meals also); a shop selling groceries, takeaway food, ice, artifacts, souvenirs; picnic/bbq/shaded area; swimming pool (guests only); tennis court; telephone; and showers for travellers ($2). Fuel includes super, ULP, diesel, LPG, oil and camping gas. Vehicle services available are: basic spares, tyres and tubes, tyre repairs and full mechanical repairs. Tourist information is available.

Open all year, opening hours 7am-11pm. Credit cards accepted (Bankcard, Mastercard, Visa), ph (089) 560 984.

EWANINGA ROCK CARVINGS CONSERVATION RESERVE

6ha (15 acres)

Location

35km (22 miles) south of Alice Springs on the Old South Road.

Characteristics

Set in red sand plain country beside a small claypan just west of the Ooraminna Ranges, this small reserve protects ancient rock carvings thought to have been the work of Aboriginal artists who pre-date the area's current Aborigines. Here, on outcrops of smoothed soft sandstone, are the art galleries, featuring a great variety of symbols and designs, including snakes, spirals and animal tracks. The carvings cannot be dated accurately, and local Arrente Aborigines have no knowledge of their origin or meaning.

Natural weathering has caused some damage and a cast of some of the carvings will at least be a record of the designs (the replica is on display in the Alice Springs Museum), and you can help preservation by not climbing on the galleries.

There's plenty of wild life and plant life here, despite its arid surrounds. Two hundred species of plants, 100 bird types and thirty reptiles have been recorded. The claypan, when full of water, is irresistible to birds and larger animals such as red kangaroos, euros and dingoes.

The carvings are best photographed in the early morning or late afternoon when shadow effects highlight the shallow engravings more. Also, these times are more comfortable for viewing, particularly in summer.

The Ooraminna Rockhole Paintings nearby are a more recent art form expression, and access to the rockhole is via a 4WD track that turns east off the road 3km (1 mile) south of Ewaninga. The track may be difficult to find as heavy rains sometimes cause washouts, and there's a 1km stretch of deep sand that often causes problems. At the site, the cave, covered with Aboriginal paintings, shelters the rock hole that in the early days was a stock watering place, and water source for prospectors trekking to the Arltunga goldfields. On the rocks, south of the rockhole are the most significant paintings.

How To Get There

The Old South Road is flat bladed and has sandy patches and plenty of dust. With care, conventional vehicles are okay. South of Ewaninga, the road leads to Maryvale Station and Chambers Pillar, but this stretch is 4WD only.

Services and Facilities

Barbecues, tables and a pit toilet have been installed at Ewaninga.

Visitors are asked by the Conservation Commission not to collect wood for fires from this area as this will upset plant and animal life. Information signs along the walking trail provide a guide to the carvings and Aboriginal use of the area. Camping is not permitted, and there is no water provided. Mobile rangers from the Conservation Commission patrol and maintain the reserve, and are most helpful with information and road advice. Dogs allowed by permit only.

FINKE

Population 300

Location

On the fringe of the Simpson Desert, 180km (112 miles) east of Kulgera from the Stuart Highway.

Characteristics

People of the Yankunytjatjara language group live in the town, governed by the Aputula Aboriginal Council. It is basically an Aboriginal settlement where tourists are welcome, and while no alcohol is allowed (it's a designated dry area by order of The Aboriginal Councils and Northern Territory Licensing Commission), permits to visit and stay are not required. There's a general store, fuel services, garage, an art and craft centre, a basic camping ground, and some old buildings associated with the town's earlier railway function.

While most Aboriginal settlements, for various reasons, remain closed to tourists, the Aputula Council has a positive attitude towards visitors and they are in the process of developing tourist facilities. Even for many white Australians, there is a similarity between being in an Aboriginal community and visiting a foreign country. Respect and sensitivity toward differences can be the basis for rewarding and genuine cross-cultural experiences, and the area provides an ideal opportunity for this. Visitors are asked not to take photographs or use video cameras here without first asking permission. (Signs to this effect have been posted. Aborigines feel this is an invasion of their privacy, just as you would if some strangers poked a camera over your suburban fence and filmed your backyard bbq party!)

History

The town was named after South Australian pastoralist William Finke, and developed as a railway settlement with the building of the line between Adelaide and Alice Springs. It was quite a flourishing township, and on a few occasions the pub's resources were exhausted when floodwaters stranded the Old Ghan train here. It hosted many a race meeting, and during one the race was held up while Australian Inland Mission patrol padre, Arthur Cottrell, conducted a baptism. The proud parents persuaded him that it was the ideal spot as "we're all here, you, us, the baby, and our friends!"

The railway station, cranes and water tower are still there, while the pub has been renovated for the community's Art and Craft Centre.

How To Get There

From Kulgera, it is a formed gravel surface that's suitable for conventional vehicles, provided care is taken. Check road conditions at Kulgera.

Accommodation

A small camping ground is located just outside town. It has power and water only, and until facilities are up-graded, no charges apply. Toilet facilities in the town are limited. Sometimes the camping ground may be closed as the area is a bereavement place when there is a death in the community.

Services and Facilities

The community store sells a range of food, drink and artifacts, super, ULP and diesel fuel. Opening times for the store are 9-11am and 3-4.30pm weekdays, Saturday 8.30-11am, ph (089) 560 968. The garage undertakes repair work during normal trading hours.

FINKE RIVER CROSSING - BLISSEY'S TUCKER BOX

Location

125km (78 miles) south of Alice Springs on the Stuart Highway.

Characteristics

Above the gum-girded Finke River is the location of the Territory's most unusual roadhouse - a converted bus. It's a popular stop for truckies, and speciality of the 'coach' is marinated, underground mutton. Joanne Bliss sells a range of take-away food, and you will have to ask her about the underground mutton bit!

FINKE GORGE NATIONAL PARK

45,856ha (113,264 acres)

Location

138km (86 miles) south-west of Alice Springs, via Larapinta Drive and Hermannsburg.

Characteristics

Prehistoric palms, tranquil rock pools, and startling rock formations are the highlights of a visit to this national park that straddles the Fink River between the Krichauff and James Ranges. The park principally protects an amazing botanical oddity; the unique cabbage palms growing along Palm Creek, a tributary of the Finke. Within this magnificent wilderness region, the variety of wind and water sculptured rock structures and prolific flora and fauna offer plenty of scope for naturalists, photographers and bushwalkers.

History

Explorer Ernest Giles came this way in 1872 on the first of his five expeditions into the Red Centre. He basically followed the Finke north-east from Chambers Pillar, and about 3km (2 miles) south of where Ellery Creek joins the Finke River, Giles found some species of cabbage palms, along with tall river gums, thin melaleucas, and a great variety of bird life. He named the grove, Glen of Palms. Here Giles collected many plant samples and from sketches, his patron for the expedition, Baron Von Meuller, a scientist and Director of Melbourne's Botanic Gardens, identified the palms as Livistona

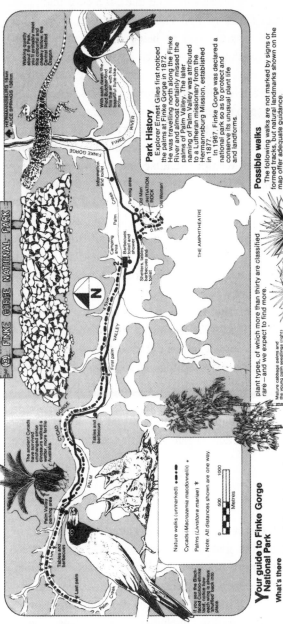

FINKE GORGE NATIONAL PARK

HERMANNSBURG 16km
ALICE SPRINGS 138km

FINKE RIVER

FINKE GORGE

Information and toilet

Parking area

Old Man/INITIATION ROCK
Old Woman

THE AMPHITHEATRE

0.5km

Palm Creek

Camping area

Barbecues, toilet and shower

Shelters, barbecues and toilet

1.5km

PALM VALLEY

First palm

CYCAD GORGE

Tables and barbecue

Palm Valley parking area

PALM

1.5km

Tables and barbecue

Last palm

Palm Creek

N

Your guide to Finke Gorge National Park

What's there

The park covers nearly forty-six thousand hectares of wilderness, including the Finke River Gorge and Palm Valley to the north and an area of sand dunes in the south. Wind erosion and the watercourses have carved impressive forms in the red sandstone. Features such as The Amphitheatre, Initiation Rock and Cycad Gorge are especially popular with photographers.

The park exists to protect one of the most comprehensive collections of living central Australian plants and in particular to help preserve the three thousand or so palms which occur nowhere else in the world. Livistona mariae cabbage palms with the scientific name Livistona mariae have survived in this area for at least ten thousand years, from a time when the climate was much wetter. The park is home to over four hundred plant types, of which more than thirty are classified rare — and we expect to find more.

How to get there

Finke Gorge National Park lies one hundred and thirty-eight kilometres west of Alice Springs, just south of Hermannsburg Mission. Most of the road is unsealed and the last sixteen kilometres into the park is termed 'four wheel drive only' since it follows the sandy bed of the Finke River. Rain may make this last section temporarily impassable but the Northern Territory Emergency Services, telephone 52 3822, can always advise current road conditions.

Commercial tour operators from Alice Springs regularly visit the park and details are available from any Northern Territory Government Tourist Bureau.

Park History

Explorer Ernest Giles first noticed the palms at Finke Gorge in 1872. He was travelling north along the Finke River and almost certainly missed the palms of Palm Valley. The later naming of Palm Valley was attributed to a Lutheran missionary from the Hermannsburg Mission, established in 1877.

In 1967, Finke Gorge was declared a national park so as to protect and conserve its unusual plant life and landforms.

Possible walks

The following walks are not marked by signs or formed tracks, but natural landmarks shown on the map offer adequate guidance.

1. Initiation Walk

The short climb up Initiation Rock offers good views of Palm Creek and The Amphitheatre area.

This rock was once the site of initiation ceremonies for Aranda youths. The Commission has declared that the Aboriginal custodians of this area accept your use of the rock as a vantage point, but as a guest you must respect the site and leave it unmarked.

2. Palm Valley Walk

From the map you'll see that this walk is in two sections. The first, about 1.5km, one way is separated by the Palm Valley Parking Area. The walk follows the course of Palm Creek and takes you past the palms, cycads and towering sandstone cliffs for which the valley is known.

Nature walks (unmarked) ●●●

Cycads (Macrozamia macdonnellii) *

Palms (Livistona mariae) *

Note All distances shown are one way

0 500 1000
Metres

The ancient Cycads have survived unchanging since dinosaurs walked a wetter, more fertile Australia.

Mature cabbage palms and the young palm seedlings (right) which will eventually replace them.

Walking quietly about the park you'll probably meet the colourful and cheeky Spinifex Pigeon.

With each dawn the Pied Butcher Bird will fill the air with his beautiful flute-like notes.

If you see the Black-faced Cuckoo-shrike bird, notice how each wing is always shuffled back into place.

mariae, one of the world's oldest surviving trees. It's clear that Giles did not explore Palm Creek or find Palm Valley. One reason that possibly deterred him was his fear of being trapped in a narrow gorge, as Aborigines at the time were lighting fires ahead of the party. Giles felt they were attempting to frighten him into retreat. Stuart named the Finke River in 1861, after one of his benefactors, when he crossed it close to the present town of Finke.

The discovery of the greatest concentration of palms is attributed to three Lutheran Missionaries from the Hermannsburg Mission, Kempe, Schulze and Schwarz, in 1877. They explored the upper reaches of this Finke tributary and named it Palm Valley. The Horn Scientific Expedition to Central Australia, in 1894, spent some time here collecting samples and studying the environment, and few visited the region until Len Tuit and Jack Cotterill pioneered tourism in the area during the late 1950s. In fact, Tuit established a chalet near Palm Creek for the slowly developing touring industry at this time.

Apart from tourism, the discovery of sizeable reserves of natural gas and oil in the 1970s led to the establishment of the Palm Valley Gas Field. Its 9.2 billion cubic metres of recoverable gas is now being piped to Alice Springs and Darwin, via Tennant Creek and Katherine for domestic and power generation purposes.

Further west is the Mereenie Oil and Gas Deposits which have proven reserves of 38 million barrels of oil and 11 billion cubic metres of gas. Oil production began in 1984 and both fields are closed to visitors.

Flora and Fauna

The park contains one of the most comprehensive collections of living central Australian plants, of which over 400 species have been identified with more than 30 classified as rare. After rains, wildflowers carpet the ground in a spectacular blaze of colour. Ghost gums, river red gums, melaleucas, cyprus pine and the palms provide a habitat for prolific birdlife, including pied butcher birds, black-faced cuckoo-shrike, western bower birds, Port Lincoln parrots and white-plumed honeyeaters. The central netted dragon, among other reptiles, is an interesting creature.

Cabbage palms have been growing here for at least 10,000 years and evolved at a time when the climate was more suited to these tropical plants. Their nearest relatives survive at Millstream on the Fortesque River in Western Australia and near Mataranka. These relics of the sub-tropical flora which flourished over the Centre a million years ago require for their shallow root system, a stable soil structure free from scouring floods, a permanent shallow water table and protection from fierce fire. That they have survived climatic changes is due to the local geology where tiny pores within the sandstone allow rainwater to seep gradually through to the solid base rock which prevents it from escaping. This seepage, despite lengthy drought periods, maintains a sufficient supply of moisture to the palms.

About half the 3000 individual palms in the Palm Valley area are of reproductive age, and the oldest trees have an age of between 100 and 300 years, based on their growth rate of 1m every 10 years. The tallest are over 30m. In Palm Valley, about 750 mature specimens grow in this narrow rocky valley along with cycads, river red gums and melaleucas.

Cycads (Macrozamia macdonnellii), like the cabbage palms, are relict plants, remnants of earlier geological time scale periods when higher rainfall occurred. But cycad are more akin to living fossils. They evolved 200 million years before the palms, at a time when dinosaurs roamed across a prehistoric Australian landscape. While palm-like, it does not belong to the palm family. It never flowers; instead it produces male and female cones. It is a slow growing plant with a thick, usually underground trunk, while its large greyish-green leaves, and sharply pointed leaflets crowd the stem top. The cycad usually grows at the base of cliffs where there is adequate shade and moisture. They are concentrated in Cyclad Gorge and are in other parts of the MacDonnell Ranges.

Particularly after rain, crystal-clear rock pools remain in the valley and provide beautiful reflections of the long, narrow, red-cliffed walls. The towering walls of Cycad Gorge are an impressive, colourful entrance to the oasis-like Palm Valley. An equally unforgettable sight is the slow moving camel train, as Noel Fullerton leads his 'ships of the desert' along the base of the red bluffs.

Shield Rock, better known as Initiation Rock, was once the site where Aranda youth were initiated into manhood. While it is a highly significant Aboriginal place, visitors are allowed to use the site as a vantage point, and are asked to respect and leave this sacred area unmarked. **From here there are excellent views of the Amphitheatre** . These unusual sandstone structures resulted from erosion of 400 million-year-old Hermannsburg formations, originally deposits of sand under a shallow sea that were welded together by great heat and pressure and subsequently uplifted. The surrounding rocks of the Amphitheatre take on remarkable shapes, particularly at sunrise and sunset, and give rise to such names as Sundial Rock, Cathedral Rock, Battleship Rock and the Wall of a Thousand Faces.

How To Get There

From Hermannsburg, it's 4WD only along the Finke river bed. Coach tours or 4WD safaris offer a number of trips to the Park throughout the week. Contact the Information Office in Alice Springs. You can book a tour at Hermannsburg.

Services and Facilities

A large camping area features shower and toilet block (please use solar showers sparingly) free gas barbecues and water. It's an attractive area with plenty of shade. Information and the ranger residence are at the entrance to Palm Creek. Shelters, tables, bbq and toilet facilities are located near Initiation Rock. Tables and bbq are provided at Cycad Gorge and Palm Valley. Swimming is allowed.

Camping fees - $4 per person per night, or $10 per family. Pets only on permit basis.

GEMTREE CARAVAN PARK

Population 6

Location

On the Plenty Highway, 70km (43 miles) from Stuart Highway turn-off, on sealed road.

Characteristics

A new establishment in the Harts Range features natural bush camping sites amidst a rocky outcropped, mulga, ironwood and bloodwood covered landscape, where the main interest is gemstone fossicking (zircon, garnet, smoky quartz, moonstone are some). June and Graham Short will show novice fossickers the basic skills, and hire equipment ($10). For zircons, which are harder to find, June or Graham will accompany fossickers, and the charge is $25 including equipment hire. They also cut stones, have a fine gemstone display, and sell gemstones.

Accommodation

Powered sites $16 x 2; unpowered $12 x 2; bush sites $6 per person; on-site vans $37 x 2. Pets allowed, dogs leashed.

Services and Facilities

Basic shop, food (pies, pasties, drinks), ice, souvenirs, local Aboriginal artifacts, fuel (super, ULP, diesel), oil, camping gas. Opening hours 7.30am-6.30pm, 7 days, ph (089) 569 855.

GOSSE BLUFF
SCIENTIFIC RESERVE

Location

197km (122 miles) west of Alice Springs, via Larapinta Drive.

Characteristics

Gosse Bluff is an astro-geological feature; the scene of the Territory's biggest bang when a comet struck here 130 million years ago. It's one of the most significant and best documented comet impact geological structures in the world, and many of its landform features are highly significant to Aborigines. It was discovered in 1872 by Ernest Giles, who named it after Alice Springs telegraphist Harry Gosse, not the explorer William Gosse, as widely believed.

The 4km (2 miles) ring of rugged hills that rise some 200m (655 ft) above the plain is all that remains of the core of the original crater. The actual Bluff is an erosional remnant of the crater, and an estimated 2000m (6540 ft) of weathering and erosion since the impact, has removed visible traces of the outer rim which had a diameter of 22km (14 miles). Evidence for this comes mainly from satellite images which reveal a distinct halo effect, thought by scientists to show the extent of affected rock. Rings of differing vegetation (one of which is the grass tree, unique to this location in Central Australia), are surface indicators of re-arranged rock structures. Shatter cones, smaller scale structures characterised by cone-shaped fractures that result from extreme shock, are further evidence of a major impact here. From these shatter cones, scientists determined that the object was probably 600m (1962 ft) in diameter, had a low density, consisted of an agglomerate of frozen carbon dioxide, ice and dust, and a high velocity (40km/sec-25 miles/sec).

The impact force released energy equivalent to one million times that of the atomic bomb at Hiroshima. No extra-terrestial material has been found; not surprising as with all that energy on impact, the comet would have vaporised.

The sandstone rock strata that form the inner rim were uplifted from their original bed (between 1000 and 300m - 3270 and 9810 ft - below the present land surface), by the shock waves. Not only is it a scientific marvel, but also it's of great spiritual significance to Aborigines who call it Tnorala - "Father of the Mountains".

A good view of the feature can be seen from the Tylers Pass Trig Station, and the Department of Mines and Energy have an excellent brochure available.

How To Get There

Permits to travel across Aboriginal land to Gosse Bluff are required, as is an entry permit from the Northern Territory Aboriginal Sacred Sites Protection Authority (Belvedere House, Parsons Street, Alice Springs, ph (089) 526 366).

4WD vehicle is necessary for access from the Redbank/Hermannsburg Road. Check current road conditions before leaving.

HARTS RANGE

Population 120

Location

On the Plenty Highway, 215km (133 miles) east of Alice Springs.

Characteristics

This small, mainly Aboriginal, town is situated on the northern flanks of Harts Range near the centre of one of the Territory's best mineral fossicking areas. In this model Aboriginal settlement there is a police station, school, the Atitjere Community shop (a small supermarket and general store), registered airfield, and race course. While it is on Aboriginal land, no permits are required, but alcohol is discouraged.

The surrounding landscape is full of interest. The ranges are composed of rugged outcrops of strongly metamorphosed sediments and volcanic rocks with various intruded material. Many strangely shaped rock formations, and the interplay of light, provide plenty of subject variety for photographers. Vegetation includes mulga and witchetty bush on slopes and ridges; ironwood, whitewood and kerosene grasses on the flatter areas; tea-tree along the upper creek beds, and river red gums lower down. Keen fossickers will be pleased to know that spinifex is not widespread in the area.

History

The area was the scene of much mining activity in the past, the remnants of which are mullock heaps (waste rock), scattered diggings, and the foundations of many stone-walled houses that used to shelter over 100 men and equipment. These structures are part of the Territory's mining heritage and should be left intact.

Fossicking

Zircon, magnetite, moonstone, garnet, muscovite, mica, blue quartz, beryl and apatite are just a random sample of what is here. The best information on this and other fossicking areas is contained in *A Guide to Fossicking in the Northern Territory* produced by the Mines and Energy Department. It's a must for serious fossickers, and costs about $10.

Events

Picnic races are held during the first weekend in August, and everyone is welcome.

How To Get There

By road, the first 90km (56 miles) of the Plenty Highway is sealed after which it is a reasonable gravel surface to Harts Range. It's suitable for conventional vehicles. Check conditions first.

Accommodation

Camping by the racecourse.

Services and Facilities

The store has a wide range of food and general store items, ice, limited take-away food, and sells gemstones. Fuel services include super, ULP, diesel, oil and camping gas. Hot and cold showers are available. Opening hours are 9am-5.30pm throughout the week. It's cash only, ph (089) 569 773.

HENBURY METEORITE CRATERS CONSERVATION RESERVE

16ha (40 acres)

Location

On the northern slope of the Bacon Range, 144km (89 miles) south-west of Alice Springs.

Characteristics

This reserve protects a series of at least 12 craters formed about 5000 years ago when a falling meteor shattered in the atmosphere, and its pieces struck the earth's surface. The craters range in diameter from 2 to 180m (588 ft), and up to 15m (49 ft) in depth; their distribution suggests that the meteorite shower came from the south-west. The meteorite's fiery path through the sky appears to have been witnessed by Aborigines, the clue being in the translation of one Aboriginal name for the area - "sun walk fire devil rock".

Consisting of iron (90%) and nickel (8%), these high density meteorites weighed several tonnes and hit the surface at 40,000km/hr (25,000mph). The impact velocity caused 'explosive' craters; the immense energy released folded back strata of near-surface rock to form the crater rims, while fragments of nickel-iron alloy were dispersed shrapnel-like over a wide area. Over 500kg of metal has been recovered from the site, one fragment of which weighs in at 44kg, and can be seen in the Alice Springs Museum. It's suspected that a number too are used as door-stops in various places around the

Centre, but don't let that give you ideas; today, it's illegal to remove any specimens, if indeed they can be found.

The dry, rocky, crater-pitted plain resembles a small-scale moonscape that is of great scientific value. The United States National Aeronautic and Space Administration thought so, when personnel including astronauts used it for familiarisation purposes prior to and during manned moon missions. Perhaps Armstrong walked here as well!

Vegetation is sparse, except in the soaks created by the craters, there is little shade, and it gets very hot. Wildlife is migratory and includes red kangaroo, dingo, various reptiles such as bearded dragons, wedge-tailed eagles, spotted harriers and zebra finches.

How To Get There

By road, access is from the Stuart Highway via the Kings Canyon Road (Ernest Giles Road), which is a formed gravel road that can get very corrugated, and after rains can become slippery. Conventional vehicles are okay. Various tours are available from Alice Springs. Check with the Tourist Association.

Services and Facilities

Wood barbecues, benches and tables with shade shelters, and pit toilets, are provided at the entrance to the park. There is no water or wood supplies. It is a comfortable walk along a track that has detailed guide information about the craters. There is wheelchair access. Please keep to the track, avoid unnecessary disturbance of the surface, and remember that these astro-geological features are unique. Camping is allowed. Dogs are allowed in designated areas only.

HERMANNSBURG

Population 500

Location

On Larapinta Drive, 132km (82 miles) south-west of Alice Springs.

Characteristics

An historic precinct of sun-scorched stone buildings set among palms and eucalypts on the Finke River plain bear testimony to the dedication of Lutheran pastors, who brought the gospel message, medical aid and European education to the Aranda people over 114 years ago. Today, the Aranda own the old Mission and, with the help of the National Trust, older buildings are being restored while others are retained for use by a thriving community. Hermannsburg maintains its strong links with the Lutheran Church through its Aboriginal and European pastors, whose role today is a spiritual one.

Buildings include the second church built in 1880, the Bethlehem Church, a smithy (built in 1882), a school-house, and old residences, two of which house a museum and tea rooms. Although an Aboriginal settlement, visitors are welcome but a permit is required for an overnight stay. Most visitors use the settlement as a transit stop whilst on their way to Palm Valley, but it's well worth looking at for its rather unique role in Territory history. Check with the office as to what buildings you may visit, and be diplomatic with photography.

History

Original missionary Kemp said of the torrid 20 month journey from Bethany in South Australia in 1877 "...that like the journey of St Paul to Rome, it was beset with all the privations imaginable". With missionary Schwarz, they led a party consisting of five lay workers, two Aboriginal stockmen, over 30 horses for the two large covered wagons, 2000 sheep (half of which died in the heat, and the long waterless stretches encountered), 20 cattle, 5 dogs and chickens.

The settlement, named after the Lutheran Training College at Hanover, was the first mission station in the Territory. It battled not only the harsh physical conditions, but also isolation, financial problems, sickness, apathetic governments, and constant opposition of vested interests among some pastoralists. The 1880s saw the beginnings of racial problems, with the arrival of the white pastoralists. Many settlers had little regard for Aboriginal needs or rights - in fact, in many instances Aborigines were regarded as a nuisance and sub-human. Tensions and clashes between the races occurred. The drought of 1883 brought hostilities when Aborigines speared cattle for food. White reaction was swift; police stations were established, such as at Illamurta Springs (see separate listing), and Aborigines were shot. Schwarz spoke publicly of Aboriginal treatment in 1886: "In 10 years' time there will not be many Blacks left in this area, and this is just what the white man wants. With all the shooting that is taking place, it is hard to conceive that the native people have any kind of future, and our only hope is that they are rescued from this intolerable position". In later years, reserves were to be established, the first of which was at Haast Bluff in 1937, as a result of lobbying by Lutheran missionaries.

In the 1880s, about 100 Aborigines lived at the mission, and buildings consisted of a church, residences, shearing shed, wooden blacksmith's shop, and the second oldest remaining structure, 'the colonist's residence'. A vegetable garden and orchard, including date palms, were established. Under Pastor Carl Strehlow's leadership in the 1890s, the buildings that today constitute the historic core were constructed. A grammar and dictionary of Aranda language was compiled in 1891. **Albert Namatjira was born here in 1902,** and with artist Rex Battarbee's encouragement, started to paint Central Australian landscapes, using European techniques combined with an

Aboriginal eye for perspective and colour. His works achieved international recognition in a style of watercolour paintings that became known as The Hermannsburg School. Caught in a cultural cross-fire, Albert Namatjira died an unhappy man in 1952. A monument recognising his work is located on Larapinta Drive, about 2km east of Hermannsburg. The school blackboard was used in the 1940s to demonstrate drawing techniques to children. Pastor Albrecht was a powerful force behind the direction of the mission between 1926 and 1952.

Freehold title of the Hermannsburg lease was granted to Aborigines in 1982. In recent years, there has been a trend by Aborigines to return to a more traditional family-oriented lifestyle in the outstations. **One such outstation is Ipolera, west of Hermannsburg, where the Malbunka family are developing a unique tourist venture which provides an insight into traditional Aboriginal lifestyle - visits are through operators.** Check with the Tourist Association in Alice Springs.

How To Get There

The road is sealed to within 30km (18 miles) of Hermannsburg, then it's a formed gravel road that's suitable for all vehicles. There are plenty of tours from Alice Springs (see Alice Springs listing). Provided you have made prior arrangements, you can join a tour to Palm Valley (Finke Gorge National Park) from here.

Services and Facilities

There's a shop, supermarket, tea rooms and fuel (super, diesel, ULP and camping gas). It's cash only. Open 8.30am-5.30pm, ph (089) 567 411. The museum is open 9am-5pm. There is no accommodation or tours, but visitors may drive up the main road to see the historic buildings. You are not allowed near the Aboriginal residential area, and photographing Aborigines strictly requires permission. Direct any enquiries to the Council Office, open Mon-Fri 8.45am-4pm.

ILLAMURTA SPRINGS CONSERVATION RESERVE

130ha (320 acres)

Location

Approximately 235km (146 miles) south-west of Alice Springs, via Stuart Highway and Ernest Giles Road.

Characteristics

The reserve protects the permanent waters of Illamurta Springs, which was an important water source for cattle in this dry, sandy area. To prevent further environmental damage to this verdant oasis, cattle have been fenced out. The Spring is situated in the bed of a small Illbilla Creek tributary, at the foot of the James Range, and the ruins of a lonely police outpost, established here in 1891 in an attempt to reduce cattle killing by local Aborigines, is the only sign of man's intrusion. Thick scrub surrounds the old station and stockyards, which are rapidly decaying. It is a picturesque, quiet spot, where a range of wildlife can be observed at the now clear waters. Access is via a variable flat bladed road with sand ridge terrain from the Tempe Downs turn-off to the reserve. You can camp here, but there are no facilties. No animals are allowed.

JERVOIS STATION

Population under 10

Location

On the Plenty Highway, approximately 335km (208 miles) north-east of Alice Springs.

Characteristics

In addition to looking after about 5000 Polled Hereford cattle on their 2750 sq km (1045 sq miles) station property, Michael and Denise Broad offer some basic transit services to travellers going to, or coming from, Queensland.

Of interest on the property is an air raid shelter, built during the 1960s for protection against rockets being test-fired from the Woomera Range in South Australia. Jervois and other stations were under the test flight path, and before they pressed the button at Woomera, controllers would telephone the stations to let owners know that another rocket was on its way. In case the rockets fell short of their targets, the shelters were provided. Some fragments did fall on local stations!

How To Get There

From Harts Range, it is a formed road surface, and beyond here 4WD is recommended. There are two river crossings just before the turn-off to the station.

Accommodation

You can camp at the Rest Area, nearly opposite the Jervois turn-off, on the Plenty Highway. Facilities here include fireplace, table, shelter and water.

Services and Facilities

The station has a small shop selling basic items, ice, artifacts and souvenirs. Super, ULP and diesel, oil, and minor repairs are vehicle services available. There's no accommodation or camping, but you can have showers ($1.50).

It's cash only, open during daylight hours, ph (089) 566 307.

Saltlakes on the way to 'The Rock'.

KINGS CANYON - WATARRKA NATIONAL PARK

106,000ha (261,820 acres)

Location

323km (200 miles) south-west of Alice Springs, near the western end of the George Gill Range, and 95km (59 miles) west of Wallara Ranch.

Characteristics

Watarrka National Park, formerly Kings Canyon· National Park, features contrasting coloured canyon walls of a mighty cleft in the George Gill Range, dome-shaped buttresses of the 'lost city', and a narrow, verdant valley climaxing in a large rockpool called the 'Garden of Eden'. No trip to the Centre is complete without having experienced these dramatic features that are contained in a relatively compact area, and which can be seen via an exhilarating walking track. Aboriginal art and a ranger station with excellent interpretative displays are complementary features.

History

The area is homeland for the Luritja people, who have three main living areas in the park, and, in association with the Conservation Commission, they are involved with future development plans for the canyon.

Explorer Ernest Giles and his companion Samuel Carmichael were

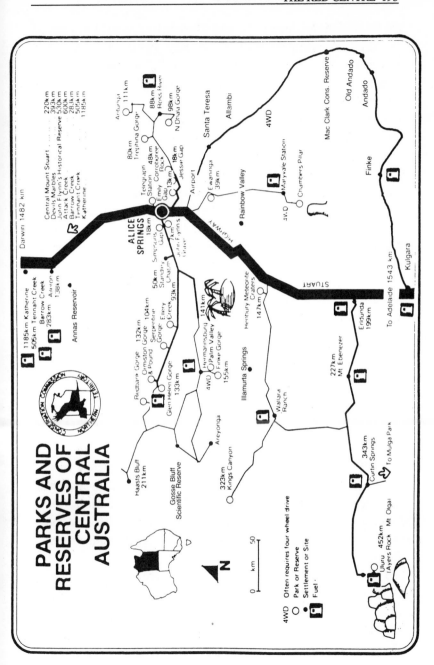

PARKS AND RESERVES OF CENTRAL AUSTRALIA

4WD — Often requires four wheel drive
○ — Park or Reserve
● — Settlement or Site
🅵 — Fuel

0 km 50

N

Darwin 1482 km

Central Mount Stuart 220km
Devils Marbles 393km
John Flynn's Historical Reserve 530km
Attack Creek 600km
Barrow Creek 283km
Tennant Creek 505km
Katherine 1185km

1185km Katherine
505km Tennant Creek
Barrow Creek
283km Aileron
138km

Annas Reservoir

Redbank Gorge 132km
Ormiston Gorge 104km
Serpentine & Pound
Gorge
Ellery 93km
Creek
Glen Helen Gorge
133km

Haasts Bluff
211km

Gosse Bluff
Scientific Reserve

Areyonga

323km
Kings Canyon

452km Mt Olga
Uluru
(Ayers Rock)

343km
Curtin Springs
To Mulga Park

227km
Mt Ebenezer

Erldunda
199km

Wallara
Ranch

4WD
Hermannsburg
Palm Valley
Finke Gorge
155km

141km

Illamurta Springs

Henbury Meteorite
Craters
147km

50km
Standley
Chasm

18km
Simpsons
Gap
7km
John Flynn's
Grave

ALICE
SPRINGS

Airport

Telegraph
Station
Emu
Gap
13km

48km
Emily Corroboree
Rock
18km
Jessie Gap

80km
Trephina Gorge

Arltunga
111km

88km
Ross River
98km
N'Dhala Gorge

Santa Teresa

Allambi

4WD

Mac Clark Cons. Reserve

Old Andado

Andado

Finke

Rainbow Valley

Ewaninga
39km

Maryvale Station
Chambers Pillar

4WD

HIGHWAY

STUART

To Adelaide 1543 km:

Kulgara

To Adelaide 1543 km

the first non-Aboriginals in the area when their expedition was forced to skirt Lake Amadeus while on its way to Mt Olga, and were attracted to this red sandstone range, in 1872. Giles named the range after his brother-in-law, and wrote enthusiastically about the creek, which he named after the expedition's main financier, Fieldon King. His glowing reports brought the pastoralists, which not surprisingly upset local Aborigines, and a few skirmishes resulted.

The Canyon takes it name from the creek, but to the Aborigines the whole locality is known as Watarrka, after the Acacia ligulata, which grows in profusion, particularly at the beginning of the walking track. William Gosse came this way a year later, and camped at Kings Creek before heading south to discover Ayers Rock, curiously missed by Giles.

In 1960, the tourist potential of the feature was recognised by the late Jack Cotterill, who established Wallara Ranch a year later to service the attraction which was described as "the tastiest tourist attraction in the Territory".

Geology

The evolutionary sequence of the canyon in Devonian Times (about 350-450 million years ago) was sedimentation (laying down of sands, silts and clays under a shallow estuary), sandstone rock formation, uplift of sandstone blocks by tectonic activity (great internal energy forces) and, according to one theory, an associated monumental splitting of the sandstone. Subsequent flood-waters of Kings Creek have, over millions of years, undercut the softer base sandstone, causing massive slabs to shear from the towering 100m high walls, thus widening the canyon.

The lower level rock consists of reddish-brown sandstone, silty sandstone, and red-green and white silt and claystone laid down about 440 million years ago, called Carmichael sandstone. Overlying this is a bed of highly permeable white quartz-rich rock known as Mereenie Sandstone, characterised by ripple and cross bedding marks from wave (water) movement and joints (fractures) from the uplift period. Traces of worm trails can also be seen, particularly on the plateau.

Features

The distinctive red colouration of the south wall's almost vertical joint face, due to coatings of iron oxide, contrasts with the creamy colour of the equally awesome one kilometre length of the north wall.

Dome-shaped structures on the plateau result from sandstone blocks being eroded along their joints, the edges of which were rounded by further weathering processes. **The end result is an amazing layout of 'houses' and paved 'courtyards' aptly named the 'Lost City'. Keep to the arrow-directed track, as it is easy to get disorientated here!**

You won't be disappointed by the 'Garden of Eden', a narrow gorge with native fig, gum and cycads lining the creek that flows into a delightful triangular-shaped rockpool, before plunging over the edge into the canyon when the rains come. The unforgettable grandeur of the canyon unfolds at this point.

Flora and fauna characteristic of The Centre are well represented. An extended walking track, foot-bridges and boardwalks now complete a round trail up to the plateau to the canyon rim and 'Lost City, down into the 'Garden of Eden', across to the south wall, then descends to the canyon floor past some Aboriginal rock paintings, and back to the car park. It's a physically demanding walk - take something to drink, wear a hat, and have supportive footwear. The climb to the plateau is particularly steep. It's a beautiful wilderness area, where even a thoughtlessly dropped sweet wrapping constitutes visual pollution.

How To Get There

From the Ernest Giles/Angus Downs Roads junction (Wallara Ranch), it is a sealed road to the Canyon.

Accommodation

Seven kilometres from the Canyon on the Ernest Giles Road is the Frontier Kings Canyon Motel, with a licensed restaurant, swimming pool, barbecues - $140-180 a double room. All credit cards accepted.

Kings Canyon Frontier Caravan Park: powered sites - $20 x 2; unpowered - $16 x 2, no pets allowed.

Services and Facilities

A ranger station and visitor centre at the park entrance (about 20km [12 miles] from the canyon) have displays and literature, including an excellent Mines and Energy Department Geology and Landforms brochure. Facilities at the canyon include car park, day use (toilets, picnic, gas barbecues) camping area, water and cold showers. Because of wood scarcity and fire danger, camp-fires are discouraged. Swimming in the rockpools is also discouraged because of bacteria build-up from fouling. A memorial stone cairn at the beginning of the walking track recognises the work of Jack Cotterill.

KINGS CREEK CATTLE STATION

Population 9

Location

South-west of Alice Springs, and 30km (19 miles) east of Kings Canyon.

Characteristics

Apart from managing the cattle side of things on this 800 sq km (304 sq miles) property, Ian Conway has developed a tourist enterprise that is conveniently located close to the magnificent Kings Canyon National Park. It features a camping ground with grassed, small, individual sites, separated by natural vegetation that is the next best thing to bush-camping.

Attractions

Working cattle station. Camel rides and tours (by prior arrangement), and the nearby Kings Canyon National Park (see separate listing).

How To Get There

For access and road conditions, see Wallara Ranch and Kings Canyon listings.

Accommodation

Serviced tents including dinner, bed and breakfast, $71 per person.

Camping costs are $5 per person, and sites are powered, grassed and shaded. Pets allowed, dogs must be leashed.

Services and Facilities

The station is expanding its facilities. It has a shop selling basic items including artifacts, souvenirs and ice, a bar, bough shed where bbq meals and damper are available, take-away food, picnic/bbq/shaded areas, disabled facilities, and showers for travellers ($2.50). Fuel includes super, ULP, diesel, oil and camping gas. Vehicle services available are basic spares, minor mechanical repairs and tyre repairs. There's a 1.5km airstrip.

Opening hours as required, all year round, ph (089) 567 474.

KULGERA

Population 21

Location

On the Stuart Highway, 20km (12 miles) north of the Northern Territory/South Australian Border.

Characteristics

Surrounded by the 1370 sq km (521 sq miles) Kulgera Cattle Station and an arid landscape of mulga plains with strange rocky outcrops, this small settlement consists of a hotel/motel caravan park complex, and a police station. This is Pitjantjatjara country, where evidence of former Aboriginal presence can be seen in a number of rock painting sites in the area.

The hotel is either the first or the last in the Territory (depending on which way you are travelling), and its comfortable, friendly atmosphere gives a great introduction to the Outback, or vivid memories of it as you leave. Apart from the usual roadhouse services, owners Kay and Jeff Sutton are working closely with the Tourist Bureau and Conservation Commission in providing information facilities. For those entering the Territory, it is a worthwhile orientation and information spot, as well as being the gateway to the Dalhousie Springs area in South Australia. Since the recent discovery of the real geographic centre of Australia near Finke, the pub can now claim to be the most central in the continent.

Attractions

A new flora and fauna park is a 2ha (5 acres) enclosure that will have most types of Outback wildlife, including kangaroos, wallabies, dingoes, camels and donkeys.

The old Kulgera Homestead is near the pub, and was built in the early 1930s as headquarters for a large sheep station. In conjunction with the Conservation and Heritage Commissions, the homestead will be restored and house a museum.

Events

The showground is the venue for the annual gymkhana held during the last weekend in September. Everyone is welcome, and evening barbecues and bush dances provide plenty of lively entertainment.

Accommodation

Hotel/Motel with self-contained units - $50 a double.

Camping/Caravans - powered sites $15 x 2; unpowered sites - $6 x 2.
    Sites are grassed, with some shade. Pets allowed, but must be under control.

Services and Facilities

The hotel has a shop, a bar, restaurant, picnic/bbq/shaded areas, showers for travellers, and sells take-away food, ice, souvenirs and artifacts (locally produced and excellent value for money). A 1.3km airstrip is nearby, and the police station provides road condition information. An Information Bay near the hotel gives further detailed tourist advice.

Fuel includes super, ULP, diesel, autogas, camping gas and aviation (by prior arrangement). Oil, basic spares, mechanical repairs (qualified mechanic), tyres and tubes, and towing service are vehicle services available.

Opening hours 6.30am-11pm. Credit cards accepted (Bankcard, Amex, Mastercard, Visa), ph (089) 560 973.

MAC CLARK CONSERVATION RESERVE

Location

In the Simpson Desert, about 300km (186 miles) south-east of Alice Springs.

Characteristics

It is an area set aside to preserve a rare occurrence of Acacia peuce, of which there are only two other known locations in the world - both in Queensland, near Birdsville and Boulia. At this Andado bore location, they are known as casuarina, while in Birdsville they are called waddywood. It resembles a she-oak in shape and foliage, but whereas the she-oak bears cones or 'apples' the peuce has seed pods, hence its acacia classification.

Acacias, more commonly known as wattles, generally live for about 20 years. Exceptions are mulga, blackwood and cedar wattle, which live to about 100 years, while peuce is thought to be over 6000-years-old! It grows at a rate of 30cm every 200 years, and as many of the trees are over 10m, an indication of their age and botanical significance is seen.

The reserve honours the late Mac Clark, who owned the surrounding Andado Station for many years.

Facilities

There are none, and for road conditions and access, refer to the Andado Station listing.

MARYVALE STATION

Population 120

Location

On the Old South Road, 120km (75 miles) south of Alice Springs. 42km from Chambers Pillar.

Characteristics

A 3180 sq km (1208 sq miles) cattle station that now provides basic services to travellers, because of its location on the increasingly popular route to Chambers Pillar. It's run by Bill and Tracey Hayes, who don't mind caravans or trailers being temporarily left here, but they don't take any responsiblity for their safety. About 115

Aboriginal people live on the property, and some of their artifacts can be purchased at the store.

How To Get There

From Alice Springs, refer to Chambers Pillar listing for road description, and please keep to authorised private station roads only.

From the Stuart Highway, 103km (64 miles) north of Erldunda, a flat bladed, public road runs to Maryvale. It's rarely graded with rough patches (Hugh River crossing). Distance is approximately 115km (71 miles), 4WD recommended. Check conditions with Police or Roads Department.

Services and Facilities

There's a shop selling basic items, including snack type foods, pies, cold drinks and morning and afternoon teas and coffee. Super, unleaded and diesel fuel are available, but there are no repairs or other vehicle services. Toilets and water are available. It's cash only, open 7 days a week (closed Sunday afternoon) from 10am-5pm, ph (089) 560 989.

Camping: Camping is allowed for a minimum fee but there are no shower facilities.

MT CONNER

Location

Approximately 20km (12 miles) south-east of the Lasseter Highway at Curtin Springs.

Characteristics

This flat-topped monolith rises 350m (1444 ft) from the plain, and was named after M.L. Conner, a South Australian Parliamentarian, by explorer William Gosse who discovered it in 1873. It is the eastern-most of the 'Three Great Tors' (residual prominent rock mass - mesa is a more accurate term to describe Mt Conner, as it is an isolated tableland area with steep sides), and often mistaken for the more famous, Ayers Rock (Uluru). Unlike Ayers Rock, Mt Conner has horizontal rather than near vertical strata, and the summit is flatter. Structurally, it is a mass of quartzite nearly 3.5km (2 miles) long and up to 1km wide, with much of its surrounds boulder strewn at the base from which vertical rock faces rise sharply. Some softer layers have worn away, creating deeply honeycombed faces and cave-like rock shelters.

The precipices glow red when lit by the mellow sun, providing another unforgettable desert image.

The monolith is the remnant of a former land surface in which marine fossils suggest it was once the sea floor of an inland ocean from which Ayers Rock and the Olgas (Kata Tjuta) were also formed.

To the Aborigines, it is known as Artula, once the home of the dreaded Ninya (Ice-men), whose nightly wanderings, amongst other things, caused frosts. Two quartzite heaps near the summit are the remains of a couple of these icicle-clothed creatures. Not surprising that the Aborigines respected this place, even though legend has it that the Ninya now live beneath some salt lakes about 25km (15 miles) north of here.

There is plenty of interesting flora and fauna. Native pine and fig, corkwood, mulga, saltbush and spinifex soften the harsh red colours. On the 3 sq km (1 sq mile) summit, spinifex mainly grows. Wildlife includes large goannas, euros, dingoes, camels, emus, grass-wrens, and rare peregrine falcons in the surrounding area.

Mt Conner is situated on Curtin Springs Cattle Station, owned by the Severin family, who regretfully found it necessary to close public access because of constant damage to fence and bores. However, in conjunction with Uluru Experience, the station offers a range of tours including such activities as camping, sightseeing (ruins of Paddy De Connlley's homestead), summit climb for Ayers Rock and Olgas views, as well as a more distant vista of the Petermann and Musgrave Ranges, and swimming in the dam. It is a peaceful, wilderness environment. Contact Uluru Experience for details and bookings, ph 008 803174 (toll free)

On the Lasseter Highway, the Mt Conner Lookout and rest area is a pleasant 'cuppa' stop. Facilities include fireplace, tables, shade and water. Across the road are steps to a ridge-top which overlooks some distant salt lakes.

Mt Conner

MT EBENEZER

Population 20

Location

Approximately half-way between Alice Springs and Yulara; 183km (113 miles) east of Ayers Rock Resort on the Lasseter Highway.

Characteristics

The original part of this 40-year-old roadhouse is built out of hand-cut desert oak, which contributes to its unpretentious exterior and inviting, comfortable atmosphere inside. It is managed by Barry Ganley for the owners, the Imanpa Aboriginal Community who have their settlement nearby. Apart from providing services to travellers, a positive feature is Aboriginal participation in the enterprise, which has a training ground emphasis for Imanpa Aborigines as well as a focus on their artifacts and dot paintings. Visitors are asked not to take photographs or use video cameras without prior permission.

The roadhouse specialises in home-style cooking; the pies and bread they make are superb, while the shady, fly-screened bbq area is a popular retreat from the heat and the bush-flies. In the distance opposite, the Basedow Range and Mt Ebenezer can be seen across the shimmering red sand and desert oak landscape. The meaning of the name has a ring of optimism - 'land of hope'.

Accommodation

Motel style - $40 single, $46 double.
  Camping/Caravans - $3 per person. Pets allowed, dogs leashed.

Services and Facilities

The roadhouse has a bar; licensed restaurant (buffet style meals), breakfast from $3, dinner $8-10; shop (basic things); gift shop with an emphasis on an impressive range of local artifacts and paintings that are excellent value (Barry will explain and provide background to the artwork, as will other staff); showers for travellers ($3); ice and take-away food.

Vehicle services include super, ULP, diesel and oil.

Opening hours 7.00am-8.00pm. Credit cards accepted (Bankcard, Mastercard, Amex, Diners, Visa), ph (089) 562 904.

NEW CROWN STATION

Location

On the fringe of the Simpson Desert, approximately 185km (115 miles) east of Stuart Highway at Kulgera.

Characteristics

Francis Smith runs this large 7720 sq km (2980 sq miles) cattle property, and frequent requests for fuel resulted in the station providing this basic service for travellers. Super, diesel and limited ULP supplies are the only services available, during reasonable daytime hours. It is cash only, ph (089) 560 969.

How To Get There

For road conditions refer to the Old Andado listing.

OLD ANDADO STATION

Population 1

Location

In the Simpson Desert, 350km (217 miles) south-east of Alice Springs.

Characteristics

Historic Andado Station features the original homestead buildings of the huge 10,857 sq km (4126 sq miles) cattle property set amongst giant sand dunes of the Simpson Desert. Built out of timber and corrugated iron by the first lessee, Mr Robert MacDill in 1922, visitors can now enjoy its authentic atmosphere in the red desert environment. 18km (11 miles) away is the current Andado Homestead, where by arrangement you can see the working side of things on a cattle station, but only if there are activities like a muster, branding or camp draft - check with Molly Clark who runs the Old Andado Homestead. Molly and her husband, Mac, used to own the whole station, and if you want to learn something about remote station life, Molly's a mine of information. Her husband was tragically killed in an air crash in 1978, and the Mac Clark Conservation Reserve nearby is named in his honour. (See separate listing for this reserve.)

The drive to the station offers a stunning experience of endless stretches of the Simpson Desert, named after the President of the South Australian Royal Geographical Society by Dr Madigan, whose flights over the area in 1929 were financed by the Society. The Simpson extends much of its 48,282 sq km (18,347 sq miles) into this corner of the Territory, and has Sahara-like ridges of rich red sand that are virtually straight, parallel and continuous for nearly 150km

(93 miles). Wave-like, they roll north-west/south-east from horizon to horizon, often exceeding 30m in height.

History

There was much truth in the old saying "no wise man fools with the Simpson". Many people have died of dehydration, and it's thought that explorer Ludwig Leichhardt perished in its formidable sands, too. To cattleman, Edmund Colson, it was a challenge. Convinced that after good rains, fresh water would lie in the claypans and grass would sprout between the ridges, he set out in May 1936, after some heavy rains had fallen, with an Aboriginal companion and five camels; two for riding and three for food and water. With temperatures over 45C by day, and below freezing point at night, the 55-year-old arrived in fine fettle at Birdsville after just 16 days and 321km (99 miles). He had conquered the unconquerable, and to dispel any doubts about his feat and satisfied that he had proved his theory, he returned by the same route. However, his crossing was the first southern crossing in the vicinity of the 26th Parallel (Northern Territory's southern border follows this line of latitude). David Lindsay attempted one of the earliest crossings in the same year he found 'rubies' at Ruby Gap, in 1885. It was Madigan's 1939 expedition that made the first crossing north of the 26th Parallel, and the story is well told in his book *Crossing the Dead Heart*.

How To Get There

Leigh Goldsmith's Outback Experience 4WD Tours offer weekend trips here (all inclusive $275 adults) from Alice Springs, as well as an escort 4WD service, ph 532 666.

From Alice Springs, the Allambi Road is a formed surface to Santa Teresa (an Aboriginal settlement where no services are available and permits are not required if in transit only), and beyond. Access from the south at Kulgera is via Finke on 180km (112 miles) of formed road surface to New Crown, then 60km (37 miles) of flat bladed road to Andado. While 4WD is recommended, with care conventional vehicles can make it, but check road conditions first at Kulgera. Continuation of the Simpson Desert Loop Track south from Andado is a graded surface to Mt Dare Homestead (103km-64 miles). Roadhouse facilities here. The Track then runs north-west (40km-25 miles), north (30km-19miles) to New Crown Station. 4WD recommended. Check road conditions.

Accommodation

Bunkhouse - $17 single, $34 double; Camping - $5 per person. Pets allowed, dogs must be leashed.

Services and Facilities

Toilets and showers, station type meals for guests only (dinner $10, breakfast and lunch $5) and an airfield. No fuel services. Cash only, please phone before arrival, (089) 560 812.

ORANGE CREEK - CAMEL OUTBACK SAFARI

Location

On the Stuart Highway, 80km (50 miles) south of Alice Springs.

Characteristics

This man-made 'oasis' in the desert is where Noel Fullerton and his family keep their herd of 70 camels that provide the backbone for a range of Outback treks lasting up to two weeks. The Camel Outback Safari (formerly Virginia Camel Farm) has been operating from this site for seven years, ever since Noel moved the enterprise from Emily Gap Road. It offers visitors the option of camel rides of varying duration, a place to picnic, camp or merely to browse inside the large corrugated iron barn that has a shop, photograph-lined walls and roof, memorabilia of the past, and some interesting Aboriginal artifacts. In addition to safari work, the property has the only selective camel breeding programme in Australia, and the quality of the racing camels is such that the Fullertons have never lost the well-known premier Camel Cup Race in Alice Springs from the time they started it 17 years ago! Arab countries have expressed interest in the camels for racing purposes, and while discussions about the possibility of providing the Sheiks with racing camels has been going on, there are problems. Arabs favour long distance races, whereas the camels here are trained for sprint racing. It is a fascinating place to learn something about these animals, and equally interesting to talk with the Fullertons.

Camel Facts

The camels here are dromedaries (Camelus dromedarius), native of North Africa, Arabia and East Asia, commonly called Arabian, and have one hump, as distinct from their near relatives in Mongolia, the bactrian (Camelus bactrianus) with two humps. Like horses, there are varieties from heavier built draught beasts to light swift types bred for riding and racing. They have remarkable mechanisms designed to cope with their harsh desert habitat. The camel has the ability to use body fluids contained in tissue, and to recycle urine to prevent dehydration. This allows days without intake of water. The hump is a food store of fatty tissue that enables survival for lengthy periods without replenishment - in fact if times are hard the hump can literally disappear, so if you see a flat-topped camel you know he's quite hungry! They regulate their body temperature to adjust to outside conditions to prevent moisture loss. At night, heat is released and the coating of body hair acts as an insulator, and assists in temperature control by preventing sweating during the day.

It's interesting that the camel can be virtually dehydrated, drink 30 litres of water, and be quickly back to normal again. The secret is the elasticity of the corpuscles which, unlike humans, have the ability to expand and absorb under such conditions of stress. During sandstorms, adaptive features allow the nostrils to be sealed, while double lids and protective hair effectively seal the eyes.

Camels live for about 48 years, and certainly have distinct personalities. They are ruminants; cloven-hoofed, cud-chewing animals that regurgitate semi-digested food and grind away on it. Bull camels, particularly in the wild, can get nasty. An interesting human statistic for you to ponder over is that women are far keener on riding camels than men, in fact on the longer safari treks, over 90% of the riders are female.

An innovative feasibility trial of a camel dairy is being undertaken here. Camel milk keeps for six months without refrigeration or artificial preservatives.

It is of interest to the medical fraternity because of its low cholesterol qualities. It seems there may be a potential market for the milk from Australia's Muslim Community, and some Arab countries have expressed interest in the scheme, as well.

Camel History

Between the 1860s and 1920s, camels and their 'Afghan' camel-masters played a vital development role in an Australian Outback of relentless heat and drought that exacted a terrible toll on traditional beasts of burden; horses, donkeys and bullocks.

Camels were first imported in the early 1840s. They were few, and used for show purposes in the southern states. John Horrocks from Adelaide imported some in 1846, but most perished on the ship. Burke and Wills were the first to use camels in an organised way for exploration, and Giles, Warburton and Gosse followed suit for their expeditions. Madigan's 1939 Simpson Desert crossing was the last important use of camels in Australian exploration.

Camels carried telegraph poles for the Overland Telegraph Line, hauled rock to build repeater stations, carted minerals for mining companies, and supplied stations with goods and mail. The thousands of kilometres of camel tracks, or camel 'pads' as they were known, created a distinctive network that linked the scattered settlements of the vast interior. Although often unsung, camels and camelmen are as legendary in the Outback as the explorers, cattlemen, drovers and miners.

Some early colonists and settlers in South Australia and Victoria had experience of the usefulness of camels in the development of arid regions, and this knowledge encouraged the first large shipment to Australia in 1860 for the Burke and Wills expedition. The 24 camels were purchased in Peshawar on the Afghanistan border, and along with three 'Afghan' camelmen, arrived in Melbourne on the steamship *Chinsurah*.

Pastoralist Thomas Elder (later Sir Thomas, who founded the pastoral company in the 1860s that is today the multi-national Elders

IXL Group) and partners imported 124 camels and 31 donkeys. Thirty-one Afghans accompanied this shipment in 1865. Several varieties were brought; heavier beasts best suited to large loads from cooler mountain areas; riding and baggage breeds from the Karachi region; and swifter, riding camels from the western desert region of India. Elder established the first camel farm on the Beltana pastoral property, near Lake Torrens in South Australia, and the camel's superiority in the desert as a beast of burden assured success of the venture.

In the Territory, Afghans and their camel strings (the name given to the camel supply trains) worked mainly from the Oodnadatta railhead in South Australia to Alice Springs, where further strings travelling at 10km a day would supply settlements to the north, on a 6 monthly basis. Up to 40 camels comprised a string, and in their hey-day, 12,000 camels, many of which could carry 600kg of load each, were working the camel pads throughout the Australian Outback.

When the railway finally reached Alice Springs the train was called 'The Ghan' in honour of the Afghan cameleers.

Most Afghans had tribal associations with Afghanistan, even although some came from India. They were a nomadic people who adopted well to Australian conditions, and their wandering way was a probably reason for harmonious relationships with Aborigines. Afghans were certainly distinctive in their baggy clothing and turbans, and tended to live in 'Ghan towns' on the fringes of the main settlements, where they faithfully maintained their customs and religion. European attitudes towards them were at times ambivalent. Alice Springs commemorates the Afghans by a bronze statue situated in the railway station foyer, and the Cameleers' Memorial on the Council Lawns near the Todd Mall.

Sally Mahomet was one of the best-known Afghan camelmen, and before he died in 1984, his skills had been well and truly passed onto Australia's 'camel king', Noel Fullerton. By an ironic twist, the railway and motorised trucks which brought about the demise of camel strings worked in the reverse for Fullerton. He is an 'ex-truckie' from New South Wales, now turned camelman. While he is the reigning king, he was not the first to have this title. Frank Wallis, Alice Springs pioneer, storekeeper and forwarding agent, owned about 200 camels, which earned him the title in 1884.

With their period of usefulness over by the 1920s, many camels were left to wander free, and it is estimated that about 16,000 of these ruminants roam Central Australia today.

This stock provides a source of camels to meet breeding, circus, zoo, tourist and export demands.

Tours

Camel safaris to Rainbow Valley take 7 days and cost $699 all inclusive. A 2-week trek to the Gardiner and Krichauff Ranges, including Palm Valley, costs $1370 all inclusive. For these longer trips, moleskin or track suit type trousers rather than jeans, are advised for comfort. Other shorter tours are available, and can be negotiated to suit visitors. One-day and half-day can be organised - the latter costs $45, including light lunch. Generally shorter rides are on a $20 per hour basis. Cheapest rides are $2 for children, and $3 for adults.

Accommodation

Next door is Jim's Place, a roadhouse/pub that has accommodation and full vehicle services. It's run by Jim Cottrell, formerly of Wallara Ranch, ph (089) 560 808.

Cabins - $60 x 2; Backpackers - $24 x 2; powered sites - $12 x 2; unpowered sites $10 x 2.

Services and Facilities

There is a shop selling a range of food, including take-away and buffet style meals. Ice, souvenirs and artifacts are available. Tourist information, picnic/bbq/shaded area and showers for travellers are offered. Services and facilities are currently being extended and upgraded. Fuel includes super, ULP, diesel, oil and camping gas.

Vehicle services are basic spares, tyres and tubes, tyre repairs and mechanical repairs. There is no entry fee, and the establishment has a family emphasis.

It is open all year from 7am-5pm, ph (089) 560 925.

PAPUNYA

Location

222km (138 miles) north-west of Alice Springs

Characteristics

An Aboriginal settlement established in 1960 to alleviate population pressure at Haast Bluff. It has transit fuel services only (super, ULP, diesel), available during normal trading hours, and it's cash only. Trading hours are 9am-noon and 1.30-4pm, and 4 hours Saturday. Fuel availability and road conditions should be checked before leaving (refer to Information and Advice sections). Access is via the sealed section of the Tanami Road, then by formed road to Papunya.

RAINBOW VALLEY NATURE PARK

2483ha (6133 acres)

Location

97km (61 miles) south of Alice Springs, via the Stuart Highway.

Characteristics

The major feature of this park is a valley with free-standing sandstone ridges and bluffs, that effuse rainbow-like bands of colour when touched by the early morning and late evening sunlight. The

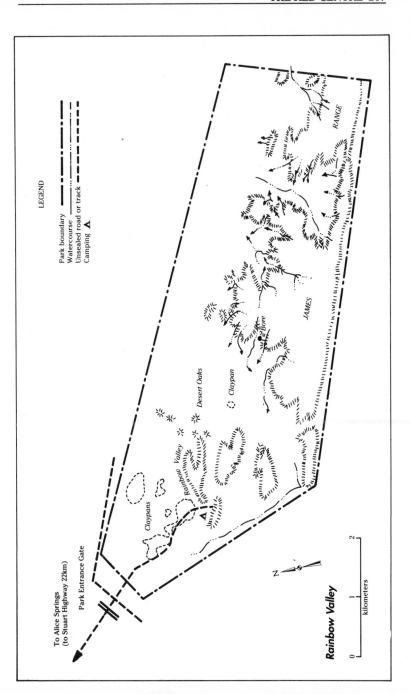

LEGEND

Park boundary
Watercourse
Unsealed road or track
Camping ▲

To Alice Springs
(to Stuart Highway 22km)

Park Entrance Gate

Claypans

Rainbow Valley

Desert Oaks

Claypan

Bore

JAMES

RANGE

N

0   1   2
kilometers

Rainbow Valley

valley forms part of the James Range, where the north-west surrounding area is characterised by spinifex-clothed sandplains with a system of interconnecting claypans that enhance the landscape when filled with water. In the southern parts of the park, dissected sandstone hills and ridges add further interest with Aboriginal petroglyphs (rock engravings) and ochre paintings that dot the area. Desert oaks, ironwoods and, after the rains, wildflowers have a softening effect.

> **It is delightful area that offers plenty of fascination for walkers, photographers, and for those who wish to enjoy some wilderness beauty and tranquillity.**

A number of tour operators include Rainbow Valley in their schedules. Check with the Information Office in Alice Springs. A novel way is by camel from Noel Fullerton's Outback Safaris at nearby Orange Creek. (See separate listings for details.)

Geology

The fine-grained quartzite layers have been inclined from their original horizontal beds, and millions of years of weathering and erosion have shaped the valley outline, rock faces and towers.

The varied colours are the result of water permeating through tiny pores in the sandstone and mixing with a range of iron oxides during earlier geological time scale periods, when rainfall was much higher. The dissolved oxides were drawn to the surface by the sun's heat, and effectively stained the surface layers, while iron deficient layers below were bleached a creamy-white. The dark red iron oxides, once percolated to the surface, formed a hard crust that is more erosion resistant, while the white sandstone below crumbles easily.

Conservation

This is a particularly fragile area, which has been damaged by thoughtless drivers. Please stay on the access track. No fires are permitted outside barbecues provided, and extinguish fires before leaving.

> Bring your own firewood (wood is scarce in the park and it is an offence, as in all parks, to remove or damage plants in any way). Pets are not allowed, take all your rubbish with you, and deeply bury all toilet waste.

How To Get There

The park turn-off is 14km (9 miles) north of Camel Outback Safari on the Stuart Highway, where a flat bladed 17km (11 miles) track, with some deep sandy patches, takes you to the valley. It is 4WD and vehicles are required to remain on this track and in the parking area only. The park is accessible year-round, with the cooler months being the most pleasant times to visit.

Services and Facilities

Fences have been put in place to confine vehicles and reduce landscape damage. Barbecues are the only facilities provided, and camping is allowed in the designated area. Sufficient supplies of drinking water must be taken in.

RYAN WELL HISTORICAL RESERVE

2ha (5 acres)

Location

Approximately 120km (75 miles) north of Alice Springs, on the Stuart Highway.

Characteristics

Sunk by Mr Ryan in 1889, the well was one of several the South Australian Government sank along the track that followed the Overland Telegraph Line, to encourage settlement through what was then its Northern Territory. In 1914, the Glen Maggie sheep and cattle station was established around the Well, and the owner, Sam Nicker, charged a small fee for its use by drovers. The ruins of the homestead which replaced the family's original mud and wattle dwelling in 1918, are reminders of these tough pioneering days. The homestead also functioned as a telegraph office and store from 1921. Despite the station being sold and incorporated into the Aileron property in 1929, the store kept going until this building was finally abandoned in 1935.

There are no facilities at the reserve.

Nearby is the Native Gap Conservation Reserve (11ha-27acres) - a scenic stopping place on the Stuart Highway, 120km (75 miles) north of Alice Springs, where travellers can appreciate a shady picnic area and Centralian scenery.

Facilities include picnic, toilet and disabled amenities. Camping is allowed, but no animals are allowed.

TI TREE

Population 362

Location

On the Stuart Highway, 193km (120 miles) north of Alice Springs.

Characteristics

The township, situated close to the Pmara Jutunta Aboriginal Settlement, consists of a modernised licensed roadhouse and general store, that's more like a supermarket, police station, medical clinic, school, post office, art gallery, garage and a small park and recreation area. While the roadhouse has a pleasant beer garden with free range kangaroos, it is the full-sized coffin behind the bar that catches the eye. Territorians have a distinctive sense of humour, and owner Greg Dick is no exception. He says it's his spirit cabinet!

History

Ti Tree takes its name from the Melaleuca glomerata which grew around the creek and waterholes about 300m to the west of the present roadhouse site. Originally named Tea Tree Wells by Dr Woodruff in 1869, the name was changed in 1981. Explorer John McDouall Stuart was the first European in the area in 1861, and in 1888 the Overland Telegraph Line declared a 5 square mile area a reserve for a station. The township is built within this area, and the lonely grave of an OTL linesman lies opposite the roadhouse.

The region is homeland for the Anmatjera people, and some interesting rocks and potholes about 2km to the east of the township is where they used to grind their grain for a type of flour. In 1971, local Aborigines were granted the least of Ti Tree Cattle Station, which now sustains an Aboriginal population of about 320. The Pmara Jutunta Settlement has a modern school, and an excellent medical clinic which is also available to the local European population of about 60.

The wells and waterholes of Ti Tree guaranteed some future for the settlement. The water was regarded as the cleanest for 160km (100 miles) in either direction, and was a welcome spot for travellers and users of the north-south stock route, so it is not surprising that one of the first roadhouses on the 'Track' was built here.

Events

Ti Tree Camp Draft is held in May, and everyone is welcome to join the day and evening frolics.

Accommodation

Motel units - $55 double, $45 single.

Camping/Caravans - powered sites $12 x 2, unpowered sites $4 per person. Sites grassed and shaded. Pets allowed, but under control.

Services and Facilities

The roadhouse has a store, bar (no take-away liquor sales), restaurant (good main serve for $10), beer garden, picnic/bbq area (coin operated), swimming pool (guests only), toilets for the disabled, and showers for travellers ($2). It sells ice, souvenirs, take-away food, and has a well-stocked store. Fuel services include super, ULP, diesel and LPG for vehicles. The roadhouse is open 6.30am-11pm, credit cards accepted (Bankcard, Mastercard, Visa), ph (089) 569 741.

A nearby garage, run by Ken Fogg, undertakes a range of mechanical repairs, including tyres. The town also has the Aaki Gallery, which has an excellent range of locally produced artifacts at prices much cheaper than the larger centres. It is located next to the roadhouse.

ULURU NATIONAL PARK/AYERS ROCK RESORT

Location

In the desert, 465km (289 miles) south-west of Alice Springs.

Characteristics

The National Park is Australia's first Aboriginal Park, and has the Territory's greatest attraction, Ayers Rock. · The Mutitjulu Community are permanent residents in the Park, and 'Uluru' is the Aboriginal name for Ayers Rock.

> The Rock is one of the world's greatest monoliths and undergoes amazing colour changes at sunrise and sunset.

The Olgas, 32km (20 miles) to the west, consist of a series of large domes whose colouring and shape are impressive. The Aboriginal name for the Olgas is 'Kata Tjuta' (sometimes written as one word).

The haunting and humbling qualities and colours of Ayers Rock are legendary, to the extent it has become a national symbol; it is to Australians what the Black Forest is to Germans, or The Grand Canyon to the Americans. The Park is owned by the Anangu, and is jointly managed by Europeans and Anangu. It's interesting to reflect that this symbolic, spiritual heart of Australia is also where two cultures have come together in a positive way in what Aborigines call ngapartji ngapartji, meaning 'you learn from me, I learn from you', or tjunguringkupai, 'working together'.

Geology

Ayers Rock (Uluru) is huge, measuring 9.4km (5.8 miles) around the base, 3.6km (2 miles) in length, 2.4km (1.5 miles) in width, and 348m (1138 ft) above the surrounding plain. It's composed of coarse, grained Arkose sandstone, and is the world's largest monolith, or rock. The Olgas (Kata Tjuta) is a conglomerate with larger material cemented together. (A conglomerate is a rock consisting of rounded pebbles or boulders cemented together in layers.)

There are varying theories as to how they were formed. Their basic composition is sandstone and conglomerates, which are derived from the worn remnants of more ancient mountains. One theory suggests that the original material came from the Mann and Musgrave Ranges in the south, the peaks of which would have constituted mountain ranges about 600 million years ago. The huge deposits of silt, gravel and boulders were laid down in beds that were not horizontal. In fact, the beds may have developed on the lower slopes of these ranges, and extended for many kilometres to the north. The striations evident today mark the way in which the beds were laid down. Along with further tilting, it offers an explanation why the rock beds are kilometres thick below the present surface level. This theory suggests that rather than having been 'pushed up' from below, Ayers Rock (Uluru) and The Olgas (Kata Tjuta) have been left behind as harder more resistant parts of the conglomerate, while the material between them has eroded away.

This contrasts with the conventional theory that the sediments were laid down under a shallow sea, compressed and inclined to the near vertical by massive internal forces. The theories are interesting, and no doubt there will be many more.

The 36 domes of The Olgas (Kata Tjuta) may have been a single dome many times the size of Ayers Rock (Uluru); weathering along weaknesses has divided it with deep chasms over the eons.

Weathering continues today. Ayers Rock surface material flakes in what is called spalling, while the red coating of iron oxide on the surface hides the underlying grey colour. It is the oxide coating that gives the magnificent hues of reds, oranges, purples and blues when struck by the various angles of the sun.

And the Anangu have a different interpretation of their formation. To Aborigines, the Tjukurpa, or creation period, is the explanation, with evidence of ancestral imprints being the landforms themselves. Whatever the origin, it evokes awe and a sense of spirituality to both Europeans and Aborigines.

History

Aborigines have lived in the Ayers Rock area for at least 10,000 years, and it continues to be of deep significance to them today. Central to Aboriginal understanding of the land is the Tjukurpa; laws which provide explanations for the origin of life as well as for all features of the landscape. The Tjukurpa is absolute and to the Anangu it gives meaning and order to all aspects of life.

Ernest Giles became the first European to sight both Ayers Rock and The Olgas in 1872, but he did not explore them. When he returned a year later, he found the 2-month-old camel tracks of Gosse at The Olgas, and his inspired description is worth recalling: "it is formed of several vast and solid, huge and rounded blocks of bare red conglomerate stones of all kinds and sizes, mixed like plums in a pudding, and set in vast rounded shapes upon the ground... it displayed to our astonished eyes rounded minarets, giant cupolas and monstrous domes...". Comparing the two features he said the Olgas were "more wonderful and grotesque", while Ayers Rock was "more ancient and sublime". Gosse was the first European to visit and climb Ayers Rock, which he named after Sir Henry Ayers, the Chief Secretary of South Australia, and later Premier.

After the explorers came prospectors, missionaries and the pastoralists. Conflict between the two cultures occurred at times. Despite European attempts to change Aboriginal thinking, and in some cases to force them off their traditional land, the Anangu maintained their strong ties and culture. When they saw increasing pastoralism, mining and tourism as dangerously impinging on their culture, the Anangu began a complex battle to protect traditional lands. Aborigines were finally granted title to Uluru in 1985. Uluru was immediately leased to the Director of the Australian National Parks and Wildlife Service, and is now jointly managed by the ANPWS and the Anangu. Uluru is the Pitjantjatjara name for a rockhole located at Ayers Rock.

Park Features

It covers an area of 132,566ha (327,438 acres) and protects extremely sensitive arid ecosystems that contain the geological masterpieces of Ayers Rock (Uluru) and The Olgas (Kata Tjuta), set on a contracting, nearly flat, sand plain. The area abounds in wildlife; over 150 species of birds, 24 mammals, and many reptiles and frogs. Over 566 species of plants have been recorded in the park. Much of the flora and fauna described in the introduction to The Red Centre is found here.

Information

See Visitors Centre under Ayers Rock Resort section. They have a booklet that offers excellent advice on visitor safety that should be read by all.

Activities

AYERS ROCK (ULURU)

Ranger guided tours (see under Ayers Rock Resort Tours).

The Climb. The climb from the base to the summit, where there is a cairn, is 1.6km (1 miles). The average time for a return trip is around

Uluru - Ayers Rock

Uluru Circuit Walk,
9km, 4hrs. Start
from either car park.

Kantju Gorge

The Climb,
1.6km, 2hrs return

Liru Walk
2km, 30mins
one way

Mutitjulu

Ranger Station,
display, toilets.

Maruku Arts & Crafts,
souvenirs, kiosk.

N

Legend
Sealed road...........
Unsealed road......
Car park................. ●
Walking track........ ●●●●●●●●●●●

two hours. It's a demanding walk, and should only be attempted by those who are fit and healthy. Visitors with the following conditions should not climb: heart problems; high blood pressure; angina; asthma; fear of heights; vertigo or dizziness. A number of people with these conditions die each year as a direct result of the climb. Water should be carried, and it can get windy up the top, too. Certain sections are very steep, although there's a chain to help and guide.

Walk around the Base. It's a fascinating 3-4 hour walk, with much to explore. Please keep away from sacred site areas. You can drive to various vantage points and do short walks to the base.

Ranger Station. The Station has display material and literature available. There's also a kiosk, and an excellent feature documentary is shown on the video. Copies are available for purchase.

Maruku Arts and Crafts. The traditional bush shelters next to the Ranger Station are where Maruku Arts and Crafts display, and have available for purchase, a range of Aboriginal artifacts from the western desert region. The enterprise is owned by the Anangu. It affords a good chance to meet Aborigines, too. Open usually 9.30am-2pm, Mon-Sat.

Sunrise and Sunset viewing of Uluru. The park is open from half an hour before sunrise until one hour after sunset. You won't miss the sunset area because of the crowds - its 14km (9 miles) south of Ayers Rock Resort, and 6km (4 miles) from Uluru, and best advice is to get there early for the spectacular parade of Uluru's colours. The Ranger Station noticeboard displays sunrise and sunset times.

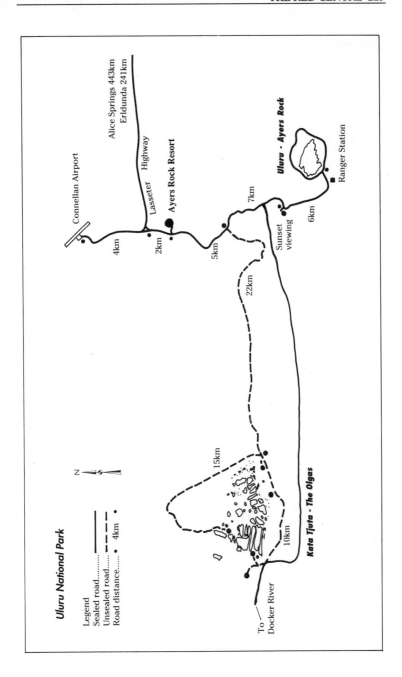

Uluru National Park

Legend
Sealed road........
Unsealed road......
Road distance...... • 4km

N

Connellan Airport

Alice Springs 443km
Erldunda 241km

Lasseter Highway

Ayers Rock Resort

4km
2km
5km
7km

Sunset viewing

Uluru - Ayers Rock

Ranger Station

6km

22km

15km

10km

Kata Tjuta - The Olgas

To Docker River

THE OLGAS (KATA TJUTA)

Walks. There are *two walks:*

1. Mt Olga Gorge Walk is suitable for the family.

2. Valley of the Winds Walk follows the creek over a small waterfall and around the base of the dome. It's a 3 hours return, 6km round trip. Check with the Ranger Station about walk details, and be properly prepared, i.e. clothing and plenty of water, and some food. Remember that temperatures are hotter in enclosed rock environments because of additional heat radiated from the rocks. Refer to Practical Information and Advice sections also. Check with the Visitors Centre or Rangers for up-to-date maps.

How To Get There

The new 50km (31 miles) access road is sealed, and there is a viewing area along the way.

The gravel road west from Kata Tjuta continues to Docker River (see page 144).

Services and Facilities

At *The Rock* there's the Ranger Station, toilets including for the disabled, kiosk (Initi store - snacks, drinks, souvenirs, T-shirts), barbecues (gas) and delightful picnic area with tables and water.

At Kata Tjuta facilities are walking trails, car park areas, toilets, sunset viewing area and picnic area.

An entry fee of $10 per adult (valid for 2 weeks) is charged (children under 16 free), payable at entry station.

Camping is not permitted anywhere within the National Park or outside the Ayers Rock Resort camping ground. Dogs must always be leashed.

AYERS ROCK RESORT

Characteristics

Located 20km (12 miles) from Ayers Rock, this highly imaginative
and innovative resort, originally named Yulara, was designed by one
of Australia's leading architects, Philip Cox. The long, low
development nestles comfortably within the swales of the region's
sinuous sand dunes, and, with its subdued ochre-painted structures, it
blends easily into the landscape.

It was built of necessity. The rapid increase in the number of
visitors to Ayers Rock was causing environmental problems. The
outcome was a $160 million resort that incorporated elements
unique in Australian design technology, while its scale and scope
and fine attention to detail made it an attraction in itself.

The serpentine-form layout results from following the natural lines
of the dunes and, to prevent 'dead' areas of activity or interest, the
hotels were located at the extremities. Between these poles, magnets
or attractions were placed, thus creating an even flow of movement
and interest along its length. A lively village atmosphere results,
complementing the natural wonders that spawned it.

Of further interest are the spaces, shapes and roofscapes, in
particular the 68 spectacular sails designed to deflect the sun's head.
2300 solar panels on the resort rooflines heat more than 70% of hot
water requirements, and for those who like statistics, transporting the
1.5 million concrete blocks and pavers used in its construction
required 380 road train loads from Alice Springs!

The resort is the fourth largest centre in the Territory. The water
comes from an underground aquifer, and is desalinated at Australia's
largest water treatment plant of its kind. It's a remarkable resort
centre where there's plenty of interest, fine facilities, and ideal places

to relax after visits to the Rock and the Olgas.

The telephone area code is 089.

Information

The Visitors Centre features imaginative displays with a wealth of excellent information on Aboriginal culture, wildlife, landscape and geology of Ayers Rock and the Olgas, video displays, and free literature. Open 9am-9pm, ph 562 240.

Video Screenings - free shows are available at The Amphitheatre every night.

Tours

There are many tours on offer to allow visitors to experience this special part of the world. Coach tours are available, and the National Parks run some free tours for people with their own transport. Rock Ayer, ph 562 345 and Skyport, ph 562 093, operate a range of scenic flights in helicopters and light aircraft with prices ranging from $55 per person for a 30 minute flight.

Full details of all the tours are available from the Visitor Centre, ph 562 240.

Uluru Experience Tours is an ecotour company based at Ayers Rock Resort that specialises in providing interesting, professional tours in small 4WDs and minibuses. A great range of tour options is offered, for example:

* The Edible Desert Experience offers the chance to learn the skills that Aboriginal people use to find bush tucker - $40 adult, $29 child. Departs daily at 8.30am.

* Uluru Walk explores the base of Ayers Rock and teaches the mysteries of the Aboriginal Dreamtime - $52 adult, $40 child (includes breakfast). Departs early every morning.

* Valley of the Winds is a spectacular walk through the central gorges of the Olgas. A photographer's delight - $52 adult, $40 child (includes breakfast). Departs early every morning.

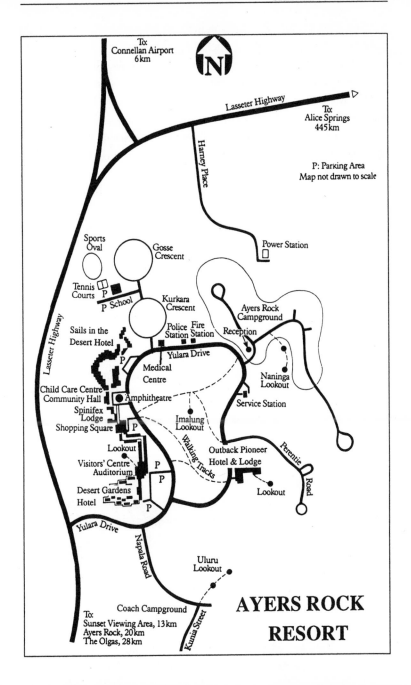

AYERS ROCK RESORT

* Star Observatory is a fascinating one hour discovery tour of the spectacular Southern Skies, including the Southern Cross and the Milky Way (weather and astronomic conditions allowing) - $15 adult, $9 child, Family $40. Several sessions are held nightly.

* Safaris into Aboriginal Lands/Kings Canyon and Mt Connor are also available.

All tours are conducted by university qualified ecoguides and operate in small groups. Passes alos include airport transfers and climb transfers.

Best value deal is a 24-hour Pass for $85 which includes airport transfers, Rock Sunrise, breakfast, Rock climb or base tour and Olgas tour. Also available is the 48-hour Pass for $165 which includes all the above as well as the Edible Desert Bush Tucker Tour, Champagne Sunset and Night Sky show.

Uluru Experience tour bookings - ph 008 803 174 (toll free).

How To Get There

See also Tours from Alice Springs.

By air: Ansett and Qantas have daily flights from Alice Springs (connecting with other domestic ports) to Ayers Rock, and the trip takes 45 minutes.

Kendall has regular flights to Conellan Airport from South Australia.

By coach: AAT Kings Tours, Greyhound, Pioneer and Bus Australia have daily schedules.

By road: The Lasseter Highway is sealed the length of the 245km (151 miles) from the Stuart Highway turn-off.

Local Transport

Sunworth Taxis, ph 562 152.

Car Rentals: Budget, ph 562 121; Hertz, ph 562 177; Territory Rent-A-Car, ph 562 556.

Marty's Bike and Moped Hire: enquire at Visitors Centre.

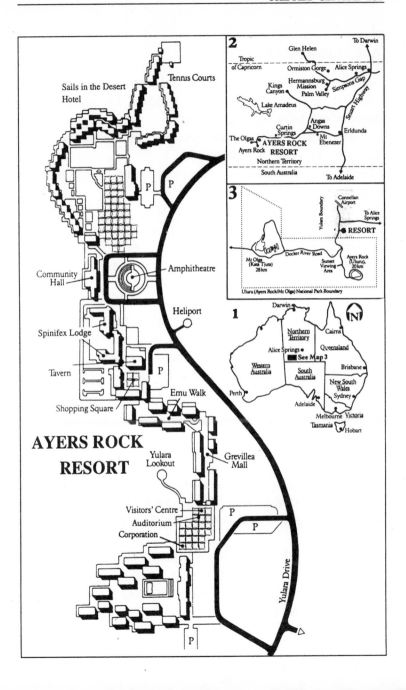

Accommodation

Superb accommodation, catering for all tastes, is provided.

Sails in the Desert Hotel: rooms from $242-273; facilities for the disabled; swimming pool; ph 562 200.

Desert Gardens Hotel: standard rooms from $280; facilities for the disabled; swimming pool; ph 562 100.

Emu Walk Apartments: 1 bedroom $105 (up to 4 persons); 2 bedroom $126 (up to 6), ph 562 100.

Outback Pioneer Hotel: rooms from $184; cabins 4 single bunk beds from $80; units and dormitory accommodation available; swimming pool; ph 562 170.

Spinifex Lodge: single, double from $90; facilities for the disabled; guests may use Sails in the Desert pool; ph 562 131.

Ayers Rock Campground: can cater up to 3,600 campers; well appointed facilities including for the disabled; bbq; swimming pool; 20 on-site vans from $60 for up to 4 persons; powered sites $25 for two adults; camp sites $10 per adult, $5 child; shade limited and ground gravelly and hard; kiosk; telephone; pets allowed, dogs leashed; ph 562 055.

Eating Out

Inexpensive meals at Outback Pioneer Hotel kiosk and The Rocks Bistro, and snacks at Yulara Coffee Shop and Takeaway. The Tavern has a courtyard bbq each evening, and reasonably priced bistro meals.

The Desert Gardens Hotel White Gums is open for dinner nightly from 6pm till late, with outdoor settings available. Silver Service at the Sails in the Desert Kunia Room; buffet and a la carte in their Desert Rose Coffee Shop.

Services and Facilities

All services and facilities are available, and credit cards are widely accepted. Most shops are open 9am to 9pm daily. There's a post office; police station; medical centre; supermarket; gift/souvenir shops; travel agent; newsagent; Bank (ANZ, Agencies - Westpac handy banks at Tavern Bottleshop, Commonwealth at Post Office); foreign currency exchange at ANZ Bank and Sails in the Desert Hotel; one hour photo processing; vehicles - full services, repairs and fuel; camping gas; child care facilities; multilingual guides (ph 562 144); church services (check with Visitors Centre); airport. At Ayers Rock itself, there's a Ranger Station (see under Uluru National Park).

Radio Station: ABC 99.7 FM. Radio 8HA can be heard on 100.5FM.

Emergency Services: Emergencies - 000 (Fire, Ambulance, Police); Doctor, ph 562 286 (Mon-Fri 9am-noon, 2-5pm); Police station opens 8am-4pm daily for enquiries; vehicle breakdown, ph 562 188.

Ayers Rock Resort

UTOPIA

Location

On Angarapa Aboriginal land, just off the Sandover Highway, approximately 195km (121 miles) north-east of Alice Springs.

Characteristics

An Aboriginal settlement that provides transit services only to travellers. A permit is not required for the road, but you will need one to make any purchases here. Utopia has a store and sells fuel (super, ULP and diesel) during normal trading hours generally. It is cash only. It also has toilets and water, but no accommodation.

How To Get There

The Sandover Highway is a formed road surface that can be negotiated by conventional vehicles, but check conditions before leaving.

WALLARA RANCH

Population 8

Location

225km (140 miles) south-west of Alice Springs, half-way to or from Ayers Rock (Uluru), near the Angus Downs and Ernest Giles Road junction.

Characteristics

The old bush pub has been demolished and a temporary structure now in place dispenses basic services to travellers.

History

Wallara is a vital link in the history and development of Kings Canyon and tourism in the Centre. The Canyon's tourist potential inspired Jack Cotterill and his son Jim, to establish the ranch in 1961 on land leased from the 3221 sq km (1224 sq miles) Angus Downs Cattle Station. Permanent water supply from Yowa Bore determined the location; it not only supplies the ranch with good water, but also the cattle which, with the cockatoos, come at night to drink at the troughs. Nearly 30 years ago, with the help of two Aborigines from Angus Downs to chart the route, the Cotterills cut a 100km (62 miles) track into the Canyon by using an old Dodge weapon carrier, which dragged lengths of railway iron welded into a solid A-frame to gouge the way. Jack Cotterill was also associated with early tourist developments at Ayers Rock and Palm Valley.

Attractions

A visit to the spectacular Kings Canyon and 'Lost City' domes, 95km (56 miles) away is a must (see Kings Canyon listing).

How To Get There

By road from Alice Springs, travel south on the Stuart Highway for 133km (82 miles), then west via Ernest Giles Road for 95km (56 miles). The Angus Downs Road, north from the Lasseter Highway and 50km (31 miles) east of Curtin Springs, is an alternative 70km (43 miles) route. Both routes are a mix of formed and flat bladed surfaces that are passable for conventional vehicles and caravans. But take care, as there are patches of deep sand and corrugations. Along the way, scenery varies from Mulga plains, red sand ridges and rocky outcrops to graceful stands of desert oaks, sometimes called 'willows of the desert'.

Accommodation

Demountables and campsites are available.

Services and Facilities

Basic store, fuel (super, ULP and diesel).

YUENDUMU

Population 900

Location

290km (180 miles) north-west of Alice Springs on the Tanami Road.

Characteristics

An Aboriginal settlement that has fuel services only available for travellers. Super, ULP and diesel can be obtained during normal trading hours, 8am-5pm weekdays, 2.30-4.30pm Sat-Sun. A permit is not required, but it is wise to check the current situation. **No credit cards are accepted.** For road description, see Rabbit Flat listing (Barkly Region).

   Mining Store: A well-stocked general store sells groceries, pies, drinks and fuel (super, ULP, diesel, aviation) and oil. Open 9am-5pm weekdays; 9am-5pm Sat-Sun, but closed between 1-4pm, ph (089) 564 040.

THE BARKLY REGION

The Barkly Region extends from the desert, through tableland, to the Gulf of Carpentaria coastline. It's the transitional zone between arid Centre and tropical Top End, and there's plenty of interest as the ochre landscape tones give way to a softer green. Renner Springs marks the geographical end to the semi-arid lands; around here is the southern limit of the Wet Season tropical rains.

Tennant Creek is the flourishing centre of this huge, sparsely populated region, which has an economy based on pastoral, mining and tourist activities. A large area around Tennant Creek is Warumungu homeland, while other Aboriginal people live in the more isolated western and eastern margins.

Within its vast boundaries are some of the Territory's largest cattle stations, longest 'beef roads', fascinating bush pubs, historic stock-routes, gold mines and settlements, interesting flora and fauna, and some outstanding geological features. You can even sail at Tennant Creek, or if you're into fishing, Borroloola is the barramundi capital of the Gulf.

Tennant Creek	J	F	M	A	M	J	J	A	S	O	N	D	Ann. av.
Temperature: C°													
Av. monthly max.	36	36	34	31	27	24	24	28	31	34	36	37	32
Av. monthly min.	25	24	23	20	16	12	11	14	17	21	23	25	19
Rainfall:													
Av. monthly mm.	105	106	67	16	9	9	9	3	11	23	36	65	459

Daly Waters	J	F	M	A	M	J	J	A	S	O	N	D	Ann. av.
Temperature: C°													
Av. monthly max.	36	35	34	34	31	29	29	32	34	37	37	37	34
Av. monthly min.	23	23	22	19	15	12	11	13	16	20	23	23	18
Rainfall:													
Av. monthly mm.	161	156	119	22	6	6	2	2	5	22	59	103	663

Climate

It has a definite Wet and Dry Season, with distinct differences in temperature, rainfall and humidity between northern and southern areas. In the south, it's hotter in summer, cooler in winter, and lower in humidity. On average, Tennant Creek has 119 days over 35C (95F), 19 of which are over 40C (104F), while winter is characterised by mainly warm days and some cold nights. Generally, the further north you go, temperatures are less extreme, while rainfall and humidity increase.

Landscape

The Barkly Tableland dominates the landscape east of the Stuart Highway, and gradually slopes until it merges west and south into the vast semi-arid lands. It's nearly a perfect plain, almost free from surface rocks with deep grey-brown soil clothed in tufted Mitchell grass. Except for the creek lines, there are very few trees. The tussocky grasses and extensive plain quickly attracted the interest of cattlemen who saw it as ideal cattle breeding country, best suited to produce young steer. Despite little permanent surface water, the sinking of bores ensures that cattle remain king on these grassy domains.

Of special interest is its geological makeup. While surrounding landscapes underwent massive geologic upheaval, it's extraordinary that the ancient rocks of **the Barkly have remained virtually unchanged since Cambrian Times - 600 million years ago.** In fact, it's one of the few places on earth where this occurs. During the Cambrian Period, the area sank, and under a shallow sea accumulated beds of shales and limestone. Later, two periods of slow uplift uniformly elevated the sea bed to about its present height. In the few places where the rocks are revealed, it is possible to see well-preserved remains of Cambrian Time marine species.

From the Barkly Highway, brown and grey termite mounds can be

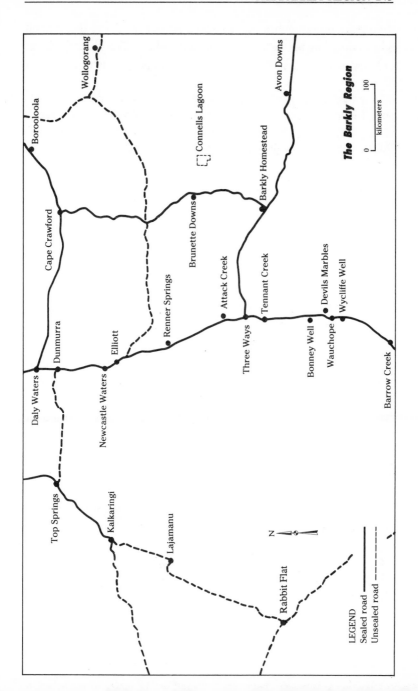

The Barkly Region

LEGEND
Sealed road ———
Unsealed road ----

seen resembling tombstones; bleached grasses stretch to the horizon and shimmer under the Dry Season sun; willie willies distantly spiral columns of dust; and relentless heat produces unforgettable images.

> To the west, the sand ridges, sand plains and stone pavements of the Tanami Desert meet the tableland and merge into undulating semi-arid lands, broken only by some rocky outcrops - the best known being the Devil's Marbles and Devil's Pebbles.

Flora

Colourful flora abounds, and it's well worth stopping for a closer look, particularly after the rains when spectacular windflower cover occurs in the more arid areas. Perennial grasses grow in clumps on the tableland - Curly and Mitchell mainly, with panic, kerosene, blue and love, lesser varieties. Spinifex or porcupine grass thrives in semi-arid areas. Distance gives the illusion of a complete grass cover - in fact, the clumps can be widely spaced with barren ground between. Other species are: *mulla mullas* which bloom fluffy mauve in the Dry Season; *cassia* shrubs, which are distinctive with their yellow flowers; *mulga* with its grey-green foliage, denser in the south but fading away north of Tennant Creek, its hard durable wood used by Aboriginal craftsmen; *lancewood*, *bauhinia* or bean tree further north; *native hibiscus* which blooms all year and has five petalled pink flowers; the native *pomegranate* has creamy petals with silky filaments and produces apple shaped fruit; *candelabra* is a large acacia bush which has cylindrical yellow flowers and twisted seed pods. (When green pods are rubbed with water on your hands, the sodium produces a lather or 'bush soap').

Main eucalypts are *snappy gum*, *yellow box*, *bloodwood*, *ironwood*, *woollybutt*, *stringybark* and the *coolabah* (Banjo Paterson's favourite shade tree). *Ghost* and *river red gums* tend to line the sandy creek beds and *red bud mallee* is common in the Tanami. But most trees give little shade.

Fauna

Cooler times of the day are best for wildlife observation. Larger animals include: *red kangaroo* (in lesser numbers now) on the treed, grassy plains - you'll need sharp eyes to spot them resting in the daytime heat; *euro* or *wallaroo* which mainly inhabit rocky outcrops; *feral donkeys* and *horses*, often in groups which can be a surprise encounter; *dingo* and of course, station cattle. *Goulds goanna* with an average length of nearly 1.3m is a most impressive reptile, and *snakes*, while present, are not really interested in meeting you.

Birdlife is plentiful - *emu* and *bustard* on the plains, while *wedge-tailed eagle*, with a 2m wing-span, *black kite* and *brown falcon* are some of the birds of prey. Waterholes attract a great range - *whistler duck*, *heron*, *egret* and *ibis* are some. Open wood and shrublands have *honeyeater*, *finch*, *cockatoo* and *galahs*.

Of the insects, *termites* (white ants) are most fascinating. They are large, whitish in colour, soft bodied, avoid sunlight, and build large clay mounds. The mound's outer shell is tough and durable - sufficiently so to wreck the suspension of a vehicle! Inside it's full of softer, woody material arranged into galleries and chambers. The queen produces thousands of eggs, conveyed by workers to the nursery chambers, where high humidity levels are maintained to assist hatching. Termites forage and harvest organic matter, and while they play an important role in soil ecology, they are bad news for wooden buildings. Most of Northern Australia's early architecture was destroyed by them.

Touring Suggestions

Take time along the Stuart Highway. There are plenty of historic spots, some coinciding with the Territory's best bush pubs that offer original Outback architecture and intriguing interiors - Barrow Creek, Wauchope and Daly Waters Pub should not be missed.

For 'off the beaten track' Outback stuff, try the narrow-sealed, all-weather Carpentaria and Tablelands Highways or 'beef roads' (so named because of the huge roadtrains and the cattle they transport), which give conventional vehicle access across the Tableland to Borroloola and the Gulf of Carpentaria.

There's much to offer the adventurous. South-east along the Carpentaria Highway from Borroloola takes you to the historic Wollogorang Station with its Gulf beach camping. To the west of the Stuart Highway at Dunmarra, try the Buchanan Highway to the Tanami desert fringes at the Top Springs and Kalkaringi outposts.

A novel way to experience the Barkly is by mail plane, for a day's flight with the 'aerial postman' to remote cattle stations and settlements. Seat availability depends on the amount of mail and freight, the first priority of operator Skyport Group. Check with their offices in Tennant Creek or Katherine, or ph (089) 526 666; costs around $200 per person.

Aboriginal rock painting

PLACES AND ATTRACTIONS

ATTACK CREEK HISTORICAL RESERVE

0.2ha (0.5 acres)

Location

On the Stuart Highway, 70km (43 miles) north of Tennant Creek.

History

Explorer John McDouall Stuart's first attempt at crossing the continent from the south ended here on June 25, 1860, when sickness forced him to return to Adelaide. There is some dispute about the role of Warumungu tribesmen who were supposed to have forced his retreat. An inscribed plaque marks the event.

10km (6 miles) north is Churchill's Head, a rocky outcrop on the eastern crest of the Old Stuart Highway, where some American soldiers stuck a log like a cigar in the 'head's' mouth. The 'cigar' has long gone, so you'll have to use your imagination. A further 10km (6 miles) north is Banka Banka Homestead, one of the few station settlements close to the highway, characterised by an attractive tropical garden including banana palms and bougainvillaea. It was used by the army during WW II as a staging camp, the second night stop for troops from Alice Springs on the run to Larrimah railhead.

Services and Facilities

Table, shade, wood barbecue, camping allowed. Dogs - in designated areas only.

AVON DOWNS

Location

On the Barkly Highway, approximately 60km (37 miles) from the Northern Territory/Queensland border.

Characteristics

Homestead of the 3939 sq km (1497 sq miles) cattle property situated just off the highway, thus allowing a glimpse of a station settlement.

Services and Facilities

A police station next door is the only public service. A roadside rest area includes fireplace, table and shelter.

BARKLY HOMESTEAD

Population 15

Location

At the junction of the Barkly and Tableland Highways, 211km (131 miles) east of Tennant Creek.

Characteristics

This modern roadhouse, established by current hosts, Bob and Lynn Rose in 1984, is a welcome 'watering hole' on the arid fringes of the Tableland where summer temperatures hit 45C (113F). It features a restaurant that offers traditional to exotic food in a comfortable, 'baronial' atmosphere. With the closure of Barry Caves, it is now the only roadhouse on the Barkly Highway.

History

Although the homestead is recent, it is named indirectly after Henry Barkly, Governor of Victoria, when William Landsborough named the tablelands after him while searching for Burke and Wills, in 1861. The tablelands were discovered earlier by Ludwig Leichhardt in 1845, and crossed by explorer A.C. Gregory in 1856. Legendary cattleman and drover Nathaniel Buchanan opened up the area for settlement between 1877 and 1878, and by 1884 there were over 100,000 sheep on the Barkly. Sheep were short-lived when cattle were found to thrive better in the harsh heat conditions, and they have been dominant ever since. A police station was established at Anthony Lagoon (about 226km-140 miles north of Barkly Homestead) in 1895 to protect the stock routes. It closed in 1979. The Barkly Highway was constructed during the Second World War with the assistance of United States finance.

How To Get There

While the Barkly Highway is sealed, there are some narrow sections with rough shoulders. Although infrequent, flood waters may cut the road.

Accommodation

Motel - $62 single, $72 double.
  Cabins - $35 x 2
  Camping - powered sites $16, others $3.50 per person. Dogs must be leashed.

Services and Facilities

A bar, restaurant, shop, accommodation and 'bush' swimming - dam with pontoon. Meals from $9, take-away food, ice, souvenirs, camping gas, fuel (super, ULP, diesel, autogas), oil, basic spares and repairs, towing service and limited aviation fuel. Showers for travellers ($2). A 1.2km dirt, non-registered airstrip is unusable when wet. Credit cards accepted (Bankcard, Mastercard, Visa) Open 6am-1am all year, ph (089) 644 549.

BARROW CREEK

Population 12

Location

284km (176 miles) north of Alice Springs, on the Stuart Highway.

Characteristics

This tiny township nestles at the foot of a table-top range and consists of the oldest roadhouse on 'The Track', and the historic Barrow Creek Telegraph Station. If you're beginning to think that real Outback pubs are a myth, try 'The Barrow'. Its well-worn comfortable atmosphere reeks of history, beer and cattlemen - the sort of place Crocodile Dundee would meld into, except there's an inquisitive emu or wallaby to greet you instead of a croc!

The bar walls are a pictorial essay of mainly humorous artwork, strongly suggesting that the more isolated the pub, the more creative are the people who flourish around it. Its crowning glory is the wall of dollar notes of all denominations and currencies behind the bar, called the 'bush bank'. Patrons make sure they're never caught short of cash by simply signing a note and pinning it to the wall of 'The Creek Bank' and withdrawing it if necessary at a later date. According to 'bank managers' and publicans, Les and Bev Pilton, the house always wins. No-one has claimed money yet without spending it at the bar first. The pub is an art gallery, museum, theatre, community centre and living shrine, that can provide the casual caller with a memorable, even if fleeting, insight into an isolated Outback community.

History

The area was first explored by Stuart in 1860, and named after South Australian politician John Henry Barrow. The Telegraph Station, built in 1872, was one of a series the OTL needed at about 250km (155 miles) intervals to boost the signals along. The stone fortress-like structure was surrounded by a 200 sq km (76 sq miles) grazing reserve - in such remote locations, the operators had to be well protected from hostile Aborigines and virtually self-sufficient. But, in a surprise attack by Kaytej tribesmen in 1874, linesman John Franks and station master, James Stapleton, were killed. The station is now preserved as a memorial to them, and their graves are close by. The station was used for communications during World War II, and the yellow house, built in the 1950s, was a post office and residence until the early 1980s. The station is open to visitors.

The hotel was built by Joe Kilgariff in 1930, and there's a store of amusing tales about the ringers, prospectors, telegraph linesmen and travellers who have passed through. About 40km (25 miles) to the north are the concrete slab remains of New Barrow, which was a large wartime staging camp, the first night stop for troops travelling by army truck between the Larrimah and Alice Springs railheads.

Events

The desert golf course is the venue for the 'Barrow Open' held in October. The Creek Races are run over the long weekend in March, and the annual cricket match between the 'Barrow Bottlers' and Ted Egan's 'Eroes' from Alice Springs, takes place in mid-September.

Accommodation

Hotel room - $20 single, $35 double, $45 triple; Dongas $20.
  Cabins - $35 x 2.
  Camping - Caravans $7 for 2 persons, $2 extra for power. Tents $3 per person. Some grassy, shady sites. Pets allowed, dogs must be leashed.

Services and Facilities

A bar, dining room ($9 for a generous main course serve), accommodation, shop, tourist information, swimming pool (guests only), shaded bbq area, shade shelters for vehicles (bough sheds), 6-hole golf course, 1km airstrip, ramps for the disabled and showers for travellers ($2). Take-away food, ice, fuel (super, ULP, autogas, diesel), oil, camping gas, basic spares, tyres, tubes, tyre and minor mechanical repairs, towing service and souvenirs are all available.

It's cash only. Opening hours 7am-11pm daily, all year, ph (089) 569 753.

BONNEY WELL

Location

On the west side of the Stuart Highway, 85km (53 miles) south of Tennant Creek.

Characteristics

A National Trust administered site featuring one of the last remaining original water improvements on the Overland Telegraph Line Stock Route. Alfred Giles, who later overlanded cattle for his Springvale property near Katherine, began the first well here in 1879, to provide water for mobs of sheep being driven up from Alice Springs. Well sinkers, who were excavating the bank of Bonney Creek were instructed to stop, as rains had provided sufficient surface water for the sheep. The well was completed later by the Telegraph Department in 1844, further altered in 1892, and finally abandoned in 1936. Much of the original solid stonework remains intact.

Services and Facilities

Roads Department rest area with fireplace, table and shelter.

BORROLOOLA

Population 800

Location

Situated on the McArthur River, 60km (37 miles) from the Gulf of Carpentaria, 116km (72 miles) north-east of Cape Crawford, on the

Carpentaria Highway.

Characteristics

Borroloola is thought to mean 'place of the paperbarks', and locally it's known as 'The Loo'. The town consists of timber, fibro and iron buildings scattered over a few square kilometres, and serves the cattle and tourist industry. It has an Aboriginal population including the Mara, Yanyula and Garawa people. Borroloola's 're-discovery' is based on the river which teems with barramundi, hence the 'Barra Capital of the Gulf' tag. And, there are plenty of saltwater crocs. A laid-back atmosphere, colourful history, and stunning landforms and coast, make Borroloola an extraordinary community in the Outback.

History

Explorer Ludwig Leichhardt crossed here in 1845 on his epic walk to Port Essington. Overlanders Cahill, Buchanan, the Duracks and MacDonalds used it as a drovers' camp in the 1880s, and the pub was built in 1885. It became a port too: supplies and materials for the Barkly Stations were shipped to the Gulf and landed at Borroloola, and its colourful history began as 'a wild and lawless outpost where everyone wore Colt revolvers'. Its early days were further described as 'a resort for all the scum of Northern Australia', with robberies, drunkenness, prostitution and sly grogging rackets rife among the mainly male population. Not surprising that a police station was quickly established in late 1886!

The early town consisted of two hotels with general stores attached; two general stores with grog shanties attached; two butchers' shops; three saddlers' huts; a bakery, blacksmith, Chinese market garden and dairy farm. The permanent population of about 30 was often boosted to over 100 by drifters, and there were some conflicts between Europeans and Aborigines.

Borroloola began with a bang and seemed destined to end in a

whimper - the victim of isolation, high settlement costs and slow pastoral development on the Barkly. For 50 or so years, it was a backwater. The few Europeans who remained had little contact with the outside world, and subsisted around the few dilapidated buildings left.

The police station continued to function, and there's a lovely, but disputed, story about one of its officers, Corporal Power, who was so bored with lonely outpost duties, that he asked the Carnegie Foundation in New York for a book or two to read. He got them alright - a whole classics library! The library became something of an institution, continued to acquire books until the 1930s, and nourished the mind of many a bushman. Outback raconteur and writer the late Bill Harney (the first Ranger at Ayers Rock) read most of them in gaol. He had plenty of time, five months in fact, while waiting for his appeal against cattle duffing (stealing) charges to be upheld. He was freed when the papers eventually arrived from Darwin.

It's the story of the last old white men that makes Borroloola a legendary place. Described as hermits and eccentrics, they cut biblical figures with their beards and bush staves as they hobbled around their Utopia. David Attenborough made a film about them in 1963. One, Roger Jose, arrived here in 1916, lived in an upturned corrugated iron water tank, and was widely read (he had read all the books in the library before it disappeared - the termites not only ate most of the books, but the building too!). He rarely left the town where he lived with his Aboriginal wife. He wore a heavy coat 'to keep out the hot air', and died here in 1963. He hated material things, saying "man's true wealth is the fewness of his wants", while about Aborigines he said, "...No one could ever make converts of them. They had too strong a culture of their own, a profound attachment to nature that transcended the white man's materialistic creed". Jack Mulholland, another 'hermit', lived in the old hotel until it crumbled away in the early 1960s, by which time the main street doubled as an airstrip.

There is not much left of the old town, but there is a wealth of stories about both its notorious past, and its legendary 'lotus eaters'.

Attractions

The old Police Station is the oldest surviving example of such an outpost in the Northern Territory, and houses a museum and information centre under the control of the National Trust.

The cemetery has some interesting headstones on the pioneers' graves, and other isolated graves, including some of the 'hermits', are in the bush. Most visitors come for the barramundi - a large fish, highly prized for its fighting spirit and delicate taste. A guide to the best spots and lures is available in town, and Ross Potts and Greg Lord at the pub will give you plenty of good advice and information, as will other friendly locals.

Outlying Attractions

King Ash Bay (Batten Pt.) 40km (25 miles) north-east of Borroloola. A popular fishing and camping spot on the coast with a ramp facility.

Billengarrah Station. Approximately 80km (50 miles) south-west of Borroloola. A homestay working cattle station (2124 sq km-820 sq miles) which offers specialist interest activities (photography, fishing, safaris - $100 per day per person), bush camping, safe swimming, participation in station action (mustering, yard work) and tours of the stunning natural features in the area. Homestay costs $60 per day per person, ph (089) 759 949.

Landforms. 'Lost City' type rock formations, pandanus-lined pools, Paradise Pools, Glyde River and Abner Range, and prolific birdlife are in the process of being declared a National Park. Contact NTTC for details regarding access. Located approximately 80km (50 miles) west of Borroloola.

Tours

Most focus on the river, reef or gulf.

Croc Spot Tours - fishing charters, croc spotting, scenic river and gulf island camping charters, ph (089) 758 734.

Brolga Air - scenic flights, ph (089) 758 791.

Billengarrah Station - see under Attractions.

Events

The 'Barra Classic' at Easter is a premier fishing competition; Rodeo in August; and the District Show is held in early July.

How To Get There

By road: The narrow sealed all-weather Carpentaria Highway is about a five hour, 378km (234 miles) trip from the Stuart Highway at Daly Waters, and gives all year access. From the south, the Tablelands Highway gives similar conventional vehicle access over 391km (242 miles) from the Barkly Highway turn-off.

By air: Air North operate a twice weekly flight from Katherine (Tuesday and Thursday) - $180 per person one way.

Accommodation

Borroloola Inn - 3 single rooms, $40 per room, ph (089) 758 766.

Borroloola Holiday Village - single from $72, double from $84, economy single from $48, bunkhouses from $26, ph (089) 758 742.

McArthur River Caravan Park - on-site vans $30 x 2, powered sites $12.50 x 2, camping sites $9 x 2. All sites grassed and dogs must be leashed, ph (089) 758 734.

Services and Facilities

The range is sufficient to satisfy most tourist needs, but credit cards are not widely accepted. There's a supermarket, 2 general stores, pub, garage, fuel outlets (super, ULP, diesel, aviation, camping gas), butcher, hospital, post office, police station, health clinic, church and local government offices. Bank agencies are Westpac (Chicken

Shop) and Commonwealth (post office and Bulk Discount).

Boating and fishing requirements, hire boats (Black Jacks), souvenirs and Aboriginal artifacts are available. Three boat ramps, sealed airstrip, swimming pool (Borroloola Inn - for guests and patrons only) are the main recreational facilities.

There is a choice of take-aways, and The Restaurant (Borroloola Inn) has main courses from $10.

Radio Stations: ABC 103.7 and 107.7 FM.

BRUNETTE DOWNS

Population 100

Location

On the Tablelands Highway, 140km (87 miles) north of Barkly Homestead Roadhouse.

Characteristics

This huge cattle station, owned by Australian Agricultural Company and managed by Geoff Wagstaff, covers 12,250 sq km (4655 sq miles), making it the 3rd largest in the world. It has 2,200km (1364 miles) of fencing, and runs 53,000 Santa Gertrudis cattle. The homestead settlement is town-like and clusters close to the Brunette Creek. While established in 1883, it's not the oldest or the largest, but its far-flung reputation, based on quality stock, characters and incidences, gives Brunette Downs a legendary status amongst cattlemen of the Outback.

Events

The station hosts an annual event in mid-June that's being going since 1910 - The Brunette Downs Bush Races, featuring campdraft on Friday, racing Saturday and campdraft finals, rodeo and gymkhana on Sunday. It is held 20km away from the homestead and the 'Club' even has its own corrugated iron hall and bar. The 'locals' come from hundreds of kilometres away by plane or road, and a carnival atmosphere exists in the campsites near the track. Bush dances, bbq and bar ensure lively evenings. Anyone is welcome, camping is free, and meals cost around $10 with bar prices for drinks. Toilet facilities are limited. The station is closed to visitors at all times. The race track area only is open to visitors during the event.

How To Get There

By road, via the Barkly or Carpentaria Highways to the Tablelands Highway. It is sign-posted, and access is okay for conventional vehicles. By air: an airstrip for light plane travellers is located at the western end of the race track. Prior arrangement only for use of station airstrip.

CAPE CRAWFORD

Population 6

Location

At the junction of the Carpentaria and Tablelands Highways, 275km (170 miles) east of the Stuart Highway at Daly Waters, and 383km (237 miles) north of Barkly Homestead Roadhouse.

Characteristics

Cape Crawford consists of a roadhouse only, intriguingly called Heartbreak Hotel. Many stories circulate as to how it got its name -

the most likely seems that when being constructed about ten years ago, spasmodic supplies caused the builder to constantly exclaim in frustration to anyone who would listen "... it breaks your bloody heart!" And, why is a place so far from the sea called a cape? It is thought that the land shape as the Tableland drops resembled a coastal feature to the Telegraph survey party, who named it after one of their officers. Lack of ocean was obviously immaterial!

Attractions

A new National Park (see Borroloola listing), tours with Savannah guide offered by the hotel, and other scenic attractions.

How To Get There

By road, via the narrow sealed Carpentaria or Tablelands Highways. Conventional vehicles are suitable for this all-weather road.

Accommodation

Rooms - single $36, double $42. Camping - 44 powered sites, $12 for two persons, each extra $3; unpowered $6 for two, each extra $3. Grassed sites, pets allowed, dogs leashed.

Services and Facilities

It offers good homestyle accommodation, meals around $8 with bbq Saturdays, take-away food, shop, bar, ice, camping gas, picnic area, showers for travellers ($1) and swimming pool (guests only). Vehicles services: fuel (super, ULP, diesel, autogas), oil, tyres, tubes. Credit cards accepted (Bankcard, Mastercard, Visa). Open 7am-11pm, ph (089) 759 928.

CONNELLS LAGOON CONSERVATION RESERVE

25,890ha (634,948 acres)

Location

East of Brunette Downs Station. Turn off from the Carpentaria Highway just north of the station.

Characteristics

An area set aside to preserve and protect the Mitchell grassland ecology from pressures of grazing. There are no facilities, or lagoon (except after rains). No animals are allowed.

How To Get There

Access is via a formed road to this reserve.

Aboriginal rock painting

DALY WATERS

Population 20

Location

3km west of the Stuart Highway, 374km (232 miles) north of Tennant Creek, and 260km (161 miles) south of Katherine on the Stuart Highway.

Characteristics

Tucked away from the hustle of the highway, and situated near a creek and large waterhole, this small township centres around a quaint, bougainvillaea-draped pub and offers a rare blend of Australian bush and traditional architecture that should not be missed. In its tropical woodland setting, Daly Waters consists of the Territory's oldest pub, six houses, caravan park, the remains of a telegraph station, and Australia's first international airfield. It is surrounded by the nearly 4000 sq km (1520 sq miles) Kalala cattle station. Apart from the delight of finding an unspoilt (and plastic-free) Outback spot, it has quite a few historic surprises in store, too!.

History

Explorer John McDouall Stuart's final expedition discovered a small creek which began "improving wonderfully", broadened, deepened, became "splendidly grassed", and was surrounded by ironwoods, lancewoods, bloodwoods and crimson-blossomed bauhinias. Stuart was obviously delighted with his May 23, 1862 find, and named the place after Sir Dominic Daly, the then Governor of South Australia.

But words written here by Stuart also tell of the enormous physical and mental strain of the expedition, "I feel this heavy work much more than I did the journey of last year; so much of it is beginning to tell upon me. I feel my capability of endurance beginning to give way...". There's a tree about 800m from the pub on which Stuart, or a member of his party, is said to have carved the initial 'S', and the large waterhole bears his name.

An overland telegraph repeater station was built here in 1872, and until the lines were joined near Dunmarra later that year, a pony express plugged the gap between Daly Waters and Tennant Creek. A West Australian expedition, led by Alexander Forrest to explore the Kimberley, might have perished in the desert had it not been for the telegraph line and Daly Waters. Striking north-east from the De Grey River on the west coast in 1879, the party failed to find a way through the precipitous Kimberley gorges, and dwindling rations forced Forrest to abandon attempts to trace the Ord River outlet. They struck east to the telegraph line, surviving on weaker horses, snakes and birds. When some members became ill about 160km (99 miles) from the line, Alexander Forrest and Arthur Hicks rode for two days and nights for help; found and followed the line to Daly Waters, where a rescue party was hastily organised. The point where Forrest found the line is commemorated today by an inscribed roadside cairn, approximately 50km (31 miles) north of the township.

The nearby creek and waterhole became a drovers' camp for overlanders moving cattle along the north-south stock route from Queensland to the pastoral expanses of the tropical north and Kimberley. It wasn't too long before some enterprising bloke took out a Drover's Licence for the area, set up a tavern, and sold grog here. What sort of building preceded the present pub is not clear, but the fact that liquor has been dispensed from this site since 1893 (the date when the licence was thought to have been granted) supports the pub's claim to holding the longest, continuous licence, and so to being the oldest pub in the Territory. It's likely that the original pub was built from local timbers, which no doubt were destroyed by the voracious white ants. Mr and Mrs Bill Pearce didn't make the same mistake when they built the present pub in the 1920s (probably around 1927). From the north they brought supplies of Maranboy Cypress Pine, known to be disliked by white ants, and built the pine and corrugated iron pub that architecturally remains unchanged today.

Daly Waters was eventually put on world maps by two Australian World War I fighter pilots, Hudson Fysh and P.J. McGuinness, who in 1922 purchased two war-surplus biplanes and began the Queensland and Northern Territory Aerial Services (Qantas). When Qantas started its first international service between Singapore and Brisbane in 1934, Daly Waters was the refuelling stop, and nearly all who travelled to Australia by air during the 1930s came via here. Pianist Arthur Rubenstein flew in from London in 1936 and coincidentally met violinist Bronislaw Huberman, who had arrived from Perth - a most unlikely meeting place for the two famous musicians who had not seen each other for 15 years. Many other well-known and titled people passed this way, as did the Australian pioneer aviators. These aviators didn't impress overland telegraph linesman Waldemar 'Wallaby' Holtze. He loved the solitude of the Outback and complained that Daly Waters was too noisy. Kingsford Smith had just roared in with the first airmail for London and for a few months 'Wallaby' endured such mad fliers (as he called them) as Bert Hinkler, Amy Johnson, Jimmy Broadbent and Ray Parer. 'Wallaby' Holtze applied for, and was granted, a transfer to Tennant Creek in 1932. (He didn't find much peace there either - the gold rush had just begun!)

Bill Pearce's pub thrived under this unexpected aerial bonanza, which increased further with the development of internal air services. All of this happened well before the Stuart Highway was built! For a while Daly Waters was the major junction of these early air routes, and the first inland international airport in Australia, both of which give it a unique place in Australian aviation history.

The airport was an important United States and Australian Air

Force base during World War II, mainly for the US Flying Fortress Bomber Squadrons, and after the Japanese bombing of Darwin in 1942, an RAAF hospital was established here. The 2000m runway is still used, mainly by light aircraft, while the hangar and staff quarters building are reminders of earlier, action-packed days.

Attractions

Daly Waters Pub. One of the Territory's best Outback pubs that has a 'bush bank', plenty of interesting nooks and crannies and memorabilia, a friendly kangaroo, loads of hospitality, and a sign over the bar which offers credit to any woman over 80 who is accompanied by her mother! Phil Mewett is an affable host who runs the power and meteorological stations in Daly Waters as well, and aims to maintain the pub's authentic charm. The Airfield and Stuart's Tree can be visited, but Stuart's Swamp, which teems with birdlife when full (pelicans, black cockatoos), is on private property accessible only by an organised tour.

Telegraph Station. The original wooden structure was destroyed by fire, and burnt foundation posts are all that remain. The usual stone construction for telegraph stations was not possible here because of lack of accessible rock.

Events

The Daly Waters Rodeo runs for three days over the last weekend in September.

Accommodation

Motel units - $25 single, $35 double.
  Camping/caravans - powered sites $10 two persons, unpowered $3 per person.
  Sites grassed and shaded, pets allowed - dogs must be leashed.

Services and Facilities

Most are centred around the pub and include a general store, bar, restaurant (3 course meal around $12, 'beef and barra' bbq each night), Commonwealth Bank and post office agencies, picnic/bbq shaded area, 2000m airstrip, and showers for travellers ($1). Ice, take-away food and souvenirs are also available. Fuel includes super, ULP, diesel, aviation, oil and camping gas. There are basic spares, tyres and tubes, tyre and limited mechanical repairs for vehicles. Credit cards accepted (Bankcard, Mastercard, Visa), open 7am-11pm, ph (089) 759 927.

DALY WATERS JUNCTION - HI-WAY INN

Population 10

Location

At the junction of the Stuart and Carpentaria Highways, 4km (2.5 miles) south of Daly Waters township turn-off, and 400km (249 miles) north of Tennant Creek.

Characteristics

Often mistaken for Daly Waters (the historic township, 4km north and 3km west of the Stuart Highway from here), the Hi-Way Inn is a 1974 vintage roadhouse that offers a 24 hour service to travellers. Confusion comes from its closeness to Daly Waters; it's known by some locals as Carpentaria, while to others it's Daly Waters Junction, a 'suburb' of Daly Waters that is more conveniently located on the Stuart Highway.

Accommodation

Motel style - $40 single, $50 double.
 Caravans/Camping - powered sites $10 x 2, unpowered $3 per person.
 Sites shaded, pets allowed - dogs must be leashed.

Services and Facilities

It has a shop, restaurant (seafood, grills), bar, tropical beer garden, picnic/bbq area, swimming pool (for patrons), and showers for travellers. Take-away food, ice and souvenirs are available. Fuel includes super, ULP, diesel, autogas, aviation fuel by prior arrangement (airfield at Daly Waters) and oil. For attractions see Daly Waters listing. Credit cards accepted (Bankcard, Mastercard, Visa, EFTPOS facility), ph (089) 759 925.

Devil's Marbles

DEVIL'S MARBLES CONSERVATION RESERVE

1828ha (4515 acres)

Location

On both sides of the Stuart Highway, 104km (65 miles) south of Tennant Creek.

Characteristics

An extensive rocky outcrop scattered across a wide, shallow valley features a collection of gigantic granite boulders, some of which perch precariously on top of one another. It has an aura reminiscent of Stonehenge, and is a Dreaming Place of the Warumungu, who believe that the Rainbow Serpent laid them. They are a photographer's delight.

Geology

The 'marbles' were formed from an original granite mass. As it cooled and uplifted slowly, the mass developed three main sets of joint planes (cracks) at right angles to each other, breaking the granite into three to seven metre rectangular blocks. Erosion along the joints associated with flaking away of thin slabs from the surface, widened and rounded the corners to their present shapes. Where the surrounding granite has worn away, these boulders are left, one upon the other.

Flora and Fauna

Ghost gums cling to some boulders, and spinifex is the main ground cover. Pygmy spiny-tailed goanna frequent crevices; the larger sand goanna prefer spinifex. On the underside of over-hanging boulders, fairy martin mud nests may be found; painted and zebra finch are numerous.

Conservation

It is a fragile, arid environment. You can help preservation by keeping vehicles to existing roads, and taking your litter away with you. Fires should be lit only in places provided, and wood must not be collected in the reserve as trees are sparse, and decomposition of fallen branches is an important part of the food chain for birds and reptiles. Defacing the 'marbles' in any way is an offence.

Facilities

Information signs along a short walk. Wood bbqs, picnic area, and basic toilet. Camping is allowed, but there is no water. For supplies, Wauchope is 10km (6 miles) south. Dogs allowed in certain areas.

DUNMARRA

Population 12

Location

On the Stuart Highway, 350km (217 miles) north of Tennant Creek, and 44km (27 miles) south of Daly Waters.

Characteristics

Roadhouse, pub, store and restaurant, the Shell Wayside Inn, is a convenient stop after the dry stretch from Elliott. The original pub, built by drover Noel Healey in the 1930s, was replaced in 1971 by the present structure. Opposite are remnants of one of the original telegraph poles, and an area of the former Dunmarra Cattle Station was a wartime RAAF base. An interesting historic marker about 20km (12 miles) south, commemorates not only the Overland Telegraph Line construction, but is also near the spot where the wires were joined in 1872. The Buchanan Highway turn-off to Top Springs is 8km (5 miles) north of Dunmarra.

Accommodation

Motel units - $35 single, $40 double, extra person $5.

Caravans/Camping - powered sites $6 couple, $1 extra person; unpowered sites $2.50 per person. Pets allowed.

Services and Facilities

It has a bar, shop, restaurant, accommodation, camping and shaded barbecue area. Take-away food, ice, super, ULP, LPG for vehicles, diesel, tyre and minor mechanical repairs are available. Credit cards accepted (Bankcard, Mastercard, Visa), open 6am-midnight, ph (089) 759 922.

ELLIOTT

Population 600

Location

Approximately half-way between Alice Springs and Darwin on the Stuart Highway - 790km (490 miles) north of Alice Springs, and 735km (456 miles) south of Darwin.

Characteristics

Elliott is a small, friendly regional service centre and cattle town, that has a wide range of services available to travellers, including a hotel/motel, camping grounds, supermarket, dining rooms, vehicle services, including 24 hour fuel, police station, post office, medical centre, airstrip, school, and various local government offices. It's an attractive settlement, set in an open woodland landscape, and surrounded by the 4000 sq km (1520 sq miles) Newcastle Waters Cattle Station.

It had its origins during World War II, when it functioned as a staging camp for troops on the move between Darwin and Alice Springs. The name is after Captain Elliott from Adelaide, the officer in charge of the wartime camp, and its development was assisted by both the decline of Newcastle Waters township, and the more convenient location on the Stuart Highway. It got a boost when the Junction Hotel licence at Newcastle Waters was transferred to Jimmy Munckton's Elliott Hotel in 1962, and the pub today is a good place to meet the locals, and like the town, it is unpretentious.

Attractions

The nearby historic droving township of Newcastle Waters is worth visiting (see separate listing). Visitors should be aware that nearby Lake Woods is on private property and, contrary to information in many publications, it is not available for public use of any kind.

Accommodation

Elliott Hotel - share shower $25 per person; units $30 per person, $45 double (prices lower in off-season). Open 24 hours. Shaded sites, pets allowed, bbq area, pool, ph (089) 692 069.

Midlands Caravan Park - cabins $40 x 2, $5 extra person; unpowered sites $5 per person; powered sites $15 x 2, bbq area, swimming pool, shop, pets allowed on leash. Open 6.30am-6pm, ph (089) 692 020.

Halfway Caravan Park - camping/caravan sites $10 for powered site. Pets allowed, pool. Open 6am-10pm, ph (089) 692 025.

Services and Facilities

There is a well-stocked supermarket (Halfway Caravan Park open), and general store (Midlands Caravan Park).

Bank Agencies: Westpac (BP Roadhouse), ANZ (Mobil Service Station), Commonwealth (Midlands Caravan Park).

Licensed dining room meals at Hotel, BP Roadhouse and Mobil Service Station (BYO). Take-aways from Mobil and BP Roadhouse.

Fuel: 24 hour service at Hotel (super, ULP, diesel), aviation fuel; BP Roadhouse (super, ULP, diesel); Mobil Station (super, ULP, diesel and LPG), camping gas; Midlands Caravan Park (super, ULP, diesel).

Vehicle repairs are available at the BP Roadhouse (24 hour mechanic, basic spares, AANT Agency, 24 hour towing) and at the Mobil Station (mechanical repairs, spare parts).

Medical services are available at the health clinic; ice - Mobil and Pub; Aboriginal artifacts - BP and Pub; showers for travellers - Midlands Caravan Park $2.50 (swim and shower $3) . The town has an airstrip and major credit cards are widely accepted.

Emergency Services: Ambulance, ph (089) 692 060; Police, ph (089) 692 010.

KALKARINGI

Population 250

Location

On the fringe of the Tanami Desert, 460km (285 miles) south-west of Katherine.

Characteristics

Set among low hills, plains of spinifex and stunted eucalypt, Kalkaringi (formerly Wave Hill) basically services the Dagaragu Aboriginal settlement and local cattle stations. For travellers, it is the only petrol and food outlet, and is the half-way point between Halls Creek and Katherine on the Buchanan Highway. There is some fishing in the Victoria River (swimming too, after the Wet Season), but hardly prolific, while for rock hounds, there are prehnite, amethyst, agate and jasper fossicking areas.

If you come this way, don't miss the ramshackle and bizarre atmosphere of the spinifex-roofed and wall-less Frank's Bar and Grill. Frank's is headquarters of the cricket club, where 'locals' drive for hundreds of kilometres from stations for a Saturday match played on a dusty pitch. In fact, the small European population (about 25) formed the club just to get a bar licence, and it is the most popular spot in town after 4pm. Local Aborigines are not allowed membership by order of their own council. Kalkaringi is a dry area (alcohol restrictions apply).

The 12,580 sq km (4780 sq miles) Wave Hill Cattle Station nearby is one of the largest in Australia, and the most common question asked of locals is "how the hell can you live in a place like this?".

History

Dagaragu, 8km from Kalkaringi, originally called Wattie Creek, is significant in the Aboriginal Lands Rights Movement, being the site of the first grant of land ownership to an Aboriginal group. Led by Mr Vincent Lingiari in 1966, 200 Aboriginal stockmen and their families protested about their poor conditions on Wave Hill Station, and later demanded ownership of their traditional land. Because Wave Hill's Wattie Creek was sacred land - the main place of Guringi Dreaming and site of sacred totem paintings - the issue evolved into the first land rights claim. Mr Whitlam's Labour Government granted the Guringi people a pastoral lease in 1975, on 3200 sq km (1216 sq miles) of the Wave Hill property, and in 1986, they were formally granted ownership. Land rights pioneer Vincent Lingiari died in 1988, and Dagaragu is a purely Aboriginal settlement where tourists are not welcome.

How To Get There

Best access for conventional vehicles is from Katherine during the Dry Season, via the sealed (mainly narrow) Victoria Highway, Delamere Road and Buchanan Highway. From the Stuart Highway (turn-off near Dunmarra), the Buchanan Highway is compacted gravel - with care, suitable for conventional vehicles. The Buchanan Highway from Halls Creek is gravel; reasonable after grading (generally twice a year) but can become corrugated - 4WD recommended. During the Wet Season (between January and early March), it is 4WD only, as floods at creeks and rivers can occur on both sides of Kalkaringi.

Accommodation

Camping/caravans only. Powered sites $10 for 2 persons; tents $5 for 2 persons; extra person $2. Sites grassed and semi-shaded. Pets allowed - dogs must be leashed.

Services and Facilities

It has a service station, supermarket and caravan park as one enterprise - The Kalkaringi Service Station, open 8am-6pm Mon-Sat, 3-6pm Sun. Cash only, ph (089) 750 788.

There is also a police station, and a health clinic with twice monthly doctors' visits, open 7am-3pm Mon-Fri, on call other times.

Other facilities include tourist information, a licensed Cricket Club (tourists welcome), CBA Agency (Mon, Wed, Fri mornings), airstrip, and showers for travellers ($2). Services include take-away food, ice, fuel (super, ULP, diesel), oil, camping gas, mechanical and tyre repairs (Council workshop, 7am-3pm weekdays), tyres and tubes.

LAJAMANU

Location In the Tanami Desert, 104km (65 miles) south of Kalkaringi on the Lajamanu Road.

Characteristics

Lajamanu is an Aboriginal settlement with transit services only for tourists. A permit is required for fuel purchases, but not for the Tanami to Lajamanu Track, which is a public road through Aboriginal land. Fuel (super, ULP and diesel) is available during normal hours, cash only. Access from the south is via the Tanami-Lajamanu Road, a 243km (151 miles) 4WD track.

NEWCASTLE WATERS

Population 10

Location

3km (2 miles) west of the Stuart Highway, 24km (15 miles) north of Elliott.

Characteristics

This old droving township, situated at the intersection of the Murranji and Barkly stock routes, and by the intermittent waters of Newcastle Creek, **features historic buildings including the Junction Hotel, and a recent National Trust acquisition, George Man Fong's House, now known as Jones' store.** Interspersed are old houses occupied by Newcastle Waters Station employees, three of whom, Margaret McLean, Donna Schubert and Kirsten Squires, act as custodians. The 1988 opening of the Drovers' Memorial Park, historic trail and Jones' Store, with its memorabilia, is the first preservation and commemoration stage of Newcastle Waters' legendary droving heritage.

At the beginning of The Last Great Cattle Drive from here (the Northern Territory's major Bicentennial event in 1988), it must have been gratifying for the oldest living drover, 95-year-old Tommy Williams, to see the place much as it was in his hey-day. The ersatz 'traditional' buildings now appearing in the Territory are sad reminders of how much of Australia's Outback architectural heritage has been lost. At Newcastle Waters, as elsewhere, the National Trust, along with other local groups, has done a magnificent job in ensuring the preservation of, and making available for public appreciation, this significant architectural and historic site.

At this stage, the township has no facilities or services, and visitors are asked to respect private station roads and property.

History

Explorer Stuart was the first non-Aboriginal in the area in 1861, and he named the stretches of water after the Duke of Newcastle who was Secretary of State for the Colonies. The waters are known locally as Longreach Waterhole, and lie between the old town and Lake Woods to the south. The thick, savage scrub and dry stony plains proved too much of a barrier for the party, and concern for his men and supplies led Stuart to abandon any further movement north on this expedition.

The settlement developed primarily as a droving town in two distinct phases. In the first, between 1919 and 1930, it was a depot for construction gangs working on watering facilities for the east-west stock route. When government bores provided reliable water points after 1930, the second phase began, which saw the establishment of stores and the hotel. Apart from the police station, the fledgling township relied entirely on stock routes and their users for its livelihood.

The Junction Hotel, so named because of its location at the meeting place of two of the world's longest stock routes, has been described as "seeing more good-natured fights and non-malicious brawling than any other pub on the Track". In its hey-day, it is also claimed the place saw about one fight per gallon of beer! It is not surprising, when the most common drinks taken in excess were beer and rum with a 'Rankin Bomb' being a popular mix - an 8oz glass filled almost with neat rum and topped off with port to sweeten it!

It did not cost Newcastle Waters storekeeper Jack Sargent much to build the 'Drovers Pub' in 1932. Old windmill blades found abandoned at stock route bores provided materials, while those who owed him money at the store "wiped their slates clean" with their labour. It certainly had plenty of atmosphere with its galvanised iron walls, iron bars on the windows, and hitching rail outside for the horses. Busiest times were at the beginning of the Wet Season when up to 14 droving plants camped here, and with no cattle to look after, the men had plenty of time for drinking. Max Schober, who ran the pub between 1935 and 1956, was as colourful as he was enterprising - he would travel for hundreds of kilometres, first by wagon, then in later years by motor vehicles, to meet the drovers with stores and food supplies. His successor, Dutch-born Oscar Schank, loved to prepare exotic food and despaired when his culinary delights were spurned. "All they want", he said, "is steak and eggs mate, always steak and bloody eggs!"

By the early 1960s, the widespread movement of cattle by motorised roadtrains, the construction of 'beef road' networks, one of which by-passed the Murranji stock route, and its location off the Stuart Highway, meant the end of both drover and pub. Oscar sold the licence, which was transferred to Jimmy Munckton's new establishment at Elliott in 1962, and the pub reverted to a store and bottle shop for the cattle station, until it finally closed in 1975.

The main part of Jones' store was built in 1935, and run by Arnold Jones from 1936 until 1949 as a store and butchery. In the late 1950s and early 1960s, George Man Fong, when he wasn't out on trips as a Boss Drover, worked from the premises as a saddler during his occupancy of the store. Architecturally, the store represents a traditional style common in the Territory; having had many owners and roles it has been adapted to meet each new need. Its construction of mud-brick walls, large bush timbers, corrugated iron and bamboo slatting that has withstood a harsh environment, along with its important function in the town's community life, highlight the building's significance. It's open for a few hours each day. The house next to the pub was built in 1942 as a telegraph repeater station for World War II communications, and is now a private residence. The large group of buildings away to the left is the homestead complex of the 4000 sq km (1520 sq miles) Newcastle Waters Cattle Station, first leased by Dr Browne from London in 1883, and established by the mid-1880s. Today, it runs between thirty and forty-five thousand cattle, mainly Santa Gertrudis, Brahman and some Charolais breeds, and is managed by Ken Warriner for media magnate owner Mr Kerry Packer.

In more recent times, the town was close to decay and used by itinerant Aboriginal families and station workers for housing, but never with any permanency. 1983 saw Newcastle Waters station bring about a revival by housing married staff in the town and renovating the run-down condition of the buildings. An active community consisting of station personnel, Aboriginal families, contract workers, and a teacher, has now breathed new life into this old droving town. You can wander through the old settlement, store and pub, and along the short, information posted, historical trail.

Drovers and Droving

The explorers first made known the pastoral potential of the Outback, but it was the overlander and drover who filled these huge spaces with cattle and sheep, often in epic treks that lasted many months, covered hundreds of kilometres and broke open new land. There were considerable profits to be made from these animals, and wealthy pastoralists and financiers in New South Wales, Victoria and South Australia eagerly snapped up land options in the Territory and Kimberley. The only way to stock these frontier lands was to overland livestock from the Southern and Eastern states. Once established, the stations were the source of a steady supply of cattle droved along a network of stock routes that criss-crossed the continent to the southern railheads and markets.

The linchpin of this whole operation was the drover, a nomadic horseman who for nearly 100 years 'punched' the cattle across the vast, often arid, tracts of the Outback. In the late 1800s, they became "a symbol of the young nation's spirit; their stoicism, sardonic humour, mateship and restlessness expressed in folklore and balladry gave them legendary status and laid the basis of character traits much revered and regarded as typically Australian today".

Droving cattle long distances was a well-ordered operation. A drove of 1500 cattle would require eight to ten men, a cook and horse-tailer (the man who tended the horses at the stock camp). Gear (food, water, general equipment and personal belongings) would either be carried by pack-horse, or in a sturdy wagon pulled by horse teams, and driven by the cook. Usually, there were about eight saddle-horses per man, and at least forty night horses. The leader was called a Boss Drover and 'ringers' were expert stockmen, so named for their ability to circle the herd at night to quieten them, and the term is quite distinct from the southern meaning - the fastest sheep shearer in the shed. A 'jackaroo' is an apprentice stockman who acquires his skills on the station, and the team of drovers was called 'a plant'.

Drovers operated in stages, moving the cattle about 12km (7 miles) a day (for sheep it was about 10) along nearly one kilometre wide designated stock routes. When a plant was passing through their property, station owners rode by to make sure their land was not being eaten out by some 'grass pirates'. Journeys were undertaken during the Dry Season, and for water they depended on natural surface supplies, until permanent bores at regular intervals along the routes were sunk

It took great skill to control the cattle, many of which would not have been mustered for two years, and so could be wild and unsettled. The drovers' greatest fear was the sudden rush or stampede, and a few lost their lives in this terrifying way. Night watches were kept; the horses for this were carefully selected for their dark colour and ability to see well and move unobtrusively at night so as not to disturb the cattle. Drovers got to know each individual beast, helped by the fact that cattle adopted set positions in the herd.

Drovers were expert stockmen, horsemen and bushmen, and almost Aboriginal-like in their intimate knowledge of the land. They were independent, courageous and had to cope mentally and physically with the loneliness and rigours of the vast empty spaces.

> The harsh environment had an important bearing on their attitude towards life. Drought, heat, floods, and stampedes shaped fatalistic outlooks expressed in their dry and often sardonic humour. They were thinking men too, and many carried books in their saddlebags including histories and philosophical works, which were read and discussed during the long waiting hours.

Many wrote poetry. The drover was distinguishable by his generally long, lean frame, weather-beaten hat, flannel shirt, moleskin trousers, and riding boots. Beef or mutton, damper (unleavened bread) and billy tea was the staple diet, and the latter are a popular legacy with Australians today.

King of the drovers was Nat (Bluey) Buchanan, "legendary for his sense of locality and skill in uncharted country", and there were others; Tommy Williams, Charlie Swan (he drove cattle for 60 years from Queensland to the Kimberley), Les Griffiths, Matt Savage, Clarrie Pankhurst, and John Hagen, to name a few. Drinking and droving did not go together, and it's hardly surprising that at the end of long hazardous droves, many 'cut' their wages at the nearest pub. Banjo Paterson's words "...the drover's life has pleasures the townsfolk never know..." provide some insight into the strong attachment they had to the bush, and the story of drovers, droving and stock routes is well worth reading in Keith Willey's book *The Drovers*.

The Murranji Stock Route

Victoria River properties received their cattle via Top Springs along the Murranji Track, which took its Aboriginal name from the desert frog that was capable of living for long periods underground without water. It was the shortest route to the Eastern States from the Victoria River region; 234km (145 miles), in comparison with an extra 644km (399 miles) that the northern route through Katherine and the Roper River area entailed. The Murranji, opened in 1886, tapped into the pastoral lands of legendary owners and overlanders, Kilfoyle, Bradshaw, Buchanan, MacDonald and Durack, and between 50,000 and 70,000 cattle were brought down this track each year, reaching a peak of 77,000 in 1951.

It was the toughest track of them all: limited water until the bores went in; witchwood scrub with spiked branches that could spear stock, horse and rider; and a horror stretch of limestone country, called 'drummy' ground, that reverberated under the hooves and caused cattle to take fright and stampede. All contributed to the route's deadly reputation. A 'Rankin Bomb' at the Junction Pub was clearly understandable after the Murranji!

How To Get There

From the Stuart Highway, access is by a 3km sealed road through Newcastle Waters township.

RABBIT FLAT - TANAMI DESERT

Location

In the Tanami Desert, on the Tanami Road, 604km (374 miles) north-west of Alice Springs, and 77km (47 miles) from the Western Australia border.

Characteristics

One of the most remote Outback pubs in Australia consists of a small cluster of buildings, the largest of which is a corrugated iron structure that functions as a store, cafe and bar, and is the last fuel stop before Halls Creek in Western Australia, 488km (302 miles) away. It's surrounded by the 160,000 sq km (60,800 sq miles) Tanami Desert (an area more than twice the size of Tasmania), and is a region of searing furnace-like heat in summer, with little permanent surface water. Such a trip is not advisable in summer, and is best suited to the experienced and well-equipped 4WD Outback traveller.

Basic services are available only on Friday, Saturday, Sunday and Monday. On Tuesday, Wednesday and Thursday, the roadhouse is completely closed. In view of this partial closure, intending travellers should check availability of services prior to leaving.

History

With the determination and spirit reminiscent of the early pioneers, Bruce and Jacqui Ferrands established the roadhouse here in 1969. They ran a weather station and sent off daily reports to the Meteorological Department. In 1975, Rabbit Flat was headline news when the settlement's population doubled overnight - Jacqui gave birth to twins, helped by Bruce who followed radio instructions from the Royal Flying Doctor Service. The Ferrands continue to run the roadhouse.

Accommodation

It's camping only, which is free of charge, but there are no powered sites.

Services and Facilities

It has a bar, a shop selling basic things, ice and take-away food. Fuel services include super, ULP, diesel and oil. It's cash only, open 7am-10pm on Fri, Sat, Sun and Mon only, ph (089) 568 744.

THE TANAMI DESERT

Characteristics

An advertisement that appeared in the Alice Springs paper a few years ago said: "For sale. One rain gauge. Two years old. Never used. As is, where is. Apply Mongrel Downs Station". Mongrel Downs, before it was abandoned, was within a hundred kilometres of Rabbit Flat, and the advert gives some idea of what the climate is like.

It's a semi-arid region with average rainfalls peaking at about 140mm in January, dropping to below 10mm between July and August, with yearly totals between 300 and 900mm. Rainfall is erratic, and high evaporation rates leave little surface water. Average maximum temperatures are just over 40C (109F) in November and December at Rabbit Flat, while the average temperature in December and January is 39C (106F)! Between June and August, average minimum temperatures are as low as 10C (50F) at Rabbit Flat, so nights can get cold, and sometimes freezing.

The landscape is characterised by: gently undulating sand plains, the dominant feature; sand dunes, occur in many places with major dune fields about 60km (37 miles) south of Rabbit Flat, vary in colour from yellow to red, and in height; ranges, rises and rocky outcrops are generally low reflecting the degree of degradation of the ancient Precambrian granites and sandstones by erosion over millions of years; salt and freshwater lakes tend to be found in the central and south-western parts of the desert, the former often appearing as dried-out salt lakes, while freshwater form in depressions such as Lake Surprise near Rabbit Flat, or in claypans and river floodouts. **Other features are distinct low depressions of drainage systems which collect and divert rainfall without forming channels, particularly around Rabbit Flat, and provide a habitat for**

termites *(Nasutitermes triodiae)*, whose red mounds are dominant landscape features. Limestone outcrops and Eucalyptus-lined creek beds complete the landscape picture.

Flora and Fauna

Spinifex, grasses, shrubs (acacia, grevillia, mulga, witchwood) and trees, particularly along watercourses (river red gum, coolabah, melaleuca) give the landscape further interest. The surprisingly abundant flora of the desert is due to the closeness of its northern part to the sub-tropics, and so is an interface between sub-tropical and semi-arid plants.

> The Tanami hosts a fascinating array of wildlife, deemed so important that 37,529 sq km (14,261 sq miles) was protected by Wildlife Sanctuary status in 1964.

It's also been subjected to a number of wildlife studies in recent years, that have revealed some of its biologically unique and pristine characteristics. Facts from studies show a rich wildlife occurrence; 2 species of fish; 17 amphibians; 90 reptiles; 188 birds; and 41 mammals. Five new species were found for the Northern Territory - the lesser hairy-footed dunnart, skinks and frog. Greater bilby, spectacled hare-wallaby and northern nailtail wallaby are common in some areas, as well as the rabbit-sized Rufous hair-wallaby, known to the Walpiri people as the Mala - once widespread throughout much of semi-arid Australia.

The Tanami also seems to be a biological paradox - while appearing to be a refuge for species once more widespread in Australia, there's also the extinction of about 58% of medium sized mammals in an area relatively free of European pressures. This constitutes a loss to conservationists and the Walpiri, whose culture incorporates these animals in song, dance, dreaming tracks and dreaming sites.

The current theory, according to D.F. Gibson of the Conservation

Commission Research Division, is that fires (or lack of them) may have been the cause. With the decrease in traditional Aboriginal hunting methods, which is directly related to the increase in European occupation in the last 50 years, came the decrease in the number of small, controlled, patchwork burning activities. Naturally sparked fires from lightning could now spread for hundreds of kilometres, instead of being checked by limited plant growth - large animals, being more mobile, could escape, medium sized ones were either killed or died because of lack of food. This consequence emphasises how arid and semi-arid regions can become ecological disaster zones if fires are not controlled - that is one reason why the Conservation Commission is providing more gas barbecues in parks and reserves that are more susceptible to fire damage, and why it is important to conform to regulations regarding fires in the open.

Tanami Desert History

This little-known region mirrored the trends of European development in the Territory - exploration, then mining, followed by attempts at pastoral activities.

Traditionally, the Tanami is homeland for the Walpiri people, with inter-facing Walmanpa to the north-east, Alyawarra and Kayetj to the south-east, Kurintji to the north, and Pintupi to the south-west. In recent times, Land Rights claims led to the granting of 90,000 sq km (34,200 sq miles) of the Tanami, including the Wildlife Sanctuary, as freehold title to the Walpiri Aboriginals.

Explorer A.C Gregory and his expedition members were probably the first Europeans to see the Tanami when, in 1855-56, they reached an area near Lajamanu. Other explorers tended to skirt the desert. The first crossing is attributed to Nat Buchanan in 1896. Thorough explorations were made in 1900 by Alan Davidson, who discovered gold at The Granites in the same year, and Michael Terry in the 1920s and 1930s.

Pastoral development, with the exception of Suplejack and Tanami

Downs Stations (both within 100km [62 miles] of Rabbit Flat), was never a great success in the central areas. The abandoned Granites and Mt Doreen Stations are reminders of the hardships.

Tanami and The Granites

Both are old gold mining sites discovered by British prospector, Alan Davidson, in 1900. Between 1910 and 1911, there were about 200 men working in the Tanami fields. However, the heat, severe water shortages, and little returns saw most miners leave after 1911. Spasmodic workings at both sites continued into more recent times, and by 1961 the fields had yielded over 12,000oz.

North Flinders Mines has an agreement with Aboriginal land owners to mine gold at The Granites site, which began operations in 1986, with production in 1988 reaching 80,000oz. Mine staff fly in and out of Alice Springs, with a roster operation on the field, and cost of producing an ounce of gold from the underground mine is $250.

How To Get There

The road begins 20km (12 miles) north of Alice Springs, where there is a sign warning that conventional vehicles are not suitable west of Tanami. 4WD however, is preferable for the road that is sometimes referred to as a track, and best time to travel on it is during the winter months. The first 118km (73 miles) is sealed, after which it's a formed road with some gravel stretches to Rabbit Flat. Beyond Rabbit Flat is definitely 4WD, on a flat bladed road characterised by sand build-ups in the middle, interspersed with rocky outcrops. Places along the way include three rest areas with water, Chilla Well Homestead, and The Granites.

A permit to travel on this road through Aboriginal land is not required, but it's advisable to check in case of changes. Also, check road conditions and fuel availability before leaving, and remember that Rabbit Flat is closed on Tues, Wed and Thurs of each week. Water at some bores along the way is undrinkable.

TILMOUTH CROSSING ROADHOUSE

Population 4

Location

On the Tanami Road, 190km north-east of Alice Springs. See Tanami Desert listing for road conditions.

Characteristics

Located by the wide Napperby Creek Crossing, this establishment serves stations and travellers heading across the Tanami Desert. There's plenty of wildlife, and the roadhouse has camels and kangaroos. The 9-hole desert golf course must be one of the most remote in Australia. Nearby salt lakes add interest.

Accommodation

Bunks, including breakfast, $20 per person; camping. $5 per vehicle.

Services and Facilities

It has a shop selling a range of general goods, take-away food, artifacts, fuel (super, ULP, diesel), oil, basic spares for vehicles. Open 7 days, ph (089) 568 777.

RENNER SPRINGS

Population 18

Location

On the Stuart Highway, 158km (98 miles) north of Tennant Creek.

Characteristics

It is a well-weathered wayside inn that has a rough and ready charm
about it, and is surrounded by the 5047 sq km (1918 sq miles) Helen
Springs Cattle Station. The roadhouse offers comfortable
accommodation, good value homestyle food (3 course meal $10.50),
and has a small collection of historic objects. The proprietors are very
proud of their home-baked bread, made in brick ovens, and they offer
the '600 mile Sandwich'. It is so large that you eat half when you buy
it, and the other half for the next meal when you are 600 miles away!

The building itself is a museum piece. Basically, it's an old army
hut, hauled from Banka Banka Station in 1949, where it was used to
quarter troops during the war. The construction reflects the
resourcefulness of immediate post-war roadhouse builders, who
faced short supplies of materials, and Renner Springs is one of the
few buildings of this period left along the Stuart. Higher rainfall here
marks a climatic change reflected in the vegetation, which becomes
lush and green. At the turn-off to Helen Springs on the eastern side of
the Stuart Highway, there is an amethyst and smoky quartz fossicking
area.

History

The freshwater springs nearby were named after Dr Renner, an OTL
engineer, but today water at the roadhouse is from a bore. The first

'roadhouse' consisted of three tents (one a dining room, one a kitchen, and one a house) pitched by proprietors Jack and Dorothy Doyle before they converted the army hut in 1952.

A prominent feature of the plains to the east of the highway and 4km (2.5 miles) south, is a flat-topped mesa called Lubra's Lookout (Lubra = Aboriginal Woman). In the Dreamtime it is thought that the plains were a significant meeting place for Aboriginal clans who came from hundreds of kilometres away; the local women sat on the lookout to report arrivals to their men below.

Accommodation

Hotel/Motel style SC units - single $40, double $50.

Camping/caravans - powered sites $10 for 2 persons, $1 for each extra, other sites $7 for 2 persons.

All sites grassed and shaded, and there are barbecue facilities. Pets allowed - dogs must be leashed.

Services and Facilities

It has a shop, bar, dining room, camping ground, airstrip, and showers for travellers (50c). Take-away food, ice, souvenirs, fuel (super, ULP, LPG, diesel), oil, basic spares, qualified motor mechanic, tyres, tubes and repairs, towing service, camping gas, are all available, with aviation fuel on request.

Credit cards accepted (Bankcard, Mastercard, Visa). Open usually 7am-11pm but heading towards 24 hour opening, so phone ahead, ph (089) 644 505, fax (089) 644 525.

TENNANT CREEK

Population 3200

Location

On the Stuart Highway, 507km (314 miles) north of Alice Springs, and 675km (419 miles) south of Katherine.

Characteristics

Apart from Katherine, Tennant Creek is the only major town between Alice Springs and Darwin. Situated in the centre of the Territory, this modern, progressive town with an attractive, wide, tree-lined main street, serves mining, cattle and tourist industries, and has all the facilities and comforts of the city. It is also the centre for the Warumungu people who, along with Walpiri, Warlmanpa, Alyawarra and Kaytej Aborigines, refer to Tennant Creek as Jurnkurakurr after a significant Dreaming Pace.

Tennant Creek's past as a Telegraph Station outpost and tough goldrush town is the stuff of Outback legend; the remnants of this era can be seen at the old mine sites which dot the rocky outcrop landscape. Its colourful mining history, fascinating geology, and modern tourist facilities, make a few days' stay a rewarding interlude between the Centre and Top End.

History

Stuart discovered the slow-moving creek, 11km (7 miles) north of the present town site, in 1860, and named it after South Australian pastoralist, John Tennant. The OTL repeater station was built beside it in 1872. Legend has it that the town stands where it does today because that's where the beer cart broke down. Rather than manhandle beer and building materials for the intended hotel back to the creek, everyone simply moved camp! There is the story too, that the establishment of a government reserve around the Telegraph Station prevented any commercial development here. In fact, the pub and shops were built on the present site because it was closest to the goldfields; miners didn't want to walk 10km from the creek each day! Water had to be carted from the creek as bore water was too salty. The high cost of water (5/- for a 40 gallon drum) led many miners to believe that it was cheaper to drink beer, a habit that was hard for them to break when water supply systems improved!

Gold discoveries in 1932, and the boom town conditions that briefly followed, put Tennant Creek on the map. It became the site of the last major goldrush in Australia. More than 100 separate mines were in operation before World War II - most were shallow and small with only 22 producing more than 1000oz (31kg) of gold. The first mines, some with names reflecting the optimism of the 'gougers' (miners were called gougers as they used a 'hammer and tap' method to gouge their way through the granite), included Great Northern, Shamrock, Peter Pan, Rising Sun, Pinnacles, Nobles Nob, Weabers Find, Peko and Eldorado. Eldorado produced 175,000gr of fine gold between 1932 and 1958. The great Peko Wallsend Mining Company had humble beginnings here when Joe Kaczinski and Bill Bohning pegged Peko Mine (named after Joe's dog) in 1933.

Tennant Creek was in danger of becoming a ghost town after the goldrush, but sizeable copper deposits breathed new life into the town during the 1950s. There is still plenty of mining - gold, silver, copper and bismuth - in the area, and a few of the goldrush miners sometimes relive the 'old days' at the local pubs.

Tennant Creek's major mining company, Poseidon Gold, has the White Devil Mine, currently Australia's highest grade gold supplier.

Geology

Tennant Creek is situated on an area known as the Warramunga Geosyncline. This consists of a considerable thickness of

TENNANT CREEK

1 ANGLICAN CHURCH — E13
2 ANZAC HILL LOOKOUT — E12
3 AUSTRALIAN INLAND MISSION — E13
4 BARKLY T.A.F.E. — E13
5 BLUESTONE MOTOR INN — E13
6 C.W.A. HOSTEL — E13
7 CIVIC CENTRE & LIBRARY — E13
8 ELDORADO MOTOR LODGE — E12
9 GOLDFIELDS HOTEL MOTEL — E12
10 GOVERNMENT BATTERY — F13
11 GOVERNMENT CENTRE — E13
12 HISTORICAL DISPLAY — D12
13 HOSPITAL — E13
14 KARGURU PRIMARY SCHOOL — E13
15 MEMORIAL CLUB — E13
16 NATIONAL TRUST HEADQUARTERS — E13
17 N.T. TOURIST BUREAU — E12
18 OLD SCHOOL MASTER'S HOUSE — D13
19 OUTBACK CARAVAN PARK — F13
20 POLICE STATION — E13
21 POST OFFICE — E13
22 R.S.L. CLUB — E13
23 RACECOURSE & SHOWGROUNDS — F12
24 ROMAN CATHOLIC CHURCH — E13
25 SAFARI LODGE MOTEL — E12
26 SPORTS GROUND — E13
27 SWIMMING POOL — E13
28 TENNANT CREEK CARAVAN PARK — E12
29 TENNANT CREEK HIGH SCHOOL — E12
30 TENNANT CREEK HOTEL — E12
31 TENNANT CREEK PRIMARY SCHOOL — E13
32 TENNANT CREEK SPORTING CLUB — E12
33 UNITING CHURCH — E13
34 YOUTH HOSTEL — E13

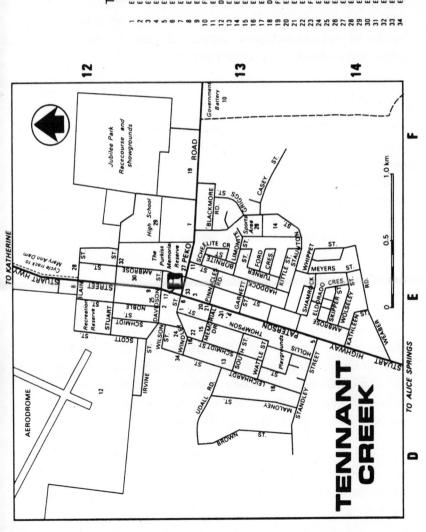

TENNANT CREEK

inter-bedded sandstones and siltstones which were originally laid down under a shallow sea. Over millions of years, much upheaval and change has occurred and scattered within these sediments are iron-rich horizons and intrusive and extrusive quartz porphyries (dark, purplish red igneous rock with small felspar crystals). Ironstones, consisting of black to metallic grey magnetite and hematite in fine-grained sedimentary rocks are widespread on the surface. They offer mineralogical interest as they may contain fine specks of gold, bluish-green copper, or veins of red jasper, cross-cutting white quartz and black hematite.

Attractions

The Tennant Creek Regional Tourist Association is located at the Transit Centre, Paterson Street; it's the place for local information and bookings. Open Monday-Friday, 9am-5pm, ph (089) 623 388.

Bill Allen Lookout is one of the best places for views and orientation. Located 2km east along Peko Road.

National Trust Museum, build in 1942 as a wartime Army Hospital, is one of the few historic buildings left, and houses an interesting display of early day reminders. Located in Schmidt Street, open weekdays, 4-6pm - other times by appointment.

Church of Christ The King. This Catholic church has certainly been places. Built in Pine Creek in 1904, dismantled in 1935, trucked to Tennant Creek, washed overboard by floodwaters near Daly Waters, and finally re-erected in Windley Street. It's no wonder that the corrugated iron and timber structure is called the 'longest Church in Australia'! It has historic building classification.

Airport Memorial. The engine of a DH914 aircraft, which crashed at the present Goldfields Hotel site in 1929, is on display at the Airport Terminal, and also recognises the work of the early pioneers.

Telegraph Station. Established in 1872, this stone structure is now a museum, where visitors are welcome. Located by the creek, 10km (6 miles) north of the town.

Isolated Graves. Near the Telegraph Station at what is known as the Seven Mile, are two graves; one of Tom Nugent, who was supposed to have been a member of 'The Ragged Thirteen' - a notorious bland of cattle duffers (thieves) who ranged the Territory in the early days. The other grave, to the south, is that of OTS telegraphist Archibald Cameron, who died around 1918.

Devil's Pebbles. A geological formation consisting of rounded boulders scattered in heaps across a large area. They have resulted from the weathering of a 1700 million-year-old intruded granite mass (similar in formation process to Devil's Marbles). Their makeup is an unusual mixture of minerals - circular pink feldspar crystals surrounded by blades of black biotite, outcrops of porphyry (similar to granite but with distinctive bluish quarts fragments) and various types of feldspar. The evening sun enriches the natural granite tones to produce magnificent colours for photographers. Ghost gums, spinifex and rock wallabies complement this outstanding geological feature. Camping is allowed, but there are no facilities. Located 11km (7 miles) north on the Stuart Highway, then left onto a dirt road (suitable for conventional vehicles) for 6km (4 miles).

Mary Ann Dam. This delightful recreational reserve features a man-made lake, where you can enjoy swimming, sailing and boating (non-powered only), but there are not boat hire outlets. Facilities include boat ramp, pontoon, bbq, picnic and toilet, making it an ideal family leisure stop. For the energetic, there's a bicycle track connection to the town, and bush walking tracks in the nearby Honeymoon Ranges. Located 6km (4 miles) north of the town.

Purkiss Reserve Travellers' Rest Area. Located on the corner of Ambrose and Peko Roads, this reserve has shade, bbq, playground equipment, swimming pool, and toilets.

Battery Hill, home of the Tennant Creek Gold Stamp Battery. Here gold-bearing hematite-quartz ores from local claims are crushed in the first stage of extracting the fine grain gold. Flushing processes complete the task. The battery was originally built in 1946, and during the day you may watch it in action, making it one of the few working museums in existence. There are also various displays - historic artifacts and former battery site and buildings. Shaded bbq area and toilet facilities are available. Tour times - 8am, 9.30am and 4pm daily. Cost, $4 adult, $2 child, $10 family. Located 1.6km (1 mile) along Peko Road.

Nobles Nob Mine. Actual mining in this huge open cut mine stopped in 1985. It was one of the richest gold mines, producing $65m worth of fine gold. It was discovered in 1934 by Jack Noble and William Weaber. When the main pillar collapsed in 1967, it was converted to an open cut operation, and at its maximum size, the mine measured 910ft long, 480ft wide and 270ft deep. It is located 16km (10 miles) east on the Peko Road.

Burnt Shire Mine. So named when co-founder Bluey McIlroy accidentally scorched himself when burning off nearby spinifex. Access is by conducted tour only. Check with the Tourist Bureau.

Fossicking. The Moonlight Rock Hole locality, north of Warrego mine, is available for gold fossickers. Check with the Visitor Information Centre for details.

Riding. Trail riding at Kraut Downs is available by appointment only. Check with Tourist Bureau.

Tours

Ten Ant Tours offer local town historic tour, flora and fauna and Burnt Shirt Mine - value at $12 per person.

Dot 6 Mine Tours offer a journey into the past with washing and gold panning - $5 adults, children under 12 years free. Ph Colin Bremner on (089) 622 168.

Aboriginal Corroboree

Events

Races - St Patrick's Day; Tennant Creek Race Day in May. Renner Springs Races are held here over East weekend - also include camp-draft (Good Friday), Rodeo and horse events on Sunday.

Show - July.

Go-Kart Grand Prix - May.

Golf Open - June.

How To Get There

By coach: Greyhound, Pioneer Express and Bus Australia run daily services between Alice Springs and Darwin. Coaches stop at the Tennant Creek Transit Centre, which has all facilities.

By air: Skyport.

Accommodation

There are 4 motels, 1 hotel/motel, a youth hostel, and 2 caravan/camping parks. The telephone area code is 089.

Goldfields Hotel/Motel, Paterson Street, ph 622 030 - $65 a double.

Bluestone Motor Inn, Paterson Street, ph 622 617 - pool, disabled facilities - $79 a double.

Eldorado Motor Lodge, Paterson Street, ph 622 402 - pool - $75 a double.

Safari Lodge, Davidson Street, ph 622 207 - $69 a double.

Desert Sands, Paterson Street, ph 621 346 - $55 a double.

Youth Hostel, Leichhardt Street, ph 622 719 - $9 per person.

Outback Caravan Park, Peko Road, ph 622 459 - on-site vans from $35 for 2; cabins (en-suite) $45 for 2, $50 family - pool and spa. No pets.

Tennant Creek Caravan Park, Paterson Street, ph 622 325 - on-site vans from $40 for 2; powered sites $14 for 2 - pool, pets allowed, dogs leashed.

Eating Out

The Dolly Pot Inn, Davidson Street, is one of the Territory's most highly regarded restaurants (main course around $13). Others offer reasonably priced meals - *Bluestone, Eldorado, Goldfields and the Hotel* (all in Paterson Street). *The Memorial Club*, Memorial Drive, and *Sportsman Club*, cnr Ambrose and Stuart Sts, give further choice. *Rocky's Pizza, Mr Perry's* and *Barkly Bakehouse* offer take-aways. Novel eating out - Mulga Track Tours' Silver Service Bush Dinner Party ($60 per person).

Services and Facilities

The wide range includes all vehicle needs - fuel available until 9pm (24 hour fuel at Threeways), LPG at Lone Star Mobil Station, AANT - Wyatt Motors, Irvine Street.

Hire vehicles: Budget, Newsagency, Paterson Street; Barkly, Paterson Street ; Hertz, Outback Caravan Park.

There is a full range of shopping services: chemist; banks - Westpac (auto teller), ANZ Branches, Commonwealth Agency (PO); medical - hospital, clinic, visiting dentist and chiropractor; churches - Anglican, Catholic (both Windley Street), Uniting, Aboriginal Inland Mission (both Paterson Street).

Credit cards are widely accepted.

Local radio station call sign and frequency - 8TC 684 (ABC).

Emergency Services

Police, Paterson Street, ph 621 211.
Fire, Thompson Street, ph 622 000.
Ambulance, Windley Street, ph 622 000.
Road Service, ph 622 468 - AH 622 312 (Wyatt Motors).

Recreational Facilities

Swimming pool, Purkiss Reserve; golf course; bowls; squash; tennis; speedway; cycling.

THREE WAYS

Population 25

Location

25km (15.5 miles) north of Tennant Creek, at the junction of the Stuart and Barkly Highways.

Characteristics

A roadhouse, motel, roadtrain 'mecca', and hitchhiker 'get stuck' point, located at the Territory's major intersection in the heart of heat, scrub and dust country. It was originally established in the 1950s and rebuilt in 1974. A large stone cairn commemorates the founder of the Royal Flying Doctor Service, Rev John Flynn.

Accommodation

Motel - $50 double, $45 single.
  Dongas (cabins) - $20.
  Caravans - powered sites $12 for two; tents $8 for two.
  All sites grassed, pets allowed on leash.

Services and Facilities

It has a shop, bar, licensed restaurant ('steak and vegetables' type meals $10), tourist information, picnic/bbq area, accommodation, and pool for guests only. Take-away food, ice, souvenirs, fuel (super, ULP, diesel), oil, basic spares, and showers for travellers ($1) are available.

Open 24 hours. Credit cards accepted (Bankcard, Mastercard, Visa, Shell), EFTPOS facility, ph (089) 622 744.

TOP SPRINGS

Population 15

Location

At the junction of the Buchanan Highway and Delamere Road, 289km (179 miles) south-west of Katherine.

Characteristics

Top Springs consists of the aptly named Wanda Inn, that offers some real Outback hospitality and reaffirms the Territorian liking for a beer or two - they get through 9 tons of it here a week! Apart from the increasing tourist trade, it serves the surrounding cattle stations including the huge Victoria Downs property (12,359 sq km-4696 sq miles), Dungowan (4456 sq km-1693 sq miles), Montejini (3142 sq km-1194 sq miles), Killarney (2839 sq km-1079 sq miles), and the roadtrain 'truckies'.

You can swim in the nearby pools that give name to the place, or visit the original settlement site 16km (10 miles) away, where in 1954, the 40-year-old hotel was burnt down. Near this site, the Yarrlin people have a small settlement. The historic Murranji stock route, along which overlanders skirted the Tanami Desert in their westward cattle trek to the Victoria River and Kimberley regions, passes close to Top Springs. In 1988, the route rang again to the sound of stockmen when the Bicentennial 'Droving Australia' event retraced the trail of those early drovers.

How To Get There

From the Victoria Highway near Timber Creek, the Victoria River Downs Road is compacted gravel - with care, suitable for conventional vehicles during the Dry Season, but check conditions at Timber Creek. For other routes, see Kalkaringi listing.

Accommodation

3 motel units - $45 single; $55 double; $65 family.
  Camping/Caravans - $5 per caravan, including power; $2 for tents.
  Grassed, semi-shaded sites. Pets allowed; dogs must be leashed.

Services and Facilities

The Wanda Inn has a bar, dining room (3 course meal $8-$12), accommodation, general store, picnic/bbq/shaded area, swimming pool (guests and patrons only), showers for travellers ($2), and disabled persons facilities. Take-away food, ice, souvenirs, artifacts, fuel (super, ULP, diesel), oil, basic spares, minor mechanical and tyre repairs, tyres, tubes, and limited towing service are available.
  Cash only. Open 24 hours (as required) all year, ph (089) 750 767.

WAUCHOPE

Population 6

Location

113km (70 miles) south of Tennant Creek, on the Stuart Highway.

Characteristics

Pronounced 'walk up', this bougainvillaea-draped hotel invitingly hugs the highway, exudes character, and is a branch of the 'bush bank'. Owner Bob Richard thinks it was named after one of the OTL surveyors, and it celebrated 50 years as a pub in June 1988. Apart from the usual roadhouse services, the hotel offers comfortable accommodation and good country-style food.

History

It began as a Post Office and Store, serving miners from the rich Wauchope and Hatches Creek wolfram fields, discovered in 1914. Prior to War World II, there were about 200 Chinese helping at the diggings, a few of whom began a soft drink factory here as well. Imminence of war stimulated demand for the tungsten ore which was used to harden steel. They brought it out by camel, then dray, and finally by truck load, slaking their thirst at Wauchope before the long haul east. Soft drink was not the stuff of miners in the searing heat, and in 1938, the Post Office and Store became a rather lively pub.

Like most of the old pubs of 'The Track', Wauchope stories are as rich in imagination as they are in truth - it's even said that the pub changed hands in 1946 as the result of a poker game. There is no Post Office now, but the Wauchope versus The World cricket match around mid-July each year gives it a present day interest.

Accommodation

Motel - room only $25, double $55.
  Camping/caravans - powered sites $9 x 2; sites $6 x 2; tent $3.50.
  All sites grassed. Dogs must be leashed.
  Cabins - $25 x 2.

Services and Facilities

There's a bar, shop, dining room (3 course meal $11), bbq, accommodation, a 1.2km airstrip, and showers for travellers cost $1. Take-away food, ice, souvenirs, fuel (super, ULP, diesel, autogas), aviation fuel by prior arrangement, camping gas, tyres and tubes are available. There is also a tennis court and a zoo (camels, kangaroos, emus).

Credit cards accepted (Bankcard, Mastercard, Visa). Open 24 hours, ph (089) 641 963.

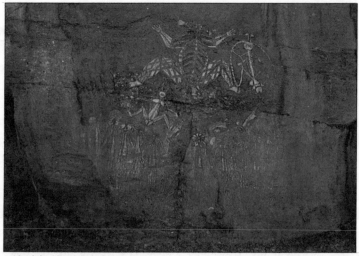

Aboriginal Rock Painting.

WOLLOGORANG

Population under 10

Location

286km (178 miles) east of Borroloola in the NT and 285km (177 miles) west of Burketown in Qld, on the Carpentaria Highway.

Characteristics

The station's licensed roadhouse not only offers supplies and accommodation, but also superb fishing, and a taste of real-life on a cattle run. This 'Gulf Gateway to the Territory' straddles the Northern Territory/Queensland Border, and covers 5767 sq km (2191 sq miles), including about 80km (50 miles) of beautiful, sandy beach frontage onto the Gulf of Carpentaria. Paul Edmonds, who manages the station, will tell you where the fish bite best, and he doesn't need much of a cue to talk about one of his favourite subjects - local history. Wollogorang is a weather station, and temperatures between December and March can reach 45C (113F); coldest is down to 7C (45F) in June/July.

History

The station was established in 1881 by Chisholm, who came from a property near Goulburn (NSW), and is the longest continually settled cattle station in the Northern Territory; other properties were settled before this but were later abandoned. The ruins of the original homestead hut can be seen; the existing homestead, built in 1926, was extensively renovated in 1984.

When established, its situation hear Settlement Creek was on the only road into the Territory from Queensland that guaranteed water.

Since the Creek was presumed to be on the Queensland/South Australian Border (in the early days, what is now known as the Territory was part of the South Australian colony - an area South Australia later abandoned), the employees of drovers bringing cattle to the West demanded 'the settlement' of their wages as they entered the Northern Territory - hence the name of the creek. Once they were outside Queensland and the jurisdiction of its courts, they could not force employers to pay their wages.

In August, 1886, Carruthers completed the task of surveying the Northern Territory/Queensland Border, and in 1986, a small group of surveyors from Queensland, Northern Territory and South Australia met on the coast and celebrated the centenary of Carruthers' great work by replacing his original, final post with a concrete one with an inscribed plaque.

Near Seigals Creek is a small Aboriginal settlement - the Waanyi Garawa People, some of whose artifacts and paintings are for sale at the roadhouse.

Attractions

You can visit the survey post on the coast, but 4WD is necessary, or fish and camp on the unspoilt Gulf beaches - many visitors spend a week or so here, it costs $10 per day per car. Swimming is not advised. Aluminium boats and outboard motors are available for hire ($35 per day), but you take them yourself for the 80km (50 miles) 2 and a half hour trip to the coast. Special fishing and safari type tours can be arranged to meet your requirements.

How To Get There

By road from Borroloola, is 260km (161 miles) of good, formed gravel surface, and it takes between 3.5 and 4 hours. From Burketown, also about 260km (161 miles), the surface is rougher - about half is formed and gravelled, the rest has bad bulldust patches, and the trip takes about 5 hours. Conventional vehicles do come through, but 4WD is preferable. Check road conditions.

By air, a weekly service from Tennant Creek by Chartair's Barkly mail plane, is an interesting alternative.

Accommodation

Motel type - $55 double. Twin rooms in Roadhouse with shared facilities - $33 single, $44 double, $60 family.

Camping - $3 per head (school age children free).

All sites grassed and pets are allowed - dogs leashed.

Services and Facilities

The station has accommodation, bar, dining room (large station type meals $10), general store, registered aerodrome, picnic/bbq area, tourist information, and showers for travellers. Take-away food, ice, fuel (super, ULP, diesel), oil, aviation fuel, basic spares, minor repairs, tyres, tubes, towing service, are available. Artifacts and souvenirs are also for sale. It's cash only. Open 24 hours, or as demand requires, all year, ph (089) 759 944.

WYCLIFFE WELL

Population 15

Location

On the Stuart Highway, 135km (84 miles) south of Tennant Creek.

Characteristics

A surprisingly well-stocked store, and recently modernised pre-war roadhouse. It's a beer connoisseur's delight, too - Irwan Farkas reckons he has the largest selection of foreign beers in Australia (300 types). You can even watch local Warumungu craftsmen making artifacts, which can be bought. A large windmill and a lake with plenty of birdlife is nearby. A few kilometres away is Ali Curung Aboriginal settlement, with a population of around 400.

In the early days, Wycliffe Well was a watering hole for the stock route, and during the war, vegetables and fruit were grown and flown out daily to supply the troop camps along The Track.

Accommodation

Motel - $68 double, $53 single. Cabins from $25, on-site vans from $35, cabins from $25.

Grassed camping sites $6 x 2, powered sites $14 x 2, and large indoor swimming pool ($2). Pets allowed on leash.

Services and Facilities

It has a licensed restaurant (Hungarian Goulash specialty), shop, motel units, pool (guests only), take-away food, ice, liquor, artifacts, souvenirs, fuel (super, ULP, diesel, autogas), oil, range of spares, mechanical repairs, tyres and tubes, and towing service. Tourist information, showers for travellers ($2), shaded picnic/bbq area, are available.

Credit cards accepted (Bankcard, Mastercard, Visa). Opening hours as required, ph (089) 641 966.

THE
TOP END

Characteristics

Whereas landform and red sand dominate the Centre, the main features which unify the Top End are climate and the luxuriant greenness it spawns during the Wet. Stretching from Larrimah in the south, the Top End encompasses vast woodland tracts, flood plain, escarpment and plateau, before meeting long, lazy beaches on its northern, eastern and western boundaries.

Darwin is the thriving heart of a huge hinterland whose life-blood is cattle on the sprawling runs, tropical agriculture, mining, defence, and tourism based on the wonders and delights of Kakadu National Park, Litchfield Park, Katherine Gorge and Mataranka. Cosmopolitan Darwin, tropical beaches and islands, turquoise waters, mystical Arnhem Land, crocodiles, and hunting and fishing, all give a unique colour and flavour to a region that's more like another country than a part of a fledgling mainland Australian state.

Climate

The Top End has a tropical monsoon climate which means two distinct seasons: The Wet or Green from November to March; The Dry from May until September, with April and October transitional months.

> **The Wet Season coincides with the highest temperatures, humidity and rainfall.**

It's hot and oppressive, and locals describe it as the 'suicide season'. Torrential rains can begin from November (the real rains generally start in December) and continue to March, dumping on average 1659mm (over five feet) of water on the land. Sometimes tropical cyclones form, and while damage has been severe when populated areas have been struck, their occurrences are fortunately infrequent. At Katherine, rainfall is less than Darwin, but temperatures are higher.

DARWIN	J	F	M	A	M	J	J	A	S	O	N	D	Ann. av.
Temperature: Av. monthly max.	32	31	32	33	32	30	30	31	32	33	33	33	32
C° : Av. monthly min.	25	25	24	24	22	20	19	21	23	25	25	25	23
Rainfall : Av. monthly mm.	409	353	316	99	17	2	1	6	18	72	142	224	1659
Relative humidity: Av. 9.00am	81	83	83	75	67	63	63	68	71	70	73	76	73
: Av. 3.00pm	69	71	67	52	42	38	38	41	47	52	58	64	53
Sunshine Hours: Average	5·6	5·9	6·6	8·7	9·5	9·9	10·1	10·2	9·8	9·4	8·4	7·2	8·4
Thunder Days: Average	15	11	11	4	0	0	0	0	1	5	12	15	74

KATHERINE	J	F	M	A	M	J	J	A	S	O	N	D	Ann. av.
Temperature: Av. monthly max.	35	34	34	34	32	30	30	32	35	37	38	36	34
C° : Av. monthly min.	24	24	23	21	17	14	13	16	20	24	25	24	21
Rainfall : Av. monthly mm.	234	214	166	33	5	2	1	0	7	31	86	193	972
Relative humidity: Av. 9.00am	77	81	76	64	58	55	52	51	51	55	61	70	63
: Av. 3.00pm	53	55	49	36	34	31	27	25	24	26	33	43	36
Thunder Days: Average	3	3	2	0	0	0	0	0	0	1	3	4	16

Source: Bureau of Meteorology

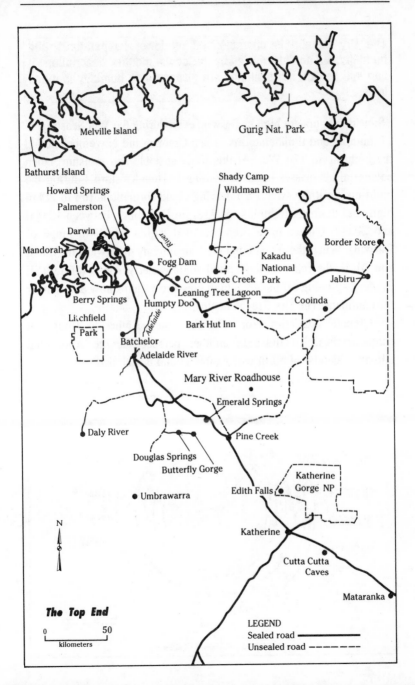

The Top End

0 ___ 50
kilometers

LEGEND
Sealed road ————
Unsealed road - - - - - - -

> **The Dry Season is characterised by lower temperatures and humidity, but don't be misled by the 'cooler months' description - it can still be hot, but evenings are pleasant and humidity is much lower.**

Sunshine hours are high in Darwin, even during the Wet Season.

Lightning and thunderstorms in late October and November herald the build-up to The Wet. At this time, unstable and moisture laden equatorial air masses begin to dominate. Thunder storms during the build-up are impressive for towering cloud formations (up to 20km high) and dramatic lightning displays (in December, between 10,000 and 20,000 flashes have been recorded within an 80km range of Darwin). When the moist equatorial air retreats northward in March and April, the rains diminish, and south-easterly winds follow (SE Trades), spinning off the great high pressure systems now dominating the continent. The Dry Season begins.

Climate statistics for Darwin and Katherine highlight characteristics. To illustrate another perspective, the Aboriginal climatic calendar of north-east Arnhem Land is included.

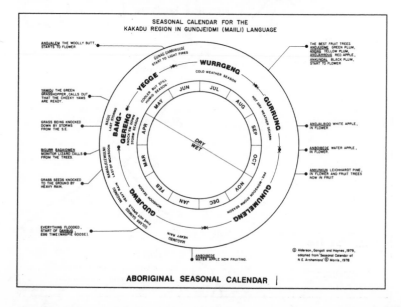

ABORIGINAL SEASONAL CALENDAR

Landscape

The mainly flat to undulating landscape is interrupted by a belt of broken rocky country that ranges north-eastward from the Victoria River region to the great sandstone massif of the Arnhem Land escarpment. The escarpment and the vast spread of the gorge-cut plateau it backs, is the dominant and most scenic landform feature in the region, best seen at Kakadu. The sweep of coastal floodplain provides contrast, while shallow seas, reefs, long sandy beaches, and mudflats, characterise the coast. The Roper and Katherine-Daly drainage systems, rising from limestone springs, are the only rivers that permanently flow along their entire length; others may dry up beyond the tidewater marks. Whereas landform lines are sharply delineated in the Red Centre, they are subdued in the Top End by the relentless cover of tropical woodland. Before the land bakes and dries in the rainless days of winter, the mantle of softer, lush-green landscape tones dominate.

Flora and Fauna

Tropical eucalypt woodland covers 85% of the flat to undulating landform of the Top End.

Dominated by the Darwin *woolly-butt* (Eucalyptus miniata) and the Darwin *stringybark* (E. tetrodonta), their canopies are sufficiently spaced to enable plenty of sunlight to the understorey of shrubs and grasses. Often, the landscape has a more open savannah character. *Ironwood* (Erythrophleum chlorostachys), smooth-stemmed *bloodwood* (E. bleeseri), the attractive *salmon gum* (E. alba) are other eucalypts. Smaller species are *billygoat plum*, also known as a vitamin C tree (Terminalia ferdinandiana), *green plum* or *wild mango* (Buchanania obovata), *sand palm* (Livistona humilis), and acacias. Tall *spear grass* (Sorghum intrans) flourishes during the Wet season.

Species of the low-lying areas, floodplains, escarpment and plateau are highlighted.

Crocodiles

Of the two species found in northern tropical waters, the salt-water, 'saltie', or estuarine crocodile (Crocodylus porosus) is definitely the most dangerous to man (attacks in recent years have resulted in a few deaths). The smaller, freshwater type (Crocodylus johnstoni) is considered relatively harmless unless provoked. Both types demand utmost respect! Crocodiles in a way are living dinosaurs - the last remaining members of the class Archosauria, the ruling reptiles of the Mesozoic era (between 70 and 200 million years ago) that have changed little since roaming with their Tyrannosaurus rex and Brontosaurus relatives.

Crocodiles are now totally protected. Prior to 1971, they were shot for skins, and numbers declined dramatically. Since 1971, numbers have increased, as has their size.

Salt-water Crocodile facts:

Salt-water is a misnomer - they do inhabit tidal rivers and inland freshwater billabongs and lagoons. (See map of distribution).

Size - males can grow to 6m (19ft), most large ones are around 4m. Males mature at about 3-4m, at an estimated age of 16 years. Females rarely exceed 4m, and may nest at 2-3m, around an age of 10 years. They live to about 100 years.

Appearance - apart from their large size as adults, salties are distinguishable by their broad snouts, but small salties may be difficult to recognise at a distance.

Food - young feed on small animals (crabs, prawns, fish, occasional snakes and mammals); adults on a range including larger mammals and man! Prey behaviour may well be observed before attacks. Large males can reach speeds of 40km/h in water, and can stay submerged for up to 2 hours. Smaller crocs are 'slower' underwater, and

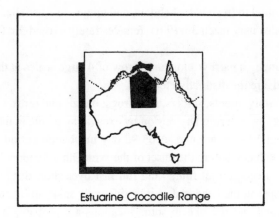

Estuarine Crocodile Range

submerged time span is less. A third eyelid assists better underwater vision, while a flap seals the nostrils. Very large males can lunge with awesome speed from the water to take a buffalo drinking at the edge, drag, roll, and drown it, in what has been described as 'the death roll'. Once locked, the jaws exert a pressure of 5 tonnes per sq cm. A fleshy valve at the back of the throat prevents the crocodile from drowning. On land, smaller salties can reach speeds up to 20km/h (12 mph) over short 20m (65 ft) distances, while larger ones are much slower. But they rarely move too far away from water, preferring to bask on mud-banks where their 'slides' may be seen.

Breeding - Nesting occurs in the Wet season. A large mound of vegetation and soil is built. About 50 eggs are laid, covered and guarded by the female. Crocodiles are particularly aggressive at this time. The hatchlings squeak for assistance when they are ready to emerge at the end of the 90-day incubation period. Only a small number survive to become mature adults.

Freshwater Crocodile Facts:

Mainly found in freshwater habitats, and unique to Australia.

Size - males may reach 3m (9 ft); females rarely exceed 2m (6 ft) in length.

Appearance - a narrow snout and a row of 4 large scales at the base of the head, are the distinctive features.

Food - mainly insects, spiders, fish, frogs, lizards and birds.

Breeding - nest during Dry season by excavating a hole in the sand, where about 12 eggs are laid. A 65-90 day incubation period allows the young to hatch before the onset of the Wet. Other features include its ability to rise 'on all fours' and run fast over short distances. A sensory organ in the head makes it instinctively snap, so 'attacks' on air mattresses and the like in some locations are probably a reflex action. Behaviour is not entirely predictable, and best advice is to give them plenty of space and respect.

Be 'Crocodile Wise':

People and crocodiles can 'co-exist' if a few simple rules are followed.

* Observe the warning signs. Absence of a warning sign does not mean the area is safe.

* Seek local or expert advice about crocodiles before swimming, camping, fishing or boating.

* There is a potential danger anywhere salt-water crocodiles occur. If there is any doubt, do not swim, canoe, or use small boats in estuaries, tidal rivers, deep pools, or mangrove shores.

* Be aware. Keep your eyes open for large crocodiles. Children and pets are at particular risk in the water, or at the water's edge.

* Do not paddle, clean fish, prepare food, or camp at the water's edge. Fill a bucket with water and do your chores at least 50m away. Returning daily or regularly to the same spot at the water's edge is dangerous.

* Do not lean over the edge of a boat, or stand on logs overhanging

water, and don't hang articles over the edge of the boat.

* Stand at least a few metres back from the water's edge when fishing. Crocodiles have not been known to attack well away from the water.

* Dispose of food scraps, fish offal and other wastes properly, and away from your camp site.

A visit to the Crocodile Farm can be a useful introduction to these creatures, before seeing them in the wild.

Protect Yourself

In the tropics, it's essential to wear a hat, advisable to use sun-cream, and always carry sufficient water, even on short walks. Confine strenuous activities to the 'cooler' parts of the day. Face nets and insect repellents are useful bushfly and mosquito deterrents. Mosquitoes, in particular, can be a nuisance, and nets are advised for campers. Water from billabongs must be boiled before drinking. Clothing ideally should be light, cotton material, which 'breathes' better in the humid conditions.

Saltwater Crocodile

Fishing

The Top End and fishing are synonymous, and there's plenty of scope for this popular recreational activity. So, don't forget to include your Jarvis Walker or whatever rod you use if your itinerary includes the tropical north. Australia's premier native sport fish is the legendary fighting barramundi, a superb table fish as well.

Salt-water crocodiles, all year, and box jellyfish, between October and May, are dangers associated with fishing. Tidal range in Darwin can be 8m (26ft) leaving boat ramps high and dry on spring lows! Tide charts are essential. Darwin Harbour has 3 artificial reefs - sunken ships called fish aggregate devices (FAD), designed to attract fish. Another FAD is at Lee Point. For regulations and bag limits refer to the Information and Advice section. Special bag limits apply for barramundi fishing in the Mary River system. Many Fishing Tour specialists operate out of Darwin and other locations - check places listings.

The following fishing guide is a sample of the main fish species found in these northern tropical waters.

Type Best times	Location and Characteristics
Barramundi or Giant Perch All year but pre and post Wet ideal.	Coastal and inland waters (rivers, lagoons). Arnhem Highway-Kakadu Region, Darwin Harbour arms, Roper and Daly Rivers good locations. Succulent table fish.
Bream All year.	Same as for Mangrove Jack.
Black Jewfish All year.	One of the biggest reef fish. Can exceed 50kg but schools 5–15kg most common. Deep holes in river mouths, rock ledges and rocky headlands and sunken wrecks.

Queenfish All year.	Rocky headlands, exposed reefs at creek and river mouths. Islands, Darwin Harbour, Gurig Peninsula.
Spanish Mackerel June, July August.	As for Queenfish but also inhabits waters above shallow reefs next to deeper waters.
Longtail Tuna June, July, August.	Inshore Waters.
Giant Trevally Most of year.	Shallow reefs and strong tidal flow Areas. Vernon Islands good location.
Barracuda Most of year.	Shallow reefs but not in great numbers.
Threadfin Salmon All year but prior to Wet best.	Similar location to barramundi.
Sailfish and Marlin All year.	Deeper waters off coast. Arnhem Land Coast.
Golden Snapper and Fingermark Bream. All year.	Shallow inshore and estuarine reefs. Sometimes found in deeper waters. Fine table fish. Generally 2–5kg but up to 10kg.
Saddle Tail Snapper All year.	Called red fish. Inshore/offshore reefs. Fine table fish 1–2kgs.
Red Emperor All year.	Deeper reefs. 3–5kg but up to 10kgs. Fine eating.
Rock Cod All year.	Wide ranging, non-schooling reef dwellers.
Coral Trout All year.	As for rock cod but a better table fish.
Moonfish All year.	Inshore reefs and estuaries. Schools of 1–2kg common.
Mangrove Jack All year.	Shallow estuarine reefs, rockbars, mangroves and tidal rivers.

Hunting and Shooting

Wild buffalo, pig, banteng cattle and sambar deer may be hunted via licensed safari operators in some ideal tropical wilderness country. Trophy and non-trophy is offered for the experienced and novice hunter, mainly in the Cobourg Peninsula and Pine Creek areas (check these listings for details). The Howard Springs Hunting Reserve (Conservation Commission) offers duck and geese shooting during the declared season. Refer to Information section about hunting regulations.

Touring Suggestions

While Kakadu is a must, try to spend a few days there and explore some of the attractions on the way - a round trip from Pine Creek is well worth considering, as is a flight over the floodplains and escarpment.

For its raw wilderness, perennial waterfalls, and 'lost city' landforms, Litchfield Park is highly recommended. For those seeking some tranquil retreats, the Daly River area won't disappoint. A definite must is Mataranka, an ideal 'R and R' spot, where you can explore the Roper River, too.

Four Wheel Drive enthusiasts can try the overland journey to the Cobourg Peninsula, and for Aboriginal cultural experiences, Melville and Bathurst Islands, or Wigram Island and Arnhem Land, afford ideal opportunities. Darwin is a good base for a range of city and outlying attractions, while remote Nhulunbuy, with its tempered climate, is a great spot for relaxation and fishing. Katherine Gorge is another must, but don't forget the attractions Katherine itself has to offer.

Adventure seekers and sportsmen are well catered for. From thrills of canoeing along the Daly or Katherine with the experts, Breakwater

Canoe Safari, ph (089) 412 899, and fishing for the fighting barramundi, to sailing tropical waters and safari hunting, are some of the exciting outdoor activities offered.

Some travellers even use Darwin as a base for short trips to Asian destinations (fares are much cheaper from Darwin). It's well worth adding a bit more icing to the Outback cake, by incorporating in your Top End visit, a taste of the stunning **Kimberley landscapes**.

Only 40 minutes away by air is Kununurra, which is an ideal base for the frontier Gibb River Road Country, and flights to the Bungle Bungle, Lake Argyll and the diamond mines. Ansett has regular flights, while Sling Air's two-hour flight to the Bungle Bungle from Kununurra is spectacular.

PLACES AND ATTRACTIONS

ADELAIDE RIVER

Population 146

Location

On the Stuart Highway, 110km (68 miles) south of Darwin.

Characteristics

A colourful township on a river of the same name, is noted for its wartime history and proximity to the picturesque Daly River area. Adelaide River consists of a hotel/motel; general store and camping ground complex (Adelaide River Inn); Post Office and general store; BP country store; Shell Service Station; Police Station; health centre; art gallery; and racecourse.

Apart from a tourist function, the township serves surrounding cattle properties and gold mines. A fascinating wartime role, local scenic river and wildlife features, and some down to earth Territorian hospitality at the Bushranger pub, merit a visit.

History

The Kungarakan were the first people in the area. European discovery, and naming of the river, was by two crew members of HM Survey ship *Beagle* in 1849. The name honours the then Dowager Queen, Queen Adelaide. The Overland Telegraph Line construction in 1870, laid the basis for permanent settlement when a depot was established. The taking up of pastoral leases and the extension of the North Australia Railway Line in the 1880s, consolidated its economic base, and the railway station and bridge were built in 1888-89.

Because of the township's strategic position and railway, it was the centre of much military activity during World War II. A major armaments depot was established at nearby Snake Creek, the buildings of which still remain. Partly for their own protection, Aborigines were moved out of northern areas during the war, and placed in camps at Adelaide River and other locations. They contributed to the war effort in many ways; tending the extensive army fruit and vegetable gardens, handling ammunition, driving army vehicles, and stripping down engines for re-conditioning. Today, the old army depot and cemetery are reminders of the war on mainland Australia.

Information

The Tourist Information Centre is located in the Old Railway Station, open Mon, Wed and Fri, 4-5pm.

Attractions

Adelaide River War Cemetery. Australia's largest war cemetery has the graves of those who were killed in the Darwin bombing raids of 1942, in a well-maintained, lawned and garden setting.

Railway Station. Now a National Trust property, this restored station was the only one on the North Australian Line that had a refreshment room for passengers. Also known as the '77 mile', the station is a fine example of railway architecture in isolated regions. The catering in the 1930s was interesting. At a time of no refrigeration, Mrs Eve Sack who ran the refreshment rooms, was a lateral thinker, and enterprising as well when the red meat supplies ran low. She recalls, "... **We'd give them roast fowl then plenty of**

goats - call it mutton - nobody knew it was goat- they all liked it!"

Indirectly, she was responsible for the township's first liquor licence. While her premises had a licence only to serve grog half an hour either side of the train being in the station, she managed to get one that allowed all travellers to imbibe - with the help of the local constabulary. The policeman, rather thirsty after a patrol, was understandably annoyed when refused a drink; a full licence soon followed! Beer came in bottles, four dozen to a box, packed in straw, and covered with wet hessian to keep them cool. At the end of World War II, a full hotel licence was granted, and accommodation was provided at the rear of the building. The Licensees decided to purchase a large army hut located in the railway yard, and the Fawcetts used this as the basis of the 'new' pub in 1951 - this building remains as the present Adelaide River Inn.

Patsy Fawcett (a niece of the original pub owner) runs the Tourist Information Centre and Library now housed in the Station. A resident caretaker looks after visitors when the Information Section is closed. Entry fee is $1.

Railway Bridge. Also built in 1888-89, it was the largest on the North Australian Line, and even doubled as a road bridge when the low level one was under water during the Wet.

Snake Creek Arsenal. It was established in 1942 as an armaments depot and large wartime military camp. The basic structures, although deteriorating, remain intact, and visitors are allowed. Keys are available from the police station.

Robin Falls. Located approximately 15km (9 miles) south on the Old Darwin to Katherine Road, the 12m (39 ft) falls are at their best during the Wet season. Interesting rock formations, gorge and tropical vegetation, make it a popular picnicking spot, but there is about a 10 minute walk into the falls. Continuation on this road leads to the Daly River attractions (see separate listing).

Tours

Special interest and general tours to Kakadu and Litchfield Park can be arranged through the hotel.

Events

Show and races - third weekend in June.

Accommodation

Adelaide River Inn and Motel - single $35, double $65.

Shady River View Caravan Park - powered sites $15, unpowered sites $6 x 2.

Sites grassed, shaded; pets allowed on leash. Open 6am-11pn, all year.

Credit cards accepted (Amex, Bankcard, Mastercard, Visa), ph (089) 767 047 for both establishments.

Services and Facilities

The township has most basic services. Three stores, ice, souvenirs, take-away food, Dining Room (Inn - general serve costs around $10, their Bull & Barra burgers are a delight!), 3 fuel outlets (super, ULP, diesel - emergency petrol, night bell at the Big Bowser), camping gas, vehicle repairs and AANT Agent (Shell Auto Port), church (Catholic), health centre, and police station.

Emergency Services

Police, ph (089) 767 042; Ambulance, ph (089) 279 000; Fire, ph (089) 767 047.

PARKS AND RESERVES OF THE TOP END

All distances marked are from Darwin. Local distances are in brackets. Not drawn to scale.

Gurig National Park

Bathurst Island

Melville Island

Beagle Gulf

Van Diemen Gulf

DARWIN

Howard Springs Nature Park 31 km
Fogg Dam 68 km

(35 km)

STUART

Wildman River
(192 km)

Jabiru
252 km

Kakadu National Park

Berry Springs Nature Park 57 km

Batchelor

Litchfield N.P.
(111 km)

Adelaide River 113 km

(134 km)

Road often closed in wet season

(63 km)

Daly River Nature Park

(38 km)

Douglas Hot Springs Nature Park
(17 km)

(72 km)   (38 km)

Butterfly Gorge Nature Park

(22 km)

Pine Creek 227 km

Umbrawarra Gorge Nature Park

(44 km)

Edith Falls

(46 km)

Katherine Gorge National Park

Katherine Low Level Nature Park

KATHERINE 317 km

(5 km)   (27 km)

Cutta Cutta Cave Nature Park

(7 km)

Mataranka Pool Park

Mataranka 444km
(3 km)

(5 km)

Gregory N.P.

HWY

Keep River National Park 784 km
Kununurra 825 km

Tenant Creek 981 km
Alice Springs 1486 km

ARNHEM HIGHWAY - KAKADU REGION

Characteristics

The superb all-season, sealed, and sometimes elevated, Arnhem Highway is the gateway to the Territory's fastest growing tourist destination: World Heritage listed Kakadu National Park. It's an area of extraordinary wildlife, pristine wilderness, and the most elaborate Aboriginal rock paintings in Australia. It's also the domain of the prehistoric salt-water crocodile, and for fishermen, it is one of the top Territory spots for barramundi. Along the way, there are a number of worthwhile places of interest including Conservation Commission Reserves, and the broad expanse of the Marrakai Plains gives a taste of floodplain, billabong and birdlife delights to come. Although the Wet season restricts some access, travel to a number of attractions and all commercial establishments in Kakadu is possible at this time.

Entry fee to the Park (valid for 2 weeks) is $10 per adult. There is no fee for children under 16 years.

A camping fee of $7 applies to developed campgrounds at Merl, Muriella Park, Mardugal and Gunlom.

A special annual fee applies to regular visitors and local residents.

Permits are required to camp outside designated areas, and can be obtained from the Park Visitor Centre, ph (089) 799 101.

Attractions

Places and attractions for the region are sequentially listed from the Stuart and Arnhem Highway junction. Landscape, flora and fauna representative of the region are detailed under the Kakadu National Park listing, and climate is outlined in the introduction to The Top End.

Crocodile Country

Salt-water crocodiles lurk in billabongs, rivers and coastal areas, while freshwater crocs may inhabit the pools of the escarpment and gorge country. Salties are definitely dangerous and lethal; respect the crocodile warning signs and ANPWS advice. There are a number of safe ways to see these huge reptiles, and any notions that literature and croc warning signs are designed to add a touch of drama to Kakadu, are totally without foundation. Crocodile attacks, resulting in a few deaths, have happened! Freshwater species, while generally regarded as being harmless to man, have been known to attack air mattresses in Kakadu at Twin Falls. Don't be blase about 'freshies', and do not provoke them!

Swimming

Salt-water crocodiles in the region, and the sometimes unpredictable behaviour of freshwater crocodiles, do not guarantee absolutely safe swimming in natural waters anywhere in the region. While it is common for people to swim in the pools at Twin Falls, Jim Jim Falls, Gunlom and Barramundi Gorge at Kakadu, and at Leaning Tree Lagoon, it is at the swimmers' own risk. ANPWS advice for Kakadu is simple: No swimming anywhere in natural waterways.

Fishing and Hunting

With a few exceptions, fishing is allowed throughout the region. Because of pressures, fishing in the Mary River system has special bag limits - 2 barramundi per person per day, and they must be over 50cm in length. For other areas, Territory bag limits and regulations apply. Fishing is allowed in designated places in Kakadu. Refer also to fishing in the Information and Advice section. Hunting is not allowed unless through licensed safari operators (no hunting in Kakadu).

Pets and Parks

All pets are prohibited from Kakadu National Park. All Conservation Commission Parks have new regulations - check with their offices.

Environmental Respect

All parks and reserves are fully protected, and visitors are asked to be mindful of regulations designed to maintain their wilderness quality.

Touring Suggestions

For the independent traveller, a round trip beginning either at Pine Creek via the Kakadu Highway, or the Arnhem Highway, avoids back-tracking. Budget several days if you can - once you have read through the range of attractions, it will be appreciated that a day trip to Kakadu gives only a cursory insight. Fogg Dam for birdlife is highly recommended while in Kakadu, at least the Yellow Water cruise, and visits to art sites and escarpment and waterfalls in the south of the park should be undertaken. If possible, take a half hour flight over floodplain, lowland and Arnhem Land - it's good value at $50 per person.

The Arnhem Land tour (Lord of Kakadu Tours) is brilliant for its unique Aboriginal art sites and landscape interpretation.

Extended touring via Arnhem Land to the Cobourg Peninsula (Gurig National Park) is another option, but there is a limit on vehicle numbers allowed to enter Arnhem Land each week, so you may need to make early application for permits.

HUMPTY DOO

Population 4000

Location

On the Arnhem Highway, 11km (7 miles) east of the Stuart Highway, and 45km (28 miles) from Darwin.

Characteristics

The world's largest crocodile replica, complete with red-lit eyes and boxing gloves, leaves no doubt that you are entering 'croc' country and Humpty Doo. The settlement is mainly a service centre for the Darwin rural belt, and has most basic facilities and services.

History

The Humpty Doo Rice Growing Project, initiated in 1956 using water stored by nearby Fogg Dam, provided the basis for the township. Rice was first grown here in the 1890s to supply Chinese miners. While the abandonment of the scheme in the early 1960s depressed the township's development, recent growth of rural small-holdings and tourism have given it new life.

The derivation of Humpty Doo is the cause of much conjecture amongst locals. At one stage it was spelt Umpty Doo, and some feel it is a shortened version of a 26-letter Aboriginal word.

Attractions

Crocodile Replica. Outside the Bush Shop supermarket complex.

Graeme Gows Reptile World. Located on the highway in the township, the establishment features an excellent representative collection of Australian snakes and lizards, including a few film stars! Crocodile Dundee's snake called 'Hoges', along with others which have starred in movies, can be seen. Open 9am-5.30pm daily, costs $4 adult, $3 pensioner, $2 children, ph (089) 881 661.

Fogg Dam. See separate listing.

Humpty Doo Hotel. While it's of 1972 vintage, the pub exudes plenty of Territorian character, and the walls are adorned with some interesting memorabilia, including a set of buffalo horns measuring 178cm (5 ft 10 ins) between tips. Highlight of the year is the annual Darwin Stubby Drinking Competition, held in September. The 2 litre stubby (the world's largest bottle of beer) was downed in the record time of 90 seconds a few years ago!

Bebbie's Place. Waldo and Sue Bayley run a home-based leather and barramundi skin craft industry which includes buffalo horns as well. You can watch Waldo in action, purchase goods (horns from $70), indulge in a 'barra' bbq lunch ($15, min 6 persons), drink free coffee or tea, or be photographed with their pet buffalo. Located in Acacia Road, open 7am-6pm, credit cards accepted (Bankcard, Amex, Visa), ph (089) 881 258.

Accommodation

Humpty Doo Hotel - Rooms $35 double. Open 10am-10pm, credit cards accepted (Bankcard, Mastercard, Visa), ph (089) 881 372.

Services and Facilities

Hotel, Dining Room (Hotel - Bistro, main $15, entree $7, counter meals from $5.50), take-away food, 2 supermarkets, post office. Commonwealth Bank agency, ice, souvenirs, medical, full vehicle services, fuel (super, ULP, diesel), church, golf course.

FOGG DAM CONSERVATION RESERVE

1569ha (3875 acres)

Location

6km (4 miles) north of the Arnhem Highway, from the turn-off 11km (7 miles) east of Humpty Doo.

Characteristics

The reserve features a low dam that provides a refuge and breeding ground for large numbers of water birds, including magpie geese, ducks, herons, egrets, ibis, brolgas, and the rainbow pitta. During the Dry season, the permanent water attracts birds from the dried billabongs to the east, and sunrise and sunset are the most spectacular times for viewing this abundant and diverse wildlife.

The dam was built in the 1950s to regulate water for an ambitious, but short-lived, rice growing project. Its failure was due to management, bird, buffalo and insect problems. The magpie geese even became adept at intercepting the aerial-sown seeds before they reached the ground!

How To Get There

An all-weather sealed road makes it accessible for all vehicles.

Facilities and Activities

Basic picnic facilities. Future plans include toilets and general upgrading. Camping and pets are not allowed. Fishing is not permitted, nor is boating. Salt-water crocodiles prevent swimming.

****

ADELAIDE RIVER CROSSING

Location

27km (17 miles) east of the Stuart Highway.

Features

Two and a half hour river cruises on *The Adelaide River Queen* depart from the pavilion, located on the western bank of the wide, grey-green waters. The double-decker, shallow drafted vessel cruises about 12km (7 miles) upstream, and allows some fine viewing of wildlife including crocodiles, pigs and diverse birdlife. 'Croc' feeding sessions from the boat demonstrate the awesome speed and power of the reptile as it lunges from the water to grab its 'prey'.

Tours

The tour schedules vary so it may be a good idea to book ahead - PO Box 37913, Winnellie, NT, 0821, ph (089) 888 144, fax (089) 888 130. There are two tour options: a 2.5 hour cruise leaving from the pavilion - $28 adult, $14 child; a half-day tour, with pick up from Darwin hotels, and travel in air-conditioned coach to the Adelaide River via Fogg Dam or another attraction - $55 adult, $45 child.

Services and Facilities

On board, the lower deck is air-conditioned and has snack/drinks galley. The Pavilion includes a kiosk, coffee shop and toilets. Open 8am-5pm, credit cards accepted (Bankcard, Visa, Amex, Diners), enquiries - ph (089) 878 989.

****

LEANING TREE LAGOON NATURE PARK

101ha (249 acres)

Location

On the Arnhem Highway, 46km (28 miles) from the Stuart Highway.

Features

A large, isolated freshwater lagoon is a refuge for water birds during the Dry season, and a popular spot for picnickers, campers and canoeists. Technically, it's a shallow, perched (raised) billabong that is regularly checked by salt-water crocodiles by Conservation Commission Officers.

How To Get There

The track leading from the Highway provides conventional vehicle access.

Services and Facilities

Limited facilities. Camping is allowed. No fishing. Dogs - designated areas only.

****

CORROBOREE PARK TAVERN

Population 5

Location

On the Arnhem Highway, 67km (42 miles) from the Stuart Highway turn-off.

Characteristics

Located on the Marrakai Plains, this roadhouse has an attractive setting and offers travellers a wide range of services. It is an information centre, and even has an albino buffalo.

It is 1km from the turn-off to good fishing at Corroboree Lagoon.

Accommodation

Rooms $46-$60 per night.
  Caravans - powered sites $12.50. Camping - $5 per person.

Services and Facilities

It has a bar, bistro meals, take-away food, ice, souvenirs, artifacts, and fuel (super, ULP, diesel), oil and camping gas. Open 7am-10.30pm (bar opens 10am) 7 days, all year, ph (089) 788 920.

****

CORROBOREE CREEK AND LAGOON

Location

On the western side of the Mary River System, 8km (5 miles) due west of Wildman River Station, or 15km (9 miles) north-east of Leaning Tree Lagoon.

Characteristics

The Creek links a number of billabongs, of which Corroboree Lagoon is most noted as one of the best barramundi fishing spots in the region. It is also a wildlife mecca - rich in birdlife and crocodiles, and where buffalo, pig, wallabies, as well as the occasional dingo, may be seen. Even if you are not keen on fishing, the diverse wildlife and wetland billabong scenery offers plenty of interest. Houseboats, moored along the creek, are a novel way of leisurely exploring the billabongs. Contact Mary River House Boats, ph (089) 886 197, for self-contained 4 or 6 berth, drive yourself, boat hire details. Bookings well in advance are advised.

How To Get There

Public access is via Wild Boar Station (no permission required) from the highway turn-off, 200m (218 yds) east of Leaning Tree Lagoon. The 15km (9 miles) track, while rough in places, can be negotiated by conventional vehicles. An alternative way is by boat from the Rock Hole (Wildman River Reserve) through a system of channels and billabongs - a distance of 7km (4 miles).

Services and Facilities

Basic camping only at the lagoon.

****

MARY RIVER CROSSING RESERVE

2590ha (6397 acres)

Location

At the Mary River Crossing (just off the Highway), 25km (15 miles) east of Leaning Tree Lagoon.

Characteristics

Another delightful spot which features several permanent billabongs, floodplain vegetation, Dry season habitat for many water birds, salt-water crocodiles, and barramundi. The floodplain landscape is broken by rocky granite outcrops, which provide a home for the black wallaroo and short-eared rock wallaby. It is a popular area for fishing, boating, wildlife and scenery. Large salt-water crocodiles prohibit swimming.

How To Get There

With care, the tracks are suitable for conventional vehicles during the Dry season. Early or late rains can cause problems.

Services and Facilities

Picnic, toilet, bbq and boat ramp. Fishing and camping allowed. Dogs must be leashed and confined to designated areas.

****

BARK HUT INN

Population 15

Location

On the Arnhem Highway, 81km (50 miles) east of the Stuart Highway.

Characteristics

The long, low roadside inn is an architectural replica of the original Annaburroo Station homestead, established in 1918. The stout bush timber construction, and vast array of historical artifacts and hunting trophies hanging from the inside walls, gives the inn a well-worn welcoming character, despite its recent establishment around 1975. It is a popular pub on the way to Kakadu, and owners Jeff and Sharon Swaine have added a wildlife enclosure which includes buffalo, pigs, donkeys, kangaroos, wallabies and emus.

Accommodation

Budget motel, powered and unpowered grassed, shaded camping sites. Pets are not allowed.

Services and Facilities

General store, bar, counter meals, take-away food, ice, artifacts, souvenirs, showers for travellers, and picnic/bbq/shaded area. Vehicle services include fuel (super, ULP, diesel), oil and limited spares. Open all year, 7 days, 7am-midnight. Credit cards accepted (Bankcard, Mastercard, Visa), ph (089) 788 988.

****

WILDMAN RIVER RESERVE
24,649ha (60,883 acres)

Location

Approximately 25km (15 miles) due north of Bark Hut Inn.

Characteristics

The reserve straddles billabongs, floodplains and paperbark forests of the Mary River system, and takes its name directly from the Wildman Station homestead (now owned by the Conservation Commission), not the Wildman River which is further east in Kakadu National Park. It offers plenty of scope for boating, barramundi fishing, bird watching, crocodile spotting, and landscape appreciation. A notable feature is the Rock Hole - a large billabong that's a popular fishing spot.

At the end of the access road is Point Stuart, the place where explorer John McDouall Stuart finally reached the north coast, after his heroic south-north crossing of the continent in 1862.

Tours

Wimray Safaris operate a number of tours from their Lodge near the old station homestead (refer to Wildman Safari Lodge listing).

How To Get There

The park is closed to all vehicles during the Wet season. Access is via the Point Stuart formed gravel road for approximately 15km (9 miles), then left for about 6km (4 miles) to the Rock Hole. The Point Stuart Road turn-off is 18km (11 miles) east of Bark Hut Inn. A further 10km (6 miles) along the Point Stuart road leads to a left hand turn-off to The Wildman Safari Lodge, while Shady Camp lies another 25km (15 miles) to the north. With care, conventional vehicles and trailers can reach these places, but check road conditions first.

Services and Facilities

Basic picnic only and boat ramp. Camping and fishing allowed. Please use only dead litter for firewood - for environmental reasons it's preferable to take in your own, or use gas for cooking. Animals by permit only.

****

WILDMAN SAFARI LODGE

Location

In the middle of Wildman River Reserve, 200m (218 yds) from the Wildman River Station Homestead.

Characteristics

A safari lodge, situated in rainforest, floodplain, billabong terrain of the Mary River system, is base camp for a range of activities (fishing, crocodile spotting, birdwatching, photography) run by Wimray Safaris. Ray Allwright leads some exciting excursions into tropical wetland wilderness, and knows the best spots for the prized barramundi. Visits are by prior arrangement only, and safaris can be tailored to suit individual or group needs.

How To Get There

By air: Wimray operate transfers from Darwin to their Lodge airstrip, or you can fly in by private light aircraft.
By road: Wimray can arrange transport. For independent visitors, the Lodge is 25km (15 miles) north along the Point Stuart Road, then a sign-posted track to the left leads 7km (4 miles) to the Lodge. For road conditions, refer to Wildman River Reserve listing.

Tours and Accommodation

Safaris, including lodge accommodation, cost $180 per day per person. Day tours are also offered from Darwin. Contact Wimray Safaris, ph (089) 410 015, fax (089) 452 731.

****

SHADY CAMP RESERVE

Location

On the Mary River, approximately 56km (35 miles) north of the turn-off, 18km (11 miles) east of Bark Hut Inn.

Characteristics

An attractive floodplain billabong, fringed with pandanus and swamp paperbarks, offers excellent barramundi fishing, prolific birdlife, and some fine camping spots. It is also the confluence of tidal salt-water and inland freshwater, so there are plenty of fish and large estuarine crocodiles about! The crocodiles can be a problem if visitors gut and deposit fish remains near the water, and it is particularly dangerous for children and dogs along the billabong banks.

How To Get There

Access is via the Point Stuart Road. Refer to Wildman River Reserve listing for details.

Services and Facilities

Boat ramp, bbq and limited picnic. Camping and animals by permit.

****

KAKADU NATIONAL PARK

19,000 sq km (7220 sq miles)

Location

Encompassing the catchments of the Alligator Rivers, 220km (136 miles) east of Darwin.

Characteristics

Kakadu National Park, included on the United Nations' World Heritage List and Wetlands of International Importance Register, is not only one of the most spectacular, but also one of the most popular parks in Australia. Dissected plateau, rugged sandstone escarpment,

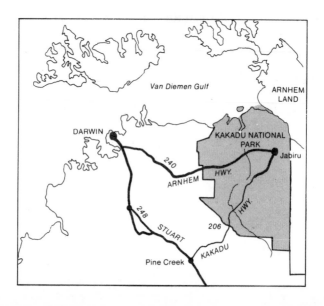

and outliers, gorges and waterfalls, lowland savannah and woodland, vast floodplain tracts, grey-green rivers and sparkling billabongs, provide a basis for diverse vegetation and prolific wildlife. Apart from the magnificent scenery and busy billabong birdlife and crocodiles, an Aboriginal presence of at least 30,000 years has left a priceless heritage of rock art, the scale and scope of which is regarded by some as being as great as, and older than, the Palaeolithic art sites of France and Spain.

Within the park, the township of Jabiru, Frontier Kakadu Village, Gagudju Lodge Cooinda and Border Stores, are establishments that provide a wide range of tourist services (these places are separately listed).

Because of the yearly rhythms of Wet, Dry and transitional seasons, marked landscape changes occur - to appreciate this you need at least a Wet or green season visit as well. Don't expect a lush tropical jungle brimming with wildlife as you drive in during the height of the Dry season. At this time, the landscape from the Southern Pine Creek entrance is a dusty-brown. But the billabongs and shaded gorges, not seen from the main access road, are verdant and teem with wildlife.

To appreciate the park's massive 200km (124 miles) north-south by 100km (62 miles) east-west dimensions, as well as its rich biological, escarpment and cultural features, a few days' stay is necessary. Some express disappointment with Kakadu - hardly surprising when they only visit a billabong and an art site on a day trip from Darwin!

Some of the most startling landscape features are Jim Jim and Twin Falls, Barramundi Gorge and Gunlom (Waterfall Creek), all to the south. Here, the isolated pools, while containing freshwater crocodiles, are mainly free of 'salties', but it pays to check at Park Headquarters. In addition to land based exploration and boat trips, a half-hour scenic flight over the park offers exciting unparalleled viewing.

History

Aborigines first set foot on the Australian continent at a time when sea levels were much lower, and a partial land bridge provided a link to Asia. The first Australians have left their traces in some 5000 archaeological sites throughout the park. These include 20,000-year-old edge-ground stone axes (one of the earliest records of stone grinding technology in the world) and paintings on the walls of rock over-hang shelters. Archaeological artifacts remain in situ at many of the sites, and must not be removed or disturbed in any way - even innocent looking stones may in fact be artifacts.

There is sufficient evidence that Aborigines have lived in Kakadu for at least 50,000 years. It is one of the few places where the original inhabitants maintain strong personal and spiritual links with their traditional lands. About 300 descendants of the original clans live semi-traditionally in Kakadu today, and many are involved in various facets of the park's operation.

> Kakadu is a phonetic rendering of Gagadju, the name of the traditional owners of the land. It's thought a European mis-heard the name, wrote down Kakadu, and it has stuck ever since. British explorer and navigator Phillip King charted Van Diemen Gulf in 1818, noted the large river estuaries, and named the Alligator Rivers after one of the ships.

Several British attempts to establish settlements on the coast (Cobourg Peninsula) between 1824 and 1840 failed, but their major legacy remains today - the buffalo. While adding a touch of bovine beauty to the park, the beasts' days are numbered because of the environmental damage they cause. From 50 or so set free with the abandonment of the Cobourg Peninsula settlements in the 1840s, their numbers increased to around 175,000 in the Top End by the 1970s. While a few thousand remain today, policy is to eradicate them from the park and commercially farm them outside. Cattle stations were established in the 1880s, but distance and disease brought about the demise of many a decade later. Pastoralist and drover Paddy Cahill held original leases here and at Oenpelli, and also hunted buffalo in the 1890s. The East Alligator River crossing is named after him.

Explorer Ludwig Leichhardt came this way in 1844 on his long trek from the east, met friendly Aborigines, reported an abundance of buffalo, and discovered some of the rock art sites.

Four major mining leases were granted before Aboriginal land rights and the park establishment. One area has been rehabilitated, and the operating Ranger Uranium Mine produces 3000 tonnes of uranium oxide (yellow cake). Its operation within the park is a continuing contentious issue for environmentalists and politicians. Today, Kakadu is owned in both traditional and contemporary law by Aborigines and leased to the Australian National Parks and Wildlife Service (ANPWS). The Gagadju Association represents Aboriginal interests, and they work closely with the ANPWS in the management and planning of Kakadu. Aboriginal people are willing to share some of their knowledge and understanding of the land in the hope that visitors will learn to appreciate the importance of Kakadu, and share responsibility for its protection.

Landscapes

While the tidal flats, floodplains and lowlands each have their unique wilderness qualities, the soaring craggy escarpment is the park's most outstanding geological feature. It varies from vertical cliffs to stepped rocky outcrops, rises to 300m (98 ft) above the lowlands, ranges for 500km (310 miles) and marks the edge of the Arnhem Land Plateau. Outliers (isolated rock outcrops), such as Ubirr (Obiri Rock) are remnants of former plateau edges - in fact, it is thought that the escarpment is retreating at a rate of 1m (3 ft) every 1000 years.

The rock is quartz sandstone, horizontally bedded over older granites and formed by sand deposits under a shallow sea about 2,000 million years ago. Consolidation and probably slow uplift created this vast sandstone block criss-crossed with joint planes (faults). Eons of weathering and the action of running water have deeply dissected the plateau along these fault lines, leaving impressive gorges, and fragmenting the escarpment rock into huge angular blocks, some of which perch precariously one on top of the other. The awe-inspiring, weirdly weathered shapes of the escarpment are further highlighted by the suffusion of soft, golden colours in the late afternoon sun.

During the Wet season, massive volumes of water pour from the plateau, and spectacular waterfalls thunder over the edge. The intricate river systems swell and not only inundate the floodplains, but also link and lend life to the various Kakadu landscapes.

Flora

Over 1000 plant species find a niche in Kakadu.

Tidal Flats: 22 mangrove varieties, pandanus, acacia and eugenic rainforest, while samphire, sedges and grasses grow on the mud flats.

Floodplains: Annual grasses, sedges; swamp paperbarks, freshwater mangroves fringe billabongs. Red lotus lilies float on, while yellow flowering lilies grow near billabongs. On higher ground grow acacias, pandanus and ficus (fig).

Lowlands: Are characterised by closed forest pockets, open woodlands and grassland with local variations due to soil, water and micro-climatic differences. Eucalyptus miniata (Darwin woollybutt) and E. terodonto (stringybark) dominate. Others include ghost gums, banyan, grevilleas and acacias.

Escarpment/Plateau: Rainforests in gorges and shady areas include Allosyncarpia ternata, cottonwood, mosses, ferns and orchids. On the plateau are heaths, spinifex and grasses.

Fauna

There are at least 50 mammal, 275 bird, 75 reptile, 25 frog, 55 fish, and approximately 10,000 insect species. Buffalo, pig, horse, cattle, cats and dogs are feral species. During the Dry season, the lagoons and billabongs, creeks and rivers magically reappear as the plains drain and dry, thus concentrating wildlife. Early morning is the best time to see and photograph birdlife as this is prime feeding time. Birdlife represents one-third of all Australia's types, and the vast flocks of magpie geese around the billabongs are a fascinating and photogenic sight. **King of this domain is the awesome salt-water crocodile, now the trendiest in the popularity stakes of Australia's diverse wildlife.**

A sample of wildlife in the Park is as follows:

Tidal Flats: Boobies, cormorants, curlews, greenshanks, herons, ospreys, oyster catchers, plovers, rails, sand pipers, egrets, mangrove robins, and warblers, are some birds. Estuarine crocodiles, dugongs, turtles and snakes.

Floodplains: Burdekin duck, magpie and pigmy geese, pelicans, ibis, pied and white-faced herons, egrets, jabiru (stork), lotus bird, honey eaters, king fishers, sea eagles, letterwing kite, yellow chat and brolgas. Agile wallaby, dingo, crocodile, water python, feral animals, reptiles and frogs. Silver barramundi or giant perch, ox-eye herring, fork-tailed catfish and mullet are some freshwater species of interest to fishermen.

Lowlands: Wedge-tail eagle, sparrow hawk, black and whistling kite, honey and bee eater, friar bird, flycatcher, finches, cuckoo shrike, parrot, cockatoo, pheasant concal, and quail, with bustard and emu rarer. Termite hills, dingo, bandicoot, kangaroo, hare wallaby, euro, quoll (native cat), snakes and smaller reptiles.

Escarpment/Plateau: In rainforest areas, jungle fowl, rainbow pittas, Torres Strait and banded pigeons, white-lined honey eater, while on the plateau, chestnut quilled rock pigeon and white-throated grass wren. Animals include goanna, bat, flying fox, agile wallaby in rainforest; narbalek, short-eared rock wallaby, echidna and snakes elsewhere.

Information

The Park Visitor Centre, on Kakadu Highway, is open daily 8am-5pm, and has a wealth of information and displays about the Park. Enquiries and bookings for tours can be made at the Jabiru Tourist Centre, ph (089) 792 548; from Kakadu Air, ph (089) 792 411; Gagudju Crocodile Hotel; Gagudju Lodge Cooinda; Frontier Kakadu Village; and Frontier Lodge and Caravan Park, Jabiru.

Attractions

Yellow Water. As the billabong contracts during the Dry season, the concentrated nutrients produce an algae which gives the waters a distinct yellow tinge. A two-hour boat trip where you can spot crocodiles at close range and observe an incredible array of birdlife in a paperbark, mangrove fringed billabong, is a must. See Cooinda listing for details. Facilities include toilet and boat ramp. Fishing allowed, but no camping.

Rock Art Sites. Three major sites are open to visitors during daylight hours (closed at night): *Anbangbang* and *Nanguluwur* Galleries at *Nourlangie* and *Ubirr (Obiri Rock)*. Aboriginal art reflects much deeper spiritual and cultural relationships with the natural environment than the outwardly simplistic drawings of animals, beings and objects suggest. Artists evolved highly stylised symbols among others, designed mainly to communicate traditional cultural beliefs. Paintings are not an idea of the moment, as in much western art; rather it is a honed down record of essential aspects of their

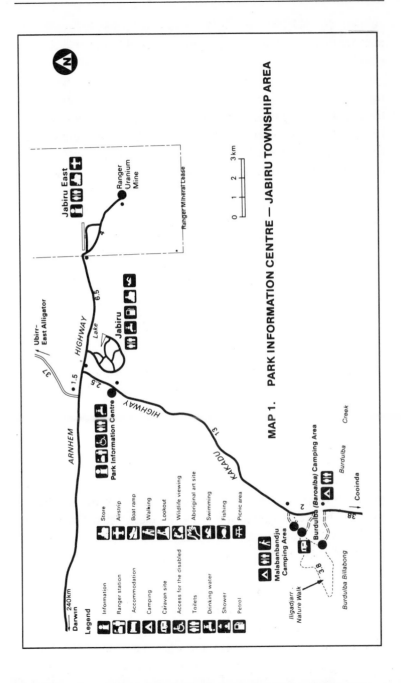

MAP 1. PARK INFORMATION CENTRE — JABIRU TOWNSHIP AREA

culture, the precise meaning of which is generally obscure to non-Aborigines. All art has strong mythological links to the past and some sites are sacred because of the special knowledge they contain.

Other Aboriginal art forms, such as bark and sand paintings, also represent similar links with the past, and contemporary works follow the tradition of significant messages being economically conveyed. Historically, environmental differences throughout the Territory and Kimberley have spawned a wealth of subject and artistic styles, while further evolution and complexity is seen in the works of present-day artists.

Periods of the various styles and motifs provide a useful basis for art appreciation in Kakadu. The early period (more than 20,000 years ago) features object imprints; animals such as the Thylacine (Tasmanian Tiger) at Ubirr represent a Naturalistic Period (up to 20,000 years ago); Stylisation and Symbolism is typical of 15,000 years ago and characterised by animals, humans, weapons and mythological figures, while the intricate 'X-ray' depictions which show the internal organs and skeletons of barramundi, crocodile and 'Lightning Man', introduce a Realism period. The last 1000 years saw the evolution of more decorative 'X-ray' subjects, while contact with Macassans (people from the Indonesian Island of Sulawesi) and Europeans, produced depictions of boats, buffalo, horses and guns. Apart from their intrinsic value to Aborigines, the subject matter offers a fascinating window on past environmental conditions and human activities.

Rock Art Conservation. To protect the ancient rock art, visitors are asked to observe two simple rules: Do not touch painted surfaces or interfere with sites in any way, and follow directional signs by keeping to marked paths and walking trails.

Ubirr (Obiri Rock) Art Site. The main gallery contains some of the best examples of Rock Art in Australia, while another rock overhang has a series of paintings including a Warrior frieze. A loop walking track provides access designed for wheelchairs too. The outlier

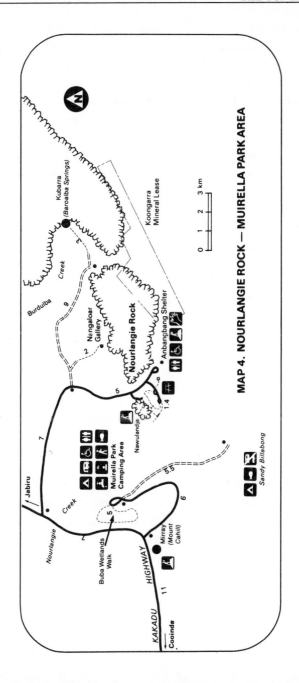

MAP 4. NOURLANGIE ROCK — MUIRELLA PARK AREA

shapes add landscape interest, and a walk to the lookout gives sweeping views across lowland and plain. Facilities include a carpark, picnic, drinking water, toilets including for the disabled, interpretative display and brochures (it's wise to get one at park headquarters first). Ranger guided tours during the season. Open 2pm-sunset (December 1 to May 31); 8.30am-sunset other times.

Other things of interest in the **Ubirr East Alligator River Area** include a day-use area (toilets, boat ramp, fishing), Bardedjilildji and Manngarre short walks, Cahill's Crossing to Arnhemland (a permit is required to enter Arnhemland so please obey signs at causeway), Border Store (see separate listing), Youth Hostel, Merl camping ground and ranger station. **A formed gravel road, dusty with corrugations in the Dry, impassable during the Wet, and suitable for conventional vehicles, leads to the site**.

Nourlangie Rock Art Site. The Anbangbang Shelter has been a home for Aborigines for at least 20,000 years and archaeological evidence points to more frequent usage during the last 6000, when environmental change brought a more hospitable climate and abundant food resources. The gallery, smaller in scope than Ubirr, has some magnificent mythological figures including 'Lightning Man'. An interesting nature trail to a lookout leads from the gallery.

Nangaloar Gallery is another art site on the northern side of Nourlangie Rock (Burrung-gui). An interesting 3-4km walk (about 1.5-2 hours return) leads to the gallery which has mythical beings, hand stencils and a ship of the contact art period.

Facilities include car park, access tracks to main art galleries suitable for wheelchairs, interpretative displays, walks and lookouts, picnic and toilet, including for the disabled. There's a good sealed road to the site.

Jim Jim Falls. Located in the southern part of the park via a 4WD only track, the falls plunge dramatically 200m (654 ft) from the escarpment edge. While little or no water falls during the Dry, awesome volumes provide spectacular viewing from the air during the Wet season. Rugged escarpment scenery, deep plunge pool, freshwater crocodiles, sandy beaches, exhilarating walk to the plateau, and fine camping, make it one of the scenic highlights of the park. Facilities include pit toilets, walks and camping area.

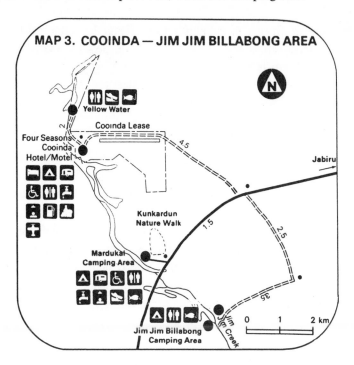

MAP 3. COOINDA — JIM JIM BILLABONG AREA

Twin Falls. Located 10km (6 miles) south of Jim Jim via a 4WD track which includes fording Jim Jim Creek. Extreme care is needed with this crossing. Most visitors take the 'easiest' route to the falls - via a series of short swims and rock scrambles up the gorge, but it's definitely for the fit and energetic, and some find an air mattress helpful. But, freshwater crocodiles are present, and you take this route at your own risk. The other alternative is by a rugged walk and climb.

Not only does water cascade down in two places, but ferns and other greenery give the stepped waterfall face a hanging garden appearance. A fine natural pool, sandy verges, and pockets of rainforest, make it an idyllic spot. Freshwater crocodiles and a walk to the top add further interest. **There are no facilities and camping is not allowed. 4WD tours to Jim Jim and Twin Falls are available.**

Barramundi Gorge. A delightful walk along the rainforest-lined series of pools, rapids, and beaches of the gorge, leads to a large main waterhole. There is plenty of birdlife and freshwater crocs in this verdant spot. Camping is allowed - pit toilets are the only facility. Located in the southern part of Kakadu, access is via a 10km (6 miles) 4WD track from the Kakadu Highway.

Gunlom (Waterfall Creek). Formerly Waterfall Creek Nature Park managed by the Conservation Commission, this feature is now incorporated into the Third Stage of Kakadu National Park. Access is suitable for conventional vehicles and caravans during the Dry Season, but check road conditions first. One of the locations for the film *Crocodile Dundee*, Gunlom features a 100m (327 ft) waterfall, a huge, deep pandanus and paperbark fringed pool, sandy beaches, large flat rocks to meditate or sun-bathe on, freshwater crocodiles and energetic bush walks. It has all camping amenities.

Fishing and Boating

All fishing in the park is by hand line or rod using lures only. Cast nets, live bait, traps, spear guns and crab pots are not permitted. These items may be left at Park HQ for safe keeping. Upstream areas are closed for fishing, but check with rangers where fishing is allowed and regulations, as these are subject to change. Territory bag limits apply.

Be aware of crocodile dangers when fishing, and you could be placing yourself and others at risk if you clean fish or leave food waste near water. People in boats should keep away from both species of crocodiles and not harass them.

The East Alligator River is within the park, but please note that the eastern or left bank (when facing upstream) is Arnhem Land (Aboriginal Land) and boats are not allowed to land on this bank. Boating downstream in this tidal river is hazardous - mud bars can span up to 90% of the river channel at low tide; there is no drinkable water downstream of the crossing, and some of the largest crocodiles in Kakadu inhabit the waters. The Visitor Information map details fishing areas and boat ramp locations.

Walking Trails and Lookouts

A number of short and extended tracks provide access to different park habitats. Information on these is available in brochures, Park Information Centre, and on signs along the tracks. Wear a hat and take ample water (billabong water, unless boiled, is unsuitable for drinking). Lookout spots throughout allow excellent landscape viewing. Check with Rangers first if you plan longer walks.

Park Protection and Hazards

Remember that all natural and cultural features in the Park are protected. Don't provoke wildlife. Hunting and firearms are not allowed in the park, and because of bushfire risk, confine all campfires to the fireplaces provided. The cutting of live vegetation is prohibited.

Drive carefully - roads are dusty, and buffalo and other animals on roads, particularly at night, pose a danger. At times areas of the Park may be closed for buffalo eradication purposes - a major reason why visits to remote parts should be checked with rangers first.

Obey crocodile warning signs and be mindful of their presence. Do not 'souvenir' croc warning signs - such action could result in the deaths of other visitors. Buy a replica sign instead, available from souvenir shops and Park HQ. At the risk of repeating myself, do not leave fishing scraps or other wastes around camping areas, boat ramps or water's edge, as these attract crocodiles. Put all scraps in bins provided, or take them away with you. Keep children away from the edges of all natural waterways.

Tours

Plenty of tours within the park, including 4WD, are available through Gagudju Crocodile Hotel, Gagudju Lodge Cooinda, Frontier Kakadu Village and Jabiru East Airport (see also under separate listings). ANPWS offer guided tours in the Dry season.

How To Get There

A number of tour operators and large coach companies offer day and extended tours from Darwin. Air North and Kakadu Air have regular services into Jabiru East from Darwin.

If you fly in, 4WD hire allows independence - if you are not used to these vehicles, Budget (Cooinda and Crocodile Hotel) will give you instruction for their Sierras, but you need to book well in advance. Within the park, roads and tracks (some 4WD) provide conventional vehicle access to the main attractions.

By road, the all-weather Arnhem Highway provides year round access to Frontier Kakadu Village and Jabiru, while the Kakadu Highway provides similar road conditions from Jabiru to Cooinda. The Kakadu Highway from Pine Creek, while gradually being upgraded, is a good formed gravel surface in the Dry, with two river crossings. It's dusty too, with some rough patches in the Dry and with care, suitable for conventional vehicles and trailers. During the Wet it is often closed.

Park Accommodation

Apart from commercial establishments (see separate listings) and Youth Hostel (see Border Store listing), there are four ANPWS camping sites which have showers, flushing toilets, disabled facilities, hot water and drinking water - Gunlom, Mardugal, Muirella Park and Merl (Mel). Along with Malabanbandju, these camping sites are suitable for caravans. All campsites, with the exception of Mardugal, are subject to closure during the Wet season. More isolated designated camping areas are: Two and Four Mile Holes on the Wildman River (the latter is 4WD and has no facilities, Two Mile has pit toilets); Burdulba, Sandy Billabong, Jim Jim Billabong and Alligator Billabong have pit toilets only, while on the Old Darwin Road, Black Jungle Creek Springs and South Alligator River Crossing have no facilities. ANPWS sites have no power, and permits are required for camping outside designated camp grounds.

Facilities

Jabiru township and other commercial establishments have a wide range of services that are detailed following the Kakadu listing. Boat ramps (concrete) are located at the South Alligator River/Kakadu Highway Bridge and at the East Alligator River. Unsealed ramps are found at Muirella Park and Mardugal, Yellow Water, Gadjuduba and Djaburluku Billabongs.

****

FRONTIER KAKADU VILLAGE

Location

In Kakadu National Park, 186km (115 miles) from the Stuart Hwy.

Characteristics

Rainforest, bushland, billabong and grassed areas provide an attractive setting for a complex that offers a range of facilities, accommodation and tours to suit all types of travellers. You don't have to be a guest to enjoy the facilities offered.

Tours

Daily South Alligator River cruises offer an interesting wetland, river and wildlife perspective: the larger vessel *Kakadu Princess* and smaller *Pathfinder* and *Explorer* offer popular 2 hour cruises - adults $24.50. There is a 3-hour cruise ($45 adults) and a 'Wetland Magic' 2.5 hour cruise, Wet Season only, ($28.50 adults).

Accommodation

Motel - double from $110, units suitable for the disabled are available.

Budget - from $27.50 per person (4 share basis).

Camping - powered sites $20 two persons, $7 each extra; unpowered $7 per person.

Sites grassed, shaded. Pets not allowed.

Services and Facilities

The resort has a mini-supermarket, bar, licensed restaurant (3 course meal $25), cafe (blackboard menu, around $10 main course), take-away food, ice, artifacts and souvenirs. Fuel includes super, ULP, diesel and oil. Picnic/bbq areas, billabong rainforest walking track, tennis courts and swimming pool (guests only) are recreational facilities offered. Open 7am-10pm, credit cards accepted (Bankcard, Mastercard, Visa, American Express, Diners), ph (089) 790 166.

****

Jabiru

JABIRU

Population 1500

Location

In Kakadu National Park, 218km (135 miles) from Darwin.

Characteristics

A modern mining town relocated from its former East Jabiru site and established to service the nearby Ranger Uranium Mine. With the popularity of Kakadu, it now has an important tourist function and offers visitors a range of services from the compact, attractively laid-out town centre.

Attractions

Jabiru Lake. A large man-made lake on the residential zone fringe has a small sandy beach, pontoon and gently sloping grassy, shaded banks that make it an ideal family picnicking, boating, sailing and swimming spot. Facilities include picnic, barbecues and toilets.

Gagudju Crocodile Hotel. A 250m long 30m wide, crocodile-shaped and coloured two-storied hotel, where guests enter through the jaws, sleep and dine in the belly and head, may seem rather bizarre, but this is what the Gagudju Association have built. Outwardly, the unique design may appear trendy - in fact the Ginga or giant crocodile is a spirit ancestor of the Gagudju people, and a highly respected totemic figure. From this perspective, the symbolism embodied in the design is appropriate. The reptilian theme dominates the 110 room complex. The circular car parking areas represent crocodile eggs; gaping jaws complete with teeth herald visitors, while ventilation units are housed within the slatted yellow eyes. The head section contains foyer, shops, restaurants and bars. All guest rooms are located within the belly section overlooking an internal courtyard. The shaded pool and barbecue in the courtyard represent the heart, the walkway the spine, and the flowing billabong is the croc's alimentary canal. A lushly landscaped courtyard and a paving representation of an X-ray bark painting complete an innovative internal design.

Facilities include bars (11am-2am), restaurant ($15-20 main course, 4 course buffet style $32, specialties are barramundi, crocodile and buffalo), craft and coffee shop (open from 10.30am). It is a tour-booking agent, and also runs conducted tours of the hotel according to demand.

Tours

Ranger Uranium Mine: 60 minute conducted tours of the mine depart from Jabiru East Airport, $8. Telephone (089) 792 411 for tour times, or book through Gagudju Crocodile Hotel or Gagudju Lodge Cooinda.

Kakadu Air: Scenic half-hour and hour flights over the floodplains escarpment and Arnhem Land are highly recommended for an exhilarating, wider perspective of landscape and wildlife. Cost is $90 one hour, ph (089) 792 411.

Accommodation

Gagudju Crocodile Hotel: rooms from $168 a double. Credit cards accepted (Bankcard, Mastercard, Visa, American Express, Diners), ph (089) 792 800.

Frontier Lodge and Caravan Park, Jabiru: rooms from $80 (including linen) - 4 persons, or $22 per person on a share basis.

Camping - powered sites $20 for two, unpowered $8 per person. Disabled facilities, ph (089) 792 422.

Services and Facilities

Jabiru provides a wide range of services; open 6 days 8am-5pm, and credit cards are widely accepted. There is a police station, post office, medical centre, dentist, supermarket, newsagent, chemist, bank (Westpac) take-away food, ice, artifacts and souvenirs. A church is being used by Catholics on Saturday evening and Uniting Church on Sunday. Territory Rent-A-Car (Gagudju Crocodile Hotel) and Cheapa (Jabiru Airport) have hire vehicles. Vehicle services, repairs and fuel (super, ULP, diesel, autogas, camping gas). A swimming pool complex is the main recreational facility.

Radio Stations: ABC 8JB 747; 107.7 FM.

Emergency Services

Police, ph (089) 792 122; Medical and First Aid, ph (089) 792 018 or 792 102.

****

GAGUDJU LODGE COOINDA

Location

In Kakadu National Park, 290km (180 miles) east of Darwin, and 59km (37 miles) south-west of Jabiru.

Characteristics

Attractively sited amidst massive mango trees and fragrant frangipanni near Yellow Water Billabong, this 'experiential destination resort' offers comfortable accommodation, swimming pool (motel guests only), camping ground, restaurant and an open, shaded bistro and beer garden. It is a low key complex, ideal both as a base for park exploration, and relaxation. The name Cooinda bodes well too - it means 'happy meeting place'.

Tours

Booking agents for a range of tours. It also runs five Yellow Water Boat Tours daily - $22.50 for 2 hours, $19.50 for 1.5 hours (children half price). This tour offers intimate viewing of a billabong environment where diverse birdlife and crocodiles can be seen at a close, safe range. Tour guides give excellent commentaries and this is one tour that should not be missed. Bookings are essential.

Kakadu Gorge and Waterfall Tours offer a day 4WD excursion for $115.

Accommodation

Motel - double $116. Budget - backpacker $12 per person.

Camping - powered sites $6.50 per person. Unpowered $3.50 per person.

Sites grassed, shaded. Pets not allowed.

Services and Facilities

The motel has a bar, counter meals (purchase 'cook your own' bbq meat packs), bbq, restaurant (a la carte - main course $13-20), take-away food, mini-supermarket, ice, artifacts, souvenirs, Budget hire vehicles, tourist information and airstrip. Fuel includes super, ULP, diesel, camping gas and oil. Emergency vehicle repairs and towing only. Open all year, 7 days, 6.30am-11pm, credit cards accepted (Bankcard, Mastercard, Visa), ph (089) 790 145.

MANBIYARRA - BORDER STORE

Location

Near Obiri Rock in Kakadu National Park, approximately 40km (25 miles) north-east of Jabiru.

Characteristics

Manbiyarra, thought to mean 'old man', is a Gagadju Association operated store situated close to the rock art galleries of Ubirr and the East Alligator River, which marks the eastern boundary of the National Park. Nearby Cahill's Crossing is the gateway to Arnhem Land which provides 4WD access across Aboriginal land to Gurig National Park. Permits are required to enter Arnhem Land.

Accommodation

Youth Hostel - located behind Border Store, the hostel has a limited number of beds ($12 per person). While listed under Border Store, the Youth Hostel is an independent establishment. May be closed Dec-Mar due to regional flooding. Bookings are advised, ph (089) 792 985 when hostel is open, otherwise YHA-NT Head Office (089) 843 902.

Services and Facilities

The shop sells groceries, drinks, pies, pasties, ice, souvenirs, Aboriginal artifacts and petrol. It has a welcome shaded eating area with tables. Open weekdays 8.30am-5pm, weekends and public holidays 8.30am-4pm, cash only, ph (089) 792 474.

****

MARY RIVER ROADHOUSE

Location

By the Mary River on the Kakadu Highway 60 kms (37 miles) north-east of Pine Creek.

Characteristics

A recent colonial style roadhouse serves travellers entering the southern part of Kakadu National Park. It has bunkhouse accommodation, single rooms ($18 per person), campsites ($4 per person). Other services are takeaway food, drinks, meals, bar, ice, souvenirs, fuel (Super, ULP, diesel), oil. Open 7am-11pm and as required, ph (089) 754 564.

Billabong, Kakadu National Park

ARNHEM LAND

Population 5000

Location

Stretches east from the East Alligator River to the Gulf of Carpentaria.

Characteristics

A huge area of dissected plateau country, first proclaimed a reserve in the 1930s, is now owned by the Aborigines who live traditionally and semi-traditionally in scattered communities. The region has a rich heritage of art sites, some of which surpass even the magnificent Kakadu galleries in age, scope and style. Artists of the oldest continuing culture in the world have left their traces, particularly in some remarkable cave and rock overhang sites near Oenpelli. A permit is required to enter Arnhem Land, and the only way to view the art sites is by organised tour.

History

Navigator Matthew Flinders named the region in 1803 after one of the two ships of a Dutch expedition led by Jan Carstensz, who discovered this coast in 1623. More recent evidence suggests Indonesians, Malaccans and Portuguese visited the region at earlier dates. Overland explorer Leichhardt (1845) and surveyor David Lindsay (1883) were early Europeans to cross Arnhem Land. Pearling in the late 19th century, cattle stations, mission stations, and more recently Uranium mining in 1980 (Narbarlek was mined out in one season and rehabilitated) were the main European activities.

Attractions

Fascinating Aboriginal art sites, escarpment and plateau scenery, prolific birdlife, rivers and shaded, forested gorges, and an insight into a totally different way of life are the main features offered by Arnhem Land tour operator, Davidson Safaris. From their base camp near Mt Borradaile, 47km (29 miles) north-east of Oenpelli, Max and Phillipa Davidson conduct small group tours which include one art site featuring a huge Rainbow Serpent painted on a 20 feet high cave ceiling, while other sites have hand stencils, macassan praus and European figures. And, while much is undocumented, some paintings are thought to be over 30,000-years-old. Max demonstrates the abundance of the natural 'supermarket' (medicinal plants, bush tucker) and talks about the Aborigines' relationship with the environment. Meeting elder Aborigines and barramundi fishing add further excitement to what is one of the most enlightening and stunning tours in the Territory. Facilities at the camp include large tents, beds and linen, showers, toilets, covered eating area and airstrip. It costs $250 per day per person (includes accommodation, meals, air transfers, permits). Tours can be tailor-made to meet specific interests. For details ph (089) 275 240.

Umorrduk Aboriginal Safaris also have a cultural, rock art focus, ph (089) 413 882.

How To Get There

For those travelling overland to Gurig National Park, only 15 vehicles a week are permitted, and it's booked up well ahead. Oenpelli is a closed community, so no facilities or services are available, and travellers are not allowed to enter (emergencies, as in all closed Aboriginal communities, excepted).

****

BATCHELOR

Population 600

Location

13km (8 miles) west of the Stuart Highway, from the turn-off 87km (53 miles) south of Darwin.

Characteristics

Batchelor's unspoilt, lush-green woodland setting is largely due to the environmentally sensitive town plan and construction of 1952 in which removal of trees was kept to a minimum. There's plenty of colourful birdlife (galahs, cockatoos and parrots), so much so that Jackie Hargreaves calls her restaurant at the Rum Jungle Inn, 'Birdies'.

The Overland Telegraph Line and 'Track', experimental agriculture, railway siding, wartime air base and old mine sites, give a touch of history to the area. Apart from continuing mining and quarrying operations (gold, lead and zinc) and a large export beef and buffalo abattoir, Batchelor is the gateway to one of the Conservation Commissions most exciting protected areas - Litchfield Park.

A unique Aboriginal Teacher Training College and the Top End Aerial Sports Association (parachuting and gliding) based at the airport, add to the town's variety of activities. All basic services and facilities to meet tourist needs are available in the town.

History

The Overland Telegraph Line and subsequent track spawned a few pubs in the region during the 1870s, one of which, "The Rum Jungle" (located in the vicinity of the mine site), was a popular stopover for travellers. The derivation of Rum Jungle, like that of Tennant Creek, is typically Territorian. A horse and dray loaded with supplies broke down on the rough track tipping off a barrel of rum. The teamsters set up camp where the wheel and the barrel rolled off and drank the lot in the jungle-like forest!

As early as the 1880s, coffee, rubber and tobacco were grown for a short time, and a site a few kilometres south of Rum Jungle was selected for an experimental farm in 1911. The farm's object was to prove that specialised crops were viable in the tropics - in its first year of operation the pumpkin story pointed to a successful venture. It was supposed to have measured 1.3m (4 ft) in height, 1.6m (5 ft) in diameter, and 4.5m (14 ft) in circumference! Despite what appears to be the fairytale pumpkin, insects, climate and management problems saw the scheme abandoned after a few years. The site was named Batchelor in 1912 after South Australian politician Egerton Batchelor.

A legacy of a large World War II Allied air base, attacked in 1942 by Japanese bombers, is an old airstrip where General Douglas McArthur landed en route to important meetings. Army installations and other wartime relics lie scattered in the bush.

The discovery of uranium and the subsequent development of an open-cut mine in the early 1950s, gave the town its first solid economic base. The population rose to nearly 700, but with the mine's closure in 1971, Batchelor struggled to survive. An abattoir established in 1972, the Woodcutters lead, tin and zinc mine, gold mining and more recently tourism, promise a bright future.

Information

Rum Jungle Inn, Batchelor Caravillage and Pearce's Paradise offer detailed Litchfield Park information and maps.

Attractions

Wartime Relics. Airfield and army installations.

Karlstein Castle. A miniature, detailed replica of a Bohemian castle is a major eye-catcher, located on a rocky outcrop in front of the police station.

Batchelor Recreation Lake. Sometimes called Rum Jungle Lake, this large spring-fed tract of water is a popular boating (non-powered only), sailing, canoeing, swimming and picnicking spot. Located 5km (3 miles) from town, with a sealed road to the Lake.

Rum Jungle Mine Site. Uranium ore bodies were discovered by Jack White in 1949. The mining project began in 1952 and Batchelor was established as a town for miners in 1954, with the official opening of the mine. The actual mine ceased in 1963 as the remaining ore was uneconomic to treat. The treatment plant closed eight years later when the stockpiled ore had been processed. The area has been rehabilitated, but visits are by organised tour only, through Caravillage. There's a fossicking locality nearby.

Aerial Sports Association. Based at Batchelor Airport, parachute and gliding clubs have weekend instructional flights, including tandem free-fall parachuting. It's by appointment only, enquire at the airport. Scenic flights are available, ph (089) 760 023.

Pearce's Paradise. A mini circus featuring performing camels and ponies is something rather unexpected, but worthwhile visiting. Performances according to demand throughout the season, $4 adult, $2 child. Phone for bookings. Ex-rodeo rider, drover and bushman, Ron Pearce, also runs 4-hour trail rides along some magnificent stretches of the Finniss River, including artesian springs, billabongs and rainforest accessible only by horseback. Costs $35 per person, including lunch. Ron has resurrected some of the old bush cooking skills and implements with a corrugated iron galley (open fire bbq) where you can indulge in a bush meal and hear some of his Territory Tales!

The Windmill Caravan Park has powered sites for $12 x 2. Bush

campsites ($8) are shaded and within easy reach of the river and
billabongs. Bunkhouse, including 3 meals, $25 per day, or $10 for a
bed. Pets allowed - in fact Ron has quite a few unusual ones of his
own! Caravans and trailers are not recommended in the Park - you
can leave them here. Crocodiles (both types) inhabit the waterways -
even 'Sweetheart', the saltie now peacefully resting in Darwin
Museum was caught a few kilometres from here. For details of tours,
bbq meal and camping, ph (089) 760 070. Open all year, located 8km
(5 miles) west of Batchelor on Litchfield Road. Look for the sign on
the roof.

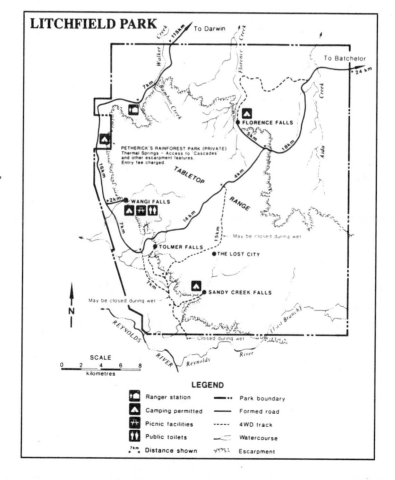

LITCHFIELD PARK

To Darwin
To Batchelor

FLORENCE FALLS

PETHERICK'S RAINFOREST PARK (PRIVATE)
Thermal Springs - Access to 'Cascades'
and other escarpment features.
Entry fee charged.

TABLETOP

RANGE

WANGI FALLS

May be closed during wet

TOLMER FALLS

THE LOST CITY

SANDY CREEK FALLS

May be closed during wet

N

REYNOLDS

Closed during wet

RIVER   Reynolds   River

SCALE
0   2   4   6   8
kilometres

LEGEND

Ranger station		Park boundary	
Camping permitted		Formed road	
Picnic facilities		4WD track	
Public toilets		Watercourse	
Distance shown		Escarpment	

LITCHFIELD PARK

Located 13km (8 miles) east of Batchelor, this 65,700ha (162,279 acres) nature park boasts an area of pristine wilderness including permanent waterfalls, palm-fringed pools, hot springs, tracts of monsoon rainforest and fascinating flora and fauna. The rugged beauty of the ancient dissected sandstone plateau and escarpment extends across much of the park, and contrasts with the vast black soil, billabong dotted plains.

Landscape

The plateau called Tabletop Range and escarpment that dramatically drops to the woodlands and plains, is the dominant landform feature. A botanical wonderland includes cascades of ferns on the shaded gorge and cave walls, four species of cycad, zamia and carpentaria palm and pandanus, as well as the taller, dense stands of rainforest. Springs rising near the escarpment face feed creeks that spill over the edge into the pools below. Elsewhere, the drier plateau supports an open woodland vegetation cover.

The black-soil plains are covered with tall green spear grass (Sorghum intrans) during the Wet season. This rapid growing annual grass is one of the most common that forms the under-storey for large areas of tropical woodland in the Top End and Kimberley. It literally grows 'as high as an elephant's eye', producing a dense, movement-restricting cover. The lush green colour dries to straw tones when it dies after the Wet, and is fuel for huge bushfires which sometimes raze these landscapes. Controlled burns of such areas may take place in the Top End. Eucalypts, mainly Darwin woollybutt (Eucalyptus miniata) are prevalent species, while kapok bush (Cochlospermum fraseri), acacia varieties, fern-leafed grevillea (Grevillea pteridifolia) and the purple flowering turkey bush (Calytrix extpulata) add colour and variety to the lowlands and hills.

Wildlife in its many forms add interest. There are around 28 known species of mammals and marsupials; bats abound in the cave recesses, including the orange horse-shoe, among other species; marsupial mice and prolific birdlife including the rare bush-hen (Gallinula divocea). Undoubtedly, more species of both flora and fauna will become known as scientific research proceeds.

On the exposed plain areas 'magnetic' termite mounds (so named because their shape has a definite north-south orientation), dot the landscape. Many billabongs attract a great array of water birds, including many of those seen at Kakadu, and their surrounds provide a wallowing ground for the feral water buffalo.

The most colourful land-based birds are the red-collared lorikeet, known as the rainbow lorikeet and also distinctive for its yellow front (Trichoglossus haematodus), red-tailed cockatoo (Calytorhynchus magnificus), black cockatoo, sulphur-crested cockatoo (Cacatua galerita), northern rosella (Platycercus venustus) and honey-eaters attracted to the delicate orange nectar-laden fern-leafed grevillea flowers. Black and whistling kites ride the thermals high above the plateau, and if you fail to see the flash of the blue-winged kookaburra, its raucous laughter will be heard.

Animals include wallabies and kangaroos, seen best at dusk and dawn, while the sighting of the northern quoll (native cat) is extremely rare.

There are snakes and smaller reptiles, and water monitors inhabit some streams. There are no crocodiles (salt-water or freshwater) in the falls area of the park, so swimming in these areas is regarded as safe. But the Finniss and Reynold Rivers are known as salt-water crocodile habitats! There are thousands of noisy fruit bats (flying foxes) too.

Park Features

Florence Falls. Picturesque 'twin falls', shallow valley and rainforest surrounded pool make this an ideal camping and swimming spot. It has a camping area, toilets, conventional vehicle access, and is 45km (28 miles) from Batchelor.

Tolmer Falls. These plunge from the end of a narrow gorge into a large deep pool - a swimmers' delight! Horseshoe-shaped caves harbour hidden delights - bridal falls, pools, and even a warm thermal cascade and pool. Above the falls are a series of rock pools, and an impressive sandstone arch creating a natural bridge. Other weathered rock formations provide plenty of landscape interest for photographers, but take care around the sinkholes and sheer cliffs. Camping is not allowed, there are no facilities, but has conventional vehicle access. Located 16km (10 miles) from Florence Falls.

The Lost City. Sandstone blocks, weathered into curious formations, resemble ancient city ruins in their plateau, woodland location. Located approximately 6km (3 miles) directly east of Tolmer; access via 4WD track and walk - no water.

Sandy Creek Falls. Another attractive set of falls and pool from which Sandy Creek flows through a small forest of tall paperbarks. Located 18km (11 miles) south-east of Tolmer Falls; camping allowed, no facilities, 4WD access. The main track continues south from the Sandy Creek Falls turn-off to the southern park boundary. About 12km (7 miles) south of the boundary is a turn-off to Surprise Creek Falls (swimming is not recommended as salt-water crocodiles could be present); ultimately the main track leads south to either Daly River, or back to the Stuart Highway.

Wangi Falls. One of the park's main attractions features permanent spring-fed falls and a large pandanus-fringed pool with a gently sloping sandy entrance. It's a delightful spot for swimming. Located 15km (9 miles) north of Tolmer Falls; camping allowed; picnic facilities, toilets, and it has conventional vehicle access.

Pethericks Rainforest Park. A privately owned park offers walks, escarpment scenery, cascades and falls, rock pools and thermal springs in some dense monsoon rainforest. For those interested in flora, trees along one walk are identified. Facilities include camping (toilets, showers), bbq. Entry and camping fees. Located approximately 10km (6 miles) north of Wangi.

Walker and Bamboo Creeks. Bush camping sites are a good base to explore rainforest and rock pool terrain. There's a ranger station nearby, and access to Walker Creek is 4WD. No facilities. Located approximately 10km (6 miles) north-east of Pethericks Park.

Bushwalking

One of the best spots in the Territory for this activity. On extended walks you should take one or more topographic maps (1:100,00 Reynold River Sheet No 5071, 1:50,000 Mt Tolmer Sheet No 50714, Rum Jungle Sheet No 50711), and inform rangers of your intended route and return time.

Crocodiles

There are no crocodiles in the Falls area of the Park. Estuarine crocodiles do inhabit the waters of the Finniss and Reynold Rivers.

Conservation

Please help to keep this area in its unspoilt wilderness state. Collect dead timbers for fires before arriving at your campsite, avoid using soaps and detergents in the waterways as they pollute streams and kill aquatic life, generators disturb fellow campers and wildlife (don't use them in the park), no shooting, and 4WD owners, please keep to designated tracks. Six Rangers are most helpful with any queries you may have about the park. The park's southern boundaries have been extended.

Pets

By permit only. Check with the Conservation Commission.

How To Get There

The park can be reached via either the Cox Peninsula/Wangi Road, or via Batchelor. The loop road through the park has a good formed surface suitable for conventional vehicles, but access to some features requires 4WD. The park is open all year, but check road conditions, particularly during the Wet season when flooding may restrict access (in fact only on a few days does the Finniss River cut the road, and generally only for a few hours). Roads into the park are now being sealed.

Tours

Litchfield Park Tours conduct full day tours to Litchfield Park (9am-7pm); all inclusive - meals, etc, costs $90 adults and $70 child. Enquire at Caravillage where Bob Davis will give you plenty of good advice about the Park. Tours from Darwin can also be undertaken (see Darwin listing).

Pearce's Paradise offer 4-hour trail rides along some superb Finniss River wilderness. Cost is $35, and it is highly recommended.

Batchelor Air Charter, ph (089) 760 023, has scenic flights over Litchfield Park, Victoria River region and Kakadu from Batchelor Airstrip. A 50 minute flight costs $60.

Accommodation

Rum Jungle Motor Inn - motel from $68 single; $78 double; $88 triple. Facilities for disabled, swimming pool (guests only), credit cards accepted (Bankcard, Mastercard, Visa), open all year, ph (089) 760 123.

Batchelor Caravillage - cabins/on-site vans from $40. Powered sites $17 for two, tent sites $7 per person. Grassed, shaded sites, bbq, kiosk, ice, camping gas, pets not allowed. Credit cards accepted (Bankcard, Mastercard, Visa), open all year, ph (089) 760 166.

Pearce's Paradise - see Attractions listing.

Services and Facilities

Hotel (Rum Jungle Inn), supermarket, health centre, ambulance station, police station, post office, garage (full range vehicle repairs) and service station (fuel - super, ULP, diesel - camping gas, oil), churches (Catholic, Uniting, Seventh Day Adventist), bank agencies (Westpac at Caravillage, Commonwealth at post office), restaurant (Rum Jungle Inn, generous serve - roasts, steaks, seafood from $7.50), take-away food outlet, kennels (Pearce's Paradise) and airstrip. Recreational facilities include public swimming pool, bowls and tennis courts. Credit cards widely accepted. Shops open all weekend.

Radio stations: ABC, 105.7 FM.

Emergency Services

Police, ph (089) 760 015; Ambulance, ph (089) 279 000.

BATHURST AND MELVILLE ISLANDS

Population 2500

Location

Off the mainland coast, about 80km (49 miles) north of Darwin.

Characteristics

Two islands separated from the mainland by the Clarence and Dundas Straits are themselves divided by the very narrow Apsley Strait. Together they cover an area of 8000 sq km (3040 sq miles), and Melville is the second largest island so near the Australian coast after Tasmania. Relatively flat, mangrove-lined rivers, indented coastline, rocky shorelines and long white sandy beaches fringed by she-oaks, are some of the landscape features. Colourful birdlife, and an abundance of marine life including estuarine crocodiles, add interest.

The Islands are owned by the traditional Aboriginal inhabitants, the Tiwi people, whose contact with mainland Aborigines was limited until about the late 1800s. The Tiwis, meaning 'people'; 'we, the people', or perhaps 'we, the chosen people', are outgoing and relatively confident, and have a culture that differs in significant ways from mainland Aborigines. This confidence and proximity to Darwin in recent times is reflected in the progressive Nguiu community, which has a well-developed range of commercial activities. Of interest is the Tiwi Design screen printing workshop, Tiwi pottery and wood carving, Bima Wear clothing and Tiwi Pima Art Centre. Nguiu is the main centre with a population of 1200 administered by the Tiwi Land Council. Milikapiti and

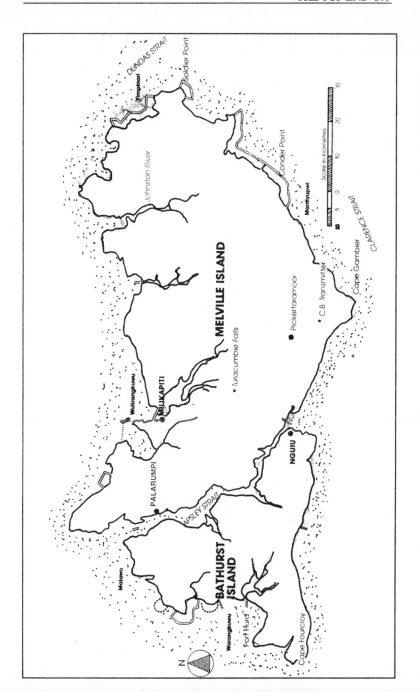

Pularumpi are the two main communities on Melville, with a population of around 300 in each. In conjunction with the Northern Territory Government, the Tiwi people have established a forestry enterprise which will be a major supplier of Caribbean Pine to the mainland.

Visits and accommodation are by packaged tours, and each offers a unique opportunity to meet Tiwi people and experience something of their comparatively dynamic culture. Permits are required to enter.

History

The first authenticated sighting of the islands by Europeans was by the Dutch in the early 1600s. Colonial power Great Britain established a presence on Melville Island in 1824 at Fort Dundas (near where Pularumpi is today) in order to counter growing Dutch interest in the area. Captain Bremer of the Royal Navy was empowered to set up a military settlement, but tropical diseases, poor relations with the Tiwi, and isolation, all contributed to its failure and abandonment in 1829. This was the first European attempt at settling the North Australian coast, and very little remains of it today. Phillip Parker King landed on and named the islands in 1818. Bathurst was named after Earl Bathurst, Secretary of State for the colonies. King found the Tiwi knew some Portuguese words, suggesting earlier exploration and contact with these Europeans.

Macassan fishermen were the only other overseas visitors, and contact led to trade in some areas with the Tiwi - in fact with the steel blade axes, the Tiwi were able to forego traditional bark canoes and build dugout ones.

Nguiu began as a Catholic Mission in 1911, and mission activities have had a strong influence on the lives of the Tiwi. During World War II the first ever Japanese bullets on Australian soil came from a strafing raid on February 19, 1942, the same raid that bombed Darwin. A Tiwi captured the first Japanese prisoner, a pilot who crash-landed on Melville.

In the early 1980s, the advent of tourism and other enterprises added another dimension to both Tiwi culture and European understanding.

Attractions

Tiwi Culture. Meeting Tiwi people, visiting their art, wood carving, pottery and screen printing workshops at Nguiu (purchases may be made). Milikapiti community and a Tiwi pukamani burial ground featuring tall, elaborately carved and decorated totems, give insights into local culture. Traditional living skills can also be experienced.

Fishing. The local coast offers some fine fishing, including barramundi, mackerel, trevally, threadfin salmon, tuna, marlin and sailfish. These are some of the 17 species regularly caught. Huge tides characterise coastal waters.

Turacumbie. Lush tropical vegetation, waterfall and a large pool offering welcome swimming, is located in the centre of Melville Island. While there are large salt-water crocodiles around the islands, they don't frequent this pool.

How To Get There

Basically, it's through organised tour only.

See under tours. Independent boat or yacht owners should check with the Tiwi Land Council in Darwin, ph (089) 410 224, or Bathurst Island, ph (089) 783 991, for details of permits, regulations and areas where fishing is not permitted.

Independent private aircraft visitors using the gravel airstrip at Nguiu must make prior arrangements with the tour operators, and have permits.

Accommodation and Tours

Tiwi Tours - Three day tour of both islands includes visits to Aboriginal art, carving and screen printing workshops, the old mission precinct, Turacumbie Falls, Milikapiti, and a burial site. Costs around $590.

Day Tour Bathurst Island is a busy tour of the Nguiu and the Pukamani burial site. Costs $230. Both tours include return airfares from Darwin, lunch, morning and afternoon teas, and entry permit fees. Special interest tours are negotiable, ph (089) 815 144.

Barra Base Lodge - Lodge-style rooms, swimming pool, bar and dining room with a wide verandah and basic shop, is the base for guided fishing trips to some of the Territory's best spots. Fishing for a wide variety of species (see Attractions) all year. Wet Season fishing is a delight for before and after storm cloudscapes (you don't fish during the storm!). Minimum of 2 days, costs around $400 per day including lodge accommodation, fishing guides, return air fares to Darwin, meals and fishing gear. Located on the western side of Bathurst at Port Hurd, ph (089) 811 088.

Australia Kakadu Tours - A four day tour visiting Nourlangie/Ubirr Rock Aboriginal art-sites, cruising the Wildman River and Yellow Water Lagoon, before returning to Drawin, and flying to Bathurst Island. Cost is $812 adult, ph (089) 815 144.

Services and Facilities

Nguiu has a store for those things you have forgotten. Barra Base sells basic items from its store, and except for the special licensed bar at Barra Lodge, no alcohol is permitted on the Islands. Purchase of local products requires Australian currency or Bankcard, Mastercard, Visa, American Express or Diners Club credit cards.

BULLO RIVER STATION

Population 14

Location

Approximately 470km (292 miles) south-west of Katherine, and 130km (81 miles) east of Kununurra.

Characteristics

This 1627 sq km (628 sq miles) property run by Sarah Henderson, has 8000 Brahman Cross cattle, straddles some magnificent Kimberley type country, and offers small groups (6-8) a rare experience of life on a remote tropical Australian cattle station. You'll understand why the legendary overlanders settled this Victoria River country when you see it. Visits are by prior arrangement only.

Attractions

Working cattle station where you can assist too. Scenic - rocky ridges, startling gorges, prolific wildlife (turkeys, goannas, wallabies, fresh and salt-water crocs), boabs and ghost gums, and permanent water where you may fish, swim or boat.

How To Get There

The turn-off from the Victoria Highway is 110km (68 miles) west of Timber Creek, or 130km (81 miles) east of Kununurra. The 77km (48 miles) road leading to the homestead is formed gravel, suitable with care for conventional vehicles during Dry season. Arrangements to fly you in can be made.

Accommodation

Private homestead rooms, all inclusive, $300 per person per day. The homestead has a swimming pool and tennis court, ph (091) 687 375, for bookings.

CUTTA CUTTA CAVES NATURE PARK

1499ha (3702 acres)

Location

West of the Stuart Highway, 27km (16 miles) south of Katherine.

Characteristics

The park protects two aspects of a typical karst or limestone landscape; a series of limestone caves with classic stalactite and stalagmite formations, and weirdly weathered pillar formations of limestone on the surface called tower karsts. Other characteristics of karst country are evident on the surface, namely the sink holes (doline or swallow-hole), conical depressions in the limestone. Geologically, the Tindal limestone was formed some 500 million years ago, and a noticeable feature of the caves is their dryness. Only during the Wet season (at which times the caves are closed to visitors) does the water seep through and cause growth of the stalactites and stalagmites. The geology of the caves is well explained by Rangers, who run thrice daily tours.

Flora and Fauna

On the surface, carbeen gum (Eucalyptus confertiflora), small-leaf bauhinia (Lysiphyllum cunninghamii), native fig, and tropical grasses which grow to 3m during the Wet season, are common. The flora and rocky terrain harbour a host of fauna. Rock wallabies, brown tree snakes, which are venomous but as the fangs are located at the back of the mouth they are not regarded as dangerous to man, and the harmless Children's python, are a few. The caverns provide a habitat for Ghost Bats and the rare Golden Horseshoe Bat, two of six species in the caves, while two rare species of blind shrimp live in cave pools.

Tours

Ranger guided tours operate 7 days a week during the Dry season on the hour 9-11am, 1-3pm. Tickets may be obtained in the car park 15 minutes prior to the tours ($6 per adult). Entry to the caves is by guided tour only.

How To Get There

By road, it is via the Stuart Highway. There are a number of Katherine tour operators who include the Caves in their programme (see Katherine listing).

Services and Facilities

Toilets are the only facilities in this day-use park, which opens at 7am and closes at 5pm. No animals are allowed.

DALY RIVER

Population 250

Location

On the Daly River crossing, 110km (68 miles) west from the Stuart Highway turn-off near Hayes Creek.

Characteristics

A quiet place on the appealing Daly River consists of a Roadside Inn, police station, church, Aboriginal Mission, store and health clinic, with some accommodation retreats in the vicinity. It is tropical, lush and tranquil; an idyllic spot to 'go bush' for a few days, where the river barramundi, salt-water crocodiles, and some fine natural camping sites are the main attractions.

History

The river was named after Sir Dominick Daly, Governor of South Australia (1862-1868) by Explorer Stuart in 1862, and the later settlement took its name from that source.

A short-lived copper mining venture in the 1880s brought a sharp clash between cultures when three miners were murdered by Aborigines in 1884. White retaliation was ruthless. The Jesuit missions established in 1886 provided a buffer between the races, and today Aborigines run the old mission through their Naniyi Nambiyu Council. The Mango Farm Safari Camp occupies part of the former mission property, including historic ruins and huge old mango trees planted by the Jesuits.

A few agricultural ventures were attempted in the region - sugar cane in the early 1880s; peanuts between the 1920s and 1950s, and even dairying in 1915 - all with little lasting success. Pastoral runs established in the 1880s are the most enduring agricultural activity. Mrs Nancy Polishuk has written a detailed account of the local history, entitled *Life on the Daly River*. Along with her family, she runs the Bamboo Creek Rainforest Park.

Attractions

Daly River Nature Park. The 60ha (148 acres) reserve preserves a scenic area at the lowest Daily River crossing point. Barramundi fishing and boating activities are popular. It has picnic facilities, and camping is allowed. The pub has a pet croc!

Activities

Barramundi fishing (best times during the Dry Season, or just after the Wet), boating (hire boats, Mango Farm, $85 per day, $50 half-day, $13 per hour, includes fuel), canoeing (hire canoes, Bamboo Creek Rainforest Cottage, $15 per day, $20 deposit), walking and flora and fauna appreciation.

Tours

Bamboo Creek Rainforest Park. Guided motor-bike tours (bring your own bike) include historic sites and croc spotting.

How To Get There

From Stuart Highway between Hayes Creek (38km-24 miles) and Adelaide River (32km-20 miles), the Daly River Road runs for approximate 72km (45 miles) to Woolianna Road turn-off, and a further 4km takes you to the crossing. The Daly road is sealed except for a 24km (15 miles) section, which, like Woolianna Road, is a formed surface, suitable for all vehicles.

Accommodation

Daly River Roadside Inn, ph (089) 782 418 - motel, from $53 a double.

Caravan Park - powered site $10-14 x 2, unpowered $7 x 2, pets allowed, dogs leashed. Open all year, 7am-11pm, credit cards accepted (Bankcard, Visa).

Woolianna on the Daly Tourist Park, ph (089) 782 478 - powered sites $18 x 2, unpowered $15 x 2, swimming pool, spa, no pets.

Mango Farm Safari Camp, ph (089) 782 464 - cabins from $63, units from $90; Camping - hire safari tents $12.50 adult, $9 child (includes bedding). Sites $6.50 adult, $3.50 child. No powered sites, no pets. Swimming pool (guests only). Located 5km south, then 7km from a well sign-posted turn-off. All vehicles okay on the dirt road. Open all year, credit cards accepted (Bankcard, American Express),

Bamboo Creek Rainforest Park - 2 bedroom cottage $54, 3 bedroom cottage $60. Camping only in conjunction with cottages, $5 per person. No pets allowed. Located 12km up Woolianna Road. Open all year, ph (089) 782 410.

Other Camping - There are many fine, free spots in the area, but be mindful that salt-water crocodiles inhabit creeks and billabongs.

Services and Facilities

Police station; Catholic Mission has a supermarket (open Mon-Fri 9am-5pm, Sat 9am-noon, Sun 5-6pm); church (Catholic); resource centre (Aboriginal silk screen printing, batik, artifacts); The Roadside Inn has a bar, licensed restaurant, and Ian and Mandy Noble also offer counter meals ($12 barramundi steaks), ice, take-away food. Commonwealth Bank Agent (Mission).

Allan Hagstrom and Murray Brown at the Mango Farm have a bistro/restaurant, BYO. Fuel - super, ULP, diesel (Roadside Inn and Mission), camping gas (Mission). The Sandbar General Store is located up the Woolianna Road. The Mission has an airstrip, and there is a natural boat ramp. No permits are required for the Mission, but check with the Council Office as to where you can go on the Aboriginal land.

The Merpeena Arts Festival is an annual event featuring the work of local Aboriginal artists. Phone the Mission, (089) 782 422, for details.

Radio stations: ABC 106.1 and 107.7 FM.

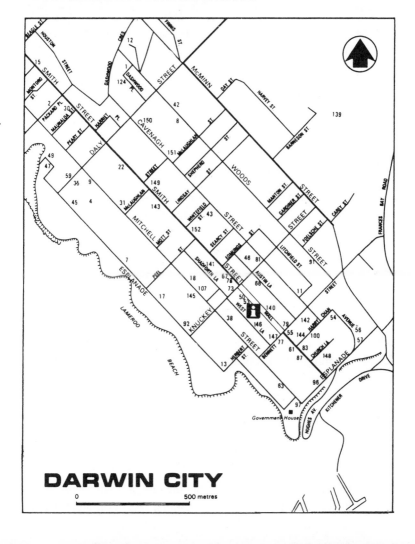

DARWIN CITY

0   500 metres

DARWIN

Population 73,000

Location

Astride a Beagle Gulf Peninsula, on Australia's northern coast, 1482km (918 miles) north of Alice Springs.

Characteristics

Darwin is a truly tropical city with a distinct cosmopolitan flavour, given by the 47 or so nationalities residing there. The cultural mix, torrid zone climate, tropical coastline, experience of man-made and natural disasters, hard-drinking frontier-town reputation, proximity to Asia and great distance from anywhere in Australia, are the basic ingredients that give Darwin flair, colour, and an easy-going and racially harmonious life-style.

The dominant population centre in the Territory is also the capital city of an embryo state, and Australia's 'newest' city by virtue of an almost complete reconstruction after being flattened by Cyclone Tracy in 1974. It's a vibrant and relaxed city that enjoys one of the highest daily sunshine hours in Australia, even during the Wet season when some of the most beautiful cloudscapes, sunsets and lightning displays highlight the many sparkling white buildings and luxuriant verdant vegetation.

City Centre

A geographical paradox of the town centre site is that you have to drive south to enter it. It's a modern, but mellow, centre with huge shady trees in the squares surrounding the hub of it all, Smith Street Mall. The variety of shops, plazas, cultural mix, lush-green palms and the bougainvillea-splashed 'Vic' walls, is a tropical delight for first-time visitors. Early morning is an ideal visiting time; it's cooler, good for photography, and pleasant for walking. A number of fascinating food places are open too - first to open, at 6am, is The Taco House in Darwin Plaza, for the early birds looking for coffee or breakfast; others in the plaza open soon after. The Mall has plenty of atmosphere, and a favourite activity is people-watching from the outdoor table settings.

Car Parking Around the City
Nothing dampens enthusiasm more than a parking ticket, and wardens are very strict here on 15, 30, 60 and 120 minute parking zones. It's better to use the West Lane Car Park.

History

The present sites of Government House and Stokes Hill were the Aboriginal camping grounds of the first occupiers of the peninsula area, the Larrakeyah people. In 1839, Captain J.C. Wickham and John Lort Stokes of the HMS *Beagle* were the first authenticated European discoverers of Port Darwin, and Stokes named it after his friend, the famous naturalist Charles Darwin. No attempt at settlement was made until 1869, when the South Australian Government despatched Surveyor-General Goyder to map out a settlement. It was an instant settlement too - Goyder's party numbered 135! The street pattern was laid out; streets were named after surveyors in the group, and with remarkable foresight, the Esplanade was designated as a public reserve. The embryo town was officially named Palmerston, after the British Prime Minister of the time, but was popularly called Darwin.

The building of Government House in 1870, the completion of the Overland Telegraph Line in 1872, the first newspaper *Northern Territory Times* in 1873, and a town council in 1874, all reflected an optimistic outlook for the town, despite the harsh hinterland and previous ill-fated attempts at settlement on the north coast.

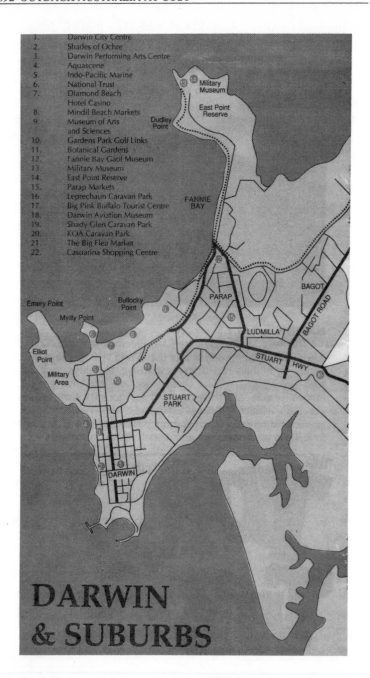

1. Darwin City Centre
2. Shades of Ochre
3. Darwin Performing Arts Centre
4. Aquascene
5. Indo-Pacific Marine
6. National Trust
7. Diamond Beach
   Hotel Casino
8. Mindil Beach Markets
9. Museum of Arts
   and Sciences
10. Gardens Park Golf Links
11. Botanical Gardens
12. Fannie Bay Gaol Museum
13. Military Museum
14. East Point Reserve
15. Parap Markets
16. Leprechaun Caravan Park
17. Big Pink Buffalo Tourist Centre
18. Darwin Aviation Museum
19. Shady Glen Caravan Park
20. KOA Caravan Park
21. The Big Flea Market
22. Casuarina Shopping Centre

DARWIN
& SUBURBS

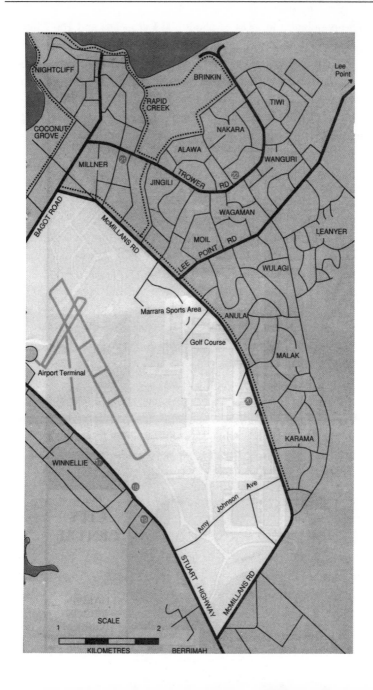

The population in 1874 of about 600 Europeans and 180 Chinese and Malays, rose rapidly at the time of the Pine Creek Goldrush of the 80s and 90s, to 4898 in 1891, but dropped to less than 1000 when the gold petered out. Pearling began in 1884, and the first motor car from Adelaide to Darwin was in 1908 when Dutton and Aunger made the incredible crossing. In 1911, the name was officially changed to Darwin at which time the population was 944, and already the basis of its cosmopolitan character today was in evidence.

World War II

This saw the port as an important naval base, and the Japanese bombing of Darwin on February 19, 1942, interestingly paralleled the attack on Pearl Harbour the year before. Non-essential civilians, women and children were evacuated from Darwin in 1941, but the suddenness and ferocity of the first attack curiously caught everyone by surprise. Recent evidence suggests that over 1000 people were killed rather than the 243 as officially stated. Altogether the city was bombed over 60 times in 1942, with massive structural damage resulting. Many of those killed are buried at Adelaide River.

The war highlighted Darwin's strategic position, and its defence role in the post-war years has been one of its major functions. Improved communications and facilities, important mineral discoveries (uranium at Rum Jungle in the 50s), increasing trade drawn from its huge pastoral hinterland sustain growth, while more recent mineral finds have been a further catalyst to expansion.

Cyclone Tracy

Struck on Christmas Day in 1974, wrought a level of destruction that saw few buildings left standing, and 66 people killed. Temporarily quelled by the magnitude of the disaster, the indomitable spirit of Territorians brought about a remarkably rapid return to normal functions. And some time later, a bright, vibrant, modern, tropical city emerged and added large scale tourism to its range of other functions.

Information

The telephone area code for Darwin is 089.

Darwin Regional Tourism Association has an information centre at 33 Smith Street Mall, ph 814 300, and at the Airport which services all incoming flights.

Free booklets produced by Top End Tourist Associations are widely available. They provide useful up-to-date information.

The National Trust, 52 Temira Crescent, Myilly Point, ph 812 848 - excellent value for historic walks and similar material.

NT Conservation Commission, ph 894-411.

Attractions

Around Darwin - an Historic Walk.

Lyons Cottage. A delightful little bungalow-style dwelling in local stone. Built in 1925, it originally housed an officer of the Britain-Australia Telegraph Company.

Former Admiralty House. Now an art gallery - which also serves delicious morning and afternoon teas. This tropical-styled house was built to a 1927 design. One of only a few of its type remaining in Darwin.

Government House. Construction of this superb example of colonial architecture began in 1870. Nine year later the current Government House, known as the 'Seven Gables', took shape as we see it today.

Old Post Office. Built in 1872, the Old Post Office survived until a Japanese air raid on Darwin.

Police Station, Old Court House. The Police Station (nearest Mitchell Street) and Court House with cell block behind on the

Esplanade between Mitchell and Smith Streets, were built in 1884.

Christ Church Cathedral. Originally built in 1902, this Anglican church was totally destroyed by Cyclone Tracy early on Christmas Day, 1974. Part of the ruins were incorporated into the new Cathedral.

Tree of Knowledge. Don't miss it. An ancient, spreading Banyan tree, situated behind the Civic Centre.

Browns Mart. A building of stone with a romantic past. Now a small, well patronised theatre, Browns Mart was first a mining exchange, later became a fruit and vegetable market and is also supposed to have been first a police station, and then a brothel.

Old Town Hall. The Town Hall was built by the District Council in 1883 during the mining boom.

The Commercial Bank. With its facade now fully restored, this building was constructed in 1884.

The Victoria Hotel. Last restored in 1978, this fabulous old hotel, known affectionately as 'The Vic', was designed and built in 1894.

The Star Village. Site of Darwin's first moving picture house.

Indo-Pacific Marine. The aquarium features one of the few places where living coral reefs have been successfully transplanted from the sea, and a fascinating variety of tropical marine fish including the deadly blue-ringed octopus and box jelly fish (sea wasp). Located by the Roundabout, Smith Street West, ph 811 294.

Doctors Gully. Every day at high tide, hundreds of fish come in from the sea to be fed at Aquascene. Milkfish, catfish, mullet, bream, batfish and rock cod, are some of these delightful free-loaders. Check the local tourist magazines for times and tides. Located at the end of The Esplanade. Costs $3.50 adults, $2 children, ph 817 837.

The Botanical Gardens. It features a variety of native and imported trees and shrubs, including a fine display of orchids. A delightful place to stroll around.

Museum of Arts and Sciences. A magnificent museum with outstanding South-east Asian and Oceania anthropological galleries. Aboriginal art figures prominently, and in the natural history section you can see 'Sweetheart' - a 5.1m mounted crocodile. There's a fine Arts Gallery as well as an exhibition one. A pearling lugger adds interest outside, and the facilities offered include The Beagle restaurant, coffee shop and toilets. Located in Conacher Street, 4km from the City Centre.

Fannie Bay Gaol. The oldest part of the gaol was built in 1883, the infirmary in 1885, and the gallows, a replica of England's notorious Newgate Gallows, were established in 1952 for the last hanging in the Territory. Located at East Point Road, Fannie Bay. Open throughout the week 10am-5pm.

Artillery Museum. Gun emplacements at East Point are grim war reminders. Open daily 9.30am-4.30pm.

Audit House/Giese Residence. An excellent example of tropical architecture amidst a beautiful matching garden. It was built in 1938 for public servants. Viewed from street as it's only open 4 days in the year. Located 50 Temira Crescent, Myilly Point.

Chinese Temple. The first temple was built on the site in 1887, but was nearly destroyed by a cyclone in 1937. The more recent Temple serves a thriving Chinese community. Entry is free. Located in Woods Street.

Outlying Attractions

Crocodile Farm. See Noonamah listing.

Yarrawonga Zoo. A few stars of the Crocodile Dundee films reside here, along with many other animals. Many are free range, ready to be patted by the kids, or to steal some picnic goodies. The train rides are also very popular. The Zoo is run by private enterprise, and is open daily 9am-6pm. Admission is $4 adult, $2 child (2-14), $10 family. The restaurant in the front of the zoo is open much longer (heading for 24 hours), and after 6pm you can BYO wine, etc. No alcohol is allowed during zoo hours. Located near Palmerston, 20km (12 miles) south of the city, ph 832 267.

Historical Home Museum. Nostalgic historical homes situated at the '18 miles' (28km south of Darwin), are two of Darwin's oldest remaining tropical houses, built by Harold Snell in 1913. Period decor and memorabilia feature inside, while Devonshire Teas add a nice touch to this historic place. Open 10am-4pm, adults $4, children $1.50.

Holmes Jungle Nature Park. A 250ha (617 acres) Conservation Commission reserve protects delightful patches of wet monsoon rainforest accessible by elevated walkways, and there's a popular picnic area too. It was called Jungle Creek during World War II, when it was used as a convalescent camp by the army. Approximately 17km (10 miles) from the city, via Stuart Highway, Bagot Road, Trower Road and Vanderlin Drive.

Casuarina Coastal Reserve. A 1180ha (2915 acres) semi-natural area of coastline, notable for pockets of rainforest, World War II gun emplacements, and an area set aside as a free beach where nude bathing is allowed. Located off Trower Road.

Howard Springs and *Berry Springs* are separately listed, as are other outlying attractions, eg Batchelor.

Other attractions are associated with the natural recreational resources - the fine turquoise waters that offer much for fishermen and sailors alike.

Tours

Like Alice Springs, there's a huge variety offered, with a focus on the Kakadu region for extended tours. All activities including safari hunting, Aboriginal culture tours, sailing, cruising, fishing and diving are catered for. AAT Kings are major operators, complemented by a number of smaller, specialist ones. Tours can also be tailored to meet your specific requirements. Generally there are concessions for children. Refer also to listings in Kakadu Region, Bathurst and Melville Islands, Gurig National Park and Batchelor for tours.

Some samples and costs:

Darwin Day Tours: Offer range of city tours - historic, city sights, museums, Doctors Gully fish feeding and crocodile farm. Half-day from $29, ph 818 696.

AAT Kings: Darwin in a Day Tour covers the city and attractions out as far as Howard Springs, for around $79 adult; Wangi Falls, Litchfield NP and Rum Jungle 1-day Tour, $85; Kakadu and Katherine Gorge, 3 days, from $395, ph 471 207.

Go-Anna Safari: 3-day 4WD Kakadu-Litchfield Safari includes Tolmer and Wangi Falls, and costs around $260 adult, ph 813 833.

Adventure Terra Safari Tours: 3-day Kakadu tour costs $390, ph 412 899.

Tiwi Tours: Bathurst Island one day (see also under Bathurst and Melville Islands listing), ph 815 144.

The Tour Tub: A different way to see Darwin, in an open bus. Costs around $14, ph 854 779.

Breakwater Canoe Tours: 4-day safari on the Daly River, $520, ph 412 899.

Keetleys Tours: 2-day Katherine, including Mataranka and Gorge cruise, around $300 including accommodation and meals, ph 814 422.

Wimray Safaris: Hunting and fishing (see also under Gurig and Wildman Safari Lodge listings), ph 452 755.

NT Barra Fishing Trips: Day or extended, from $200 per day, ph 451 841.

Ferry Trips: Day trip to Mandorah via MV *Darwin Duchess*, Darwin Harbour Ferries, ph 785 094 (see also Mandorah listing), $14 return. Mandorah Jet Shuttle, ph 853 167.

Barra Base Lodge (see Bathurst and Melville Islands).

Willis's Walkabouts: Choose your own bushwalk, from $65 per day, ph 852 134.

Groves Helicopters NT: Flights over Litchfield Park from $50 for 15 minutes.

There are many more tours available. Check with the Information Offices.

Events

In keeping with its laid-back tropical image, Darwin hosts a few zany events.

St Patrick's Day Race Meeting - March 17.

On the Beach Carnival, in May, celebrates the retreat from Darwin Waters of the lethal box jellyfish, and the beginning of the swimming season.

North Australian Eisteddfod - May 22 to June 2.

Bougainvillea Festival, June, celebrates the peak flowering time of this tropical flora.

Beer Can Regatta is Darwin's answer to Alice Springs' 'Henley-on-Todd' boat race. Crafted entirely out of beer-cans, it's a zany boat race with a few surprises. Held in the sea and on the beach in June.

Royal Darwin Show is held in July.

The Darwin Cup, August, is the high point on the Territory's racing calendar, and part of the six week Cup Carnival.

Mud Crab Tying Competition - an annual barefoot competition that's interesting to say the least. It's held in August.

Darwin Rodeo - an international event held in August.

Oktoberfest - a traditional beerfest, obviously held in October.

How To Get There

By air: Ansett Australia operate extensive daily services between Western Australia and Darwin, within the Territory (Gove, Katherine, Tennant Creek, Alice Springs and Ayers Rock), and from other Australian States.

Qantas flies from all capital cities.

Major international airlines servicing Darwin include Qantas, Singapore Airlines, Garuda and Royal Brunei.

By coach: Daily express road coaches include Pioneer Express, Bus Australia and Greyhound.

By road: All-weather roads link Darwin to other areas of the Territory.

By sea: Regular calls are made by cruise liners. For further details, refer to Introductory How To Get There section.

Local Transport

Buses: There's an excellent public transport system serving the city area, and connecting with suburbs including Palmerston. Buses and taxis serve the airport. A special tourist trip is available (see under Tours).

Taxis: Darwin Radio Taxis, ph 818 777; Darwin Combined Taxis, ph 411 777.

Ferry: See under Tours.

Hire Vehicles: All the big names are here, plus one with a difference, Rent A Rocket. Budget are conveniently located near the airport (500m). They are also at 1427 Stuart Highway, Winnellie, ph 844 388.

Others include: Avis, ph 819 922; Brits Rental, ph 812 081; Territory Rent A Car, ph 818 400; Hertz, ph 410 944; Rent A Rocket, ph 413 733; Thrifty Rent A Car, ph 818 555.

Caravan Hire: Trans Australia Caravan Hire, ph 813 955.

Motor Cycle Hire: Top End Motor Cycle Hire have mopeds, motor bikes, scooters, trail bikes, ph 812 661.

Bicycle Hire: U-Rent, 50 Mitchell Street, have bicycles and camping gear, ph 411 280.

Shopping

There are a number of souvenir shops and galleries selling a range of Aboriginal art - Tiwi Totems, Arnhem Land paintings, carvings, boomerangs, screen prints from Bathurst Island, and pottery, are some of the items. Other interesting places are Weavers Workshop and Potters Place in Parap Shopping Village, The Opal House in Smith Street Mall, and there's a duty-free shop in the Mall. The Buffalo Shed on the Stuart Highway, offers buffalo horns, hats and leather-ware. And, while we hope it's for a laugh, a Crocodile Attack Insurance Police from the TIO is an unusual item to take home. Then, of course, there's the world's largest bottle of beer - the Darwin Stubby.

Markets

Darwin has plenty of these - in fact, for its size, more than any other city in Australia. The Asian influence is strong in this area of marketing, and adds further to the exotic quality of Darwin. Magnificent Asian food is a feature of the Mindil Beach Market held every Thursday night (May-Sept). All year on Saturdays, there is a market at Parap; and on Sundays at Rapid Creek, from 8am-2pm. There's a food market by the Bus Transit Centre in Mitchell Street each Friday night.

They are colourful, different, and worth a photograph or two.

Accommodation

By overseas standards, Darwin offers plenty of quality, reasonably priced hotel/motel accommodation. There's a good choice in medium priced, and budget too, while close in camping grounds tend to be the only disappointing feature.

Some examples are:

Premier Class: All Seasons Atrium Hotel (single/twin from $135), Esplanade, ph 410 755; Beaufort Hotel (single/twin from $195), Esplanade, ph 829 911; Marrakai Luxury Apartments (from $185), 93 Smith Street, ph 823 711; Diamond Beach Hotel (single/twin from $150), Gilruth Avenue, ph 462 666; Darwin Travelodge (single/twin from $140), Esplanade, ph 815 388; Sheraton Hotel (single/twin from $175), 32 Mitchell Street, ph 820 000.

Beer Can Regatta, Darwin.

Medium Range: Top End Frontier Hotel (single from $90), Mitchell Street, ph 816 511; Tops Boulevarde Motel (single from $68), 38 Gardens Road, ph 811 544; Mirambeena Tourist Resort (single from $87), 64 Cavenagh Street, ph 460 111.

Budget: Leprechaun Motel (around $50), Stuart Highway, Winnellie, ph 843 400; Park Lodge (single $35), 42 Coronation Drive, Stuart Park, ph 815 692; Ross Smith Guest House (single from $18), 49 Parap Road, ph 818 457; Sunset City Backpackers Haven (from $11 per person), 144 Mitchell Street, ph 817 326; YMCA (from $12 per night), Esplanade, ph 818 377; Darwin YHA Hostel (from $11), Beaton Road, Berrimah, ph 843 902; YWCA (from $20 single, backpackers $10), 119 Mitchell Street, ph 818 644; Backpackers International Hostels, 88 Mitchell Street, ph 815 385; Darwin Transit Centre (from $12 per person), 69 Mitchell Street, ph 819 733.

Camping: See also Howard Springs listing. Costs listed are for 2 persons: KOA - powered sites $17, grassed, shaded sites, no pets, McMillans Road, Malak, ph 272 651; Palms Caravan Park - on-site vans from $35, powered sites from $14.50, unpowered from $12, 2333 Stuart Highway, Berrimah, ph 322 891.

Other parks include: Lee Point Village Resort, Lee Point Road, Lee Point, ph 450 535; and Shady Glen, Stuart Highway, Winnellie, ph 843 330.

Eating Out

There are plenty of inexpensive places including take-aways in and around the city centre, many reflecting the city's cosmopolitan character. Plazas off the Mall often reveal some gourmet delights, and don't forget the colourful food markets. There are pubs too, which offer counter and sit down meals, while the restaurant scene is as exciting as it is varied.

Indian, Japanese, Chinese, Cantonese, Thai, Indonesian, French,

Greek, Italian, Danish, Malaysian, Mexican and, of course, Australian, are the major nationalities represented. Not surprisingly, many specialise in seafood, while some have a Territorian flavour of Barra, Buff and Croc. Some names and addresses:

The Beagle - features sunset dinners from its attractive beach location, and specialises in seafood. Located at the NT Museum of Arts and Sciences, Fannie Bay, ph 824 211.

Uncle John's Cabin - Territorian specialities (croc, buffalo, kangaroo, seafood), 6 Gardiner Street, ph 813 358.

Rooftop Restaurant - good food, good views, Darwin Frontier Hotel, ph 815 333.

Rock Oyster - seafood emphasis in an open-air atmosphere with dance floor and live entertainment on the weekends, Cavenagh Street, ph 813 472.

Mississippi Queen - silver service, Creole style specialty, 4 Gardiner Street, ph 813 358.

Le Breughel - Flemish paintings give atmosphere to this French restaurant, Smith Street West, ph 812 025.

Night Tokyo - Japanese restaurant, Asti Motel, Smith Street West, ph 817 484.

Rasa Sayang - Malaysian and Chinese emphasis in an intimate atmosphere, Cavenagh Street, ph 813 981.

Tai Hung Tol - enjoys the reputation of one of the best Territory Chinese restaurants, 36 Parap Road, ph 816 474.

Night Life

There's plenty of choice, from pub entertainment to theatre.

Theatres: Darwin Performing Arts Centre, Mitchell Street, ph 819 022; Darwin Theatre Group, ph 818 424; Corrugated Iron Youth Theatre, ph 815 522; Browns Mart Community Arts, ph 815 522; Cavenagh Theatre Group, ph 480 049; Territory North Theatre, ph 204 257.

Cinemas: Darwin Cinema Centre features 4 theatres, Mitchell Street, ph 815 999; Casuarina Cinema, ph 450 174.

Casino and Bars: Diamond Beach Hotel Casino - gambling floor, Keno and slot machines, Sun-Thurs 1pm-3am, Fri-Sat 1pm-4am; Sweetheart's Bar - live entertainment Tues-Sat after 10pm; Sheraton Darwin Hotel - regular evening music in the Lobby Bar, until late; Hotel Darwin - offers a varied fare, Thurs-Sun.

Nightclubs: Fannies, 3 Edmunds Street, ph 819 761; 1990's, 21 Cavenagh Street, ph 411 811; Squires, Edmunds Street, ph 819 761; Vic Hotel, The Mall, ph 814 011; Circles, The Beaufort Hotel, ph 829 911; Beachcombers Disco, cnr Daly and Mitchell Streets, ph 816 511; Monsoons, 70 McMinn Street, ph 815 530.

Services and Facilities

As one would expect, there's a full range of services offered from the City Centre and the huge air-conditioned suburban Casuarina Shopping Square. Supermarkets and the like are open all weekend, and credit cards are widely accepted. Major banks are well represented and offer auto teller services. Full vehicles services are available, including 24 hour fuel (all types).

Radio Stations - 8DR (ABC) 657 medium wave; 8DN (Commercial) 1242; 8 TOP FM (Community Radio) 104 FM Band; ABC FM 105.7 and 107.3.

Churches - Anglican, Apostolic, Assemblies of God, Baptist, Catholic, Community, Church of Jesus Christ of the Latter Day Saints, Church of Christ, Full Gospel, Greek Orthodox, Islamic Centre and Mosque, Lutheran, Presbyterian, Uniting, Baha'i Faith, Salvation Army, Seventh Day Adventist, Christian Outreach, Darwin Christian Assembly.

Emergency Services

Dial 000 for emergency Ambulance, Police, Fire, otherwise:
  Police, ph 278 888; Fire Brigade, ph 410 000; Ambulance,
ph 279 000; Royal Darwin Hospital, ph 228 888;
Night and Day Medical and Dental Service, Casuarina Square,
Bradshaw Terrace, 8am-10pm, ph 271 899; Central Darwin Dental
Surgery, 59 Smith Street, ph 411 899; Darwin Chiropractic Clinic, 53
Ross Smith Avenue, Parap, ph 814 773.
  Chemists - Bardens Pharmacy, Parap, ph 812 013; Trower Road
Night and Day, ph 277 857.
  Veterinary - Darwin Veterinary Hospital, 8 Vanderlin Drive,
Wagaman, ph 279 033 (24 hours).
  Vehicle Breakdown, AANT, 24 hours service, ph 813 837.
  Disabled Persons Bureau, ph 227 213.

Recreational Facilities and Activities

Cycling - a very good system of bicycle tracks allows many city
attractions to be seen in this way.
  Golf - Darwin Golf Club, ph 271 322, and a 9-hole Municipal
course, ph 816 365.
  Swimming - Pools at Casuarina, Darwin, Nightcliff and Winnellie.
  Ten Pin Bowling - In association with Squash, ph 854 416.
  Tennis - Darwin Tennis Centre, ph 852 844.
  Gliding and Ballooning - Mainly from Batchelor.
  Diving - Arafura Diving and Salvage, ph 279 283; Dive North, ph
812 150; Territory Diving Services, ph 817 665.
  Fishing - For local fishing information contact Fishing Tackle
Shops, ph 816 398, 271 706, 274 656.
  In addition there are many sporting clubs.

DOUGLAS HOT SPRINGS AND BUTTERFLY GORGE NATURE PARKS

Location

On the Douglas River, approximately 42km (26 miles) south of Hayes Creek from the Stuart Highway turn-off, and 204km (126 miles) south of Darwin.

Characteristics

Douglas Hot Springs Park (3107ha-7674 acres) features a number of thermal pools, one of which, Hot Springs Lagoon, is the most popular with its 40C (104F) water temperature. Other pools are cooler. It's located on an attractive stretch of river that offers good camping under the shade of tall paperbarks.

A rough, corrugated 17km (10 miles) road beyond the hot springs leads to Butterfly Gorge Nature Park. This 104ha (256 acres) reserve has a series of large, deep rock pools, some small waterfalls, a gorge with 70m (228 ft) high cliffs, and tropical forest. It was named for the large number of butterflies often present near the warm springs at the gorge entrance. Tall stands of Melaleuca (paperbark) and Leichhardt Pines guard this entrance, where the Douglas River has cut some 300m (981 ft) through a sandstone escarpment.

Both parks are ideal for walking, swimming and fishing (barramundi, black bream). No animals are allowed in the parks.

How To Get There

From the Stuart Highway at Hayes Creek, it's a good sealed surface, apart from 15km (9 miles) of gravel. With care, it is suitable for conventional vehicles. From the Hot Springs to Butterfly Gorge, 4WD is still recommended.

Accommodation

The Corn Patch Riverside Holiday Park. For those seeking more comfortable accommodation, the holiday park has a 3 bedroom house ($90) and camping and caravan sites (powered van sites $12 x 2, unpowered $10 x 2, tent sites $4 per adult). Sites are grassed, and pets are allowed, dogs leashed. Services and facilities include: general store, bar, counter meals $10, ice, take-away food, souvenirs, fuel - super, ULP, diesel, oil and camping gas. Open 7 days, all year 7.30am-10pm (bar, etc open until 2am Thurs-Sat), ph (089) 782 479. Cash only.

Lukies Farm. On the main road to the parks, on-site vans from $30, camp sites $10 per vehicle. Boat hire, cruises available, ph (089) 782 411.

Services and Facilities

Douglas Hot Springs has picnic, bbq, toilet and camping facilities. There are no facilities at Butterfly Gorge, and while camping is allowed here, trailers and caravans are discouraged. Using soap to wash anything in the river is not permitted.

EDITH FALLS - NITMILUK NATIONAL PARK

189,190ha (467,299 acres)

Location

Located at the western extremity of Nitmiluk (Katherine Gorge) National Park, 62km (38 miles) north of Katherine.

Characteristics

The waterfalls, as the Edith River cascades over the Arnhem Land escarpment edge, and the large, deep plunge pool fringed by tropical vegetation and pandanus palms, are the main attractions of the area. Walkers taking the track to the top of the escarpment will be rewarded by some magnificent scenery, including numerous smaller pools and rapids. Generally there is plenty of birdlife, and wallabies may be seen too. Although it is a half-hour climb, the effort is well worthwhile.

The Falls were named after Lady Edith, wife of the Governor of South Australia from 1864 to 1873, Sir James Fergusson. The Fergusson River was named after Sir James.

How To Get There

The road into the Falls is sealed. A 76km (47 miles) walk along a track from Katherine Gorge is an alternate, more energetic way into the Falls area. (It's for experienced bush walkers only, and the rangers at the Katherine Gorge Visitor Centre should be notified.)

Services and Facilities

Picnic, bbq and toilet facilities are provided. Camping is allowed. People swim here despite freshwater crocodiles. Dogs are allowed by permit only.

EMERALD SPRINGS

Population 3

Location

On the Stuart Highway, 22km (13 miles) north of Pine Creek, and 198km (122 miles) south of Darwin.

Characteristics

An old roadhouse set amidst tropical vegetation and bougainvillaea, is a comfortable refreshment stop along 'The Track'. The Springs after which it was partly named have dried up, while fossickers still occasionally probe nearby localities in the hope of finding precious minerals which gave the settlement its first name. Gold is the main objective of rock hounds today. Owner of the roadhouse and pub, Michael Pepper, will tell you where the fossicking areas are, and how to get to Douglas Hot Springs.

The original roadhouse structure, an old tin shed built in the 1930s, still stands, and the current building was constructed after World War II. Mining activities in the area, including Pine Creek, during the 1930s and increasing traffic along 'The Track', provided enough custom to warrant a roadhouse.

Attractions

The fossicking localities, and the hot springs on the Douglas River (see also Douglas Hot Springs listing).

Accommodation

Motel - demountable units (shared facilities) - single $15, double $25; self-contained units - $55.

Camping/caravans - powered sites $8, unpowered $5; tent sites $4.

Services and Facilities

The roadhouse has a bar with homestyle meals from $8 (excellent steak sandwiches), take-away food, shop, ice, souvenirs, picnic/bbq area, and showers for travellers are free. Fuel - super, diesel, ULP, autogas, oil and camping gas. Credit cards accepted (Bankcard, Mastercard, Visa, EFTPOS), open all year, 7 days a week, 24 hours, ph (089) 782 320.

GURIG NATIONAL PARK AND COBOURG MARINE PARK

220,700ha (545,129 acres) and 22,900ha (56,563 acres)

Location

On the Cobourg Peninsula, 200km (124 miles) north-east of Darwin at the second most northerly geographic point of mainland Australia, after Cape York Peninsula.

Characteristics

The Parks beyond Kakadu encompass a vast area of virgin, mainly inaccessible wilderness, and the protected marine foreshores and coral reefs are their emphasised natural features. On the United Nations Wetlands of International Importance Register, especially as a migratory waterfowl habitat, these little known parks also feature magnificent bays and beaches, prolific marine and wildlife, and offer excellent hunting and fishing. A rich Aboriginal presence, relics of the Macassan trading era and the forlorn ruins of early attempts at European settlement are Gurig's cultural attributes. So significant are these early relics in Gurig that they have been placed on the National Estate Register.

The traditional owners, an amalgam of clans called the Gurig people, number about forty, many of whom live near the Black Point settlement, where some are involved in tourist services. A few choose to live semi-traditionally in the park. The Gurig people also work closely with the Conservation Commission in the joint management of the park, and a Gurig Clan Elder is chairman of the management committee.

Permits to enter are required, and access by land via Arnhem Land is very restricted. Only fifteen groups or vehicles are allowed at the park's camping ground at any one time. Early applications are necessary as peak times are already heavily booked for the next two years. Most visitors fly in from Darwin. Black Point, a tiny settlement with a population of about twenty-five, consists of a ranger station and visitors centre, store, jetty and a few houses.

History

Early European navigators included the Dutch in 1636, Abel Tasman in 1644, Matthew Flinders in 1803 and Phillip King, who in 1818 named Port Essington after a Royal Navy Admiral. The second attempt at establishing a permanent settlement on the north coast was at Raffles Bay on the Cobourg Peninsula (about 65km [40 miles] north-east of the Victoria Settlement site). While relationships with Aborigines were much better than at Fort Dundas (Melville Island), the Fort Wellington settlement established in 1827 failed commercially and was abandoned two years later.

Yet another attempt was made in 1838, when Victoria Settlement was built at Port Essington. Suspicion of French intent in the area was a major reason for the Colonial Office's decision; others included a base for Asian trade. The site was described as "the friendly hand of Australia stretched out towards the north...", but before it too was abandoned in 1849, it was a 'friendly hand' for Ludwig Leichhardt, who ended his overland journey here from near Brisbane in 1845. Apart from the buildings the British abandoned, there are the descendants of their cattle, buffalo, pig, deer and horses, which still roam wild over Cobourg, with the buffalo spread right across the Top End.

Macassans were earlier visitors; trepang collecting and pearl gathering mainly. In 1906, trepangers were prohibited from visiting the north coast. Other early European activities included timber mills, pastoralism and pearling, the latter still continuing today.

Flora and Fauna

Tropical eucalypt forest, mainly Darwin stringybark and woolly-butt, covers the undulating landscape, with enclaves of monsoon rainforest, swamp paperbark and mangroves in the wetter areas.

Gurig is the first southern hemisphere stopover in spring for thousands of migratory birds, a reason for its United Nations listing in 1974. Brolgas and jabiru delightfully grace the wetlands and margins. The coastal waters have salt-water crocodiles, dugong (sea cow), turtles, and a great variety of fish. The park is inhabited by banteng cattle from Bali, sambar deer from India, buffalo from Java, ponies from Timor, pig (Javanese boar) from Java, all of which were imported by the British at Victoria Settlement. Dingo and wallaby are the main large indigenous species.

Conservation

The parks have a preferred marine and coastal focus which means the interior, apart from licensed hunting safaris, is closed. Strict controls on numbers of vehicles entering the parks is to maintain environmental quality. Driving is strictly on designated roads only. No pets are allowed.

Information

Rick Hope at the Ranger Station at Black Point knows everything there is to know about the area, and is more than willing to help, ph (089) 790 244.

Attractions

Victoria Settlement Ruins. Extensive and some surprisingly well-preserved ruins of a British garrison town, established by Captain J.G. Bremer in 1838, lie in the bush. Up to 300 lived here at its peak, including a significant military element. Remnants include: powder magazine (half-buried); stone chimneys and walls; lime kiln; walls of a hospital kitchen; and foundations of other buildings. A cemetery is a reminder of the extreme hardships here. And, to commemorate the 150 year anniversary of the 'Red Coat' Garrison town, a visitor centre incorporating a small museum was opened at Black Point in November, 1988.

Facilities include picnic area, toilets, and an interpretive walking track. A pamphlet available at the visitors centre details the history, and identifies particular ruins. There is no water, so take adequate fluids with you. Access is by boat only. Peter Watton, of Dekime, runs trips to the ruins, with a bit of fishing on the way, for $50 per person (minimum 6 persons). Arrangements can be made at the shop at Black Point, ph (089) 790 262.

Independent boat users should advise the ranger before leaving. It's a full day trip, and you should provision yourself accordingly.

Fishing. The waters offer superb all year round fishing, and most listed in the fishing guide frequent these waters. Sandy Island No 2 is a sacred site and no landings are permitted. Tides have a lower range than Darwin - a maximum of 2.4m (8 ft).

Contact Dekime, ph (089) 790 262, for details of fishing safaris.

Hunting. Guided trophy hunting of Banteng cattle and Sambar deer is available. Costs $8500 for 5-day hunt, including trophy, fees, accommodation, transport. Contact Wimray Safaris, ph (089) 452 755. Davidson Safaris also offer hunting trips, ph (089) 275 240.

Marine Park. All foreshores and reefs have marine park designation. Beautiful sandy white beaches are ideal for walking and beachcombing for some fabulous shells. Coral reefs, tropical fish, turtles, and oyster beds add fascination. People do swim, but sharks and salt-water crocodiles make it dangerous, as do box jellyfish during the latter and earlier parts of the year. There are plenty of idyllic beaches to discover.

How To Get There

By road: it's 600km (372 miles) and 9 hours driving time from Darwin. The surprisingly good, but 4WD track only between the East Alligator River and Gurig has some rough patches, and is closed during the Wet season (between November and early April generally). Permits and bookings are required, available from the Northern Territory Conservation Commission.

By air: Wimray Safaris operate a regular mail plane that leaves Darwin at noon each Friday for the one hour flight. One-way fares are $90 per person, plus $1 per kilo freight (luggage). If you are travelling in a group, it could work out cheaper to charter a plane when you add up the weight of all your luggage.

Day trips are available in a single engine, five-seater plane, with two hours free on the ground - $390 per person. Package tours involving overnight or extended stays can be arranged by Noel Bleakley, Wimray Safaris, ph (089) 452 755.

By boat: You can cruise in independently, provided you have permits.

Accommodation

Conservation Commission: a small camping area nestles under a large stand of casuarinas, and has showers, toilets, picnic and bbq facilities. The use of generators at night is not permitted.

Gurig Park, between Black Point and Smith Point, has four cottages for rent (around $125 per day) and tent sites for $10 per person. Bookings can be made at Gurig Park Store, ph (089) 790 262 (3-7pm).

Seven Spirit Bay Resort: a wilderness retreat hotel - $330 per person plus $245 per person transfer from Darwin, ph (089) 790 277. Included in room costs is a guided tour of the Victoria Settlement. They can also arrange fishing safaris.

Services and Facilities

At Black Point and nearby, there's a ranger station and visitors centre that houses an interesting historic section; Gurig Store, basic items and foodstuffs, fuel (super, diesel, marine fuel), camping gas, ice, and there is a resident mechanic at the store; airstrip (near Smith Point); jetty and launching ramp. It's cash only at the store.

HAYES CREEK

Population 15

Location

On the Stuart Highway, 136km (84 miles) north of Katherine, and 174km (107 miles) south of Darwin.

Characteristics

Hayes Creek consists of a Wayside Inn that is a convenient stop along the highway. Not too far away in the bush, are major gold mining operations with a work force of about 200 men who live in camps near the mineral sites. Bob and Val Fisher run the popular Hayes Creek Wayside Inn, and they will cheerfully tell you about rather surprising local and outlying scenic attractions.

Attractions

The turn-off to the Douglas Hot Springs and Butterfly Gorge Nature Parks is 7km (4 miles) to the north of Hayes Creek, also the turn-off to the secluded and scenic Daly River area.

Accommodation

Motel - $27 single; $39 double; demountable $18 and $32.
  Camping - tents only, $3.50 per person.
  Pets allowed, dogs leashed.

Services and Facilities

It has a bar, outside dining area (main course $7-$11), shop, take-away food, ice, souvenirs, post office agency, picnic area and swimming pool (patrons only). Fuel - super, ULP, diesel, oil, LPG and camping gas. Credit cards accepted (Bankcard, Mastercard, Visa, American Express, Diners), EFTPOS machine, open 7 days, all year, 6am-11pm, ph (089) 782 430.

HOWARD SPRINGS

Population approximately 4000

Location

34km (21 miles) south of Darwin, on and around the Stuart Highway.

Characteristics

Situated in the rapidly growing area of Darwin's rural fringe, Howard Springs is a scattered settlement which has the Howard Springs Nature Park as its prime feature of interest. Also, there's the Territory's only Hunting Reserve (water birds) nearby, and a road from Howard Springs leads to the remote Gunn Point fishing spot on the coast.

A number of caravan/camping parks make it a useful base for Darwin and environs exploration. All major services, including a tavern, are conveniently located here, too. Howard Springs takes its name from the river which honours the work of Frederick Howard, a naval officer who spent much time in the late 1860s mapping the north coast.

Attractions

Howard Springs Nature Park. The 1009ha (2492 acres) park offers the closest and most attractive public fresh water swimming pool to

Darwin. With its beautiful, clear, spring-fed waters surrounded by monsoon rainforest, it's a very popular spot - even more so when the box jellyfish prohibit beach swimming around Darwin during the Wet season.

In the waters, numbers of barramundi and longtom may be seen, while the backdrop of rainforest species such as red ash, white cedar and camphorwood, among others, host a large variety of birds. In fact, 125 species of birds and over 50 reptile types have been recorded here. Other wildlife include agile wallabies, flying foxes, and the occasional echidna and bandicoot. A walking track through the forest helps identify flora, and you may walk to the source of the waters.

The area now used for swimming was originally established as a water supply, partly to service Vestey's meatworks. During World War II, the weir was built to boost the capacity, and at this time it became a popular recreation area with its huge shady trees, landscaped lawns, facilities, and all year round swimming. Its popularity continues.

Facilities include picnic, wood barbecues, toilets, kiosk and ranger office. It is a day-use park, open 8am-8pm. Pets are not allowed.

Howard Springs Hunting Reserve. Located next to the Nature Park, this area of floodplain and swamp near the Howard River mouth is the Territory's first duck and goose hunting reserve. A permit is required, and hunters need to check the declared season dates (enquire at Police Station or Conservation Commission about permits, regulations and season). Cleaning areas are provided, and shooters should be aware that this area is the home of the salt-water crocodile. Access off the Gunn Point Road is suitable for conventional vehicles during the hunting season.

Gunn Point. An isolated fishing, boating, camping and beachcombing spot on the coast lies approximately 55km (34 miles) north of Howard Springs. Fishing is the major interest for most at places along, and in deeper waters off, the coast, while others are content with beachcombing for shells. In fact, a world game-fishing (4kg line) record for a barracuda (23kg) was established in a catch off the Vernon Islands. There's a boat launching ramp, but watch out for crocodiles, and because of the great variation in tides, it's advisable to have a tide table. Access is along the mainly formed gravel Gunn Point Road.

Accommodation

Howard Springs Caravan Park - on-site vans $30; powered sites $14 x 2; unpowered sites $10 x 2, $3 child. Shaded, grassed sites, no pets, bbq, swimming pool, camping gas, shop. Credit cards accepted (Bankcard, Mastercard, Visa), open daily 7.30am-8pm, Whitewood Road, ph (089) 831 169.

The Nook Caravan Park - cabins $40; units $35 x 2 (communal facilities); on-site vans $27; powered sites $12 x 2; unpowered $8 x 2. Shaded, grassed sites, pets allowed - dogs leashed. Facilities: kiosk, bbq, camping gas. Open 24 hours, all year, credit cards accepted (Bankcard, Mastercard, Visa). Morgan Road, ph (089) 831 048.

Coolalinga Tourist Park - cabins $55 per night; powered sites $16-20 (own toilet/shower) of $12-17 (shared facilities); tents $5 per adult, $1 per child. Sites shaded, grassed, pets allowed ($40 bond), dogs leashed. Mini-supermarket, camping gas, ice, fuel (super, diesel, ULP) and swimming pool. Open all year 6.30am-7.30pm, credit cards accepted (Bankcard, Mastercard, Visa). Located 6km (3 miles) north of Howard Springs on the Stuart Highway, ph (089) 831 026.

Eating Out and Entertainment

The Howard Springs Tavern, run by Bob and Pauline Kerr, offers bistro-type meals in an outdoor patio setting (main meal, steaks costs around $10) and seafood specialities at their Manor Inn restaurant (main course from $12). The Tavern is open 10am-11.30pm, Sunday noon-11.30pm, and features live entertainment. Credit cards accepted

(Bankcard, Mastercard, Visa), ph (089) 831 463.

Services and Facilities

Most essential services are available; if not, Palmerston is only a few kilometres away. There's a supermarket, pub (tavern), restaurant, take-away food outlets, ice, newsagency, post office and 3 fuel outlets (super, ULP, diesel, 24-hour fuel on highway near Palmerston), vehicle services, camping gas and squash. The shopping centre is located in Whitewood Road. Credit cards are widely accepted.

Emergency Services

For Police, Ambulance and Fire, telephone 000.

KATHERINE

Population 9372

Location

330km (205 miles) south of Darwin, on the Stuart Highway.

Characteristics

Katherine, best known for its famous nearby gorge, is a lively, rapidly growing town that in itself has much to offer visitors. From its river-side and tropical woodland setting, the third largest centre in the Northern Territory is the hub of a huge agricultural region ranging from torrid cattle country to local specialised farms which produce fruit and vegetable crops.

The magnificent Katherine Gorge has given it a major tourist function, while the construction of Australia's largest Air Force Base to accommodate the front-line fighter squadron of F-18s at Tindal has boosted the population considerably. As a result, the town boasts all the comforts and facilities of a modern, small city. A strong sense of history and a range of delightful scenic spots add interest to the town.

For the road traveller, it's also the place where you turn off to the west for the Kimberley Region. Even if you are not planning a round trip of Australia, a visit to the Eastern Kimberley of Bungle Bungle fame, via the sealed Victoria Highway, is highly recommended. Reference to the Kimberley Region attractions and places along the way will assist in your decision.

History

The land around Katherine is most closely associated with people of the Dagoman and Jawoyn (sometimes spelt Djauan); the latter occupying areas north and north-west from the high level bridge, along the Edith and Cullen Rivers towards Pine Creek, and eastwards along the Stuart Highway to Beswick and beyond. The traditional Dagoman lands stretched south from the low level weir. Today, these northern lands, including Katherine Gorge, are owned by Jawoyn Aborigines.

While the river was named by explorer Stuart on July 4, 1862, after Katherine, the daughter of James Chambers, who was a major patron of the expedition, the first known European here was Leichhardt in 1844. 'The' Katherine was the first permanent waters north on the trek through the Centre, and 'The' emphasises the river's importance. Pronunciation is Kath-rhyne!

The Overland Telegraph Line construction gave substance to the original settlement site at Knotts Crossing - a tiny enclave of European civilisation and node for the gradual growth of pastoral and mining pursuits. The first pastoral lease in the Territory was at Springvale Homestead in the 1870s, the establishment of which was forerunner to increased overlander activity, and the laying down of firm foundations for a viable cattle industry that continues today.

With the railway came the town's second site, but the first official one was at Emungalan on the west bank of the river. Surveyed and gazetted as a town site in 1917 in anticipation of the railway, the railway bridge opened in 1926, and then attracted the settlement on the current town site. Little remains of Emungalan today.

During World War II, numerous airstrips were built between Katherine and Birdum, and RAAF and Army personnel were stationed in the area. The original construction of Tindal known as Carsons Airfield, was started in 1942 by a US Engineer Regiment, and completed by the Victorian Country Roads Board by 1944. Although designed for B24 Liberator sized bombers, the airfield was never used operationally and was renamed Tindal after Wing Commander A.R. Tindal, CO No 2 Squadron based in Darwin in 1941. He was killed in action in 1942 during the first Japanese

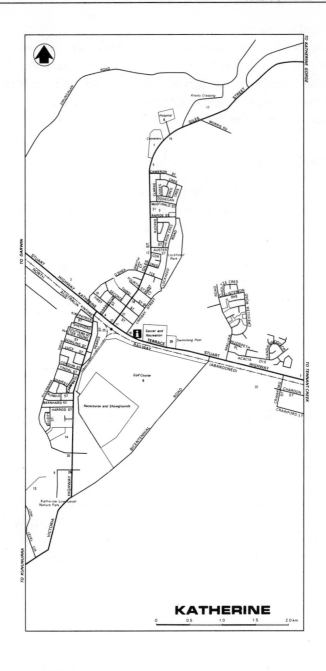

KATHERINE

0   0.5   1.0   1.5   2.0 km

air-raid on Darwin.

In recent times, Katherine's growth has been stimulated by its function as a regional base for construction (roads and Tindal), regional administration, agricultural and pastoral service centre, and tourism associated with the Katherine Gorge and Cutta Cutta Caves National and Nature Parks.

Tourist Information

The Katherine Region Tourist Association has an excellent Visitors Centre, located at the southern entrance to the town. Open Mon-Fri 8.45am-5pm, Sat 9.30am-2.30pm, ph (089) 722 650.

The BP Roadhouse and Travel North headquarters (almost opposite the Visitors Centre) offers information and takes tour bookings. Open 7am-7pm, ph (089) 721 044.

The Conservation Commission has an office in Giles Street, open weekdays, which offers a large selection of flora and fauna publications.

Attractions

Museum and Historical Park. Located on the original airport site in the former terminal building, the museum houses a fine visual display that takes you through Katherine's colourful past. Inventor of a peanut harvester, collector of relic machinery, pig and peanut farmer, are a few of the things Wally Christie has done since arriving here in 1946. He's often at the museum, and is fascinating to talk with. The restored Gypsy Moth belonging to the Territory's first flying doctor, Dr Clyde Fenton, can be seen here, along with all the medical instruments of the time (while the Rev John Flynn flew, he was not a pilot). Picnic area, teas and toilets. Open 10am-4pm weekdays, 10am-2pm Sat, 2-5pm Sunday. Giles Street (opposite hospital), ph 723 945.

School of The Air. You can watch the action as teachers contact students for lessons via the radio. Visits during term time, weekdays, 9.30am-12.30pm, costs $4 adult (children free). Located in Giles Street.

Knotts Crossing. This is the original Katherine site where the modern town had its beginnings as a tiny bush settlement that consisted of a 'pub', store, police station and telegraph station. It was named after an early settler. The old pub, called the 'Sportsman Arms and Pioneer Cash Store', is situated at the top of the river bank. The Northern Times Newspaper described it in the year of its establishment, 1888, as "The Sportsman is well fitted with all the requisites of a first class country hotel where the comfort of visitors is studied". The pub is now a gallery, open Tues, Thurs and Sat 10am-2pm.

Jeannie Gunn crossed here in a punt (now at the museum) whilst on her way to Elsey Station, in 1902.

The original Overland Telegraph Pylons are located across the river, and the one on this side can be seen about 1.5km from the crossing turn-off on Gorge Road. Access to Knotts Crossing is from a left hand turn-off just past the hospital. It's an interesting historic spot where you can picnic, fish, or swim.

Katherine Railway Station. Along with the railway extension from Pine Creek, it was completed in 1926 to service the cattle industry - meat company interests such as Vesteys were keen to transport live cattle for processing in Darwin. It was headquarters for the North Australian Railways during the war, and the track was called 'The Never Never Line'. An interesting display of railway memorabilia is now housed here, and the story of the North Australian Railway is well related in J. Y. Harvey's book *The Never Never Line*. It's a National Trust property. Open 11am-1pm weekdays (April-October). Railway Terrace.

O'Keeffe Residence. A fine example of some traditional Territorian architecture. It was built from bush poles, clad in corrugated iron and asbestos with fly-wired walls for maximum ventilation, for use by Army Engineers as an Officers' Mess during the war. Following the war, it was named after one of a number of its tenants, Sister Olive O'Keeffe. It has been restored by the National Trust, and is located on Riverbank Drive, opposite Campbell Terrace.

Heritage Trail. The Katherine branch of the National Trust have devised a heritage trail which identifies 10 sites and features of historic interest. The self-guide brochures are available from information centres and the National Trust office in the Old Railway Station.

Katherine Low Level Nature Park. Maintained by the Conservation Commission, this 1104ha (256 acres) scenic tract of the river is a popular picnicking, fishing and swimming spot. Swimming is safe during the Dry season, but care must be taken in the Wet when floods make it hazardous. Always check the swimming safety sing, as during this time the river can rise at a rate of 5m (15 ft) per hour! The old Katherine River road causeway, pleasant grassed woodlands, gas barbecues, picnic and toilet facilities make it an ideal destination for families.

Flora in the park is diverse. Common species include greybox (Eucalyptus tectifica), white-leafed bloodwood (E. foelscheana), red-flowering kurrajong (Brachyciton paradoxum), wild kapok (Cochlospernum fraseri), paperbarks (Melaleuca ssp) and fresh water mangrove (Barringtonia acutangula).

Barramundi, black and bony bream, rifle fish, garfish and catfish inhabit the waters. Fishing is allowed. Sometimes freshwater crocodiles and tortoises may be seen. On the land, agile wallabies are common; flying foxes (fruit bats) and brush-tail possum are nocturnal. There's plenty of birdlife - over 120 species have been recorded in the park. Camping is not allowed, and dogs must be leashed. Location is south-west of the town centre, via the Victoria Highway to the Low Level turn-off.

Springvale Homestead and Katherine Gorge. These two attractions are listed separately.

Tours

Travel North (BP Roadhouse) is the major tour operator for the Katherine region, and their extensive range includes Gorge cruises, canoe and boat safaris, Springvale Homestead, night crocodile spotting, Aboriginal corroboree, and extended tours.

Sample types and costs: Gorge cruise with coach, 5.5 hours, departs on a regular basis from BP Roadhouse, or pick up from motels, costs $33 adult, $17 child (5-15 years); Gorge scenic helicopter flight, 30 minutes, costs $85 adult and child.

Bill Harney's Jankangyina Aboriginal tours are recommended. Cost from $240, ph (089) 722 650.

Skyport offers Outback Mail flights, Wed, Thurs and Fri, but seat availability depends on freight and mail, their first priority. Costs: Wed $115, others $167 (longer flights), ph (089) 717 277.

Events

Show and Rodeo in July; Red Cross Canoe Race, and Show in June (Queen's Birthday weekend); Flying Fox Festival in October.

How To Get There

By Coach: Greyhound, Pioneer Express and Bus Australia operate daily services from Alice Springs and Darwin.

By Air: Skyport has regular flights from Alice Springs and Darwin.

Accommodation

Katherine boasts some first-rate motel/resort type accommodation. Generally, costs range from $50 single, $70 double. Most have swimming pools, and newer ones have facilities for the disabled. The telephone area code is 089. Some names:

Frontier Motor Inn, South Stuart Highway, ph 721 744 - facilities for the disabled.

Katherine Hotel-Motel, Katherine Terrace, ph 721 622.

Knotts Crossing Resort, Giles Street, ph 722 511 - facilities for the disabled.

Pine Tree Motel, Third Street, ph 722 533 - facilities for the disabled.

Paraway Motel, O'Shea Terrace, ph 722 644 - facilities for the disabled.

Riverview Motel, ph 721 011.

Beagle Motor Inn, ph 723 998 - facilities for the disabled.

Budget

Prices range from $10 dormitory.

Springvale Homestead (see separate listing).

Backpackers Lodge, ph 722 722, has a hostel division ($12 per person).

Youth Hostel, Victoria Highway, $10 per bed, ph 722 942.

Kookaburra Lodge, Lindsay Street, $12, ph 710 246.

Victoria Lodge, Victoria Highway, $13, ph 723 464.

Camping/Caravans

Springvale Homestead (see separate listing); *Gorge Caravan Park* (see under Katherine Gorge listing);

Frontier Motor Inn Van Park, South Stuart Highway, ph 721 744 - powered sites from $10 for two, plus power; unpowered sites $5 per person. Pets not allowed.

Riverview Caravan Park, Victoria Highway, ph 721 011 - sites from $10 for two persons. Pets not allowed.

Shady Lane Caravan Park, George Road, ph 710 491 - on-site vans $30 per night; powered sites $12 x 2; unpowered $4 per person. Pets allowed, dogs leashed.

Red Gum Caravan Park, Knotts Crossing, ph 722 239 - powered sites $16 x 2; unpowered $7 per person. Pets not allowed.

Pets

Most accommodation places don't allow pets. Dogs and cats can be boarded at Lazy L Stables (at entrance to Springvale Homestead) $5 per day, ph 722 618, or Simbani Kennels, Florina Road, ph 722 561.

Eating Out

There's the predictable range of take-away food, and Katherine has a good selection of restaurants. Some names and addresses:

Matildas Bistro, Frontier Motor Inn (steak and seafood); Golden Bowl (Chinese), Katherine Terrace, ph 721 449; Katherine Hotel, counter meals and Kirby's restaurant; Buchanan Restaurant is highly regarded, Paraway Motel, ph 722 644; Alfred Giles Restaurant (station type), Springvale Homestead, ph 721 159.

Night Life

The Crossway Hotel now features Burkes Bistro and Wings Disco. Springvale Homestead has live Country and Western music each night.

Services and Facilities

Katherine has a full range of shopping and specialist services including medical, supermarkets, vehicle (24-hour fuel - super, ULP, diesel, LP gas for vehicles and camping), banks (ANZ, Westpac,

Commonwealth, all with auto tellers), and Aboriginal artifacts at Mimis in Lindsay Street. Normal shopping hours during week, Sat 9am-noon, supermarket open all weekend. Credit cards are widely accepted.

Hire Vehicles

Territory Rent-a-car, BP Roadhouse, ph 721 044; Hertz, Jetabout, Mike Jackson Travel, ph 723 080; Avis, Hobbits, Victoria Highway, ph 721 482.

Churches:
Anglican, Catholic, Uniting, Lutheran, Assembly of God, Bethel (AIM), Baha'i Faith.
Radio:
8KN (Radio National) 639; ABC (Regional FM) 106.01; National (Hot 100) 765.

Recreational

Golf course, swimming pool, horse riding (3 places), tennis, squash, canoeing (hire canoes Springvale Homestead and Low Level Caravan Park), gun club, boat ramp and fishing. Hire mopeds (from $25 per day), bicycles (from $8 half-day), ph 710 728.

Emergency Services

Ambulance, ph 721 200; hospital, ph 729 211; police, ph 702 111, fire, ph 721 000; doctor, ph 721 677; dentist, ph 721 422; veterinarian, ph 722 893 (AH 711 127).

Road Service, Beresfords (AANT Agent), ph 722 733.

KATHERINE GORGE SECTOR - NITMILUK NATIONAL PARK

180,352ha (445,469 acres)

Location

32km (19 miles) north-east of Katherine, via the Katherine Gorge Road.

Characteristics

This huge park protects spectacular gorge and escarpment country, where the permanently flowing Katherine River has carved 13 deep canyons through the Arnhem Plateau sandstone.

It's one of the Territory's 'Big Three' tourist attractions, along with Ayers Rock and Kakadu, and the second largest park.

The variety of landscapes include plateau, escarpment, gorges and valley floors, while the ruggedness of the terrain is heightened by the regular, rectangular dissection pattern slashed by the Katherine and Edith Rivers. During the Wet, the full fury of the Katherine is awesome, when the gorge fills and becomes a thundering torrent of brown water, many metres above its normal tranquil level. During the Dry season, the waters contract to form a series of deep pools.

Geology

The original base material is around 2,300 million-years-old. Folding and lifting, and associated volcanic activity, formed the bed on which the massive sandstone block rests. This block which forms the plateau and escarpment, evolved after millions of years of sedimentation. Volcanic intrusions, and deposition of gravels and sands, have produced an array of geological structures made more complex by later uplift. Amazingly, the Katherine Gorge was formed just 25 million years ago, by the river that exploited the rectangular lines of weakness in the great sandstone blocks. From the air the evolution of the gorge is easily understood, and the Visitors Centre has excellent models explaining the gorge origin, the time frame of geological events, and various rock samples.

Gorge Features

Sheer rock faces up to 75m high contrast with the swirled surrealistic patterns deeply engraved into the gorge's hard stone floor. The canyon walls reveal fascinating histories from the geological to the Aboriginal engravings and paintings etched on some smoothed rock faces. **Most visitors take the 2-hour trip through the first two spectacular gorges, where there's a short, but easily manageable, walk between them.** Mosses and ferns cascade down wetter parts of the rugged red bluffs, Livistona palms, pandanus, silver paperbark and freshwater mangroves line or climb the cliffs, caves that are home to bats, and where fairy martin build mud nests under the overhangs, and aquatic life including freshwater crocodiles, long-necked tortoises and fish, are the main features of the gorge. Other gorges are well worthwhile visiting, on 4 and 8 hour tours, but walking between them is often more demanding.

In the picnic area near the boat ramps and jetty, the birdlife is colourful; friar birds, red-winged parrots, black cockatoos, grey bower birds, whistling and black kites, blue-faced (and very cheeky) honeyeaters and blue winged kookaburras, are common. Wallabies and goannas add interest to the picnic area.

Vegetation here includes salmon gum, northern ironwood, Darwin woolly-butt and a few boab trees. Much of the park area vegetation is medium to open eucalypt woodlands with acacias and grasses.

History

For thousands of years it has been the traditional lands of the Jawoyn people (sometimes spelt Djauan), who have been granted full ownership under land rights legislation for much of the park area. It will continue as a major tourist attraction, but will be jointly managed by the Jawoyn and Conservation Commission.

Tours

Boat tours operated by Travel North depart daily on a regular basis all week from the jetty, cost $20. They also offer an 8-hour trip of the gorge system, costs $60. Scenic flights are available, as are short helicopter flights. Bookings at Travel North in Katherine, or at the caravan park kiosk at the Gorge. Enquiries, ph (089) 721 044.

Walks

There are a number of walking tracks of varying lengths, and many involve overnight camping. The longest is the 76km (47 miles) one to Edith Falls. Bushwalkers Nelly Dykstra and Stefan Hampel described it as one of the most exhilarating they had experienced. Check with the rangers for details, advise them of your plans, and obtain a permit. A small deposit is required before departing on the walk. It is refunded on returning.

Camping

Camping is not permitted within the first 3 gorges. Register with the ranger if you wish to camp within the upper reaches of the river, or on an overnight walk.

Boats and Canoes

Boating hours between 7am and 7pm. Length and power of boats must not exceed 4m and 7.5hp, respectively. Motor powered boats are restricted to first 5 gorges, and the ranger must be notified of any boat or canoe. Kookaburra Canoe Hire offer canoes on hourly, half-day and full day basis. Located at the jetty.

Fishing and Swimming

Fishing is permitted using hand-held rod or line. Many visitors swim, but some areas are very deep (over 27m).

How To Get There

By car, it is a 32km (19 miles) sealed road from Katherine. BP Roadhouse (Travel North) operate daily bus services from Katherine ($13 one way). Gorge Tours booked from Katherine can include coach transfer.

Accommodation

Katherine Gorge Caravan Park - powered and unpowered sites, $10.50 per adult, $3.50 child. Shaded sites. Pets not allowed.

Services and Facilities

The Caravan Park has a general store/kiosk, take-away food, ice, souvenirs, telephone, fuel (super, diesel, camping gas), tourist information and tour bookings. Open all year, 7am-7pm. Credit cards accepted (Bankcard, Mastercard, Visa), ph (089) 721 253.

The Ranger Station Visitor centre - an excellent centre offers displays, park literature, video screenings, ice cold water, and duty ranger for advice.

Picnic Facilities

Treed, grassy banks, and flats have tables, toilets, showers, water, and wood barbecues.

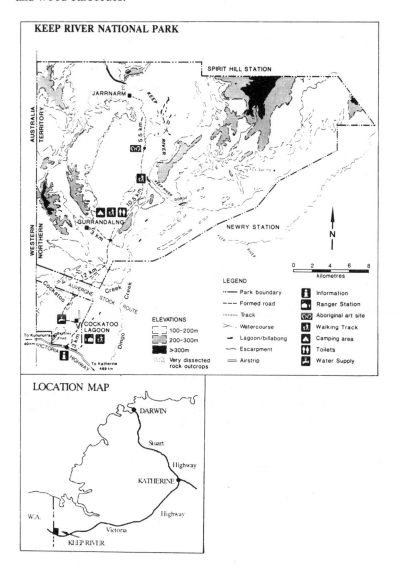

KEEP RIVER NATIONAL PARK

59,700ha (147,459 acres)

Location

On the Victoria Highway, 469km (290 miles) west of Katherine, and 36km (22 miles) east of Kununurra, Western Australia. The Western Australian State border defines the park's western boundary.

Characteristics

Noted for its striking ancient sandstone formations, and fascinating but complex geological structures, the Park also has some superb Aboriginal Art sites. It's a geologists' delight, with evidence of glacial and marine deposits and volcanic activity imprinted in the exposed rock formations. Streams leave just sandy beds during the Dry season in this isolated, wilderness area, characterised too by enormous baobab, commonly spelt boab, and known as bottle trees (Adansonia gregorii) on the open plains and rocky ridges.

The park is crossed by the Auvergne stock route, an old cattle track to the Kimberley, about 6km (3 miles) north of the Victoria Highway. Keep River is well worth visiting for its tropical savannah lands, and some spectacular escarpment and plateau sculptures.

Landforms

Several distinctive landform types characterise the park. Cambridge Gulf lowlands and plains occupy a significant area of the park in the northern and central areas. The Keep River sweeps through the centre, cutting a gorge through the sandstone, before striking north and meandering into Joseph Bonaparte Gulf. The plains are broken by uplands and dissected plateaux of cross-bedded quartz sandstones and conglomerates of the Palaeozoic era (between 250 and 500 million years ago).

The south-eastern area is dominated by Victoria River plateau terrain, with older sediments and volcanic rocks forming gently folded, undulating landscapes. Mesas and benches up to 300m above the plains, like the plateaux, are mainly composed of siltstone and sandstone, and add extraordinary colour and variety. The Halls Creek Ridge geological formations in mainly the southern part, are distinctive for low parallel ridges of metamorphic rock, while igneous (volcanic) rocks also form ridges and plateau-like formations, but with weathered domes and resistant rearing outcrops (tors). The variety of landform features make bushwalking and photographic activities most rewarding, and give a taste of the Kimberley to come. An excellent Department of Mines and Energy booklet entitled *Geology of Keep River National Park* gives detailed information. It's available from the Mines Department in Darwin.

Flora and Fauna

Many species of plantlife have been identified, the most widespread being eucalypts (bloodwoods and stringy-barks); banksias (clentata) and grevilleas are others on the lowlands. Freshwater mangroves and pandanus border the waterways and soaks. Tall tropical perennial grasses grow on the lowlands, while more undulating and rocky slopes support spinifex.

There's a range of birdlife and reptiles. Short-eared rock-wallaby, white-quilled rock pigeon and sandstone shrike-thrush find a home in the rocky dissected terrain.

Attractions

Geology and landforms. Remarkable formations softened by the light vegetation cover are enhanced by sunrises and sunsets.

Aboriginal Art Sites. The area is Miriwung homelands, and a 10-minute walking track from the car park leads to an art gallery.

Keep River Gorge. For over thousands of years, the Keep River has exploited a fault in the sandstone, and has eroded a deep, 4km long gorge. The floor provides pleasant walking conditions, and interest is added by the Aboriginal paintings at intervals along its walls.

Bushwalking

Take plenty of drinking water, and for extended walks, it's advisable to have the 1:100,000 No 4766 Keep River Topographic Map. Please advise the ranger before setting off. It's hot here - the mean yearly temperature is 30C (86F), and the hottest months, October and November have an average maximum of 37C (99F)!; sunshine hours in the Dry season average 10, while in the Wet, 7.5 hours.

Conservation

Please be mindful of fire risks. Vehicles must keep to designated roads only. Art sites, as with all natural elements in the park, are fully protected and must not be interfered with. Pets are allowed by permit only.

How To Get There

Entry to the park is 3km (2 miles) east of the NT/WA border, on the northern side of the Victoria Highway. Within the park, a formed gravel road provides conventional vehicle access, but roads may be temporarily closed during the Wet season.

Services and Facilities

A ranger station (residence only) is located at the semi-permanent waters of Cockatoo Lagoon, near the park entrance. Information is available here, as is the park's only source of drinking water.

One camp area - Gurrandalng (15km [9 miles] from the main road) - is provided. Facilities include tables, barbecues and pit toilets. Marked interpretive walking tracks are located at the **camping area.**

LAKE BENNETT

Population 4

Location

7km (4 miles) east of the Stuart Highway turn-off, 80km (50 miles) south of Darwin.

Characteristics

The privately-owned Lake Bennett Holiday Park covers over 446ha (1101 acres) of tropical wilderness, including a 105ha (259 acres) man-made lake that is ideal for a range of water-based activities, including safe swimming, wind surfing, canoeing, sailing, water cycling, and fishing. Abundant birdlife (jabiru, spoonbill, sea eagles, pelican, among many others), bush walks and pleasant foreshores, add interest. The owners have put identification tags on trees, and are knowledgeable on local landscape, flora and fauna features.

Attractions

Water-based activities. Fishing for black bream, rock cod, ox-eyed herring, and catfish. **Abseiling is by prior arrangement.**

Accommodation

Camp-o-tel (a new concept in accommodation - between a motel and a tent). These comfortable budget priced accommodation capsules consist of a raised A-frame structure, moulded fibreglass floor and fittings, and strong fabric for the walls. Beds for sleeping. Cost $15 single, $24 double, $40 for four persons (but bring your own linen).

Campsites $14-17 family; $12 x 2, $6 one person. Shady, grassed sites. No pets. Powered sites available, ph (089) 760 960.

How To Get There

A good, unsealed road from the Highway provides all year access for all types of vehicles. From Darwin, tour companies Terra Safari Tours and Dial A Safari, run trips which include Lake Bennett. There is courtesy pick-up from the Highway.

Services and Facilities

The park has a general store, take-away food, ice, artifacts, camping gas, picnic/bbq/shaded areas, and information. Water-based activity hire, with costs per hour, include: aquabikes, $10; canoes, $8; 12 ft catamarans, $20. No powered boats are allowed. Open all year, sunrise to sunset. Credit cards accepted (Bankcard, Mastercard, Visa).

LARRIMAH

Population 25

Location

On the Stuart Highway, 502km (311 miles) south of Darwin.

Characteristics

The former North Australia Railway terminus township consists of three establishments: the historic Larrimah Hotel; the Shell Roadhouse; the Green Park Tourist complex; and some scattered old houses, in an open tropical woodland setting. It is well worth an overnight stay for its character, fascinating wartime history, and a nearby ghost town.

History

The original settlement was at Birdum (about 5km away), established in the 1880s by settlers on Birdum Creek. It had a population of between 20 and 30, and reached its peak during the war when the Birdum Hotel became HQ for the US Army Forces. After the war, the town effectively moved to Larrimah, mainly due to flooding and proximity to the Stuart Highway.

Larrimah was originally known as DOMF Siding, but was re-named Larrimah by the army in 1941 - Larrimah is an Aboriginal word meaning where one encounters another. During the war it was a staging camp for troops, a major supply base, and was part of the 'Drawback Line' (a line across Northern Australia where the country would have been defended from any Japanese invasion). About 10km (6 miles) to the north, the RAAF established Gorrie Airfield, which was highly secretive and serviced aircraft. It was here that some top level Pacific Theatre wartime decisions were made by Supreme Allied Commander, US General Douglas McArthur. The longest airstrip in the Southern Hemisphere is now disused, and derelict aircraft are vivid reminders of the wartime action.

After the war, the 1920s vintage Birdum Hotel was moved to Larrimah, while the rest of Birdum was abandoned. The railway closed in 1976; a victim of lack of maintenance funds after Cyclone Tracy, de-stocking of cattle stations, and a mining slump. The Larrimah terminus is now the Shell Roadhouse. An old post office and Overland Telegraph Station remains are near the hotel.

Attractions

Historic. The old Gorrie Airstrip and WWII aircraft remains. Birdum Ghost Town. The old post office, repeater station and railway terminus.

The Larrimah Hotel. An old bush pub that is full of character, humour and wartime memorabilia. Owners Ray and Carl Drummond offer a most original menu in their dining room - Sump Oil Soup and croutons, $10; Boar's Tits on Toast, $20; and Toasted Sardines and Ice Cream, $20!

Green Park Tourist Complex. Has a 4m salt-water crocodile, 4 freshwater crocodiles, and a pet buffalo.

Events

Larrimah Irish Ashes - a cricket weekend, near March 17 each year.

Accommodation

Larrimah Wayside Inn (Hotel) - motel $10 a bed (shared facilities).
   Camping (per vehicle) - powered $5, unpowered free, backpackers free, showers $2 per person. Disabled access. Pets allowed, dogs

leashed. Open all year 7am-11pm, ph (089) 759 931.

Green Park Tourist Complex - cabins $25 single/double, $38 family. *Camping*; powered sites $12 two persons, unpowered $4 per person. Swimming pool (guests only), Shell garage facilities. Pets allowed, dogs leashed. Open all year 6am-9pm, ph (089) 759 937.

Top O' Town Van Park - cabin (en suite) $40 x 2 (up to 5 people); powered sites $12 x 2. Swimming pool (patrons only), BP garage facilities. Pets allowed under control. Open all year 7am-9pm, ph (089) 759 932.

All establishments accept credit cards (Bankcard, Mastercard, Visa).

Eating Out

Larrimah Hotel - buffalo, barramundi, crocodile and camel (from $12).

Green Park - has a licensed dining room specialising in barramundi ($12.50). While they don't have croc on the menu, they do sell Crocodile Attack Insurance!

Services and Facilities

All establishments have general stores, take-away food, ice, souvenirs, fuel (super, ULP, diesel, camping gas). Vehicle spares, repairs, tyres and tubes (Shell, Green Park; BP, Top O' Town), towing (Green Park). Showers for travellers ($2). Aviation fuel, by arrangement. Post office agency (Green Park). Picnic/bbq/shaded area (Green Park has a delightful spot).

MANDORAH

Population 100

Location

On the north-east point of Cox Peninsula, on the western side of Darwin Harbour.

Characteristics

Stretches of lonely, sandy beaches, good fishing and bush beach camping are some features of this small, attractive holiday resort situated across the bay from Darwin. Mandorah is an ideal few days' retreat spot, or a pleasant day trip destination via a 20 minute ferry ride from Darwin. An interesting corroboree performed by the local Kenbi Aboriginal people, adds interest. A supermarket, the Mandorah Inn and Golden Sands Holiday Units provide a range of services and facilities for visitors. And, because of the presence of estuarine crocodiles, there is no swimming in the coastal or inland waterways.

Attractions

Fishing. Rock fishing using lures for salmon and barramundi. Bottom fish include bream, schnapper, flathead and parrot fish. Many people fish from the jetty. For 'boaties', there's a ramp nearby.

Beaches. Interesting coastal areas are ideal for walking, and you may spot some curiously coiled shellfish - these are fossilised ammanoids, millions of years old.

Aboriginal Corroboree. In conjunction with Mandorah Inn, the local Aboriginal community perform a corroboree on the beach at 7pm Tuesday, Thursday, Saturday and Sunday nights between March and October. For its atmosphere and cross-cultural experience, it's well worthwhile, and the evening includes a meal - barramundi cooked in coals in traditional Aboriginal way, mud crabs, cold meats and salads. Costs $55 adult, $24 child, which includes return evening ferry fares from Darwin.

Magnetic Anthills. Distinctive mounds pointing north (hence the name) characterise the landscape on the drive into Mandorah.

How To Get There

By road, 125km (76 miles) from Darwin; turn-off 48km (30 miles) south of Darwin from the Stuart Highway. The road is sealed to the Blackmore bridge, then it is formed gravel of variable quality, including rough. Along the way are the Berry Springs attractions (see listing) and Belyuen, an Aboriginal settlement where there's a shop, and no permits are required to pass through.

By ferry is the easiest way. Mandorah operates *Billy-J* mainly on the days of the Corroboree, while more regular services are offered by Darwin Harbour Ferries MV *Darwin Duchess* ($14 adult return, $8 child), ph (089) 813 894 for times.

Accommodation

Golden Sands Resort - demountable self-contained units, $60 (6 persons), $40 (4 persons). Backpackers $10 per person - only *backpacker place on the beach.*

Camping - $5 per person, child under 10 free. Shaded, beach front sites, some powered. No pets allowed. Bbq, swimming pool (guests only), tennis courts. Open all year, 7 days, ph (089) 785 050.

Mandorah Inn - motel room $60 single, large swimming pool (patrons only). Camping area $5 per night. Open all year, 7 days till midnight, ph (089) 785 044. Both establishments accept credit cards (Bankcard, Mastercard, Visa, EFTPOS).

> **Beach Camping** - some camp along the coast away from the settlement, but you need 4WD for some areas.

Services and Facilities

Supermarket, bar, restaurant (Inn - bistro style, steaks and seafood around $12 main course; bbq packs $10), take-away food, ice, souvenirs, fuel (super, diesel, ULP), oil, camping gas (Inn), boat ramp, jetty and airfield. Information from accommodation establishments.

MATARANKA

Population 150

Location

On the Stuart Highway, 108km (66 miles) south of Katherine.

Characteristics

An old pub, heat and dust, and a few colourful locals, give plenty of character to a township that blends comfortably into its tropical bushland setting. Capital of the Never Never (when you reach this country you never, never want to leave), Mataranka is a small cattle and service town where the population drops dramatically during the Wet, and soars in the busy cattle and tourist season of the Dry. The nearby old Elsey Station was, in 1902, the setting for Jeannie Gunn's famous Australian outback story *We of the Never-Never* in which, as one of the very few white women in this harsh cattle country, she vividly recounts her experiences of remote station life. A varied and fascinating history, as well as the natural delights of nearby Mataranka Thermal Pool, make a stay in the area a must.

History

According to Aboriginal folklore, a wild wind swept across the region and created in its passage Mataranka, Bitter Springs and the thermal springs. The main descendants of the early Aborigines today are the Mungarai people.

The earliest Europeans in the region were Leichhardt in 1845, and Stuart in 1862. Both explored the Roper River region, while A.C. Gregory found and named Elsey Creek in 1856, after a young surgeon and naturalist attached to his party. The Overland Telegraph Line construction crews survived a massive Wet in 1872, and Warloch Ponds was named after a horse belonging to Alfred Giles (of Springvale Homestead fame) - it had an uncanny ability to find water, and twice saved the lives of men.

Elsey Station was established in 1881 by Abraham Wallace on a 6000 sq km (2280 sq miles) lease which encompassed Mataranka, then known as Bitter Springs. Melbourne-born Aeneas Gunn was appointed manager of Elsey Station in 1901 and, along with his bride Jeannie, took up the post the following year. Aeneas contracted malaria and died in 1903. Jeannie then managed the station for a short time before returning to Melbourne where she wrote her story. The film *We of the Never Never* was filmed here in 1981, and a replica of the old homestead used for the set is located at Mataranka Homestead.

A division of The Elsey in 1916 saw the formation of Mataranka Station, the homestead of which is now the tourist resort centre. Dr Gilruth, the then Administrator under South Australian Government direction, started the short-lived Mataranka Horse and Sheep Experimental Station. Dingoes, climate and spear-grass were the main reasons for its failure, and by 1919 the area had reverted to cattle.

The railway line came through in the 1920s, and about the same time the township was officially gazetted and named. The name derivation is obscure: because of Dr Gilruth's New Zealand connections, some think it is a Maori name; others say it is Aboriginal.

During World War II, Mataranka was a military camp, ammunition dump, and a base workshop for all kinds of repairs. Slab foundation remnants of the Sergeants' Mess, built in 1942, and other relics in the bush are wartime reminders. The first race meeting was run in 1943, and judging by the pedigrees of the horses supplied by local stations, the event was less than serious: 'Parched Throat' by 'Canteen' out of 'Grog'; 'Home Leave' by 'Hard to Get' out of 'Seldom Seen'; and 'Hitler' by 'Doubtful' out of 'Dam Unknown' were some.

Attractions

Mataranka Homestead and Mataranka Thermal Springs Pool. See under Mataranka Homestead listing.

Elsey Cemetery. The graves of the Elsey Station pioneers and *We of the Never Never* fame, including Aeneas Gunn, Muluka who was head of the property, and Henry Peckham ('Fizzer') the mailman, lie in the cemetery. Located 8km (4 miles) east of the Stuart Highway, from the turn-off 13km (8 miles) south of the township.

Original Elsey Homestead Site. A further 500m from the cemetery is the original homestead site, marked by a cairn. Because of frequent water shortages at this site, the homestead was relocated at McMinns Bar on the Roper River, in 1906.

Elsey National Park. Situated 7km east of the Mataranka township, this park is one of the newest in the Northern Territory and takes in the Thermal Pool and areas along the Roper River. There is an established camping ground at the 12 Mile Yards, which is suitable for tents or caravans. It does not have powered sites and generators are not permitted, but there are hot showers and toilet facilities, and a kiosk selling food and drinks. Facilities in the park include walking trails, with ranger-guided walks available; boat launching ramps at 12 Mile Yards; canoes for hire; and parking for cars and coaches. For more information on the Park, contact the Conservation Commission Matananka Office on (089) 754 560. Dogs are not permitted in Elsey National Park.

Tours

See details under Mataranka Homestead listing.

Events

Rodeo and Camp Draft (varied times).

Accommodation

Old Elsey Roadside Inn - motel units $55 double; $45 single; backpackers' accommodation $10 per person. Open 24 hours, ph (089) 754 512.

Territory Manor - more upmarket with a relaxed 'retreat' atmosphere. Motel $65 single, $72 double. Caravan park - en suites, $20 x 2. Attractive, shaded sites, swimming pool, kiosk, licensed restaurant. Reception 7am-8pm (night bell). Open all year, ph (089) 754 516. Located 300m east of water tower.

Mataranka Roadhouse - on-site vans $33 x 2.

Mataranka Homestead and Youth Hostel. See Mataranka Homestead listing.

All places accept credit cards.

Eating Out

Territory Manor: open-air dining, 3 course meals (barramundi, buffalo, beef) around $20. Also bbq buffet.

Old Elsey Inn: the colourful old pub, run by Ken Harding, serves good value counter meals (seafood, roasts, steaks - $8-12).

Mataranka Homestead: see separate listing.

Services and Facilities

Hotel, restaurant, take-away food (pizza among others), supermarket (open 7 days), store, 3 fuel outlets (super, ULP, diesel - available until at least 9pm, sometimes 11pm, AH emergency fuel at Mobil - minimum $20 worth), camping gas, oil, vehicle repairs and towing (Willy's Auto, ph 754 583), health centre, police station, post office and airstrip. Credit cards widely accepted.

Radio Stations: ABC 106.1 and 107.7 FM.

Emergency Services

Dial 000; or police, ph 754 511; ambulance, ph 721 200.

MATARANKA HOMESTEAD

Location

On the Waterhouse River, 9km (5 miles) east of Mataranka Township.

Characteristics

Set amidst tropical woodlands and bounded by the rainforest lined Waterhouse River, this delightfully treed and grassed resort is an ideal spot to relax and 'take the waters' of the magical thermal pool. Also, it's a good base from which to explore some magnificent Roper

River scenery, or try some barra fishing. Excellent campsites, an open tropical bar and restaurant, casual family oriented atmosphere, a sense of history, wildlife, including freshwater crocodiles, and plenty of activities, are the major features offered. The homestead was purchased and established as a resort after World War II by ex-serviceman H.V. Smith, who, during his wartime service, had recognised its enormous tourist potential.

Attractions

Mataranka Thermal Springs. **Located next to the homestead, the natural thermal spring and pool is surrounded by a delightful tract of tropical rainforest. It's a beautiful place for a relaxing swim and, while the therapeutic powers of the waters are debatable, it's still an invigorating experience.** The waters rise crystal clear from the deep Rainbow Spring at a rate of 16,495 litres per minute, or 23,753,945 litres (5 million gallons) a day, and maintain a constant temperature of 34C (93F). In the pool, you may see any one of four species of tortoise (Elseya spp. and Chelodina spp), as well as a variety of small fish.

Fringing the pool are the pandanus (Pandanus aquaticus and P. spiralis), cabbage tree palms (Livistona sp. and near relatives of the ancient palms in the Red Centre's Finke Gorge), paper-barks (Melaleuca spp) and yellow passionfruit (Passiflora foetida).

Birdlife is plentiful, including the colourful and noisy red-tailed black cockatoo (Calyptorhynchus magnificus), sulphur-crested cockatoo (Cacatua galerita), rainbow lorikeet (Trichoglossus haematodus), azure kingfisher (Alcyone azurea) and blue-winged kookaburra (Dacelo leachii). Thousands of black fruit bats, or flying foxes, hang from the palms and use their wings as a fan to keep cool. They darken the sky in the evening as they swarm off to feed.

The weir was constructed during World War II to provide recreational facilities for soldiers stationed in the area, and its original 'R and R' function is little changed today, as visitors use the homestead and pool as a few days' resting place before resuming their journey up or down 'The Track'.

Elsey Homestead Replica. Located at the entrance to the resort, the replica houses a fascinating pictorial, photographic and written display that provides an insight into early droving days and cattle station life at The Elsey. Open all day.

Nearby are Aboriginal Gunyas, built with the advice of the elders from the local Yangman/Mangari Tribe. Walking tours operate daily from May to October, leaving from the kiosk at the Homestead.

Activities

Bush walks, swimming (thermal pool and Stevies hole), fishing (barramundi, bream, catfish, sleepy cod, freshwater crayfish on the Roper and Little Roper Rivers), canoeing (hire from Waterhouse River Jetty), bird watching, croc spotting, tours, horse riding, helicopter and scenic flights.

Tours

The Homestead runs a Wagon Safari, which gives a 3-hour landscape appreciation of the Roper River, and includes billy tea, damper, drinks - $21 adult.

Brolga Tours, ph (089) 754 538. Doug Collins has been on both sides of the environmental fence - he was a crocodile hunter, and now leads tours that give a rare brush with nature in the Roper River system. The largest known stand of cabbage palms (Livistona rigida), historic Elsey Station, Red Lily Lagoon, and informative commentaries, are some features of his 3.5 hour tour.

A free historic homestead walking tour is offered at 11am daily.

How To Get There

By road, it's sealed to the homestead. Turn off east of the highway, just south of the township. Major coach companies include it on their daily services between Darwin and Alice Springs, or you can arrive by light aircraft.

Accommodation

Motel - $59 single, $74 double, $82 triple. Family rooms and cabins from $56. Backpacker $15 per person.

Youth Hostel - $13.

Caravan Park - powered sites $18 x 2, unpowered sites $14 x 2.

Sites shaded, grassed; some secluded waterfront sites. Pets are not allowed. Open 6am-midnight, all year. Credit cards accepted (Bankcard, Mastercard, Visa), ph (089) 754 544.

Entertainment

During the tourist season, live Country and Western music every night, and a children's show in the afternoon.

Services and Facilities

Bar, restaurant (steaks, buffalo, barramundi - main course around $17), take-away food, ice, general store, souvenirs, hire canoes, fuel (super), oil, camping gas, picnic/shaded/bbq areas (gas operated), wood bbqs (BYO wood), and airstrip (1000m, south-west approach).

NHULUNBUY - GOVE PENINSULA

Population 4000

Location

On the north-eastern tip of Arnhem Land on the Gove Peninsula, 650km (403 miles) east of Darwin.

Characteristics

Australia's most remote tropical frontier town is a modern, vibrant mining and resort centre, delightfully set amongst lush bush and woodlands on the coast where the Gulf of Carpentaria meets the Arafura Sea. The 96,000 sq km (37,056 sq miles) of Arnhem Land separate Nhulunbuy from the rest of the Territory, while the only road connection is to Katherine, over 780km (483 miles) away via a 4WD track that is inaccessible at times during the year. This remoteness means that it is relatively untouched by large scale tourism, thus allowing visitors to merge comfortably into the local scene, rather than just being a tourist. Most goods come by sea to the deep water harbour, and visitors arrive by air.

The attractively laid-out town centre offers a full range of services and facilities, and fine accommodation provides a good base from which to explore the area's attractions. Endless white sandy beaches, an excellent variety of fishing, superb sailing waters and landfall for round-the-world sailors, extensive sporting facilities including a highly rated golf course, a rich Aboriginal heritage and culture, plenty of interesting scenery and wildlife including colourful birds, salt-water crocodiles and buffalo, are some of the town's features. In

NHULUNBUY

1	ARNHEM CLUB	J6
2	CATHOLIC CHURCH	J7
3	GOLF CLUB	H5
4	GOVERNMENT CENTRE	J7
5	HIDEAWAY SAFARI LODGE MOTEL	H7
6	HIGH SCHOOL	H7
7	HINDLE OVAL	J7
8	HOSPITAL	H7
9	NABALCO OVAL	J7
10	PRIMARY SCHOOL	H6
11	SHOPPING CENTRE	H7
12	UNITING CHURCH	J6
13	WALKABOUT HOTEL	J7
14	YIRRKALA ARTS & CRAFTS	H7

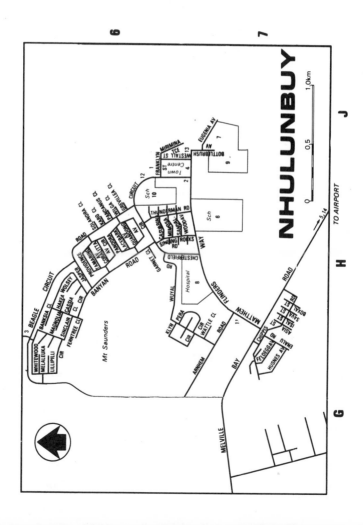

fact, it's not unusual for a buffalo or two to check out what's happening on the golf course, or in town - one was even found enjoying the waters of the pub's swimming pool one night.

The balmy, tropical climate and younger age range of the town's cosmopolitan inhabitants, most of whom work at the massive bauxite mine, have fostered possibly Australia's most sports crazy place, and outdoor oriented life style. There are over 33 sporting organisations, and many locals indulge in quite a few different sports each week. Visitors are quite welcome to join in too. The Surf Lifesaving Club tower is not for checking sharks, it's for spotting crocodiles! To a large extent, sun, sea and sand sum up this amazing tropical paradise that provides a fine environment for adventure and relaxation.

History

The prominent landform around which the town is built is Mt Saunders, called Nhulunbuy (meaning roughly 'hill by the sea') by Aborigines, which gives the town its name, while the peninsula is named after an Australian airman, William Gove, who was killed in the area during World War II.

On a human occupation time scale, a European presence of 17 years is a mere blink when compared with the possibly 50,000 year occupancy by Aborigines. The art work of their ancient but continuing culture can be seen at Yirrkala, the name of the most significant clan living here today. Macassan beche de mer (sea slug) and trepang (sea cucumber) fishermen were regular visitors from Indonesia as early as the 16th century, and this contact is shown in some Aboriginal words and art designs. Europeans and Aborigines work closely and amicably here today, and cross-cultural experience opportunities for tourists are a highlight of a visit to this area of Arnhem Land.

Navigator Matthew Flinders explored the coastline in 1803, and it's probable that Portuguese and Dutch mariners were much earlier explorers of the coastal region. Flinders noted the red coastal cliffs which were later discovered to be bauxite - the ore from which aluminium is derived.

During World War II, an RAAF airstrip was constructed on and out of bauxite, but it was not until the early 1950s that it was recognised. The town began with the mine in 1971 (construction started in 1969). While essentially established to service the mine, alumina plant and port, the climate and natural attractions encouraged tourism as an important secondary function.

Land Ownership

The area is part of Arnhem Land owned by Aborigines. Unless you are driving overland from Katherine, no permits are required to enter Nhulunbuy. However, if you travel overland independently out of Nhulunbuy, eg, up the coast, a 'recreational permit', easily and instantly obtained from the Northern Land Council Office in town, is required. Tour operators arrange permits for organised expeditions. If in doubt, check with the Lands Council office or Tourist Association.

Attractions

Climate. Because it's surrounded by water, gentle breezes have a pleasant modifying effect on temperatures, so it's not as hot or humid as other Top End places. Inland, it can be hotter. Temperatures average around 26C (79F), 18-20C (64-68F) at night (June, July), rising in average to 32C (90F) in November and December, the hottest months.

Natural Features. Beautiful sweeping beachscapes, aquamarine waters, inland waterways, billabongs and rock pools, and patches of tropical rainforest, offer much to naturalists, adventurers and walkers.

Wildlife. Large salt-water crocodiles inhabit coastal and inland waters. Buffalo range freely, while the occasional king red kangaroo may be seen. Perentie, frill-necked lizards, king brown and python snakes are around, as are dingoes. Birdlife includes blue-winged kingfisher, a range of parrots including the colourful red-shouldered lorikeet, honeybirds, white-breasted sea eagles, terns and falcons. Whilst wildlife is prolific, sightings during daylight hours are a bonus. You'll see plenty of birds, and if you are quietly observant, it's amazing what may be seen in the bush.

Fishing. Gove Peninsula offers first rate fishing. Reef fish include coral trout, cod, red emperor, sweet-lip and schnapper. Surface fish range from the fighting tuna to barracuda, queen fish, trevally and shark. In the rivers are barramundi, bream and mangrove jack. Out in the Gulf, October to May are ideal months only because June, July and August are subject to the uncomfortable south-east prevailing winds (SE Tradewinds), but the fish still bite! Charter boats are available, and reasonably priced one-day fishing trips can be negotiated with private boat owners.

Bauxite Mine. Nabalco Pty Ltd operate the open cut mine where huge 85 tonne capacity trucks haul the ore to a crusher. Once reduced, the ore is transported by a 3-tiered 17.5km (10 miles) conveyor belt system (one of the world's largest) - one to feed the alumina plant, the other two belts for direct bulk export from the deep water port at Melville Bay. The harbour here is also a safe haven for yachts. Overburden (waste rock) is used to rehabilitate area mines in the 250 million tonne reserve. About 5 million tonnes of ore are mined, producing 1 million tonnes of alumina annually, and 2 million tonnes of bauxite are exported directly. Royalties of over $1 million per annum flow to the owners of the land, the Aborigines. A 3.5-hour comprehensive tour of the mine is available on Thursdays only (see details under Tours).

Yirrkala. A former mission is now a major Aboriginal centre, best known for the Yirrkala people's historic struggle to win title in contemporary Australian law to their traditional lands. This was achieved in 1976. Aboriginal art representative of Arnhem Land is on display, and some artifacts may be purchased here. Located south of the town.

Nambara Arts & Crafts, ph 872 811, is also worth a visit.

Golf Course. A magnificent 9-hole course attracts golfers from all over Australia for the various tournaments held there. Visitors are welcome, ph (089) 872 591.

Swimming. People do swim, but with caution, as there are salt-water crocodiles in all these tropical waters, and stingers in the West season. Check with the locals about the 'safer' spots.

Tours

Cruising and Fishing: a range of charters, cruise tours of coast and islands (eg, Wigram), and game fishing (marlin, sailfish) are available. Contact Lady Sarah Charters, ph (089) 872 832.

Nabalco Mine: a free 3.5 hour tour of the mine is available every second Thursday morning only, ph (089) 875 211. This is an extremely interesting tour that is a must if you are in the area.

Events

Gove Game Fishing Classic (sailfish and marlin) is held during the third week in November.

How To Get There

By Road: it's a rough, nearly 800km (496 miles), 4WD trek from Katherine that takes about 14 hours' driving time. Some sections of the track at the Katherine end have been upgraded. Definitely for the experienced, well-equipped, no trailers or caravans, and permits to cross Aboriginal land are required (apply Northern Lands Council). Check with Katherine Police.

By Air: Qantas and Ansett Australia have regular flights. Some visit by light aircraft. There's an airport - town shuttle service for air travellers.

Accommodation

As yet there are no camping grounds, and camping in the bush or on the beaches is not allowed.

Gove Resort Hotel - double room $95, $20 for extra person. Swimming pool. Open all year, credit cards accepted (Bankcard, Master, Visa, American Express, Diners Club), ph (089) 871 777.

Hideaway Safari Lodge - budget accommodation with communal facilities, single $60, double $70; en-suite accommodation $90. Swimming pool, restaurant, credit cards accepted (Bankcard, Mastercard, Visa, American Express, Diners Club), ph (089) 873 933.

Eating Out

Hotel: An a la carte restaurant with local seafood, including mud crabs, on the menu - main course around $20; bistro with blackboard menu - main course around $10; carvery Sunday evening - $14.50 includes salads or vegetables.

Hideaway Restaurant: This delightful, intimate restaurant offers a limited a la carte menu. Apart from traditional food, it offers threadfin salmon, Carpentaria scallops and Gulf prawns - 3 course around $30. A continental breakfast costs $5, hot breakfast $10. An outdoor eating area features a lush tropical banyan courtyard with a huge fireplace/bbq.

Arnhem Club: along with other clubs in town, this offers alternative eating out, and a place to meet the locals. Contact the manager, ph (089) 871 277.

Services and Facilities

A full range includes police, post office, hospital, doctor, dentist, supermarkets, chemist, bank (Westpac), churches (Assemblies of God, Catholic, Uniting, Jehovah Witnesses), take-away food, full vehicle services and fuel (super, ULP, diesel), hire vehicles (Avis, Budget), sporting goods (including fishing), charter boats and yachts. Credit cards widely accepted.

Radio Stations: ABC 8G0 990; 103.7 FM.

Recreational

Public swimming pool, golf, bowls, tennis, squash are a few.

Emergency

Police, fire, ambulance, ph 000.

NOONAMAH

Population around 250

Location

On the Stuart Highway, 44km (27 miles) south of Darwin.

Characteristics

A small settlement consisting of a hotel/motel and store/service station is a convenient 'watering hole' at the 27-mile mark on the highway. Jock and Fran run the friendly, family-oriented Noonamah Hotel, the Aboriginal name of which means something like 'good watering place'.

The township's origins were during World War II when the RAAF built a series of fighter airstrips serviced by army field depots here. The army named the settlement Noonamah. The cluster arrangement of airstrips, supply depot, road and railway at this point was an ideal target for the Japanese, and it was attacked by a squadron of heavy bombers ·one night. The airstrips remain in remarkably good condition today, situated parallel to the highway.

Attractions

Crocodile Farm. Located 5km (3 miles) north of Noonamah, the farm is Australia's first and largest. On display is a large selection of salt and freshwater crocs; a good opportunity to see them from a close, safe range. This is home for about 7000 crocodiles which are commercially 'harvested' for their meat and skins - so it's primarily a business operation which tourists can visit. Staff give fascinating guided tours, and a visit is a very good way to learn something about these creatures before going to areas inhabited by crocodiles - for children it's one way to instil respect! Feeding times, at 2pm Mon-Sat, and 11am, noon and 2pm on Sunday, are worth seeing. There are tours at 11am every day, and on Mon, Wed and Fri another at noon.

Facilities include picnic area and children's play area, kiosk, toilets. Open daily 9am-5pm, all year, costs $8.50 adult, $3 child, ph (089) 881 450.

Accommodation

Noonamah Hotel - motel single $20, double $30, $6 each extra. Disabled facilities, credit cards accepted (Bankcard, Mastercard, Visa), open all year, Fri 10am-11.30pm, Sunday 10am-8pm, rest of week 10am-10pm, ph (089) 881 054.

Services and Facilities

Pub and beer garden, restaurant (seafood and steaks), pub entertainment Friday and Sunday, general store, ice, post office and Commonwealth Bank agencies, fuel (super, ULP, diesel - store/service station, open 6am-8pm).

Acacia store and camping ground is located on the highway about 15km (9 miles) north of the township. It offers on-site vans, powered or unpowered shady, grassed sites. Pets allowed, dogs leashed. Services include: mini-supermarket, fuel (super, ULP, diesel), camping gas, and emergency vehicle repairs. Open 7.30am-9.30pm daily.

PALMERSTON

Population 8000

Location

To the east of the Stuart Highway, 20km (12 miles) south of Darwin.

Characteristics

Palmerston is a new town, gazetted in 1980, and designed to become a self-sufficient city despite its closeness to Darwin. The establishment of extensive retail and office space in the centre will eventually be capable of providing 9000 jobs, thus ensuring its independence. It is one of the few examples in Australia of a new town developed on a virgin site, a factor which has allowed planners to apply contemporary town planning ideas without any existing constraints.

The most noticeable feature is the road layout pattern for the suburbs; roads are curved to avoid the traffic intersection problems common with traditional grid patterns. Each of the four suburbs so far developed (12 are planned) has a primary school that is also a neighbourhood community centre, while high schools double as district community centres. Residents have access to the facilities out of school hours, thus fostering stronger ties. Dominating the town centre is the 35m (115 ft) high water tower that is cyclone-proof, and has a capacity of 3000 tonnes, while the huge dishes of the Earth Satellite Tracking Station provide an interesting backdrop.

The town was named after Henry Temple, the third Viscount Palmerston (1784-1865) and British Prime Minister, after whom the original settlement at Darwin was also named. It's well worth visiting for its novel approaches to urban development, and for its shopping and recreational facilities.

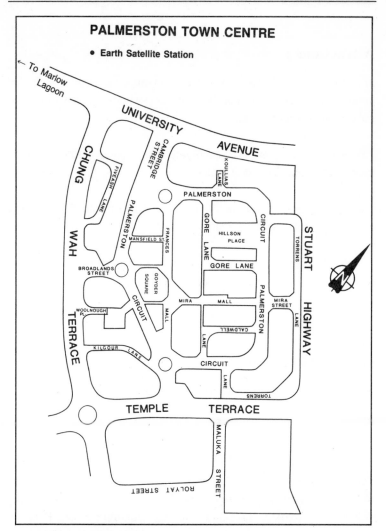

Tourist Information

Palmerston Town Council, TIO Building, open Mon-Fri 8am-4.15pm, ph (089) 321 322

Northern Territory Conservation Commission has offices in the Baywood Building, open Mon-Fri 8am-4pm, ph (089) 895 511.

Attractions

Marlow Lagoon. It features a lake and grassed, shaded barbecue areas, and is an ideal family spot for swimming, canoeing and picnicking. Elrundie Avenue.

Swimming Complex. Has an olympic size pool, children's pool, barbecues, kiosk. Tilston Avenue.

Satellite Tracking Station. Visitors are welcome to this tracking station on weekdays. University Avenue.

Each Friday evening, 5.30-9pm, there is an interesting market in the town centre, featuring exotic foods, entertainment and craft goods.

Yarrawonga Zoo. See Darwin listing.

How To Get There

There are frequent public bus services from Darwin.

Accommodation

There is no hotel or motel accommodation, but the Palms Caravan Park is located 3km away on the Stuart Highway. It has on-site vans ($38 two persons), powered sites ($14 x 2), unpowered ($5 per adult), mini-market, take-away food, swimming pool. Pets by arrangement, all major credit cards accepted, ph (089) 322 891.

Services and Facilities

For eating out, there are several take-away outlets in the town centre. The Palmerston Tavern has a family restaurant (3 courses for $10), and has entertainment on Friday and Saturday nights. The roast dinners on Sunday night are highly recommended.

There is a police station, post office, medical services (doctor, dentist, chiropractor, ambulance), veterinary clinic, chemist, supermarket, banks (ANZ, Westpac, National Commonwealth, auto teller at National). Shopping hours are as for Darwin. Vehicles - fuel (super, ULP, diesel), camping gas repairs at BP Palms, Shell Self-Serve, Stuart Highway, 24-hour fuel at BP Palms. All major credit cards are widely accepted.

Churches: Anglican, Baptist, Catholic, Christian Family Centre, Church of Christ, Lutheran, Salvation Army, Seventh Day Adventist, Uniting.

Recreation: boat ramp (Elizabeth River Bridge). It's tidal and hosts box jellyfish and salt-water crocodiles - swimming is prohibited here. Hire boats at Marlow Lagoon. Golf course and swimming centre.

Emergency Services

The telephone area code is 089.

Dial 000, or Ambulance, ph 279 000; Fire, ph 321 355 or 812 225; Police, ph 321 301 (AH 812 225); Towing, ph 321 555.

PINE CREEK

Population 500

Location

On the Stuart Highway, 230km (142 miles) south of Darwin, and 90km (55 miles) north of Katherine.

Characteristics

Pine Creek is a relatively unspoilt small town that retains strong reminders of its frantic gold rush origins. Relics of old mine workings, and a number of original buildings, make Pine Creek a significant architectural and historic site that is well worth visiting. Gold mining by large companies, tourism, pastoral and horticultural activities, sustain a thriving community today. In is undulating, tropical savannah setting, the town has modern facilities, and is one of the few places where you don't have to go too far to pan successfully for gold, or go trophy hunting for buffalo and wild pig.

History

Overland Telegraph Line builders first unearthed gold here in 1870 when digging holes for the line's construction. It triggered a gold rush. A telegraph office was opened in 1874, and in the same year, Europeans decided to import Chinese coolies to do the tough, physical work under the oppressive climatic conditions. Alluvial gold discoveries in 1877 resulted in a great influx of Chinese, so that by the 1880s, Pine Creek resembled more of a Chinatown than a European settlement. At this time, the Chinese population was about 1500, while Europeans numbered 100. Ping Que was the most astute. He not only held many mining leases, he also owned many stores and butcher's shops. European fear of Chinese dominance led to laws being passed in 1888, forbidding entry of Chinese into the Northern Territory.

In 1888, the township was officially named Playford; its present name is derived from the stands of pines that used to grow along the creek. The railway linking the town to Palmerston (Darwin) was completed in 1889. By 1905, the town consisted of a collection of galvanised iron buildings; railway station which incorporated the post office and telegraph station; police station; hotel; houses; and business premises, as well as tin shanties and Aboriginal bark humpies.

A period of stagnation occurred between the two world wars, and revitalisation came in the 1960s and 1970s with the development of short-lived uranium and iron ore mining ventures. Renewed interest in gold mining, and the advent of tourism, point to a bright future.

Attractions

The Repeater Station. Constructed at Burrundie in 1888, this iron building was dismantled and re-erected here in 1913. It is the oldest surviving pre-fabricated structure in the Territory, and is now owned by the National Trust. The Pine Creek Museum is housed here. Opening hours are 11am-3pm, entry is $2. Located on Railway Terrace.

Playford Club Hotel. Opened in 1889, it is the earliest example of a Territory galvanised iron pub still surviving. Reference is made to it in Mrs Aeneas Gunn's book *We of the Never Never* - on their way to Elsey Station in 1902, the Gunns stayed here. It is now a private residence, located on Main Terrace.

Railway Precinct. Built in 1888-89, it is of historic and architectural interest, and includes the station, goods shed, employees' residences, weighbridge, crane, and water tank. The railway closed in 1976. Adjacent is a Miners Park with an interesting array of relic mining equipment. Location is on Main Terrace, open 10am-2pm (June to October), costs $2.

Historic Sites. About 140 sites of possible historic significance have been identified in the area by the National Trust. These include old Chinese workings and mine shafts. The National Trust has devised a Heritage Trail for visitors - guides are available from the Museum.

Mary River. Pine Creek is also the southern gateway to Kakadu National Park, via the Kakadu Highway. Locals go to the picturesque Mary River where fishing is one of the main activities (barramundi, black bream, catfish). The Highway is sealed for the first 22km (13 miles), then it is a 30km (18 miles) gravel road to the river. With care, it can be negotiated by conventional vehicles, but the road is closed during the Wet season. Check road conditions at the police station.

Fossicking. Gold panning and fossicking in the area. At Frances Creek there is a Hematite locality.

Tours

Back O'Beyond offer 4 types of tours: individualised tours (fishing, local history, gold panning, Aboriginal art, etc); full-day sightseeing tours include wildlife spotting (birds, buffalo, pigs, crocodiles), swimming, fishing and escarpment terrain - cost is $400 for the day (a maximum of 6 people makes it $67 per person), lunch and morning tea provided; hunting safaris (buffalo, pig) with prices according to duration of hunt, number of hunters, accommodation and pick up requirements - hunters supply own firearms and ammunition, overseas hunters may be able to hire firearms - all hunting safaris operate only in the Dry season; a gold panning/historic tour lasts 2 hours and costs $12 per person. Earl Gano runs the tours, PO Box 12, Pine Creek, ph (089) 761 221.

Events

Pine Creek Races - last weekend in May.

Accommodation

Pine Creek Hotel - motel, single $62, double $75. Moule Street, ph (089) 761 288.

Youth Hostel - $7 per person per night. Main Terrace.

Pine Creek Caravan Park - cabins $17.50 single, $38.50 double; powered sites $13 for two persons, unpowered $5 per adult. Sites shaded, grassed, pets allowed, dogs leashed. Moule Street, ph (089) 761 217.

Eating Out

Take-away food (Shell service station and hotel). Counter meals from the Hotel Bistro ($9-12)

Services and Facilities

Police station, medical centre, post office, hotel, church (used by all denominations), supermarket and general store (both open Saturday mornings), bank agencies (ANZ, Commonwealth, Westpac), fuel (super, ULP, diesel), oil, camping gas, repairs and spares, towing service (Shell station, open 7am-6pm, (089) 761 217). Major credit cards are widely accepted in Pine Creek.

ROPER BAR

Population 9

Location

On the Roper Highway, 185km (115 miles) east of the Stuart Highway, from the turn-off just south of Mataranka.

Characteristics

Dieter and Veronica Janushka own the store/motel at this attractive tropical outpost on the Roper River, called simply "The Roper" by the locals (station people). The area is rich in exploration and pastoral history, and it is a popular boating and fishing spot for the prized barramundi. But, be careful as both salt-water and freshwater crocodiles inhabit the waters. The store is also the last fuel stop for those heading down to Borroloola, and while maps show Roper Bar as Aboriginal land, at the time of writing, no permits were required. It also serves as a meteorological station, and Veronica phones the readings through every 3 hours to Darwin.

History

Its European discoverer was Leichhardt and his party in 1845, and the river and bar were named after one of the expedition members, John Roper. Described as "a tall, vague, hungry-looking man", Friedrich Wilhelm Ludwig Leichhardt arrived in Australia in 1841 and succeeded in the greatest overland expedition in the country's history - an epic 5000km (3100 miles) trek from near Brisbane to Port Essington via the Gulf of Carpentaria and Arnhem Land. The party discovered and crossed the Roper on October 19, 1845. **In an area where fruit bats were abundant and easily caught, Leichhardt tossed some into the stew-pot and, after eating them, commented, "... a little strong"!** While he did not have a university degree, Leichhardt was an expert naturalist, and his botanical skills enabled the party to 'graze' well on the hazardous trip. It could even be said that he was Australia's original European 'bush tucker man'! Leichhardt disappeared in an expedition in 1848 - it is thought he perished in the Simpson Desert fringes. His favourable pastoral-potential reports led to the establishment of large cattle runs in the Roper region in later years.

The Roper River was part of the main supply route for the construction of northern sections of the Overland Telegraph Line; the Bar marks the navigable point of the river, originally known as Leichhardt's Crossing, and the rock bar was constructed in the early 1900s.

Attractions

Barramundi fishing. Best times are just after the Wet (April, May), and when they are 'running', the causeway is a popular spot. Other attractions are its remoteness, crocodiles, flora and fauna.

Dieter and Veronica offer individualised tours, and they can tell you much about the area's history and landscape.

How To Get There

By road, it is sealed for 140km (87 miles); the last 45km (28 miles) is a formed gravel surface suitable for conventional vehicles. From Roper Bar to Borroloola, recent road works have improved the surface - conventional vehicles with car. Keep an eye out for road trains!

Accommodation

Motel - $30 single, $40 double.

A camping/caravan park with unpowered sites, $3.50 per person. Powered sites available on request. Shaded, grassed sites, pets allowed, dogs leashed.

Services and Facilities

General store, take-away food, ice, Commonwealth Bank agency, information, boat ramp, airstrip, fuel (super, ULP, diesel), camping gas. Credit cards accepted (Bankcard, Mastercard, Visa), open all year 9am-6pm, ph (089) 754 636.

SPRINGVALE HOMESTEAD

Population 30

Location

8km (5 miles) south-west of Katherine Town Centre on Shadforth Road.

Characteristics

The oldest original station homestead in the Territory now functions as a low key tourist resort from its attractive 81ha (200 acres) Katherine riverside setting. It features the well-preserved and still functional stone homestead, and some original outbuildings constructed in 1879; a waterlily-covered billabong that's home for three freshwater crocodiles; huge shady trees; and newer unobtrusive buildings that include a restaurant, outdoor bar and motel accommodation. Staff are dressed in period costume.

Along with an Aboriginal Corroboree, Tranquillity Cruise, night Croc Spotting excursions, Bushman's Stew and Damper Night and Homestead Tour, the resort offers a cultural and historic perspective that is refreshingly different.

History

Springvale Station was established in 1878, and stretched from Pine Creek to Mataranka. It was one of the earliest settled in the Territory, and the first livestock, 12,000 sheep and 3000 cattle, arrived after an epic drove from Adelaide that lasted nearly 20 months. Alfred Giles directed the mammoth operation. The stock were broken into smaller manageable mobs in a successful operation that involved 40 men. Giles, along with his wife, Mary, managed the station for owner Dr W.J. Browne for many years. While much is made of Jeannie Gunn's 13 months at Elsey Station, there were many other women, such as Mary Giles, who endured unsung, married lifetimes in the Outback of the 1880s at places like Springvale.

Sheep were not very successful, and a succession of land uses were attempted here, even a peanut farm in the 1920s. A fascinating guided walking tour around the property covers such things as station life, history, flora and fauna. The historical focus of this tour is complemented by the river cruises run by Travel North. A booklet on the History of Springvale by Peter Forrest makes interesting reading and is available at the Homestead.

Tours and Entertainment

Springvale Homestead Tour. Two tours daily during the season, 10.30am and 2.30pm. There is no charge, and you do not have to be a guest to enjoy it.

Adventure Cruise. Night croc spotting, bushman's stew and damper, with a singalong around the campfire. Costs $31 adults, $15 children, 6.30-9.30pm.

Aboriginal Corroboree and BBQ. This is the next best thing to an authentic corroboree. Monday, Wednesday and Saturday, 6pm. Costs $15 adults, $7.50 children, dinner and corroboree $31.

Country and Western Music. Live each night in the bar area.

Accommodation

Budget Motel - $39 single, $46 double, $54 family.
  Camping - powered site $13 x 2; unpowered $10 x 2.

Services and Facilities

Bar, restaurant (generous homestyle from $10), take-away food, shop, camping gas, artifacts, souvenirs, ice, bbq, swimming pool and water slide. Credit cards accepted (Bankcard, Mastercard, Visa), open all year, 7 days, 7am-midnight, ph (089) 721 159.

"LAZY L" TRAIL RIDES

Located at the entrance to Springvale Homestead, "Lazy L" Stables, run by Liz Johnson, provide complementary tourist services: riverside wagon rides, 2 hours accompanied by an easy going chat about the history and bush, costs $30; a 2-3 hour cattle muster with experienced stockmen and an Aboriginal guide, costs $40; an 18 hour overnight campout with tall tales around the campfire, costs $80; pony rides cost $20 for 1 hour.

Liz also has kennels and a cattery, $5 per day, $30 per week; and a collection of animals (buffalo, donkeys, wallabies, wild pigs, goats and kangaroos, ph (089) 721 018.

TERRITORY WILDLIFE PARK AND BERRY SPRINGS

800ha (1976 acres)

Location

11km (7 miles) east of the Stuart Highway from the turn-off 48km (30 miles) south of Darwin, on the Cox Peninsula Road.

Characteristics

A fascinating and, in many ways, unique open-range wildlife park aims to have on show most bird, marsupial and reptile species representative of both arid and tropical zones. The Park has walkways through aviaries, a nocturnal house (the largest in Australia), an aquarium that allows underwater viewing of fish and other aquatic life via an acrylic tunnel underneath, while a special window allows a close-up view of a salt-water crocodile in its enclosure.

There are three ways to get around the exhibits, which all branch off the Park's 4km ring road. You can either walk, catch the shuttle train, or do a little of both.

A family favourite is the Kangaroos and Friends exhibit, which is all about close encounters, and provides opportunities for visitors totalk to keepers and have their questions answered. People can now mingle with free roaming Agile Wallabies, Antilopine Wallaroos, Red Kangaroos and Emus. They can also watch stately Kori Bustards, and discover for themselves if the spikes of the Echidna are as lethal as they look.

The Territory Wildlife Park has only been up and running for three years, and has already earned a place in the Northern Territory Tourist Commission's "Hall of Fame" for Best Tourist Attraction. In 1992, it was runner-up in the Australian Tourism Awards for Major Tourist Attraction.

Later stages will incorporate the existing Berry Springs Nature Park. Facilities include kiosk, displays and picnic areas, and fees are levied.

Visitors are admitted to the Park daily (except Christmas Day) 8.30am-4pm, with the gates closing at 6pm, ph (089) 886 000.

Berry Springs Nature Park

It features a delightful series of spring-fed pools surrounded by tall paperbarks, pandanus and carpentaria palms. A waterfall of warm thermal water, safe swimming, and plenty of birdlife (rainbow lorikeet, red-winged parrot, blue-faced honeyeater, blue-winged kookaburra are a few) add to the area's charm as a picnic spot for the family.

Only an hour's drive from Darwin, it's a popular weekend destination for locals.

Facilities
Facilities include picnic, wood barbecues, toilets, showers and walking tracks. A visitor centre has interesting displays explaining the area's history and ecology. It is a day-use park only, and pets are not allowed.

How To Get There
From the Stuart Highway turn-off on the Mandorah/Cox Peninsula road, it's 9km (6 miles) to the well sign-posted Berry Springs turn-off. Roads are all sealed.

Accommodation

The Lakes Resort and Caravan Park, Doris Road, Berry Springs, ph (089) 886 277, is built around two lakes - natural Lake Barden, and man-made Lake Deane - and is a one-stop holiday destination. It offers a waterslide, water skiing, canoes and paddleboats, and has a licensed restaurant.

Lakeside cabins (en-suite) $55 x 2; park cabins $42 x 2; powered caravan sites $14 x 2; tent sites $12 x 2. All sites are grassed, concreted and fully serviced, and there is a swimming pool, shop, barbecues and unlimited hot water. Dogs on leads are allowed.

Special family weekly packs are available that include accommodation, waterslides, and canoe and paddleboat hire.

Attractions in the Area

Blackmore River Conservation Reserve. Also known as Tumbling Waters, the 547ha (1351 acres) encompasses a 15km (9 miles) section of the river, and conserves riverine and estuarine mangrove ecosystems. When gazetted in 1984, it became the first area to offer any protection to the mangrove communities of the Darwin Harbour and its tributaries. The presence of salt-water crocodiles prevents swimming. The low level crossing called 'Tumbling Waters' is the local name for the reserve area.

There are no facilities at the reserve. Picnicking and fishing are the main activities, and camping is popular. Located approximately 10km (6 miles) south-east of Berry Springs.

Darwin River Dam. Located 17km (10 miles) south of Berry Springs, the dam's 260,000 million litre capacity augments Darwin's water supply. Picnic area with toilets and a lookout are facilities provided.

Southport. The ruins of Southport lie a few kilometres to the north of Tumbling Waters.

Southport was one of four towns optimistically laid out by Surveyor-General Goyder in 1869, as part of an overall plan by the South Australian Government to colonise its newly acquired north coast. It was hoped that townships, if laid out, would encourage settlers, thus providing a basis for the region's mineral and agricultural development. The South Australian Government had high hopes of good economic returns, and Goyder had not forgotten Fred Litchfield's find of a little gold in the Finniss River in 1865. In the 1880s, Southport was used to service railway construction crews. It was a sizeable shanty town, established during the gold rush days of the 1870s (small local finds but mainly a stopover and supply port for those heading to the Pine Creek diggings), at one time having four pubs and 10 stores. Southport was soon abandoned when the railway bypassed it, leaving Goyder's second town merely marked 'ruins' on the map today.

TIMBER CREEK

Population 100

Location

On the Victoria Highway, 285km (176 miles) south-west of Katherine, and 235km (145 miles) east of Kununurra.

Characteristics

An historic settlement, consisting of two road houses, caravan park, old police station/museum, police station, and youth hostel, nestles quietly near the Victoria River in an open woodland setting at the base of the Newcastle Range foothills. The Ngaringman people live nearby in four camps. Bougainvillaea adds a splash of colour to the dry township, and there are some idyllic tropical tracts along the river for fishing, but watch out for crocodiles. Timber Creek is in the heart of legendary cattle country, while to the south is the broad expanse of Gregory National Park.

History

The HMS *Beagle* sailed some 200km (124 miles) up the river, reaching a point on November 3, 1839 that was to become the Victoria River Depot. The river was named in honour of Queen Victoria, and explorer Augustus Gregory is credited with naming the township. In 1855, the expedition's ship, the *Tom Tough* was severely damaged when grounded on one of the river's many shoals, and timber found locally to repair the damage prompted the name Timber Creek. Gregory later went on to explore much of the Victoria River region, and his favourable reports led to the establishment of great pastoral holdings and European settlement.

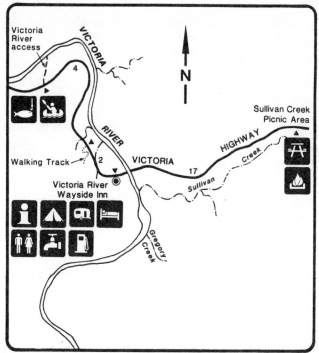

The vast 41,155 sq km (15,638 sq miles) Victoria Downs Cattle Station was the largest of the first leases granted in the early 1880s. Nat 'Bluey' Buchanan overlanded the first cattle for the station from Queensland, in an epic drove lasting many months (see Newcastle Waters listing and Barkly Region - Drovers).

A police station was established in 1898 at Timber Creek in response to hostile Aborigines, and a general feeling of mistrust existed between the races. M.C. O'Keefe, along with Aboriginal trackers, were the first police here. Today, two police officers serve an area about the size of Tasmania! Horses were the only transport, and these were busy times for officers in dealing with murders, cattle killing and racial conflicts. The original 'bough hut' station was replaced in 1908 with a more solid structure that today houses the museum.

The Victoria River Depot was established in 1891 at the furthest navigable spot along the river, where it functioned as a port for cattle station supplies. A store also made it a focal point for trade and social activity, and the Depot served the region until 1940. The first roadhouses were established at Timber Creek in the 1950s.

Attractions

Police Station Museum. Houses fascinating reminders of the police remount station days, and staff give informal accounts of events. Open 8am-5pm, $1 admission.

Victoria River Depot. The old port that is also an Historical Reserve. About 8km (4 miles) from the town.

Gregory's Tree Historical Reserve. The explorer's initials are carved on a boab tree near the site where their ship was damaged. It's located west of the town.

GREGORY NATIONAL PARK

The park is situated in a transition zone between tropical and semi-arid environments. It protects a wide range including rare species of plants and animals, and birdlife that is prolific. The park covers an area of approximately 10,500 sq km (4053 sq miles), encompassing rugged Victoria River district terrain. The main part of the park is accessible from Timber Creek. The eastern portion surrounds the Victoria River settlement, and features the river and gorge which cut through some spectacular sandstone formations. Sheer walls glow vividly at the rise and set of sun (see also Victoria River listing).

Throughout the area are the traces of Aboriginal culture, European exploration and pastoral settlement.

A number of 4WD tracks have been established within the Park, but access is by permit only. Permits can be obtained from Ranger

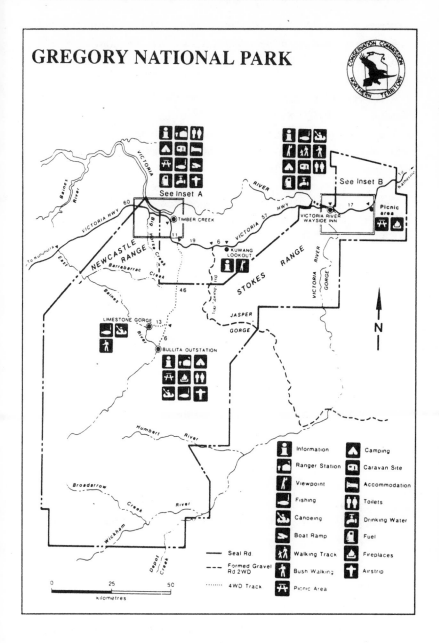

GREGORY NATIONAL PARK

Stations within the Park. Other roads are accessible by conventional vehicles, but towing trailers or caravans is not recommended. All roads, including the Victoria Highway may be impassable during the Wet Season.

Road conditions can be obtained from the Timber Creek Ranger Station on (089) 750 888.

Permits are also required if you are intending to go on an extended bushwalk within the Park. Check with the Ranger Station.

Camping areas have been established throughout the Park, and they comprise barbecues, picnic tables and pit toilets. A nominal camping fee applies.

Activities include boating, canoeing, fishing (barramundi) and walking. Facilities are marked on the map, and boat owners should note that the sluggish waters of the Dry season become raging torrents during the Wet.

Do not swim in any natural waterways as the Victoria River and its tributaries are the home of the salt-water and freshwater crocodiles.

Tours

Max's Victoria River Tours, ph (089) 750 850, run the Gregory Explorer tour that departs from Max's Information Centre, Timber Creek, daily at 8am. The 4 hour tour costs $25.

Rod and Rifle Fishing Safaris, ph (089) 750 688, have half and full day tours on the Victoria chasing barramundi, salmon, jew fish, shark and cat fish. Costs are $75 half day, and $150 full day, including safety gear and refreshments.

Events

Races: early September. Details for Racing Buffs says it all: "Timber Creek Cup. Prize - $3500. Distance - 1600m. Track - red dirt. Track condition - couldn't be drier. Tips for punters - horses which race off the pace can't see the leaders through the wall of dust; go for a front runner with an inside barrier draw".

How To Get There

By road, the Victoria Highway is sealed but narrow, and edges can be rough.

Tillair Katherine, the mail plane, flies in once a week.

Accommodation

Fogarty's Store - budget from $19, motel from $40-$60.

Circle F Caravan Park - powered sites from $11, car and campsite from $7.50. Swimming pool, shaded sites, pets allowed, dogs leashed. Open 7 days 6.30am-10pm, ph (089) 750 722.

Wayside Inn - rooms from $29 per person.

Camping - powered sites $9 per van, unpowered site $2 per person. Shaded sites, pets allowed, open 7 days, 24 hours, ph (089) 750 732.

Youth Hostel - 10 beds, $7 per bed. Located behind police station.

Services and Facilities

Police station, ph (089) 750 733, medical clinic (open 8am-4pm Mon-Fri), supermarket (Fogarty's Store), take-away food, meals (around $10), ice, bar, artifacts, souvenirs, showers for travellers (Wayside Inn and Fogarty's Store), fuel (super, ULP, diesel), oil, basic spares (both establishments), mechanical, tyre repairs, towing service (Fogarty's), Commonwealth Bank agency, hire boats (Fogarty's). All credit cards accepted by both establishments (EFTPOS facility). There's also a boat ramp and an airfield. Owners of the Wayside Inn and Fogarty's Store (Lloyd and Camille Fogarty) will advise on fishing spots and provide general information.

UMBRAWARRA GORGE NATURE PARK

972ha (2400 acres)

Location

22km (13 miles) south-west of Pine Creek.

Characteristics

Rugged gorge scenery and permanent water make Umbrawarra an idyllic location for bush camping. Aboriginal art sites and prolific birdlife add to the character of the Gorge area, where bush walking and swimming are the main activities.

How To Get There

The turn-off is west, 3km (1 miles) south of Pine Creek. It's a 22km (14 miles) formed gravel road, suitable for conventional vehicles, but rain during the Wet season makes it impassible.

Services and Facilities

Camping is allowed. Facilities include picnic, wood barbecues and toilet. No animals are allowed.

VICTORIA RIVER

Population 40

Location

On the Victoria Highway, 196km (121 miles) west of Katherine.

Characteristics

The Wayside Inn, run by Don and Frances Hoar, is attractively sited by the crossing and gorge tract of the Victoria River. Rugged sandstone cliff faces and flat-topped ranges provide an impressive backdrop to what has been described as the 'flashiest pub in the scrub'. It's a delightful camping spot, frequented sometimes by wild brolgas - my children quietly approached a pair near our campsite, imitated a 'brolga dance' and much to their delight, the brolgas joined in!

Attractions

Gregory National Park. The eastern segment of the Park surrounds the roadhouse, and features the scenic Victoria River Gorge and sandstone ranges. It's thought that their unusual shapes have been the result of massive erosion of an uplifted, ancient marine bed. The gorge scenery is best seen by boat. (Refer also to Timber Creek listing for Gregory National Park.)

Crocodiles. Salt-water and freshwater inhabit waters of the Victoria river, so swimming is not advisable.

Fishing. Barramundi and bream.

Accommodation

Motel - single $37.80, double $48.30.

Camping - $2 per person, $1 extra per site for power, and another $1 for air conditioning. Grassed, shaded sites, pets allowed, dogs leashed.

Services and Facilities

General store/supermarket, dining room (mixed grills $9), bar, take-away food, ice, artifacts, souvenirs, showers for travellers ($1), picnic/bbq area, tourist information, airstrip (Fitzroy Station). Fuel - super, ULP, diesel, autogas, LP gas (vehicles and camping), oil, aviation. Vehicle services - mechanical/tyre repairs, towing service. Credit cards accepted (Bankcard, Mastercard, Visa), open daily all year 7am-11pm, ph (089) 750 744.

THE KIMBERLEY (WESTERN AUSTRALIA)

Characteristics

The last unexploited frontier of Australian wilderness occupies the ancient lands behind the great swirl of the north-west coast of the continent. It covers 421,450 sq km (162,680 sq miles), or one sixth of the state's total area - a size which is twice that of Great Britain. Named because of its similarity to its counterpart in South Africa, the images evoked do not disappoint; nor do the grand sounding names of the inlets and bays, ranges and gorges.

A remote region that is little known in the broader Australian sense, the Kimberley is a land of spectacular contrasts. The coast is deeply indented with numerous gulfs, in which the tides have a variation of up to 10 metres. Knots of rugged ranges, deep gorges, plateau country, sandstone massifs, and some rich red plains, give the landscape a unique, savage beauty, while the savannah-like open woodland and tall grasslands present some real safari country.

The Kimberley is mainly a cattle domain, with nearly a hundred leases occupying over half its area, and the people who work the huge one-million-acre-plus runs are renowned for their indomitable spirit and adventurous lifestyle. While a sparsely populated area, the region has a vibrant economy based on the pastoral, agricultural, mining and tourist industries. Towns with colourful pasts are full of interest, and like the Northern Territory, there are plenty of things for the adventurous and curious to discover for themselves.

The Kimberley has infinite variety, plenty of characters, and above all, the stunning Bungle Bungle and the memorable fiery-red of the Cockburn Range ramparts at sunset.

Climate

The Kimberley experiences two seasons - the Wet and the Dry - but there are some differences when compared to the Top End region of the Territory. Here the Wet comes a bit later, rainfall is not so high, but temperatures can be searing. Geographical differences are noticeable, too. The northern towns generally have higher maximum temperatures, and humidity is high throughout the summer period, when the monsoons arrive. The exception is Broome, where the climate is tempered and best described as balmy. Occasional tropical cyclones form off the north-west coast during this time.

The winter brings long, dry, rainless days and loads of sunshine. For most, this is the ideal time to visit, but the Wet or green season brings a lushness to the landscape that is also well worth seeing. In fact, rivers rise and recede quickly and are not the hazards they were when roads were tracks. The climate table for Broome indicate patterns.

BROOME	J	F	M	A	M	J	J	A	S	O	N	D	Ann. av.
Temperature: Av. monthly max.	33	33	34	34	31	29	29	30	32	33	34	34	32
C° : Av. monthly min.	26	26	25	23	18	15	14	15	18	22	25	26	21
Rainfall : Av. monthly mm.	178	162	94	26	31	20	5	2	2	2	9	42	573
raindays av.	12	11	8	3	3	2	1	1	1	1	1	5	49
Humidity : Av. 9.00am	70	73	69	55	49	48	47	45	48	52	58	63	56
: Av. 3.00pm	64	65	58	42	38	36	33	33	42	51	57	60	48

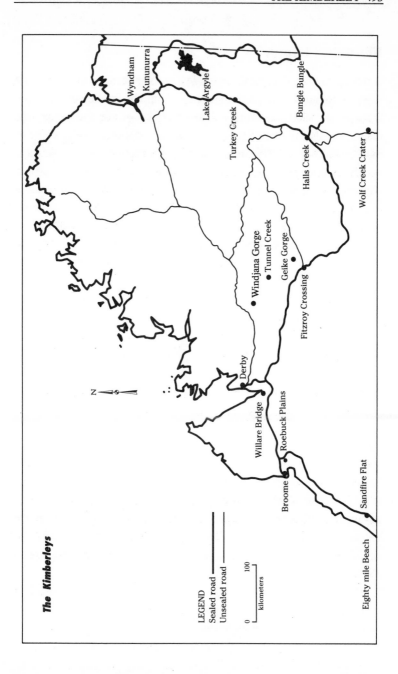

The Kimberleys

LEGEND
Sealed road
Unsealed road

0   100
kilometers

N

Flora and Fauna

A broad range of tropical vegetation is in evidence, and specialist flora is found in the mangrove belt along the sheltered coastline, amongst the sandstone gorges of the King Leopolds, and in the vine thickets of the Mitchell Plateau. A notable difference to elsewhere in the Outback is the Pindan, a complex flora association of acacias, eucalypts and the boab tree. The baobab (shortened to boab) in Australia is peculiar to the Kimberley and Ord-Victoria regions (a few grow elsewhere in the Northern Territory), has an immense bottle-shaped trunk, and reaches a height of 25m (82 ft). It should not be confused with the Queensland bottle tree. It also grows in South Africa, and it is thought seeds may have washed up thousands of years ago to produce the species here.

Details of the prolific and colourful birdlife and other wildlife are included in the listings for the various places.

Hazards

Salt-water crocodiles inhabit coastal and inland waterways, and the only safe coastal swimming is around Broome (refer to Top End region Introduction for information on crocs). The lethal fish-eating cone shell is another hazard (see Broome listing for details). Tides are enormous - up to 10m (over 30 ft) - and the navigation of northern inlets is definitely dicey. Check tide charts and seek advice if sailing these waters, or fishing along the coast. Fire in the sweeping savannah landscapes can cause enormous damage. Be aware of the danger, highlighted dramatically when 4 million hectares (9,880,000 acres) of the Mitchell Plateau was razed by a 5-month-long fire in 1988.

High temperatures, often searing in places, require sensible precautions and plenty of compensatory fluid intake, particularly on walks in areas like the Bungle Bungle.

Touring Suggestions

Kununurra is a good base for East Kimberley exploration, and allows a taste of the Gibb River Road attractions at Home Valley and El Questro Stations. Further along the Gibb Road at Jack's Waterhole, the Boab Valley Safari is highly recommended.

For the adventurous and self-sufficient, the Kimberley offers much from the Bungle Bungle to the Mitchell Plateau country. This is 4WD stuff at its best.

Highly recommended too is a flight over the Bungle Bungle, which offers not only rare views of the massif, but also the raw beauty of the Kimberley landscape. The gorges of the Western Kimberley are a must, and Broome and Derby should not be missed.

Whichever way you come, both the East and West Kimberley have much to offer.

Kimberley Region

PLACES AND ATTRACTIONS

BROOME

Population 7500

Location

On the north-west coast, on Roebuck Bay, 220km (136 miles) south-west of Derby, and 610km (379 miles) north-east of Port Hedland.

Characteristics

This delightful, tropical Nor'West town sits astride a peninsula and is bounded by the turquoise, mangrove-fringed coast of Roebuck Bay on one side, while the sweep of Cable Beach and the Indian Ocean bound the other. It has had a colourful past as the former pearling capital of the world, has been bombed by the Japanese, and blasted by several cyclones. Broad-leafed tropical vegetation, the fragrance of frangipani, tropical architecture, the old corrugated iron and timber Chinatown, the jetty area, and the beautiful white sands of Cable Beach, are characteristics of this easy going town.

Once a wild boom town, Broome has a lively economy today, based on tourism, pearling, meat processing, fishing, agriculture, and pastoral activities and mining exploration.

The rapidly growing centre is a tourist mecca in the winter season, partly because it has the only safe swimming beach in the Kimberley, and also for its romantic atmosphere and balmy climate.

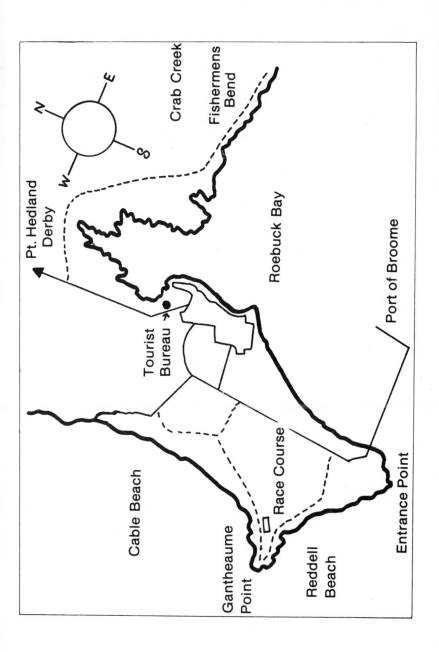

History

The first authenticated European visit was by William Dampier in 1699, and he named the bay after his ship, the HMS *Roebuck*. There is some evidence that the Portuguese may have visited Napier Bay in the 1500s, and likely early visitors were Malays and other Asians on turtle, dugong and oyster shell collecting voyages.

The settlement was named after Sir Frederick Napier Broome, the then Governor of Western Australia, in 1883. Pearling was the catalyst for the boom in the early 1900s, when Broome became the undisputed pearling capital of the world, with a fleet of nearly 400 luggers. While natural pearls were prized, the real profit was in collecting pearl shells for 'mother of pearl'. Broome became the world's leading supplier of the shell. World markets collapsed in 1914, particularly when the first synthetic buttons appeared on the market. Despite this, the demand for cultured pearls sustained a much smaller but viable industry. In 1956, a pearl farm was established at Kuri Bay, further north, and luggers supplied live shell for 'seeding'.

Broome has seen its fair share of natural disasters: cyclones of 1893, 1908 and 1910 resulted in the loss of many lives, and the sinking of a number of luggers. Seventy people were killed by Japanese bombing raids in 1942. There are many traces of its colourful past, all of which contribute to the unique character of this isolated Kimberley town.

Information

There is a very active Broome Tourist Bureau, located on the corner of Bagot Road and Great Northern Highway. Open Easter to October, Mon-Fri 8am-5pm, Sat 9am-1pm, Sun 9am-5pm, ph (091) 922 222.

The Shire of Broome produces an excellent Community Information booklet, while the Tourist Bureau has a wealth of local literature.

Attractions

Chinatown. Originally a mixture of pearling sheds, Japanese boarding houses, Chinese eating houses, billiard saloons and the Pearlers' Rest Hotel, that formed the town's commercial centre. Pearling houses still operate, with many sheds converted into retail pearl and shell centres. It is a colourful area of town, with interesting shops, and lots to see, including the world's oldest operating open air theatre, Sun Pictures, ph (091) 921 677, where current movies are shown seven nights a week at 7.55pm, and kiosk and barbecue facilities are available.

Historical Museum. Located in Saville Street, it houses a display of pearling history and relics, including diving gear. Admission is $2 adults, 50c children.

Pearl Shell and Pearls. Shell displays, pearls and curios can be seen at the Historical Museum; Shell House, in Guy Street; Paspaley Pearling Co in Short Street; Broome Pearls, the Pearl Emporium, and Linneys Pearls in Dampier Terrace; and Anastasia's Pearl Gallery in Carnarvon Street. Pearls and the like may be purchased from some of these places.

Captain Gregory's House. Captain Gregory built the largest and most profitable pearling enterprise in the town. The house, now in Carnarvon Street, has been restored, and is privately owned.

Anglican Church. Known as the Little White Church, and built in 1903, it features a mother of pearl decorated chancel, dedicated to divers who lost their lives in the 1908 cyclone.

Streeters Jetty. Built in 1879, when 400 pearl luggers served the pearling industry. Today there are only three or four.

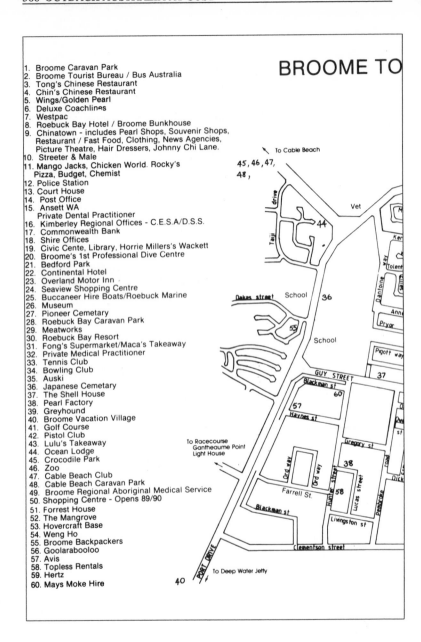

1. Broome Caravan Park
2. Broome Tourist Bureau / Bus Australia
3. Tong's Chinese Restaurant
4. Chin's Chinese Restaurant
5. Wings/Golden Pearl
6. Deluxe Coachlines
7. Westpac
8. Roebuck Bay Hotel / Broome Bunkhouse
9. Chinatown - includes Pearl Shops, Souvenir Shops, Restaurant / Fast Food, Clothing, News Agencies, Picture Theatre, Hair Dressers, Johnny Chi Lane.
10. Streeter & Male
11. Mango Jacks, Chicken World. Rocky's Pizza, Budget, Chemist
12. Police Station
13. Court House
14. Post Office
15. Ansett WA
    Private Dental Practitioner
16. Kimberley Regional Offices - C.E.S.A/D.S.S.
17. Commonwealth Bank
18. Shire Offices
19. Civic Cente, Library, Horrie Millers's Wackett
20. Broome's 1st Professional Dive Centre
21. Bedford Park
22. Continental Hotel
23. Overland Motor Inn
24. Seaview Shopping Centre
25. Buccaneer Hire Boats/Roebuck Marine
26. Museum
27. Pioneer Cemetary
28. Roebuck Bay Caravan Park
29. Meatworks
30. Roebuck Bay Resort
31. Fong's Supermarket/Maca's Takeaway
32. Private Medical Practitioner
33. Tennis Club
34. Bowling Club
35. Auski
36. Japanese Cemetary
37. The Shell House
38. Pearl Factory
39. Greyhound
40. Broome Vacation Village
41. Golf Course
42. Pistol Club
43. Lulu's Takeaway
44. Ocean Lodge
45. Crocodile Park
46. Zoo
47. Cable Beach Club
48. Cable Beach Caravan Park
49. Broome Regional Aboriginal Medical Service
50. Shopping Centre - Opens 89/90
51. Forrest House
52. The Mangrove
53. Hovercraft Base
54. Weng Ho
55. Broome Backpackers
56. Goolarabooloo
57. Avis
58. Topless Rentals
59. Hertz
60. Mays Moke Hire

BROOME TO

To Cable Beach

45, 46, 47, 48,

Taji drive

Vet

44

Ken

way

Tolent

Dantoine

Oakes street   School   36

Anne

Pryor

55

School

Pigott way

GUY STREET   37

Blackman st

60

57

Haynes st

To Racecourse
Gantheaume Point
Light House

Gregory st

Ord way

Ord way

38

Hunter street

Lucas street

road

Dick

Farrell St.

58

Blackman st

Livingston st

Clementson street

PORT DRIVE

To Deep Water Jetty

40

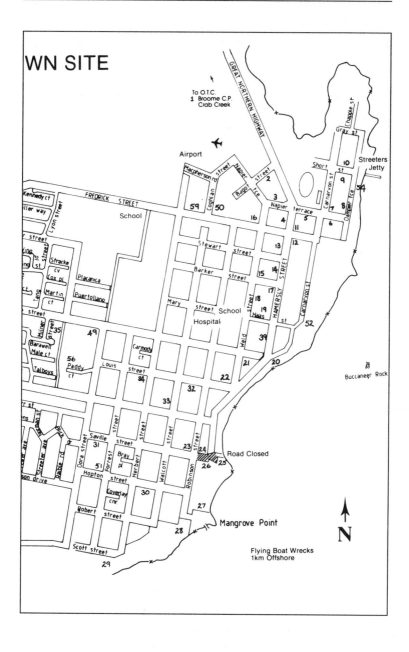

WN SITE

To O.T.C.
1 Broome C.P.
Crab Creek

GREAT NORTHERN HIGHWAY

Airport

Streeters
Jetty

Chapple st

Gray st

Short st

Macpherson rd street

Napier tce

street

Coghlan

Budge

2

Napier terrace

3

4

5

6

7

8

9

10

54

11

Carnarvon st

Dampier Tce

Kennedy ct

FREDRICK STREET

iller way

School

Lyon street

59

50

16

13

12

r street

ving

ng st

Stracke

cv

Cox pl

Placanica

Stewart street

14

15

Barker street

HAMERSLY STREET

Carnarvon st

17

18

Martin

ct

Puertollano

Mary street School

19

Haas st

52

r street

Miller st

35

Barawell

Male ct

49

Hospital

Weld st

39

Buccaneer Rock

Talboys

56

Paddy ct

Louis street

Carmody ct

21

20

34

22

32

33

Saville street

Forrest street

Herbert street

Welcott street

Robinson street

23

24

Road Closed

r st

ns

Oora street

31

Bray pl

26

25

Streeter ave

Gable rd

51

Hopton street

30

27

son drive

Robert street

Coverlay cnr

28

Mangrove Point

Scott street

29

Flying Boat Wrecks
1km Offshore

N

Buccaneer Rock

Court House. On the corner of Hamersley and Frederick Streets, and featuring an unusual architectural design. It was the telegraph station for the telegraph cable from Banjuwangi in the Dutch East Indies to Perth in 1889.

Library/Art Gallery. On the corner of Mary and Hamersley Streets, it is housed in a building that reflects the charm of early Broome architecture, and contains excellent exhibitions.

Matso's Store-Kimberley Kreations. The old Union Bank building, now located on the corner of Hamersley and Anne Streets, has been moved twice in its history; first by Sam Male and then again in 1986 when it was relocated and renovated. It now houses Kimberley Kreations Art Gallery.

Flying Boats. At Roebuck Bay at low tide, several wrecks of Allied (Dutch Dornier) flying boats lie half-submerged after a Japanese air raid, in 1942. Be careful and wear protective footwear.

Japanese Cemetery. Located in Port Drive are the graves of Japanese pearlers, the earliest of which date from the 1890s.

Pioneer Cemetery. Near the old jetty is the resting place of early pioneers.

Raou Broome Bird Observatory. Established in 1988 for research and recreational purposes, it features 247 different species of birds, and thousands of waders can be seen between October and April. The Observatory has no caged birds. Located in Crab Creek Road, off Great Northern Highway, 18km south-east of Broome.

Malcolm Douglas Broome Crocodile Park, Cable Beach Road, ph (091) 921 489. It is the only crocodile park in WA, with over 500 reptiles (freshwater, salt-water and the exotic alligator). Open daily April-Oct 10am-5pm, with feeding tours at 3pm. Check with the

Tourist Bureau for opening times Nov-April. Admission is $9 adults, $4 children, $22 family.

Cable Beach. A 22km (14 miles) white beach with beautiful waters, where you can swim safely and see magnificent sunsets.

Staircase to the Moon. This romantic phenomena can be viewed from between the Continental Motel and Seaview Shopping Centre, as the moon rises after dark. This coincides with the low-water spring tide, and is the result of moonlight reflected from the ocean bed. Check with the Tourist Bureau.

Dinosaur Tracks. Beautifully coloured and sculptured sandstone cliffs surround the area where footprints of a dinosaur, made 130 million years ago, are revealed at extremely low tides at Gantheaume Point. Cement casts of it are displayed near the beacon on the cliff.

Anastasia's Pool. A small man-made rock pool fills at high tide, and is believed to have been gouged out by a former lighthouse occupant for his crippled wife named Anastasia. Located at Gantheaume Point.

Deepwater Port. At Entrance Point, deepwater anchorage for overseas ships features a 800m long jetty. There is a beach where you can swim and picnic.

Buccaneer Rock. In Roebuck Bay, at the entrance to Dampier Creek, is a beacon and memorial to William Dampier - a colourful navigator.

Luggers. The Lugger B4 is a memorial to the late Sam Male, and is located at the entrance to the town.

Willie Creek Pearl Farm, Willie Creek, about 35km (22 miles) north of Broome. The farm produces south sea cultured pearls from the silver-lipped oyster Pinotada Maxima, and tours are offered which include the history of the pearling industry, a demonstration of seeding live half pearl sheel, and a video on divers collecting shell. It is open daily June-Sept, Tues-Sat Oct-May, with tours at 10.30am and 2.45pm - $12.50 adults, $5 children. The showroom is open 9.30am-12.30pm, 1.30-4.30pm.

Swimming. Cable Beach for surfing; Riddell Beach; Front Beach; and Gantheaume Point.

Wildlife. The coastal location is habitat to a number of water birds, including great knots, tattlers, large sand plovers, Mongolian plovers, terek sandpipers, red knots, ruddy turnstones, curlew sandpipers, and red-necked stints, as well as migratory birds from Siberia, Malaysia, Indonesia and south of Australia. Land-based wildlife includes euros, wallabies, goannas and snakes, while there is a great variety of birds - bustard or Australian turkey, brolgas, parrots, finches, eagles, falcons and kites can be seen.

Riddell Beach. Fortress-shaped rocks, coral reef and rock pools.

Fishing. Recreation fishing requires a licence. Check with Fisheries Department in Broome. Fishing is good all year. Species include - threadfin salmon, trevally, queenfish, skipjack, catfish, mulloway, barracuda or Spanish mackerel, whiting, flathead, barramundi and mud crabs. The jetty is a popular spot, and most waters are good places. Check with locals or the Fisheries Department.

Tours

Check with the Tourist Bureau about the range of shorter duration tours, such as pearling industry, helicopter rides, petrified forest, and town site historic attractions. Safari tours are available to more distant locations. Camel treks along Cable Beach operate during the season. Cruises are popular, and up to 14-days are available. They explore the magnificent Kimberley Coast. Charter boats for fishing safaris can be arranged.

Events

Shinju Matsuri (Festival of The Pearl): an annual event held mid August, the traditional time of various Asian celebrations. It features 10 days of parades, performing arts, fairs and exhibitions. The parade is led by Sammy the Dragon. Boomerang and spear throwing add interest to this colourful multi-cultural Fest.

Mango Festival: celebrates the ripening of the mango fruit, and is held in November-December.

Race Round: a series of horse races culminating in Cup Day in July.

Sailfish Tournament: held in July each year.

Hazards

Tides. Tidal range is extreme. Boaties and other fishermen, in particular, should have tide charts. Equinox or King Tides occur twice per year (March-April, September-October) with variations of 9m (30ft) or more, on a 12.5 hour cycle. Contact the Tourist Bureau for information.

Cone Shells. These occur on local beaches, and must not be touched. Stings from these are traumatic, and can be lethal. Venom attacks the nervous system and causes pain and dizziness, and death can result from respiratory failure. Apply mouth-to-mouth resuscitation, and seek urgent medical help. Wear protective footwear on rocky and mud flat beaches.

Coastwatch and sea safety planes patrol the coast daily.

How To Get There

By Air: daily flights (Ansett) from Perth and Darwin.
By Coach: Greyhound, Pioneer Express and Bus Australia operate regular express services from Darwin and Perth.

By Road: Broome is easily accessed by sealed road, 30km (19 miles) to the west of Highway 1.

Accommodation

The telephone area code is 091. Season and off-season rates apply.

Continental, Weld Street, ph 921 002 - units from $85 double, $105 family; pool, disabled facilities.

Quality Tropicana Inn, Robinson Street, ph 921 204 - from $77-$95; pool.

Mangrove Resort, Carnarvon Street, ph 921 303 - from $95 double, bed and light breakfast from $190 double; pool.

Roebuck Bay Hotel/Motel, Carnarvon Street, ph 921 221 - $95-98 double; pool.

Auski Tropical Resort, Milner Street, ph 921 183 - from $90 double; pool.

Cable Beach Club, Cable Beach Road, ph 922 505 - doubles from $225, studios from $173; highly recommended, pool.

Roebuck Bay Resort, Hopton Street, ph 921 898 - units from $80 double, studios from $96 double; pool.

Broome Backpackers, Crocker Way, ph 935 050 - from $12 per person per night.

Camping

Roebuck Bay Caravan Park, Walcott Street, ph 921 366 - metered powered sites from $17 x 2, unpowered $13 x 2. No pets.

Lambs Vacation Village, Port Drive, ph 921 057 - air conditioned cabins from $50 per day, powered sites $20 x 2; pool, tennis, shop.

Cable Beach Caravan Park, ph 922 066 - powered sites from $16; pool, shop, camping gas.

Broome Caravan Park, Wattle Drive, ph 921 776 - powered sites from $15, on-site vans from $40, camp sites from $6 per person.

Eating Out

The balmy climate and open-air eating go together well, and there is plenty of interesting food fare. There is a choice of take-away and the ubiquitous fish and chips. Many restaurants have a seafood emphasis (not surprising), and pubs offer excellent, reasonably-priced meals. Bay Bistro, Hammersley Street; Black Pearl Seafood Restaurant (Roebuck Bay Hotel); Chins Restaurant, Hammersley Street; Verandah Pearler and Asian Affair, Cable Beach Club, are some.

Night Life

Centres mainly around the pubs. The Aboriginal community has the Mamabulanjin, where dances and social evenings are held.

Services and Facilities

A full range of services and facilities are available. Seaview Shopping Centre has supermarkets and specialty shops, while the older part of town has a reasonable selection of services too. Credit

cards are widely accepted.

A hospital and full medical services; full vehicle services including all fuel (super, ULP, diesel, autogas); banks (Westpac and Commonwealth, both with auto tellers, ANZ agency); post office; police; churches (Anglican, Uniting, Catholic, Shiloh Pentecostal Church, Assembly of God); hire vehicles (Avis, ph 935 980, Hertz, ph 921 428, Woody's 4WD Hire, ph 921 791 - mopeds can be hired too); bicycle hire from Chinatown Bike Hire; boat ramps; golf course; tennis; diving; and races, are some of the facilities.

Radio stations: ABC 6BE 675; 107.7 FM.

Emergency Telephones

Police, ambulance and fire - dial 000.

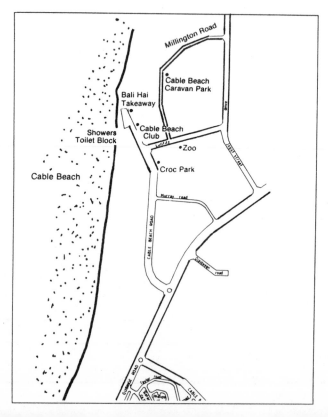

BUNGLE BUNGLE NATIONAL PARK

3200,000ha (790,400 acres)

Location

Approximately 180km (112 miles) by air south of Kununurra.

Characteristics

The Bungle Bungle is a crowded maze of gigantic sandstone whorls that tower and taper to domes and spires over 300m above the surrounding savannah landscape. Startling orange and black bands etched into the stone highlight the curious domes. The scale of the abruptly rising 'beehives' is astounding, and matched only by the geological masterpiece of it all, Cathedral Gorge. Other deep chasms, pools and a variety of flora and fauna, add to what is undoubtedly one of Australia's most exciting landform features.

Geology

The massif is a sandstone formation some 350 million-years-old, formed during the Devonian Period. A similar geological structure is found in the Hidden Valley National Park, near Kununurra, but on a much smaller scale. The rounded beehive shapes resulted from weathering along the rectangular joints of the original block, where the corners eroded more easily from eons of torrential rain, wind and heat. It is possible from the air to see 'new Bungle Bungle' in the making, as the massif continues to erode. The weathering processes and the erosive power of water have formed deep gorges and steep-sided chasms.

The sandstone is quite fragile, despite its solid appearance, and will crumble easily under hand or foot. CALM does not permit climbing because of this and visitor safety. The orange and black striations that give the 'beehive' effect (best seen towards the south near Piccaninny Creek) consist of silica (orange) and a lichen (black). The latter is a living organism, basically a combination of an algae and a fungus. Underneath, the sandstone is white to yellowish in colour.

History

To the East Kimberley Aborigines, the area of the Bungle Bungle is known as Purnululu. The name Bungle Bungle is thought to have been coined because the massif is a geological anomaly - an oddity, or literally 'a bungle'. The area was opened up initially for cattle grazing around the turn of the century. In themselves, the Bungle Bungle were of little interest to the cattlemen, who probably had more to contend with in the harsh environment, than to explore the formidable range. While the actual area of the massif is under 276 sq km (106 sq miles), the large size of the park is designed to act as a buffer zone.

Features

Individual features are Echidna Chasm, Cathedral Gorge, and for the energetic and adventurous, Piccaninny Gorge. Access is by walks of varying length and duration - one-way Cathedral Gorge is about 30 minutes, while Piccaninny is about 10 hours! Aboriginal art sites add much to the sense of timelessness evoked by these extraordinary landforms.

Walking

A wide-brimmed hat, skin protection, comfortable footwear, and above all, drinking water, are requirements for all walks. Temperatures can be searing, partly due to the additional heat

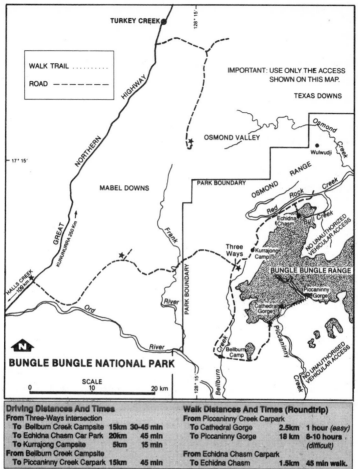

BUNGLE BUNGLE NATIONAL PARK

SCALE

0   10   20 km

Driving Distances And Times		
From Three-Ways intersection		
To Bellburn Creek Campsite	15km	30-45 min
To Echidna Chasm Car Park	20km	45 min
To Kurrajong Campsite	5km	15 min
From Bellburn Creek Campsite		
To Piccaninny Creek Carpark	15km	45 min

Walk Distances And Times (Roundtrip)		
From Piccaninny Creek Carpark		
To Cathedral Gorge	2.5km	1 hour (easy)
To Piccaninny Gorge	18 km	8-10 hours (difficult)
From Echidna Chasm Carpark		
To Echidna Chasm	1.5km	45 min walk.

radiated from the massif itself. Advise the ranger of planned longer walks, and their advice should be taken.

Conservation

This is a magnificent wilderness area, and to prevent fire devastation and ecological impact of wood collection, no campfires are permitted in the park. Please keep to designated tracks and parking areas, and do not interfere with any art sites. Firearms and pets are not allowed.

Fees

An entry fee of $20 per vehicle is charged. The park is closed during the Wet season, partly due to the rains, but also because of the fierce heat (50C - 122F) and high humidity.

How To Get There

By Road: it is 250km (155 miles) to the Bungle Bungle turn-off from Kununurra, or 110km (68 miles) from Halls Creek.

By Air: scenic flights over the Bungle Bungle from Kununurra (see Kununurra listing), Broome and Halls Creek, are available.

By Tour: tour operators from Halls Creek and other locations, offer ground tours. Check with local tourist information centres.

Access

4WD only due to rough road conditions. No caravans or trailers allowed, and a high clearance 4WD vehicle is needed. It is 55km (34 miles) to Threeways, and takes between 3-4 hours! Pick up information and maps from either Kununurra or Halls Creek for finer details.

Facilities

At Threeways, there is an Interpretive Panel of The Massif. Two camping areas are Kurrajong (just north of Threeways), which has pit toilets, water and some shade, while the other area is Bellburn Camp, with pit toilets and water from a pump. It is advisable to boil the water first before drinking. Helicopter flights are available. You need to be self-sufficient for a visit, in particular, carry extra fuel (much of the trip in is low ratio 1st and 2nd gear) and water. There is some shade, but you need to be early to get an ideal spot. There is no swimming area in the park.

DERBY

Population 4000

Location

On King Sound, 220km (136 miles) north-east of Broome.

Characteristics

A pleasant sprawling town on a coast of mainly extensive mirage-producing mud flats, backed by a zone of open woodland and savannah vegetation. A wide main street, boabs, an interesting port area where there is an 11.6m (38 ft) variation between high and low tides, and a friendly, comfortable town atmosphere, greet the visitor. It functions as an administrative centre, as well as serving a rich pastoral, agricultural and mining hinterland. It also services local Aboriginal communities, and a healthy tourist industry. While 42km (26 miles) north from the highway, a turn-off is well worth while for another dimension of the Kimberley and The Gateway to The Gorges.

History

While **William Dampier visited Cygnet Bay in 1688,** it wasn't until after 1879 that the area was settled by Europeans. Explorer Alexander Forrest led an overland expedition through the area in 1879, and filed favourable pastoral assessments. Before the Europeans came, these were the traditional lands of the Warwa people and, as in many other Outback places, initial contact between the two races resulted in spasmodic conflict. Derby was no exception. During the 1880s, hostilities were experienced, and the story of the activities of the outlaw 'Pigeon' are well told in a Heritage Trail that starts in the town. This well-presented trail gives interesting historic insights into earlier, tougher Kimberley days. In 1942, an air raid by Japanese bombers occurred, which gave the town a brief war experience.

Information

Derby Tourist Bureau is located in Clarendon Street, ph (091) 911 426, open Mon-Fri 8.30am-4.30pm, Sat 8.30am-noon, Sun 9am-4pm (April to September). Check here for tours and good tourist literature.

Attractions

Pigeon Heritage Trail. Starts in the town and outlines the legendary events of the time.

Boab Prison Tree. With a girth of 14m (46 ft), this hollow boab was used as an overnight 'lockup'. It is a popular photography spot, located 7km south of the town, and is over 1500 years old.

Myall's Bore. Located near the Prison Tree, this lengthy cattle water-trough is said to be the longest in the world at 120m (394 ft). It was used to water stock in the days of the cattle droves and drovers.

Cultural Centre. This magnificent state library and art gallery is well worth visiting. Located in Clarendon Street. Alongside is a botanic garden.

The Old Port and Jetty. A long wooden jetty, wharf building, relic machinery, and old cattle races are evidence of much busier live cattle export days, when men had to sometimes round up strays in the mud at low tide.

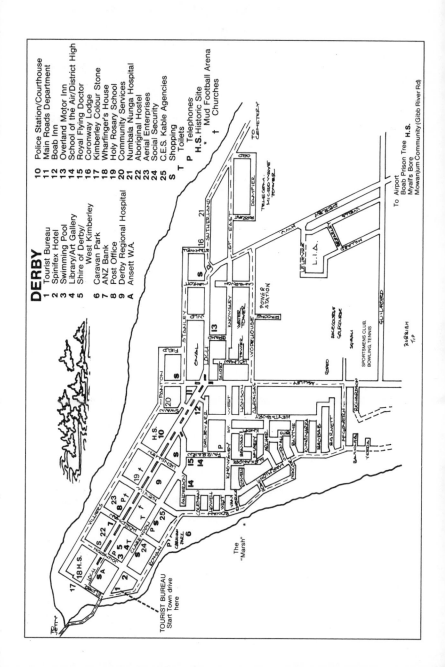

DERBY

1 Tourist Bureau
2 Spinifex Hotel
3 Swimming Pool
4 Library/Art Gallery
5 Shire of Derby/
   West Kimberley
6 Caravan Park
7 ANZ Bank
8 Post Office
9 Derby Regional Hospital
A Ansett W.A.

10 Police Station/Courthouse
11 Main Roads Department
12 Boab Inn
13 Overland Motor Inn
14 School of the Air/District High
15 Royal Flying Doctor
16 Coronway Lodge
17 Kimberley Colour Stone
18 Wharfinger's House
19 Holy Rosary School
20 Community Services
21 Numbala Nunga Hospital
22 Aboriginal Hostel
23 Aerial Enterprises
24 Social Security
25 C.E.S. Kable Agencies
S Shopping
T Toilets
P Telephones
H.S. Historic Site
* Mud Football Arena
† Churches

To Airport
Boab Prison Tree H.S.
Myall's Bore
Mowanjum Community (Gibb River Rd)

TOURIST BUREAU
Start Town drive
here

The "Marsh"

Fishing. The old jetty is a popular spot. Salmon start to run in May, skipjack in June. Others include groper, barramundi (Nov-Jan), snapper, bream and catfish. Check with the local tourist centre, and beware of hazards - big tides and salt-water crocodiles. The Fitzroy River is good for barra.

Wildlife. An interesting variety includes kangaroo, wallaby, echidna (spiny anteater), dingo and flying fox. Reptiles include 5 species of python (including the tree snake), brown snake and death adder, gecko, skink, goanna, frill-necked lizard, and bungarra. Birdlife is colourful - magpie, lark, honeyeater, budgerigar, parrot, lorikeet, galah, finch and wood swallow - while kite, falcon, eagle and kestrel are the main birds of prey. They live generally in the Pindan - a complex vegetation association of acacias, eucalypts and the extraordinary boab tree.

Wharfinger's House. An historic house in Lock Street is now a museum and art gallery. Check at the tourist bureau.

Swimming. The public pool is the only safe place to swim in town. Estuarine crocodiles inhabit coastal areas and inland waters.

Outlying Attractions include Windjana Gorge and Tunnel Creek National Parks - these are listed separately.

Tours

Kimwest Tours, ph (091) 911426, Bungle Bungle Experience Safaris, ph (091) 614 322, and Bush Track Safaris, ph (091) 914 644, are the local ground tour operators. Boat tours are provided by Buccaneer Sea Safaris, ph (091) 911 991, and for scenic flights contact Aerial Enterprises, ph (091) 911 132, or Derby Air Service, ph (091) 931 375. Contact the Tourist Information Centre for details of all tours.

Events

Boab Festival runs for 3 weeks in mid-July, with such activities as mud football, races, rodeo, mardi gras, country music, and arts and crafts. The Country Music Festival is also held in July.

Boxing Day Sports features cockroach and frog 'derbies'.

How To Get There

By Air: Derby Airport has daily flights by Ansett Australia.
By Coach: the 'big 3' coachlines stop at Derby.
By Road: a sealed road from the main highway leads to the town.

Accommodation

The telephone area code is 091.

Kimberley Motor Inn, Delewarr Street, ph 911 166 - from $79; pool.

Boab Inn, Loch Street, ph 911 044 - single around $55, double $75; pool.

West Kimberley Lodge, cnr Sutherland and Stanwell Streets, ph 911 031 - units from $30 single, family from $60.

Spinifex Hotel, Clarendon Street, ph 911 233 - rooms from $35.

Budget: *Aboriginal Hostel* - full board from $16, ph 911 867.

Kimberley Entrance Caravan Park, Rowan Street, ph 931 055 - powered sites from $14 for 2, unpowered sites from $11 for 2. Shaded, grassed sites, pets allowed, dogs leashed.

Eating Out

There is a good choice - The Boab Inn, Derby Sportmen's Club, A Chinese restaurant, The Kimberley, Spinifex and Wharfs Restaurant.

Services and Facilities

Most tourist needs are well catered for, and credit cards are widely accepted. It has a hospital, doctor, dentist, chemist, banks (ANZ, R&I, Commonwealth agency), police station, post office, supermarket, take-away food, ice, boat ramp, all vehicle services (fuel - super, ULP, diesel, LHP for cars, camping gas, aviation gas) and repairs, churches (Anglican, Catholic, Uniting, Derby Community Church, Assemblies of God, Baptist Fellowship).

Hire vehicles - Avis, ph 911 357, and Hertz, ph 911 348.

Recreational include swimming pool, golf course, squash, tennis and bowls.

Radio stations: ABC 6DB 873; 107.5 FM.

Emergency numbers

Phone 000 or: police 911 222; hospital/ambulance 911 533; Royal Flying Doctor 911 211; fire 911 222.

DEVONIAN REEF NATIONAL PARKS

Location

Near Fitzroy Crossing (Geike Gorge), extending in a north-westerly direction to near the Gibb River Road. Geike is 16km (10 miles) north-east of Fitzroy Crossing; Windjana Gorge is 145km (90 miles) north-west of Fitzroy Crossing and the same distance east of Derby; Tunnel Creek is 110km (68 miles) from Fitzroy Crossing and 180km (112 miles) from Derby. Check road conditions, as the unsealed surfaces can become corrugated.

The Parks

Geike Gorge (3135ha-7746 acres), Windjana Gorge (2134ha-5271 acres) and Tunnel Creek (91ha-225 acres) National Parks protect fascinating exposed faces of a giant 350 million-year-old horseshoe-shaped 'great barrier reef' that once extended for over 1000km (620 miles) beyond the current coastline, to join similar formations at Kununurra. Parts of it are now exposed in a series of limestone ranges, stretching for some 300km (186 miles) along the margins of the Canning Basin, south-east of Derby, once part of a shallow tropical sea. Weathering and erosive action of water have created some stunning features that are well worth seeing. The three parks are Dry season only - April to October.

Geology

In this vast warm sea, a barrier reef belt grew, built by various

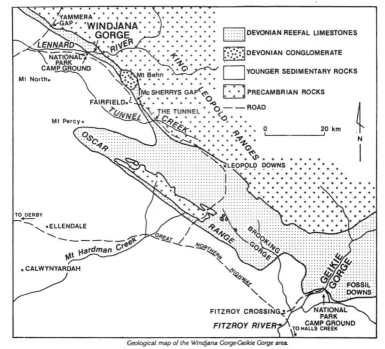

Geological map of the Windjana Gorge-Geikie Gorge area.

lime-secreting organisms that had the ability to erect wave resistant structures close to sea level - organisms included calcareous algae, stromatoporoids and corals. Stromatoporoids, now extinct, resembled modern corals, except for their internal structure. Other contributors now seen as fossils are: sponges, bivalve, brachiopod, gastropod, coral (Argutastrea), horn coral, algal stromatolites, to name some. Limestone deposits up to 2000m (6562 ft) thick and 20km (12 miles) wide were built up by these organisms.

The limestone reefs and their associated deposits wind across the landscape, reaching some 50-100m above the adjoining plains, in much the same way that they stood above the ancient sea floor. From the air, the reef is clearly delineated, aided by a complex series of geological happenings since the seas withdrew: sedimentation, uplift and erosion over millions of years. The clear topographic landform expression today results from shales and soft sediments bedded on the ocean floor in front of the reefs, having eroded to form valleys, leaving the resistant limestone reefs exposed as ranges. Except for an extensive outcrop in the Oscar Range, the reefs are backed by the ancient pre-cambrian rock structures (see map). Many reefs grew nearly vertically, but some grew outwards advancing over their own marginal slope deposits. Reef scarps were the result of slow subsidence; a black-reef limestone platform is the structure exposed and cut by erosion and river action.

Flora and Fauna

Trees in the gorges are mainly cadjeputs (tropical paperbarks), river red gums, native fig, and freshwater mangrove, distinctive for its sprays of red flowers. Surrounding vegetation is typical of the Kimberley, but with dense fringes of riverine forest near the permanent waters.

Aquatic fauna includes freshwater crocodiles in Geike and Windjana Gorges (give them plenty of space); sawfish and stingrays, whose marine ancestors, trapped by the receding seas, journeyed up the Fitzroy and adapted to a freshwater habitat; and archer fish, which shoot down insects from foliage with a jet of water. While most indigenous mammals are small, nocturnal and shy, you may see the agile wallaby, euro and rock wallaby. There is a variety of birdlife, from parrots to water birds, and in fact rangers have a checklist of over 100 species at Geike Gorge alone.

Conservation

Please be aware of the sensitiveness and uniqueness of these parks. Pets and firearms are not permitted. All litter must be properly disposed of, and fires only in places provided - it is preferred that gas is used for cooking. Rangers on site are only too pleased to answer any questions you may have.

GEIKE GORGE

Characteristics

The gorge was named after British geologist, Sir Archibald Geike in 1883, and features a slash by the Fitzroy River through the Geike Range, exposing a fine section of the Devonian Reef. It is 14km (9 miles) long, divided into two sections of approximately equal length with several atoll-type reefs in the Copley Valley area. The 30m high walls are bleached white by sun and water to a height of about 10-12m above normal river level, and fossils embedded in the limestone may be seen. Most of the gorge in its southern part is cut through back-reef limestone, while to the north, the river slices through marginal slope deposits which contain some conspicuous bivalve shells. The contact between steeply inclined margin-slope deposits and horizontally bedded reef and back-reef deposits, is well illustrated 2km south of Sheep Camp Yard.

Other Features. The colours, reflections, freshwater crocodiles, fish, freshwater stingrays, and fine camping spots, add to the park's fascinating landforms. Many swim off the sandbank, but care is needed, and there is one walking track.

The Sanctuary. Because of their significance, both banks of the river have been declared a sanctuary - no-one is allowed within 200m of either bank, and the only permitted area runs along the west bank, from the southern boundary of the park to the beginning of the west wall of the gorge.

How To Get There

The road is sealed for the 16km (10 miles) from Fitzroy Crossing. It is suitable for conventional vehicles, trailers and caravans.

Services and Facilities

Ranger station, permanently manned; the rangers run boat tours 9am-2.30pm ($10 adults, $2 children); with permission, and subject to fees and regulations, private boats are allowed on the permanent waters, but not just before the organised tour boat trip (so as not to disturb wildlife); park interpretative centre.

Facilities include boat ramp, information, bbqs, picnic, drinking water, showers, toilets including for the disabled. Day use park only, no pets. Open Dry season only.

TUNNEL CREEK

Characteristics

Tunnel Creek flows through the Napier Range in an amazing tunnel cave about 750m (2460 ft) long. The creek, once on the surface, created an underground 'channel' by solution enlargement along joints in the marginal-slope limestone to form this rather remarkable geological feature. A bench in the tunnel, 8m above the present floor, marks an older underground creek level.

You can walk through the 3m to 12m high tunnel: it is about waist-depth at the beginning, then about 0.6m-1m in the various pools along its length. It is also dark, so a torch is advised, and after about 300m, a roof collapse allows in light and fresh air. Bats frequent the tunnel, and cave paintings can be seen at the northern entrance.

How To Get There

The formed, gravel road is suitable for conventional vehicles.

Facilities

It is a day use park only, 6am-6pm. No camping is allowed. The water is cold. Display panels, tables and toilets are the only facilities provided. Dry season park only. No pets allowed.

WINDJANA GORGE

Characteristics

An attractive, narrow canyon carved by the Lennard River through the Napier Range, it is about 3.5km (2 miles) long, and up to 100m deep, with near vertical walls for most of its length. Isolated pools have fish and freshwater crocodiles, and vegetation mutes the sharp geological formations. It is of great scientific interest for the range of complex reef structures exposed. Fossil remains of huge extinct crocodiles and turtles were found in a small cave in the gorge wall, and remains of the giant marsupial Diprotodon (resembling a giant wombat) have been recovered from the river gravels.

With its classic sheer walls and restful pools, it is an ideal wilderness spot for the family, as well as to appreciate the remarkable geological happenings in this ancient landform area. Swimming is dubious because of quality and restricted space for crocs. Dry season only (April to October).

How To Get There

With care, the road is suitable for conventional vehicles.

Facilities

Walking tracks, water (be careful, it is from the river), camping allowed ($5 x 2, $3 extra person, $1 child), generator areas (restricted times), toilets, showers (cold), picnic, display panels, gas bbqs (fires being discouraged). No pets allowed. Two rangers are in residence.

EIGHTY MILE BEACH

Population 7

Location

10km (6 miles) west of the Great Northern Highway, from the turn-off 45km (28 miles) south of Sandfire Flat.

Characteristics

A 10km (6 miles) dirt track leads through huge sand ridges to provide access to this isolated caravan park and store, established in 1986 by Sandfire Flat Roadhouse. Set behind a primary dune, the camping area is a great base for exploring and enjoying an incredible stretch of wide, white sands, and the sweep of the Indian Ocean. The beach, particularly after storms and infrequent cyclones, becomes a beachcomber's paradise, with its washed up colourful shells.

Fishing is excellent for the threadfin salmon, but you have to be a smart angler - sharks like them too, when conveniently caught on the line! Talk with park managers about the fishing. While the water looks great, don't swim as it is full of sharks and sea snakes. The beach is a delight for walkers who enjoy solitude and glorious sunsets. The huge 202,429ha (500,000 acres) Wallal Station surrounds the park.

How To Get There

The turn-off is well sign-posted, 45km (28 miles) south of Sandfire Flat, and the gravel surface road in is suitable for conventional vehicles, trailers and caravans.

Accommodation

Camping - powered sites $15 x 2 persons, unpowered sites $10 x 2 persons, cabins from $55.
   There is shade, bbqs and grass. Pets allowed, dogs leashed.

Services and Facilities

The park has a shop selling basic provisions, ice, bait, fishing tackle and souvenirs. There is 24-hour power, and well appointed toilet and shower facilities. It is open all year 7am-7pm, and credit cards (Bankcard, Mastercard, Visa) are accepted, ph (091) 765 941.

FITZROY CROSSING

Population 1230

Location

On the Great Northern Highway alongside the Fitzroy River, 260km (161 miles) east of Derby, and 288km (179 miles) west of Halls Creek.

Characteristics

An old town with a tough reputation, sited on the shady banks of a river of the same name, has had a colourful history, and today, is a service town for local Aboriginal communities, stations, and the more recent BHP mining developments at Cadjebut. The nearby Geike Gorge National Park has added an important tourist function.

History

The settlement was established in the 1890s, when Joseph Blythe built one of the first structures; a shanty inn and store to serve the prospectors, bullock teamsters, drovers and the stations. It was a harsh life too, with fires, floods and droughts to contend with, as well as the hardships associated with isolation and distance.

Explorer Alexander Forrest's expedition in 1879 provided stimulus for further exploration and settlement. His favourable pastoral reports attracted pioneers from the west, and the first sheep runs at Meda River and Yeeda were stocked by overlanding livestock from Beagle Bay. By 1882, there were six stations operating in the Fitzroy area. Easterners became interested too. An exploratory trip led to the epic droves of the Duracks (Queensland), Emanuels, MacDonalds and McKenzies (all from NSW) to stock their new holdings. While they were assembling herds for the 5600km (3500 miles) trek, in 1883, Nat Buchanan, the Gordons and Paddy Cahill were already on the 'Gulf Route', basically Leichhardt's exploration route to Port Essington. It was a trek of incredible hardship and losses, but the Duracks arrived at Argyle in September 1885, while the MacDonalds struck the junction of the Fitzroy and Margaret Rivers with only 300 cattle and few horses left. The latter ended the longest and hardest cattle drove of all time at the property they called Fossil Downs.

The Fitzroy River was discovered in 1837 by George Grey in the HMS *Beagle*, and he named it after a former commander of the ship, Captain Robert Fitzroy, RN. The river flows through rugged hills and plains for 750km (465 miles), draining an area of 90,000 sq km (54,750 sq miles), before discharging into King Sound, south of Derby. While docile for most of the year, it erupts into a raging torrent up to 15km (9 miles) wide, when the rains come. It has one of the highest discharge rates of any river in Australia, with estimated flood flow rates of 30,000 cubic metres per second. The deeply gouged channel and torn up trees seen in the Dry, are reminders of its awesome power, and the pub did great business in the early days when floods stranded travellers.

Information

For Fitzroy Crossing tourist information, check with the Derby centre. A good source locally is the pub or police station.

Attractions

In the town. The old Crossing Inn, the old single-roomed tin police station, the old low level river crossing, and the pioneer cemetery, are the main features.

Outlying. Geike Gorge is a major attraction (see separate listing) and Brooking Gorge. The river is a good spot for some barramundi fishing. On the natural scene, large river red gums and paperbarks line the river, and wildlife includes freshwater crocodiles, varied birdlife (heron, ibis, cormorants, kites, brolgas) and flying foxes, wallabies and dingoes.

Tours

Geike Air Charter, ph (091) 915 068, Fitzroy Crossing Charter Tours, ph (091) 915 155, and Geikie Gorge Boat Tours are the local operators.

Events

The Rodeo in October is a lively affair and draws truck loads of people from the outlying cattle stations.

How To Get There

By Air: Ord Air Charter operates a local feeder service into the town from Derby, Halls Creek and Kununurra.
By Road: major bus companies - Greyhound, Bus Australia and Pioneer Express.

Accommodation

Crossing Motor Inn, ph (091) 915 080 - motel single around $60, double $73; cabins - from $30 for 2 persons; camping - powered sites from $13. Credit cards accepted (Bankcard, Visa).

Fitzroy River Lodge, ph (091) 915 141 - motel single from $80, double $95; safari - tented accommodation single from $60, double $73; caravan park - sites $15 for two, campsite $6.50 per adult.

Tarunda Caravan Park, Forrest Street, ph (091) 915 044 - powered/unpowered sites from $10.
Darlngunaya Backpackers, Old Townsite (former Post Office), ph (091) 915 140 - rooms from $12 per person.

Services and Facilities

Hotel, restaurant (pub), take-away food, supermarket, post office, ice, police, medical (hospital), ANZ agency, fuel at Fitzroy Crossing Roadhouse, repairs, spares, tyres and tubes, camping gas, and airfield. Credit cards (Bankcard, Mastercard, Visa) generally accepted.

GIBB RIVER AND KALUMBURU ROADS REGION

Characteristics

The most exciting wilderness area in Australia, that is the least exploited and offers the adventurous a rare view of one of the world's last remaining frontiers. The Gibb River Road, completed as a beef road for the large road trains connecting the remote Kimberley stations to the ports of Derby and Wyndham, spans 667km (414 miles) through the heart of the Kimberley. From Derby in the west, it traverses the rugged escarpments of the Napier and King Leopold Ranges, and crosses creeks and broad valleys through some magnificent gorge, ridge and sweeping savannah landscapes. Bold and beautiful, raw and rugged, sum up the last great track in Australia.

The Kalumburu Road strikes north, 419km (260 miles) from Derby, or 250km (155 miles) from the Great Northern Highway between Wyndham and Kununurra. This natural earth road ends at Kalumburu Mission nearly on the coast, 271km (168 miles) from the Gibb River Road turn-off. It traverses beautiful terrain of the Mitchell Plateau, and offers some of the most isolated features in the Kimberley. There are many attractions along the way for you to discover, and many fine camp spots, too.

Road Conditions

The first 60km (37 miles) from Derby are sealed. The surface then changes to gravel, then natural earth, due to the rocky nature of the land. It is essentially 4WD, although some risk conventional vehicles (high clearance essential). It is particularly severe on tyres, and 2 spares should be carried. While there are basic services at points along the way, extra fuel, food and water is strongly advised, and the best time to travel is between April and November. Contact authorities in Derby or Kununurra for up-to-date road reports and advice. Self-sufficiency, a well-equipped, mechanically sound vehicle, and a sense of adventure, are essentials for this part of the world. Towing caravans or trailers is not advised.

Hazards

Be on the lookout for road trains and straying stock, and take extreme care were fire.

Camping

Be exceptionally careful with fire. While not started by visitors, a huge fire which razed 4 million hectares (9,880,000 acres) of the Mitchell Plateau in 1988, illustrates how inflammable the country is. Please observe all the courtesies and environmental respect in this wilderness region.

Tours

Some coach companies operate tours through this region from Australian capital cities. Local tour operators are in evidence, too: Home Valley Station Kimberley Experience Safaris; El Questro Station Ranger Tours; Safari Trek from Kununurra take tours along the Kalumburu/Mitchell Plateau area; Aboriginal Sam Lovell's Kimberley Safaris.

Check with local tourist offices.

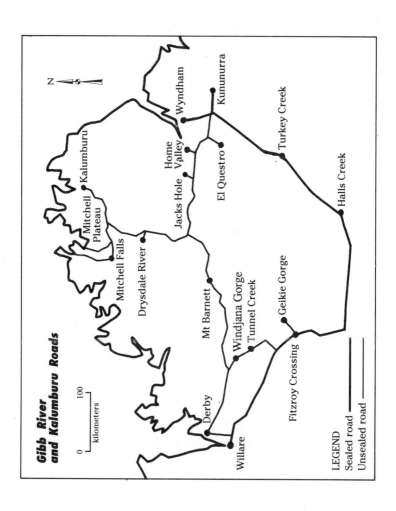

Gibb River
and Kalumburu Roads

N

Kalumburu

Mitchell
Plateau

Mitchell Falls

Drysdale River

Home
Valley

Wyndham

Kununurra

Jacks Hole

El Questro

Turkey Creek

Halls Creek

Mt Barnett

Windjana Gorge
Tunnel Creek

Geikie Gorge

Fitzroy Crossing

Derby

Willare

0   100
kilometers

LEGEND
Sealed road
Unsealed road

Along the Gibb River Road

From Derby

km (miles)	Features
0	Junction Derby Highway and Gibb River Road.
1.1	Information Bay.
34.3(21)	Meda Station turn-off. May River. Fishing, picnic, camping, watch out for salt-water crocodiles.
61.7(38)	End of bitumen.
73.4(45)	Kimberley Downs Station turn-off (4km). No access.
118.2(73)	Turn right to Fairfield, Leopold Downs Windjana Gorge National Park (21km), Tunnel Creek National Park (51km) and Great Northern Highway.
118.5(73)	Lennard River Bridge.
124(77)	'Queen Victoria's Head' on left of pass through Napier Range.
128.9(80)	Napier Downs Homestead (no access).
168.9(105)	Bridge, Bull Frog Hole.
178(110)	Inglis Gap.
182.7(113)	Mt Hart Homestead (50km rough road).
184(114)	Leopold Ranges.
194 (120)	Lennard River Gorge turn-off (4WD only-8km rough road). A 5km gorge, waterfall and pool. A delightful spot.
201.5 (125)	Cattle grid. Creek to right. Water.
204(126)	March Fly Glen. Good camping.
204.7(127)	Penguin Rock on left.
212.8(132)	Bell Gorge turn-off at Silent Grove Station (4WD only, 29km rough road).
246(153)	Mt House Homestead (store, food available).
250.1(155)	Beverley Springs Homestead (no access). Specialist groups and tours by prior arrangement - check with tourist centres.

267.5(166)	Adcock Gorge (5km). The 3 walls exceed 30m. Waterfall tumbles down stepped rock face into a small pool beside which is believed to be an Aboriginal burial ground.
285.4(177)	Galvans Gorge turn-off (700m).
301.1(187)	Barnett River.
301(187)	Mt Barnett Roadhouse.
309.2(192)	Shire West Kimberley boundary.
328.3(204)	Barnett River Gorge turn-off (3km).
337.8(209)	Mt Elizabeth Homestead turn-off (30km). Camping, store, fuel.
366(227)	Gibb River Station to left.
406(252)	Junction with Gibb River-Kalumburu Road (see listing after Gibb River).
428(265)	Russ Creek.
448.5(278)	Campbell Creek, permanent water. Undulating country with road situated mainly on ridge tops.
458.1(284)	Noble's Knob.
471.2(292)	Dawn Creek, permanent water.
486.9(302)	Airstrip on left.
495(307)	Durack River, permanent water.
500.2 (310)	Karunjie Homestead (49km), camping, meals, homestead accommodation by prior arrangement.
511.5(317)	Rollies' Jump Up - steep rise from the flat country into Mosquito Hills.
512.8(318)	Bamboo Creek. Wide creek with solid crossing. Water most of the year.
522.7(324)	Jack's Hole. Large permanent waterhole; camping, swimming, fishing, tours (see separate listing).
523.9(325)	Gregory's Jump Up - leads down from the hills to the river valley.
561(348)	Bluey O'Malley's Crossing, Bindoola Creek.
571.4(354)	Bindoola Valley from edge of Pentecost Range.

574.1(356)	Crest of Pentecost Range.
575.9(357)	Lookout, Cockburn Range, Gulf and twin rivers, Pentecost and Durack.
579.5(359)	Home Valley Station turn-off (1km); camping, homestead accommodation, tours, fuel, store (see separate listing).
588.7(365)	Pentecost River, water upstream of crossing, good fishing downstream in tidal section. Salt-water crocodiles.
588.8(365)	Old Karunjie Road to Wyndham, 4WD only.
608.9(377)	Fish Hole, water.
612.5(380)	El Questro Station (18km); camping, store, Chamberlain Gorge (see separate listing).
624(387)	Emma Gorge, camping.
629.1(390)	King River
645.9(400)	Great Northern Highway. 48km (30 miles) to Wyndham; 52km (32 miles) to Kununurra.

****

MT BARNETT ROADHOUSE

Population 130 approximately

Location

On the Gibb River Road, 301km (187 miles) west of Derby.

Characteristics

The roadhouse is the gateway to one of the many scenic surprises along the Gibb River Road - the Manning Gorge and Falls, which along with a sandy beach and delightful pools, are the main attractions. Walks, prolific birdlife, boabs, pandanus palms, fresh water crocs and fishing (black bream) add further interest. Walk to the falls is 3 hours return.

Accommodation

Camping only in the gorge area, 7km behind roadhouse - $4 per person, $8 per family - bbq, toilets, water and shady sites. Pets allowed, dogs leashed.

Services and Facilities

Take-away food, well-stocked general store, ice, souvenirs, Aboriginal artifacts, showers ($1), disabled facilities (toilet, shower), vehicle - fuel (super, ULP, diesel), oil, repairs, tyres, tubes. Open 7am-noon, 1-6pm Dry season (April-November) 7 days; Wet season 8am-noon, 2-4pm Mon-Sat, ph (091) 917 007.

****

MT ELIZABETH STATION

Population 25

Location

On the Gibb River Road, 337km (209 miles) north-east of Derby.

Characteristics

A large cattle station, named after the wife of an early surveyor, that offers a range of services to tourists. Visitors can get an insight into station life, and talk to those who live in these isolated parts. The station was established in 1946 by the late Frank Lacy, who built the original homestead of river stone. His son, Peter, runs the property today, and the Ngariyin are the local Aboriginal people.

Accommodation

Homestead (3 bedrooms and verandah beds). Dinner, bed and breakfast costs around $60 per person. Advance bookings essential. Camping - grassed, shaded sites available, power from 5pm to 9pm, hot and cold showers, toilets. $5 per adult, $1 child. Pets allowed.

Services and Facilities

Shop selling basics, artifacts, souvenirs, telephone, picnic/bbq area, showers for travellers ($1), airstrip (1300m). No credit cards. Open Dry season only, 7am-5pm, ph (091) 914 644.

****

JACK'S WATERHOLE

Population 5

Location

On the Gibb River Road, 180km (76 miles) west of Kununurra, and 523km (324 miles) east of Derby.

Characteristics

A new, but typically Kimberley architecture, corrugated iron homestead, delightfully overlooks a huge permanent pool of the Durack River. It is part of the nearly 404,858ha (1,000,000 acres) Durack River Station, run by the Sinnamons of Home Valley Station, and it is an excellent base for local exploration. Apart from the oasis-like quality, there is fishing (silver cobbler, barramundi, black bream, archer fish and sooty grunter), swimming, wildlife observation, boating (dinghies for hire), and there is even room on the water for sailing. No powered boats are allowed. It is a must for any traveller on the Gibb Road.

This was once an outstation, and the name of the waterhole is after Jack Campbell, head stockman of the station for 25 years.

Tours

Half-day safari tours are offered, as are specialist ones (bird watching, photographic, etc). The New York Jump Up, Boab Valley and Oomaloo Falls offer a rare glimpse of some stunning Kimberley scenery, where hundreds of huge boabs dot the landscape, and tall spear grass gives a real safari feel to the tour. The falls stagger down ancient broken slabs of rock to a pool fringed with greenery. Freshwater crocodiles can be seen, and the birdlife is as colourful as it is varied. The tour is highly recommended, but bookings are essential - costs $25 per person. A range of other tours is available.

Accommodation

Homestead - twin share $30; single $20. Dinner, bed and breakfast is $75 double, $45 single.

Camping - around $5 per adult, children under 12 free; hot and cold showers, flush toilets, and barbecues. Shaded sites close to the river. Pets allowed, dogs leashed.

Services and Facilities

Homestead, open bbq, dining area, meals (around $9 breakfast; $10 lunch, $12 dinner); shop (basic food and drink items) and fuel (super, ULP, diesel); tyre repairs; and telephone. Open during the dry season, cash only, ph (091) 614 324.

****

EL QUESTRO STATION

Population 6

Location

On the Gibb River Road, 100km (62 miles) west of Kununurra, and the same distance south of Wyndham.

Characteristics

The name El Questro has a particular ring about it, and along with the homestead, setting and attractions, it does not disappoint. The name means 'The Mountains', and it is surrounded by those - the Cockburn and Durack Ranges. The 404,858ha (1,000,000 acres) property offers a limited range of facilities, but plenty of beautiful natural features and scenery that are well worth seeing.

Attractions

Chamberlain Gorge. Located 9km (5 miles) from the homestead, it features a 1km stretch of deep water, best seen by boat. Fishing for barramundi, swimming, photography, walking and wildlife appreciation, are some of the associated attractions. Access by 4WD track. Thermal Springs - swimming.

Emma Gorge. 2km off the Gibb River Road, a delightful waterfall cascades down vertical, fern-studded rock faces into a pool below. Access by conventional vehicle, 20km (12 miles) from Station turn-off on Gibb River Road. Natural thermal springs, palm trees and Aboriginal rock paintings are other attractions.

Events

The Station hosts two unusual events. In May, the 35km (22 miles)

Endurance Ride (horses), and on the first Saturday in September, 'Australia's most rugged foot race' - a 25km (16 miles) Kimberley marathon!

Accommodation

Luxury air conditioned homestead with accommodation for up to 12 persons - $400 per person, all inclusive, min 2 nights stay.

Self contained bungalow for up to 10 persons, thermal springs nearby - $30 adult, $20 child.

Station camp offering backpackers accommodation - packages available from $130 per person for 2 days and 1 night, including guided tour, meals and transfer.

Bush cabins at Emma Gorge - licensed restaurant, bar and swimming pool - $40 single, $70 double.

Riverside camping - $15 per person.

Services and Facilities

Shop selling basics, emergency repairs only, and airstrip. Open all year, 24 hours, cash only, ph (091) 614 320.

****

HOME VALLEY STATION

Population 5

Location

On the Gibb River Road, 130km (81 miles) west of Kununurra.

Characteristics

The evening blazing backdrop of the Cockburn Range, flat to undulating open woodland, the sinuous tree-lined Pentecost River, and a rambling, startling white corrugated iron and partially open-walled homestead, are the immediate characteristics of Home Valley. While it is a working cattle station of 404,048ha (998,000 acres) running about 3000 brahman shorthorn cross cattle, Ian and Sue Sinnamon manage a vibrant tourist operation called Kimberley Experience Safaris as well.

Attractions

If you want to eat out in style, and experience some dry Kimberley humour, the Sinnamons host a traditional homestead silver service dinner on Saturday nights, and persons who are not house guests will need to book. Sunday is a barbecue Kimberley style, bookings essential - costs $20.

Tours

A range of personalised tours, scenic flights, such as to the Bungle Bungle, can be arranged.

How To Get There

By Road: rough in places, but with care conventional vehicles can get through, or Home Valley will pick you up in Kununurra.
By Air: flights can be arranged from Kununurra.

Accommodation

Homestead - $65 per person, dinner bed and breakfast.
  Camping - $5 adult, $1 child; hot and cold showers, toilets.

Services and Facilities

Shop with range of food and cold drinks, take-away sandwiches, telephone, picnic/bbq/shaded area, fuel (super, ULP, diesel), aviation fuel on request, airstrip, mechanical assistance can be obtained. Cash only, open all year, ph (091) 614 322.

Along the Kalumburu Road

From Gibb River Road

km(miles)	Features
0	Junction Gibb River Road and Kalumburu Road
4(2)	Gibb River Crossing, picnic and camping.
18(11)	Plain Creek, picnic and camping.
66(41)	Drysdale River Homestead left 1km, store, fuel, emergency vehicle repairs, rubbish disposal. Drysdale River Homestead is the last service point and information stop before the turn-off to the Mitchell Plateau. Trailers and caravans can be left at the homestead; the road past this point is unsuitable for most caravans. Store is open 8am-noon, 1-5pm each day, and has a wide range of goods. Bread and ice available at most times. Fuel (super, ULP, diesel) available.
67.4(42)	Miners Pool, turn right; picnic and camping. 3.5km sharp left turn, through open gateway. slow 200m to the river.
67.5(42)	Drysdale Cattle yards, right 200m. If in use, visitors allowed. DANGER WILD CATTLE. DO NOT CLIMB RAILS.
68(42)	Drysdale River Crossing; picnic and camping.
100(62)	Doongan Station - no access.
142(88)	Old Mitchell River Station Road - no access.
163(101)	Mitchell Plateau turn-off left 70km. The Mitchell Plateau area is one of extreme importance from a biological viewpoint,

including the striking Livistona Eastonii palm.
The area includes the spectacular Mitchell
Falls, King Edward River and Surveyor's Pool.
(This is an isolated area; you must be totally
self-sufficient before entering.) The Mitchell
Plateau Resources guide is obtainable from
tourist offices.

200(124) Theda Homestead - no access.

245(152) Carson River Crossing; picnic and camping.

250(155) Carson River Homestead turn-off - no access.
Drysdale National Park - no road access.
It protects and maintains an area of pristine
wilderness.

270(167) **Kalumburu Mission and Aboriginal Community**;
accommodation, store, food and fuel available.
Beware of salt-water crocodiles.
Kalumburu is situated 5km from the mouth of
the King Edward River and King Edward Gorge.
It provides a picturesque setting with giant
mango trees and coconut palms surrounding the
historic Kalumburu Catholic Mission. Kalumburu
offers visitors a variety of exciting
activities, such as fishing and trekking trips
and scenic flights at reasonable rates. Camping
is available. Stores and fuel are available
Mon-Sat 7am-4pm. Aboriginal artifacts are on
sale. An Entry Permit is required prior to
arrival at Kalumburu, and can be arranged by
phoning (091) 614 300. General enquiries, ph
(091) 614 333. Pets allowed, dogs leashed.

HALL'S CREEK

Population 1350

Location

On the Great Northern Highway, 544km (338 miles) east of Derby, and 359km (223 miles) south of Kununurra.

Characteristics

The old town, 14km (9 miles) away, was the site of Western Australia's first gold rush, and since those wild days, the new town has become the centre of a vast beef industry, and is the gateway to a number of tourist attractions. Services to mineral exploration companies, Aboriginal communities, and more recently, tourists, figure prominently among its other functions.

History

A second Forrest expedition to the Kimberley in 1883, reported favourable pastoral lands, and the suggestion that gold might be found in the rocks. Charlie Hall rode across from Roebourne and discovered the magical ore in 1855, on the creek that now bears his name. He returned to the coast two months later with his mate, Jack Slattery, and 200 fine ounces of gold. Another prospector found a 22oz nugget, and the rush was on. Between 1885 and 1887, about 10,000 men came to the Kimberley from all over Australia and overseas. Sailing vessels, luggers and schooners tied up at the fledgling ports of Derby and Wyndham, while the overlanders arrived by horse, wagon, camel, or on foot. Relentless fierce heat, waterless landscapes, resentful Aborigines, fever, thirst, starvation ·and loneliness, were experienced by those desperadoes as they trekked across the hundreds of kilometres of unknown terrain. Hall's Creek became a tough town consisting of wood, stone, canvas, tin, bark and spinifex structures, including a couple of pubs, amongst the ramshackle collection of buildings. In 1955, the town was relocated on less rugged land, so that expansion could take place - a far cry from the former shanty town of old Hall's Creek.

Information

Hall's Creek Tourist Information Centre, Main Street (opposite Swagman), ph (091) 686 262.

Attractions

Old Hall's Creek. The remnants of the original gold town can be seen, and include the old post office, and ruins of many others.

China Wall. A near vertical quartz vein projects above the surrounding rocks to form a startling white stone wall. Along with its block-like structure, it appears like a miniature Great Wall of China - hence the name. Located off Duncan Road.

Old Mines. Mt Bradley (off Duncan Road) is one of the original gold mine shafts, where care is needed as the shafts are deep. Ruby Queen Mine is a later one.

Palm Springs. A natural spring used once as a local water supply. An ideal picnic and swimming spot is where the Black Elvire River crosses the Duncan Highway.

Russian Jack Memorial. Commemorates the heroic gold rush character who, for over 300km, carried a sick friend in a bush wheelbarrow to find medical help. Located at Shire Offices on Thomas Street.

Caroline Pool. A natural waterhole near Old Hall's Creek.

Sawpit or Saw Tooth Gorge. A popular fishing and swimming spot is located off Duncan Road, where the Black Elvire River has cut through a ridge. A shaded tree-flanked pool has a sandy beach and inviting waters.

Outlying Attractions include Bungle Bungle Range and Wolfe Creek Crater National Park (see separate listings for both).

Fossicking. Check with the Mines Department for areas.

Tours

One day tours to Wolfe Creek Crater, Ruby Queen Mine and Old Hall's Creek; Safaris to Bungle Bungle, Geike and Windjana Gorges; and scenic flights are available. Tour operators are: Hall's Creek Bungle Bungle Tours, ph (091) 686 217; Kingfisher Aviation, ph (091) 686 162; Ord Air Charter, ph (091) 611 335; and Oasis Air, ph (091) 686 462.

Events

Agricultural Show is held in July, and the Race Meeting and Rodeo are held in August.

How To Get There

By air: Ord Air Charter connects to main airports at Derby and Kununurra.
By coach: Greyhound, Pioneer Express and Bus Australia.
By road: sealed surfaces connect all main centres in the Kimberley.

Accommodation

The telephone area code is 091.

Kimberley Hotel/Motel, Roberta Avenue, ph 686 101 - motel units single $60, double $73; dormitory (share facilities) $15 per person per night. Credit cards (Bankcard, Mastercard, Visa, American Express, Diners) accepted.

Hall's Creek Motel, Great Northern Highway, ph 686 001 - single from $55, double $72. Credit cards (Bankcard, Mastercard, Visa) accepted.

Swagman, McDonald Street, ph 686 060 - cabins from $45.

Hall's Creek Caravan Park, Roberta Avenue, ph 686 169 - powered sites from $12 x 2, unpowered $10 x 2, on-site vans $35 x 2; cabins from $15 per night. Shaded, grassed sites.

Services and Facilities

Most basic services are available, including: hospital, police, post office, bank agency, supermarket, taxi, all vehicle needs and fuel, camping gas, ice, restaurant (Swagman), take-away food and airfield. Credit cards widely accepted.

Radio Stations: ABC 106.1 and 107.7 FM.

Geike Gorge (see p.521)

KUNUNURRA

Population 4000

Location

Near the Northern Territory border in the north-east of the Kimberley region, 480km (298 miles) west of Katherine, and 1057km (655 miles) east of Broome.

Characteristics

Although it is a relatively new town, Kununurra, meaning 'big waters', presents a few delightful surprises from its lakeside setting, where it blends comfortably into lush tropical bushland overlooked by the rocky outcrop of Kelly's Knob. The compact town centre is dotted with palms, and provides all the necessary facilities and services for comfortable living and travelling in the tropics. Climate, as with most towns in the classic Wet/Dry climate regions of the tropical north, brings magnificent contrasts to Kununurra and its surrounding landscape. The luxuriant greenery of the Wet changes as the relentless sun of the Dry browns and dusts, while whitened grasses sharpen landscape tones and emphasise its raw beauty. During this time, the startling green of the town centre's well-watered lawns give it an oasis quality.

There is much to see and do. The Lake offers excellent fishing and a range of water based activities; if you can't make it to the Bungle Bungle, then visit the Hidden Valley miniature; the Ord scheme, dam and delights of Lake Argyle; the Gibb River Road; and varied and colourful wildlife, are a few of its attributes. While accommodation has yet to catch up with demand, there are plenty of fine camping grounds, and resorts are in the pipeline to meet future tourist needs.

Kununurra functions as a service centre for government administration, agriculture, including research based on the Ord Irrigation Scheme, pastoral, mining and tourism industries. This might well be enough for most small, tropical towns, but Kununurra has another jewel; it is Australia's diamond centre, based on the huge Argyle mine, 200km (124 miles) to the south.

Above all, Kununurra is an ideal, friendly base from which to explore a range of near and outlying attractions of the vast East Kimberley region.

History

Western Australian sheepmen and Queensland cattlemen were attracted to the region after explorer Alexander Forrest's promising description, in 1879, of the pastoral potential of the Ord and Fitzroy river valleys. Long before Forrest's expedition, Miriwun and Katjerong Aboriginal people from the broader based Dj'eragum Language Group ('Tribal' groupings and distribution are based on language more than any other characteristics), occupied these lands, and their cultural richness can be seen in art sites around Kununurra.

Alexander Forrest failed to find the Ord River outlet, and was forced to strike east for the Overland Telegraph Line in the Northern Territory (see Daly Waters, Barkly Region). Pastoralists established stations in the region in the 1880s. Among the pioneers were the Duracks who established Lissadell, Argyle, Rosewood and Ivanhoe Stations. The latter homestead was destroyed by fire and rebuilt at Ivanhoe Crossing, while the Argyle Homestead, located in the area to be flooded by the Ord Scheme, was dismantled and rebuilt on a higher site. The Duracks and the Kimberley are synonymous, and Mary Durack's book *Kings in Grass Castles* gives a vivid account of the early pastoral days (refer also to Fitzroy Crossing and Lake

Argyle for further history).

Apart from similarities in geology, space and climate to the Northern Territory, the trails of the early explorers, pastoralists and drovers, and the outlooks spawned, also strengthen the unity between these two great Outback regions.

After tropical agricultural research, the Western Australian Government began the Ord Irrigation Scheme. In 1963, the town was established to service the irrigation area, where 12,000ha (29,640 acres) of rich, black alluvial soil supports peanuts, sorghum, fodder crops, sunflower and high protein beans, while fruit and vegetables include bananas, mangoes, paw paw, melon, cucumbers and beans. The diversity of crops is the major reason why authorities are so strict, and ban fruits, etc, at the border in order to keep out pests and diseases. Other agricultural ventures include feedlots where cattle are fattened before being exported live from Wyndham.

Information

A very active Visitors Centre is open all week 8am-5pm, and located in the town centre at 75 Coolibah Drive. It has an excellent range of tourist literature, ph (091) 681 177.

The Department of Conservation and Land Management has offices upstairs in Konkerberry Drive, with good park information, maps and literature.

Attractions

Kelly's Knob. The lookout is ideal for orientation and some fine views of the town and Ord Valley. Located 2.4km (1.5 miles) from town on Speargrass Road.

Mirima (Hidden Valley) National Park. Known as the 'Mini Bungle Bungle', the park protects a valley of rugged cliffs that suffuse with colour and landform features that include amphitheatres, gullies and ridges. Mirima is the Aboriginal name, and past usage by ancestors of the Miriwun can be seen in the fascinating depictions of figures, beings and animals in the rock paintings and engravings. These art sites are fully protected, and must not be interfered with in any way.

The spectacular landforms evolved during the Devonian Period (320 million years ago) from sands laid down under shallow seas, uplifted to great blocks and weathered to the shapes seen today.

The quartz sandstone shattered from the cliffs provides an ideal habitat for the agile and short-eared rock wallabies, while their droppings, containing boab seeds, explain how the small boabs that cling tenaciously high on the valley walls got there. There's a wealth of wildlife: frogs, tortoise, geckoes, goannas, snakes and other reptiles can be seen near Lily Creek; fruit bats, dingoes and echidna; while birdlife is colourful and prolific - brown quail, peaceful dove, white-quilled rock pigeon, red-collared lorikeet, little corella, red-backed kingfisher, blue-winged kookaburra, rainbow bee-eater, common koel, pheasant coucal, northern fantail, leaden flycatcher, black-faced cuckoo shrike, brown honeyeater, bowerbird and black kite are the main types.

Walks. Views to Kununurra and over surrounding areas can be seen from a number of outlooks. Lily Pool walk is a 100m one featuring examples of stone axe grinding grooves above Lily Pool. The Wuttuwuttubin Track is a 500m return walk within a steep-sided gorge, which offers views to Kununurra. Didbagirring Track is a difficult 1km walk up steep slopes to the Bungle Bungle-like formations, and good views. **The park has picnic facilities only.**

Ivanhoe Crossing. A crossing at the Ord River near Ivanhoe Station Homestead forms a mini-waterfall, and was once part of the original road to Wyndham, before the advent of a new road across the Diversion Dam. The Ord, along with the Fitzroy and other rivers in the Kimberley, carries 86% of Western Australia's potential fresh water supply, and at a national level this comprises 16%. Before the new bridge was built, station people had to stock up prior to the Wet season, as later rains made roads and crossings impassable and gravel airfields were often unusable. Today, the crossing is closed to vehicular traffic, but remains a popular fishing spot. But be careful, it is very slippery.

Lake Kununurra. A man-made lake as a result of the Irrigation Scheme attracts an abundance of wildlife, including fish (black bream, catfish) and freshwater crocodiles and water birds. People swim here. Other activities are fishing, canoeing, windsurfing, sailing, boating, scuba diving, water skiing, and on the banks, picnicking.

Celebrity Tree Park. Located on the banks of the Lily Creek inlet of the Ord, the park contains trees planted by various celebrities visiting Kununurra. Plaques provide identification in this rather novel glade.

Black Rock Falls. A spectacular Wet season attraction where water thunders over a 30m semi-circular cliff into a pool below. Minerals in the water have stained the rockface black. Located just of Parry Creek Road, 4WD access only.

Middle Springs. A small Wet season pool and waterfall dominated by a large, slab-faced rock. Located off Parry Creek Road, 4WD access only.

Valentine's Pool. An interesting series of rock pools and sandy beaches, best seen during the Wet. A popular swimming spot.

Bandicoot Beach. A beach at Bandicoot Bar on the Ord River, just below the Diversion Dam wall. The grassy beach is a popular fishing spot. Swimming is not recommended below the dam wall as crocodiles are common.

Sleeping Buddha. A razorback ridge stands alongside the Ord River, and from a distance gives the appearance of a person lying down on his back. At the river end of the Sleeping Buddha, the rock resembles an elephant's head, complete with trunk. Best viewed on river cruises.

Waringarri Aboriginal Arts. Locally produced artifacts are on display and for sale. Located at Speargrass Road.

Pandanus Palm Wildlife Park and Zebra Rock Gallery. A range of birds, wallabies and other Australian wildlife adds interest to a drive through banana plantations of the irrigated agricultural zone, and the main feature, Zebra Rock. The only known deposits of this rock are found nearby in small reef outcrops of stratified claystone, with an estimated age of 600 million years. It is an attractive fine-grained siliceous argillite (indurated siltstone or claystone) with rhythmic patterns of red bands or spots on a white background. The workshop is interesting, and you can purchase the unique polished stone. A practical use can be seen at the hotel where the bar has a zebra rock base. Located off Packsaddle Road.

Arboretum. The Department of Conservation and Land Management are establishing a 50ha (124 acres) arboretum, with the first trees having been planted in 1980. It has both native and exotic species, and a self-guiding walk trail. Located between the irrigation channel and Ivanhoe Road, close to the town centre.

Fishing. Another great Kimberley place for the keen angler on inland or coastal waters. Types include barramundi, black bream, catfish, longtoms, mullet, tarpon, groper, threadfin salmon, archer fish and bony bream. Fishing sports are Bullocks Crossing (camping), access through Kimberley Research Station; Dunham River for barra - dam gates. Lake Kununurra and Ivanhoe Crossing are others. Check with locals for detailed advice, or the tackle shop in town. A licence is required for fishing.

Swimming. Apart from the places mentioned, the Kununurra Leisure Centre has an adventure pool, learners' pool and huge main pool and water slide. Located just beyond the Visitors Centre. Those using natural swimming places, beware of salt-water crocodiles below the Diversion Dam at Lake Kununurra

Outlying Attractions

Argyle Diamond Mine. Located at the southern extremity of the Carr-Boyd Range, 200km (124 miles) south of Kununurra, is the huge open-cut mine, with its ultra-modern village close by. It is a formidable location for the operation, which was developed between 1983 and 1985 at a cost of $435 million, and produces about 17kg of diamonds a day (5 tonnes per annum). In terms of quantity, it is the largest in the world where 4 tonnes of rock are removed to produce one tonne of ore, and each tonne gives about 7 carats of diamonds; so 4 tonnes of rock produce 1gm of diamond. Only about 5% of the output is of gem quality, 45% near gem quality, while the balance finds an industrial use (for drills, saws, etc). The gem and near gem quality are finding an outlet in jewellery settings, as the world was made known of the fine 'cognac' or 'champagne' Argyle diamonds. The finest diamond found so far has been a rare 2.11 carat pink, valued at over $1 million.

The mine can now be visited through tour groups, and the magnificent gems can be seen and purchased at Djaaru Gems, Nina's Jewellery and Kimberley Fine Diamonds. Check with the Visitors Centre for tour details. The mine can also be viewed on scenic flights from Kununurra to the Bungle Bungle.

Bungle Bungle National Park. See separate listing, and under tours.

Gibb River Road. **Highly recommended are El Questro Station (Chamberlain Gorge), Jack's Waterhole Homestead (Boab Valley Safari), and Mt Barnett (Manning Falls and Gorge). See separate listings.**

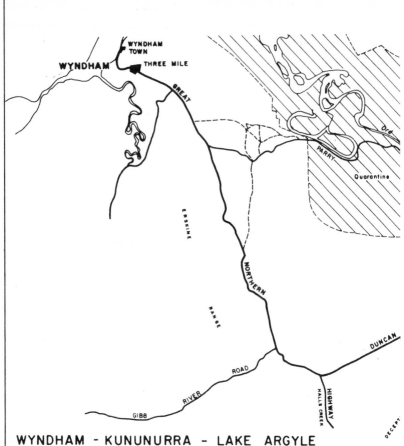

WYNDHAM - KUNUNURRA - LAKE ARGYLE

KUNUNURRA	J	F	M	A	M	J	J	A	S	O	N	D	Ann. av.
Temperature: Av. monthly max.	36	35	35	35	33	30	30	33	36	38	39	38	35
C° : Av. monthly min.	25	25	24	21	19	16	15	17	21	24	25	26	21
Rainfall : Av. monthly mm.	207	212	154	20	11	1	5	0	3	31	70	99	813
: raindays av.	14	14	12	3	1	0	0	0	1	4	7	10	66
Relative humidity: Av. 9.00am	64	71	63	44	39	37	33	34	35	41	49	57	47
: Av. 3.00pm	47	54	47	33	30	28	25	23	23	27	33	40	34

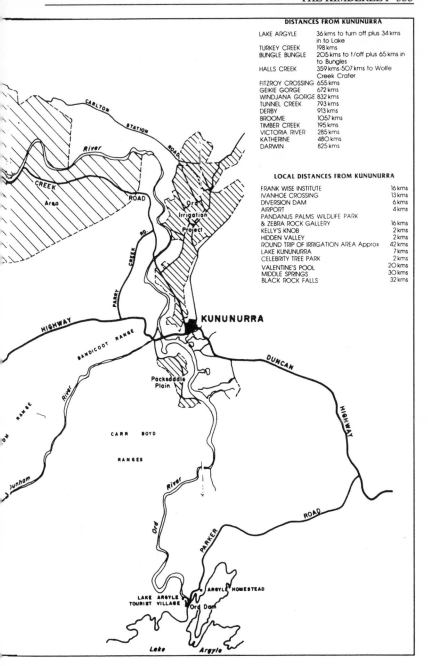

DISTANCES FROM KUNUNURRA

LAKE ARGYLE	36 kms to turn off plus 34 kms in to Lake
TURKEY CREEK	198 kms
BUNGLE BUNGLE	205 kms to t/off plus 65 kms in to Bungles
HALLS CREEK	359 kms-507 kms to Wolfe Creek Crater
FITZROY CROSSING	655 kms
GEIKIE GORGE	672 kms
WINDJANA GORGE	832 kms
TUNNEL CREEK	793 kms
DERBY	913 kms
BROOME	1057 kms
TIMBER CREEK	195 kms
VICTORIA RIVER	285 kms
KATHERINE	480 kms
DARWIN	825 kms

LOCAL DISTANCES FROM KUNUNURRA

FRANK WISE INSTITUTE	16 kms
IVANHOE CROSSING	13 kms
DIVERSION DAM	6 kms
AIRPORT	4 kms
PANDANUS PALMS WILDLIFE PARK & ZEBRA ROCK GALLERY	16 kms
KELLY'S KNOB	2 kms
HIDDEN VALLEY	2 kms
ROUND TRIP OF IRRIGATION AREA Approx	42 kms
LAKE KUNUNURRA	7 kms
CELEBRITY TREE PARK	2 kms
VALENTINE'S POOL	20 kms
MIDDLE SPRINGS	30 kms
BLACK ROCK FALLS	32 kms

Tours

Short tours include Hidden Valley; Lake Argyle; Keep, Dunham and Ord Rivers; agricultural district; and town attractions.

Cruises are available on Lake Kununurra. Fishing safaris of 2-5 days on the Ord, or by floatplane or helicopter along the coast of the Timor Sea. Ground safaris vary from 2-8 days. Specialist tours (wildlife, fishing, bird watching). Tours to Gibb River Road and El Questro and Home Valley Stations and Jack's Waterhole are recommended.

Highly recommended is Slingair's Bungle Bungle flight. In what must be one of the best scenic flights in Australia, for variety and majestic landscapes, it covers the town, irrigation district, Ord Valley, Lake Argyle (including Dam and Durack Homestead), Argyle Diamond Mine and the Bungle Bungle. It is a 2-hour flight, with 15-20 minutes over Bungle Bungle. Slingair, ph (091) 681 255.

A number of tour operators and tours stem from Kununurra. Check with the Visitors Centre.

Events

Dam to Dam Regatta - March; Kununurra Agricultural Show - July; The Ord River Festival - August; Horse Racing - August.

How To Get There

By air: Ansett operates a daily jet service between Kununurra and Perth, Darwin and Alice Springs. The Darwin flight takes about 40 minutes. Ansett's 'milk-run' flight (early morning) into Kununurra and onto Darwin is a beauty - more like a scenic flight with the sun tinting the land in orange, pinks and reds. Ord Air Charter operates a regional feeder service to Hall's Creek, Fitzroy Crossing and Derby.

By coach: Pioneer Express, Greyhound and Bus Australia service Kununurra.

By road: Kununurra is connected by an all-sealed road to other parts of Western Australia and the Northern Territory.

Accommodation

There is a good range, but Kununurra's increasing popularity as a tourist destination means it's advisable to book well in advance. The telephone area code is 091.

Kununurra Hotel, Messmate Way, ph 681 344 - single from $65-85, double $65-95; pool.

Quality Inn-Kununurra, Duncan Highway, ph 681 455 - single/double from $98, family $110; pool.

Country Club Private Hotel, Collibah Drive, ph 681 024 - single from $35, double $45; pool.

Kununurra Backpackers, 111 Nutwood Crescent, ph 681 711 - $15 per person per night.

Kimberley Court, cnr River Fig Avenue and Erythrina Street, ph 681 411 - unit, B & LtB single from $74, double $84; full facilities for the disabled.

Tropical Farm-Ord River, ph 681 056 - offers a self-contained lakeside cabin, set in a mango orchard of an organic tropical farm - around $50 double per night, $315 per week.

Raintree Lodge (Youth Hostel), Coolibah Drive, ph 681 372 - from $10 per night.

Desert Inn, ph 682 702 - Backpackers- beds $11 single, $28 double.

Camping

Town Caravan Park, Bloodwood Drive, ph 681 763 - Shire operated. No dogs, on-site vans from $50 x 2, powered sites from $11 x 2.

Kona Lakeside Park, Lake Kununurra setting, ph 681 031 - caravan sites $13 x 2, tent sites $10 x 2. No dogs.

Coolibah Caravan Park, ph 681 653 - dogs allowed, leashed (bond $20), powered sites $10 x 2.

Kimberleyland Holiday Park, Duncan Highway, ph 681 280 - dogs allowed, leashed; caravan sites $15 x 2, tent sites $12 x 2.

Hidden Valley Caravan Park, Weaber Plains Road, ph 681 790 - powered sites $14 x 2, unpowered sites $12 x 2.

Eating Out

There is Chicken Treat, Valentine's Pizza and the fish and chips outlet in Konkerberry Street, in the convenience food line.

Hotel - counter meals in the Green Room. Bistro/smorgasbord in Dining Room (around $11).

The George Room, Gulliver's Tavern, Cotton Tree Avenue, ph 681 666 - a la carte in comparatively elegant Georgian atmosphere, with a Gulliver's Travels theme depicted in prints around the walls. Main course around $18. The Tavern has counter meals.

The Country Club in Coolibah Street, ph 681 024, has Chop Sticks - a Chinese restaurant in a delightful outdoor setting (around $16); and Kelly's Bar and Grill for steak and seafood.

Quality Inn - a la carte. Good value with main course around $17.

Services and Facilities

Most services and facilities are offered, and credit cards are widely accepted. There is a hospital, full medical services, chemist, police, post office, supermarket, specialty shops, banks (National, Commonwealth, R&I, EFT/POS facility for most banks), all vehicle fuels and services, camping gas, ice, airport, boat ramp, churches (Anglican, Catholic, Uniting, People's Church), Hertz, ph 681 257; hire bicycles (Youth Hostel), fishing tackle.

Recreational facilities: Leisure Centre. Galleries: Nimberlee Art and Craft Cultural Centre, Poinsettia Street). **Emergencies: dial 000.**

LAKE ARGYLE TOURIST VILLAGE

Population 20

Location

70km (43 miles) south of Kununurra on Lake Argyle.

Characteristics

Picturesquely sited on treed, grassed slopes near the lake, the Tourist Village, including an Inn, does not disappoint after a beautiful, mountainous and winding 37km (23 miles) drive from the Duncan Highway turn-off. Apart from the wonders of this huge man-made lake and associated water activities (fishing, water skiing, boating, canoeing), it is an ideal family place for relaxation that is particularly attractive during the green season.

Lake Argyle

The nearby dam was built as a vital part of the Ord River Scheme, designed to store the massive volumes of water in the Wet season so that up to 76,000ha (187,720 acres) of heavy soils could be irrigated for tropical agriculture. Despite initial setbacks and crop failures for unforeseen reasons (the scheme was branded in some quarters as a 'white elephant'), the development, apart from the agriculture it has fostered, has silenced the critics. A wide variety of crops are grown on small holdings around Kununurra, but its biggest success is in the opening up of the region for such activities as tourism, as well as encouraging prolific wildlife.

The dam creates a surface area of 740 sq km (286 sq miles) at storage level, rising to 2072 sq km (800 sq miles) during maximum floods. It is the largest lake of its type in Australia, with a volume of water nine times that of Sydney Harbour.

Attractions

Magnificent Kimberley scenery, including drives to the dam and lookout, where in the evening there are plenty of rock wallabies.

Argyle Homestead Museum. This is the reconstructed homestead of the Durack Family, known as Argyle Downs Station. The homestead was in the area to be flooded when Lake Argyle was formed, but because of its historical significance, it now houses interesting pioneer days memorabilia, and implements from its higher ground location. A generalised history of the region is contained in the Kununurra listing.

Tours

Bower Bird Lake Cruises have two two-hour cruises leaving at 9am and 2pm - $22 per person; and a half day cruise leaving at 12.30pm and returning at sunset - $69 per person. Bookings at reception. Charter boat cruises are available. For other tours, including flights, see under Kununurra.

Accommodation

Motel - around $65 single/double.

Camping - sites $5 adult, $3 child; powered sites $12.50 x 2. Shaded, grassed sites. Pets allowed, dogs leashed.

Services and Facilities

Hotel/motel, store (limited foodstuffs), restaurant (buffet style breakfast, counter meals, country style food), take-away food, ice, souvenirs, Commonwealth Bank agency, telephone, fuel (super,

ULP, diesel), oil, camping gas, basic spares, picnic/bbq shaded area, tourist information, swimming pool, boat ramp, tennis court, mini golf course, pool table in bar, showers for travellers ($2). Open all year 7am-8.30pm. Credit cards (Bankcard, Mastercard, Visa, American Express, Diners) accepted, ph (091) 687 360.

ROEBUCK PLAINS

Population 4

Location

On the Great Northern Highway, 35km (22 miles) east of Broome, near the junction.

Characteristics

A modernised swagman roadhouse serves both road users and the locals from the nearby stations. In fact, it is a good meeting place for truckies, travellers and ringers, who add a touch of flavour to the bar. The large 303,643ha (750,000 acre) Roebuck Cattle Station, which is also a Brahman Stud, surrounds the roadhouse in an area characterised by flat to undulating country, clothed in spinifex and eucalypts.

Accommodation

Basic units - $20 single, $40 double.
   Camping - powered sites $12, unpowered $6. Sites have some grass and shade. Pets allowed, dogs leashed.

Services and Facilities

It has a bar, restaurant (steak/grills $10), take-away food, shop, ice, souvenirs, telephone, showers for travellers ($2), picnic/bbq area, tourist information, fuel (super, ULP, diesel, autogas), oil, camping gas, tyres and tubes. Open all year, 24 hours. Credit cards are accepted (Bankcard, Mastercard, Visa), ph (091) 921 880.

SANDFIRE FLAT

Population 13

Location

On the Great Northern Highway, approximately 310km (192 miles) south of Broome, and 300km (186 miles) north of Port Hedland.

Characteristics

One of the loneliest roadhouses in the north-west is located in the undulating spinifex and acacia ridge country of the vast Great Sandy Desert. There is plenty of character here where the air-conditioned tavern has hundreds of shirt sleeves hanging from the ceiling, as a fund raising effort for the Royal Flying Doctor Service. You can join the club, too; either donate about $10, or for a $2 discount, rip off your sleeve and pin it up! Ken and Barni Norton are the owners of this remarkable, remote roadhouse, and they have a store of tales about the area. Whether driving from south or north, Sandfire marks either the beginning of the Kimberley, or the memorable end.

History

The roadhouse was established in early 1970, when Ken's father put the first bore down. Mr Norton Senior had read a diary of Ludwig Leichhardt (the explorer) and was struck by a reference to sand appearing to be on fire - some years later, whilst broken down on the Great Northern Track, he saw what Leichhardt meant; the interplay of sun and desert fired the sands, hence the name of the place. The original roadhouse was like a shed, but a very welcome stop for those heading north when the road was a treacherous track.

Attractions

55km (34 miles) south is access to one of the longest, loneliest and most beautiful beachcombing sands in Australia, 80 Mile Beach (see separate listing).

How To Get There

By road: it is a sealed all-weather road serviced by the 'big three' coach companies - Pioneer Express, Greyhound and Bus Australia.

Accommodation

Motel - double between $50 and $60.
  Budget - single $20, double $30.
  Camping - powered sites $12 x 2, unpowered $10 x 2. Grassed tent sites, limited shade. Pets allowed, dogs leashed.

Services and Facilities

The roadhouse has a tavern bar, restaurant (good Aussie meals, 'steak & veg' $11, breakfast bacon and eggs $5), shop selling basics, ice, take-away food, souvenirs, telephone, showers for travellers ($2), tourist information (80 Mile Beach), fuel (super, ULP, diesel), LPG for vehicles, oil, camping gas, emergency vehicle repairs, basic spares, airstrip. Open all year 6am-midnight. Credit cards are accepted (Bankcard, Mastercard, Visa), ph (091) 765 944.

TURKEY CREEK

Population 200 (approximately)

Location

On the Great Northern Highway, 196km (121 miles) south of Kununurra.

Characteristics

A roadhouse that serves not only travellers and local stations, but also the nearby Warmun Aboriginal Community, is a welcome stop after some magnificent Kimberley landscape. It is also the gateway to the Bungle Bungle.

Attractions

The Bungle Bungle Range is 80km (50 miles) from here (see separate listing). Caravans and trailers can be left at the roadhouse for those planning the 4WD-only drive into the Range.

How To Get There

By road: it is sealed, and serviced by the three major coach companies.

Accommodation

Motel style - single around $45, double around $55.

Camping - powered sites around $15 x 2, unpowered around $5 per person. Sites are grassed with limited shade. Pets allowed, dogs leashed.

Services and Facilities

It has a general store/supermarket selling a surprisingly wide range, restaurant (a good meal at around $10), take-away food, ice, artifacts, souvenirs, telephone, showers for travellers ($1), picnic/bbq area, tourist information, fuel (super, ULP, diesel, autogas), camping gas, oil, basic spares, and airfield. It is not licensed, nor sells alcohol. Open all year, 24 hours. Credit cards are accepted (Bankcard, Mastercard), ph (091) 786 882.

WILLARE BRIDGE

Population 7

Location

On the Great Northern Highway, 56km (35 miles) south of Derby, and 155km (96 miles) east of Broome.

Characteristics

Only a good cast away from the barramundi in the Fitzroy River billabongs (actually 600m), the quaint squared roadhouse, set amidst shady trees and green lawns, is a pleasant overnight stopping or refuelling spot.

Accommodation

Old style Hotel rooms - $15 per bed.

Camping - powered sites around $10 x 2, unpowered $7. Sites grassed, shaded. No pets allowed.

Services and Facilities

The roadhouse has a dining room, general store, ice, take-away food, telephone, picnic/bbq shaded area, showers for travellers, fuel (super, ULP, diesel), camping gas, oil, basic spares, tyres and tubes. Open all year, 6am-9pm, cash only, ph (091) 914 775.

WOLFE CREEK METEORITE CRATER NATIONAL PARK

1460ha (2606 acres)

Location

Approximately 130km (81 miles) south of Hall's Creek.

Characteristics

The national park protects a huge crater, measuring about 850m in diameter and 50m deep, caused by the impact shock of a huge meteorite. To the Djaru people, who called the crater 'Kandimalal', it is deeply symbolic; the winding paths of two rainbow serpents formed the nearby Stuart and Wolfe Creeks, while the crater is where one snake emerged from the desert sands. The first recorded European discovery was in 1947. It is the world's second largest meteorite crater, and the park is day-use only. Camping facilities and services are adjacent to the park.

Origin

There is some doubt about how the crater was formed, and like the time scale in which they work, geologists are still pondering over this fascinating formation. Evidence of an impact by a meteor weighing several thousands tonnes, and travelling at a speed of over 15km/sec, are the crater shape (despite its floor today which lies 20m below the surrounding sandplain) and iron oxide balls found scattered on its slopes. The explosion that caused the crater is thought to have occurred 2 million years ago.

How To Get There

With care, the formed gravel road is suitable for conventional vehicles during the Dry season. Caravans not advised. Phone the station (see below) or check at Hall's Creek for road conditions. The turn-off to the crater is 16km (10 miles) west of Hall's Creek from the Great Northern Highway. It's also the turn-off for the Canning Stock Route Track and the Tanami Track to Alice Springs. The RAC Canning Stock Route map is good for 4WD tracks and Wolfe Creek.

Services and Facilities

An information panel and basic picnic facilities are provided in this day-use only park. Please keep to the tracks. Camping and campfires are not permitted. Carranya Station, 7km (4 miles) to the south of the crater, provides a range of tourist services: shop, refreshments, some fuel (check beforehand at Hall's Creek), camping facilities (showers, power, bbq, toilets), and souvenirs. Costs are around $2 per person, power $2 extra, ph (091) 688 927.

WYNDHAM

Population 1200

Location

On the west arm of Cambridge Gulf, 101km (63 miles) north-west of
Kununurra, at the end of the Great Northern Highway.

Characteristics

An 18m (60 ft) long and 3m (10 ft) high 'Big Croc" replica greets
visitors at the entrance to Western Australia's most northerly town
and port. It is a friendly town, too - when we had lunch in an
unshaded street, a woman invited us to use the shade under her
stilt-foundationed house - that has two sites; the original port site, and
Wyndham East on the Great Northern Highway. The latter is the
main shopping and residential area today. The older, frontier-town
part has some of the original corrugated iron shops with hitching-rails
outside, while benign boab trees dot the streetscape. The sense of
history and numerous things to see make it well worth visiting. The
pub's a good place to meet the locals, and owners, and others from
the town, will advise on fishing spots and other attractions.

History

Long before the Europeans came, the Djeidji, Dulngari and Aruagga
people are thought to have been the traditional dwellers in the region.
Lieutenant Phillip King sailed into the inlet he called Cambridge Gulf
in 1819, while 1885 saw the arrival of the *Torinda Borstel* with a
cargo for the Duracks.

The gold rush at Hall's Creek was the catalyst for settlement, and a
rough and ready town was well established by 1886, based on the

port. The influx of miners prompted the rapid erection of six hotels, but when the gold fever died down, the slowness and remoteness of Wyndham returned.

The town, named in honour of the son of Lady Broome, received new life in 1919, when the English land and livestock company, Vesteys, opened a meatworks and from the port chilled beef was exported. It became the main port for the East Kimberley. The works has had a stop-go history, finally closing in 1987, and gutted by fire soon afterwards. A thriving port today is based on mineral and live cattle exports, while the town serves the pastoral, mining and tourism industries, as well as Aboriginal communities.

Information

Wyndham Tourist Information Centre, O'Donnell Street, Wyndham Port, ph (091) 611 054, open March to November.

Attractions

Five Rivers Lookout. A fine spot at the peak of the Bastion Range, for Kimberley landscape appreciation and great orientation views of the town, port and, of course, the five rivers: King, Pentecost, Durack, Forrest and Ord. Best views are early morning, due to haze later.

Frontier-town Port site. Old buildings include the port post office, built in the early 1900s, and now appropriately housing the Wyndham Tourist Information Centre and museum, Durack's Store and Lee Tong's general store. Near the wharf offices is a display of early trains used to carry cargo to and from ships.

Crocodile Lookout. Near the wharf is the spot where effluent from the meatworks attracted many large 'salties'. Recent feeding has brought them back. Check with the Information Centre for feeding times.

Gully and Bend Cemeteries. Headstones reveal much local history. Graves date back to the early 1880s.

Three Mile Valley. The valley has all the characteristics of the East Kimberley - red gorges, rock pools, rugged terrain, and open vegetation.

Boab Trees. An enormous boab tree is located in the Three Mile Caravan Park, while a hollow one situated on the King River Road was used as a 'local lock-up' or prison.

The Grotto. This feature has a certain mystic from a vantage point overlooking the clear pool. It is a popular swimming spot, and has a carved stone staircase which leads through the greenery that fringes the rock-bound pool.

King River Pools. Many fine pools offer barramundi fishing, particularly during the Wet, while along Parry's Creek Road, stone creek crossings give access to some good fishing holes, the most popular being Crocodile Hole.

Afghan Cemetery. Contains the graves of Afghan cameleers whose camel strings brought supplies to the region.

Aboriginal Paintings. Overhanging rock walls near the Moochalabra Dam have paintings in ochre of spiritual figures and animals. This is a protected site.

Parry's Lagoon Nature Reserve. This protects a series of lagoons 20km (12 miles) south of Wyndham. Like the wetlands of Kakadu, it hosts flocks of waterbirds, which come from as far afield as Siberia in the USSR. It is an important breeding ground, too. Species include egrets, spoonbills, herons, ibis, magpie geese, raptors, pelicans, jabirus and brolgas, while aquatic life features both species of crocodiles and fish (barramundi, mullet, tarpon). Dawn and dusk are

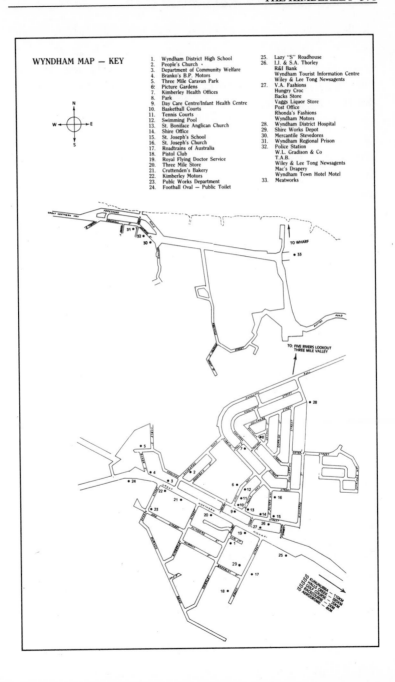

WYNDHAM MAP — KEY

1. Wyndham District High School
2. People's Church
3. Department of Community Welfare
4. Branko's B.P. Motors
5. Three Mile Caravan Park
6. Picture Gardens
7. Kimberley Health Offices
8. Park
9. Day Care Centre/Infant Health Centre
10. Basketball Courts
11. Tennis Courts
12. Swimming Pool
13. St. Boniface Anglican Church
14. Shire Office
15. St. Joseph's School
16. St. Joseph's Church
17. Roadtrains of Australia
18. Pistol Club
19. Royal Flying Doctor Service
20. Three Mile Store
21. Cruttenden's Bakery
22. Kimberley Motors
23. Public Works Department
24. Football Oval — Public Toilet

25. Lazy "S" Roadhouse
26. I.J. & S.A. Thorley
    R&I Bank
    Wyndham Tourist Information Centre
    Wiley & Lee Tong Newsagents
27. V.A. Fashions
    Hungry Croc
    Backs Store
    Vaggs Liquor Store
    Post Office
    Rhonda's Fashions
    Wyndham Motors
28. Wyndham District Hospital
29. Shire Works Depot
30. Mercantile Stevedores
31. Wyndham Regional Prison
32. Police Station
    W.L. Gradison & Co
    T.A.B.
    Wiley & Lee Tong Newsagents
    Mac's Drapery
    Wyndham Town Hotel Motel
33. Meatworks

the best times to visit this sanctuary, when thousands of birds gather.

Crocodile Farm. Located on the old meatworks site, it offers visitors a close but safe view of these awesome reptiles. Check with the Tourist Centre for feeding times.

Fishing. Wyndham offers all year fishing, both salt and freshwater. Barramundi, golden grunter, mangrove jack, threadfin salmon and huge groper, are the main types. The wharf is a popular spot, but check with the locals, too. Watch out for salt-water crocodiles.

Tours

Bushwalking and horse trekking safaris of 3-10 days' duration. Scenic flights include coastal, Bungle Bungle and Argyle Diamond Mine locations. Check with the Information Centre for details.

Events

Parry's Creek Picnic - June long weekend; Horse Racing - August; Soap Box Derby - mid-year.

How To Get There

By air: services from Kununurra.
By road: Pioneer Express, Bus Australia and Greyhound.

Accommodation

The telephone area code is 091.

Wyndham Town Hotel, 19 O'Donnel Street, ph 611 003 - self-contained rooms, single $40, double $65.

Wyndham Community Club, Great Northern Highway, ph 611 130 - rooms single $45, double $55.